EXPERT

Dr. D.G.Hessayon

First edition: 80,000 copies

Published by Expert Books
a division of Transworld Publishers

A catalogue record for this book is available from the British Library

TRANSWORLD PUBLISHERS
61-63 Uxbridge Road, London W5 5SA
a division of the Random House Group Ltd

CONTENTS

Reproduction by Spot On Digital Imaging Ltd, Gomm Road, High Wycombe, Bucks, HP13 7DJ
Printed and bound by Appl Druck, Wemding, Germany

ISBN 0 903505 58 4

CHAPTER 1

NTRODUCTION

Your home is a complex affair — so many walls, floors, doors and windows to look after, so many fixtures and fittings to care for, so many services to keep in working order. The purpose of this book is quite simple. In non-technical language it sets out to explain the basic structure of your home and to help you understand the various services, techniques, materials and pieces of equipment which are needed to make things run smoothly.

Sometimes things don't run smoothly and many pages are devoted to the problems which may crop up from time to time. Alongside the guides to preventing and dealing with problems there are the sections on home decorating — the correct way to paint surfaces, paper walls, replace glass, repoint bricks, lay flooring and so on.

This book assumes that you are a man or woman whose interest in DIY is based on a desire to do simple maintenance and decorating jobs for yourself rather than having to pay an outside contractor to do the work. It does not assume that DIY is your hobby and it does not assume that you have a cupboardful of tools. You will have to look elsewhere if you want to know how to install a central heating system or build a partition wall. There are several comprehensive DIY manuals available, but a word of caution — major constructional work calls for experience and not just clear diagrams.

Because this book is for everyone and not just for the enthusiast you will find things that rarely appear in the traditional DIY manuals. You will not find the way to hang a new door but you will find what to do if it starts to stick or if you lose the key. This book will not tell you how to lay a stair carpet but it does tell you what to do if you spill a glass of wine on it. You will have to look elsewhere if you want to know how to make a table, but it will show you how to deal with a water ring on polished wood.

The purpose of this introduction is to talk about the maintenance of your home in general terms, and so it is necessary to provide a few basic rules. First of all, consider both the advantages and disadvantages of employing a professional contractor for any major job. If you do decide to tackle the work yourself then make sure you learn the technique *before* you start, and remember that the preparatory work for painting, papering etc may well take longer than you expect. If on the other hand you feel that the job is beyond you then choose a builder, decorator, plumber or electrician with care. Check that the contractor is a member of the appropriate trade organisation and wherever possible see examples of the work he has done for others. Listen to the recommendations of your friends. Obtain a written quotation if a lot of work will be involved.

Making furniture with a saw, plane, chisel etc may well be beyond you but constructing a flatpack kit is not. With all home-assembly products you should take your time before you begin. Spread out the components and see if they are all there — read the instructions carefully to make sure you understand them and keep the box in case the kit has to be returned. Have a helper if the item to be made is large and/or awkward, give yourself ample space — now you are ready to begin.

Many troubles can be avoided by regular servicing and routine inspection — by preventing rather than tackling problems you can save a great deal of time and money. Finally, do read the sections on the services (pages 4 – 22) and on the names of the features both inside and outside the house (pages 42 – 43 and 74 – 75). Maybe this book will not make you an expert and there are many tasks you will not be able to tackle, but you will be able to understand the experts when they talk to you.

CHAPTER 2

THE SERVICES

Two basic services are on tap in virtually every home in Britain. There is water for drinking, washing and the removal of sewage, and for our comfort there is electricity for lighting and perhaps warmth. Electricity also powers an ever-increasing range of equipment — radios, computers, TVs, kettles, air conditioners, hair dryers, refrigerators and so on. But it is not used by everyone for heating the home nor for fuelling the cooker. It shares these functions with the other major source of fuel energy — gas. Most free-standing radiators are powered by electricity but the majority of central heating boilers are gas-fired. Gas requires no storage, it fares well in price comparison tables and it has lost its poisonous stigma with the advent of natural gas, but unlike electricity it is available in less than 90 per cent of the homes in Britain.

Oil has lost its place as the leading fuel for central heating despite the advent of automatic ordering systems. Solid fuels (coal, wood etc) have slipped from being the age-old mainstay of home heating to a minor source of domestic energy. Fashions change, but for some people an open fire in winter remains an important feature of the living room. Liquid fuels such as paraffin, butane and propane are not easy to use and have limited appeal. Solar energy and wind power arouse much interest but they remain novelties whose day may come.

All fuels have their advantages and disadvantages. The trade associations and suppliers of the major fuels produce excellent booklets and operate efficient advisory services. Ask for help — it won't cost you anything. There is one piece of advice that all of these people will give you — make sure that the equipment is installed properly and ensure that it is serviced regularly. Price is an important consideration, but it is no longer just a matter of choosing between electricity, gas and oil. Electricity and gas are no longer monopolies and that means you can change the suppliers of the two major fuels. Don't rush to make a change — study the price quotes carefully and don't be unduly swayed by the headline on top of the advertisement or the sales talk of the representative.

Water and fuel are of course not the only services on which we rely to make modern domestic life possible. The amount of household rubbish we accumulate each week continues to increase every year, and we rely on our local council to remove most of this for us. Recycling has become an important concept in recent years, and we now separate the items which can be reprocessed from the waste which is put in to the council-emptied bin.

Liquid waste easily outweighs the amount of solid waste we accumulate. Mains drainage is taken for granted by the urban dweller — each year over 2000 litres of washing water and foul waste per person is transported to the public sewage system without us having to give it a thought. But in some rural areas it is different — rainwater is led to a soakaway and the waste water plus foul waste go to either a cesspool (an underground storage tank which must be emptied frequently) or a septic tank (a miniature sewage works which requires emptying much less frequently).

All these services are dealt with in this chapter, but there are others which add greatly to our comfort and well-being. There is the postal service which delivers letters each day. Air waves bring us TV, radio and the mobile phone — the telephone line brings us phone calls, E-mail and the internet. All add up to an array of services which regularly come to the house but the maintenance of the equipment involved with these additional services is not a DIY job you can tackle yourself.

OIL

Until 1970 oil was the main fuel for central heating. In the years which followed, the central heating boom took place and oil lost its lead — gas took over as the major fuel for domestic boilers. The reason for this shift was twofold. The price of oil had spiralled upwards so making it uncompetitive with natural gas, and there were also the physical disadvantages. These include the need for outside storage — a 1200 litre tank is hard to conceal in a small garden, and there is also the need to arrange for supplies when the oil level in the tank runs low. This does not mean that oil has had its day. There are houses where natural gas supplies are not available and there has been a marked improvement in boiler design in recent years. In addition oil suppliers now offer an automatic topping-up service.

Oil

Two grades of oil are used for domestic central heating — the correct one depends upon the type of boiler. If in doubt consult the instruction book.
Class C2 oil (28 second oil) is the more popular type. This grade is used in Wallflame boilers and is sometimes described as Kerosene oil. It is thinner and slightly more expensive than Class D oil.
Class D oil (35 second oil) is used in Pressure jet boilers — it is sometimes described as Gas oil.

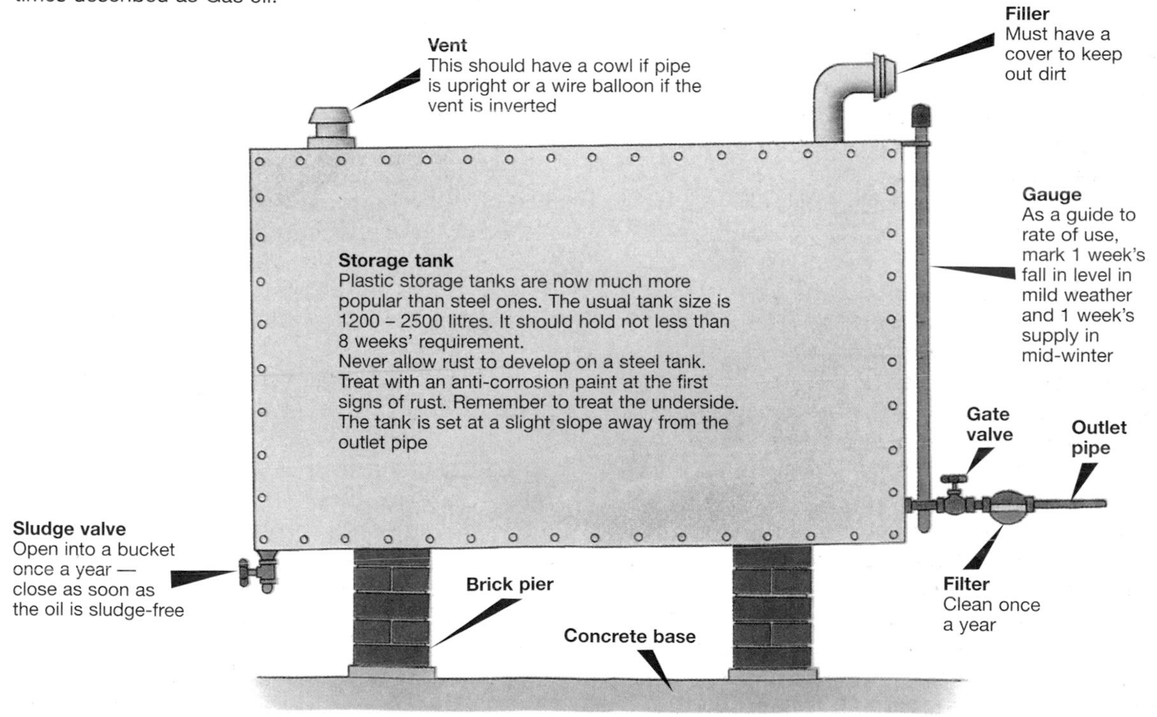

HOW TO AVOID OIL PROBLEMS

- **DO NOT LEAVE ORDERING TO THE LAST MINUTE**
  During the warm months you can order supplies when it is most convenient — keep watch for money-saving discounts from your supplier in the off-season. During winter you will find that oil consumption increases rapidly in bitterly cold weather — make sure that you order when you still have about 2 weeks' supply. Snow, ice and heavy demand can result in tanker delays.

- **HAVE YOUR INSTALLATION SERVICED REGULARLY**
  Never let a year go by without having your oil central heating system serviced. No matter how well it is running, it will be necessary to clean the burner, flue and the combustion chamber. Do not attempt to do this task yourself — have a service contract with a qualified heating engineer who will check that the installation is running at maximum efficiency.

ELECTRICITY

Power cuts rarely last more than a few hours, but they do remind us that the modern home cannot function without electricity. The basic principles are not difficult and every householder should get to know them. The reason is not to turn you into an amateur electrician — the main purpose is to avoid misuse and accidents due to ignorance.

There is no reason why you should not tackle simple jobs — fitting plugs, replacing sockets, extending flex and so on. You can be more ambitious and lay new cables — there are no regulations to stop you. However you should never attempt a major job unless you are absolutely confident that you know what you are doing. Consult a comprehensive manual and look at the Institution of Electrical Engineers Wiring Regulations in your local library.

If you have recently moved or if your system has not been looked at for many years, ask your supplier to send round one of their experts to prepare a report. It could save your home or even your life.

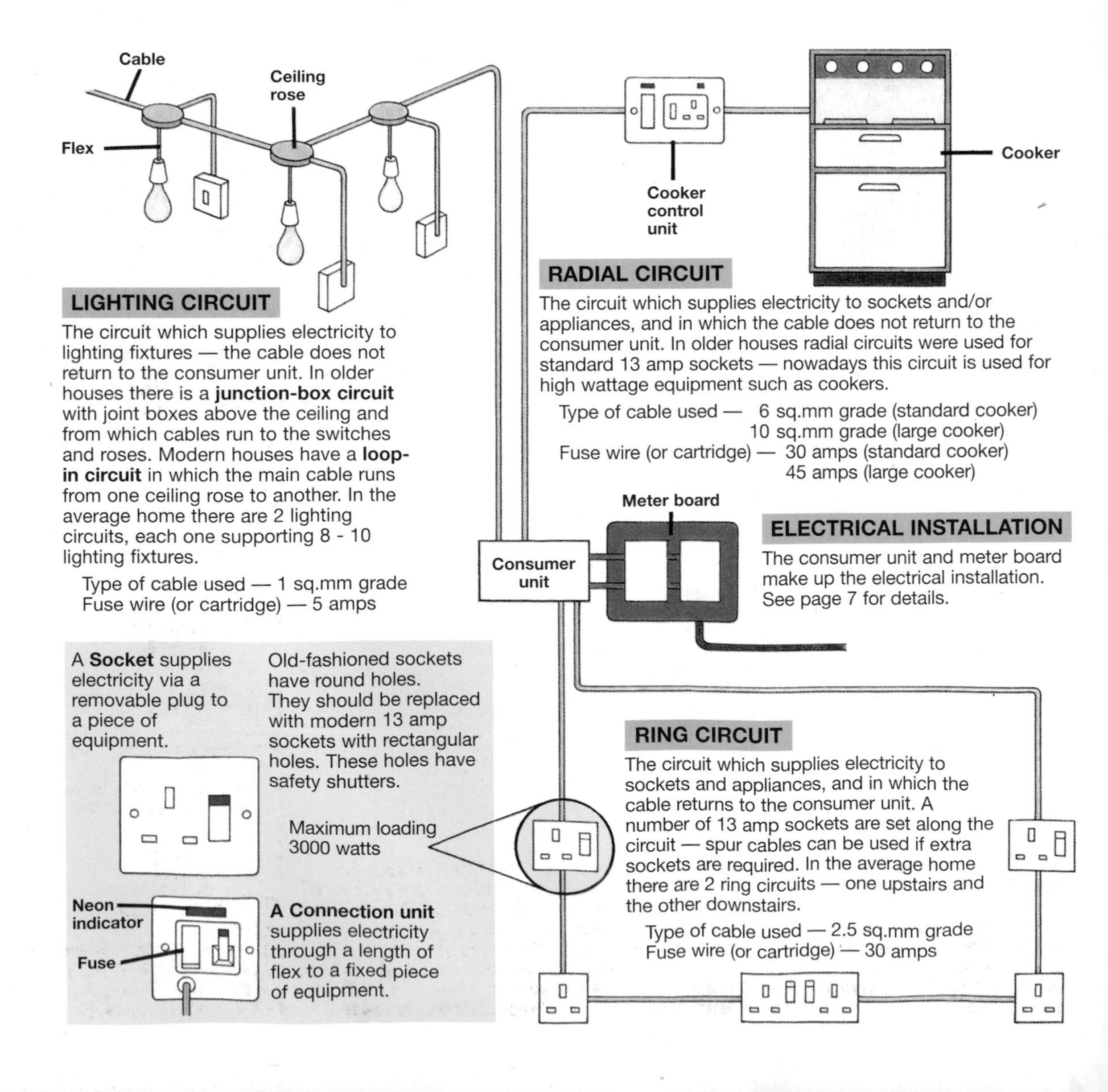

LIGHTING CIRCUIT

The circuit which supplies electricity to lighting fixtures — the cable does not return to the consumer unit. In older houses there is a **junction-box circuit** with joint boxes above the ceiling and from which cables run to the switches and roses. Modern houses have a **loop-in circuit** in which the main cable runs from one ceiling rose to another. In the average home there are 2 lighting circuits, each one supporting 8 - 10 lighting fixtures.

Type of cable used — 1 sq.mm grade
Fuse wire (or cartridge) — 5 amps

RADIAL CIRCUIT

The circuit which supplies electricity to sockets and/or appliances, and in which the cable does not return to the consumer unit. In older houses radial circuits were used for standard 13 amp sockets — nowadays this circuit is used for high wattage equipment such as cookers.

Type of cable used — 6 sq.mm grade (standard cooker)
10 sq.mm grade (large cooker)
Fuse wire (or cartridge) — 30 amps (standard cooker)
45 amps (large cooker)

ELECTRICAL INSTALLATION

The consumer unit and meter board make up the electrical installation. See page 7 for details.

A **Socket** supplies electricity via a removable plug to a piece of equipment.

Old-fashioned sockets have round holes. They should be replaced with modern 13 amp sockets with rectangular holes. These holes have safety shutters.

Maximum loading 3000 watts

A Connection unit supplies electricity through a length of flex to a fixed piece of equipment.

RING CIRCUIT

The circuit which supplies electricity to sockets and appliances, and in which the cable returns to the consumer unit. A number of 13 amp sockets are set along the circuit — spur cables can be used if extra sockets are required. In the average home there are 2 ring circuits — one upstairs and the other downstairs.

Type of cable used — 2.5 sq.mm grade
Fuse wire (or cartridge) — 30 amps

THE INSTALLATION IN YOUR HOME

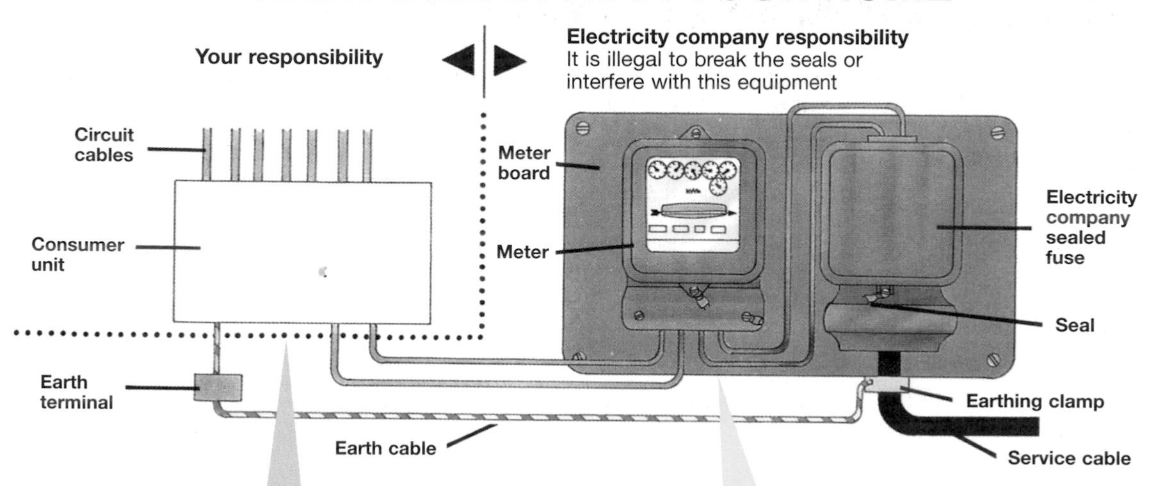

OLD-FASHIONED 'CONSUMER UNIT'
Before 1950 there were no true consumer units — each circuit had its own fuse box and mains switch.

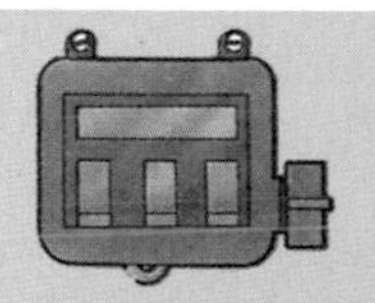

STANDARD CONSUMER UNIT
Each circuit has its own fuse, which is of the rewirable or cartridge type. The mains switch is used to cut off or restore the electricity supply to the house.

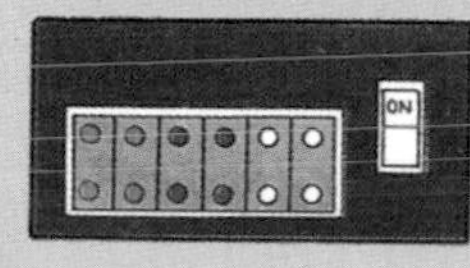

MODERN CONSUMER UNIT
There are no fuses — there are instead **miniature circuit breakers** (MCBs) which switch off if there is a fault or if the circuit is overloaded. To reset, merely correct the fault and press the button or flick the switch on the MCB. A **residual current device** (RCD) may be present instead of a mains switch or to serve just one or two circuits. It provides protection against shocks.

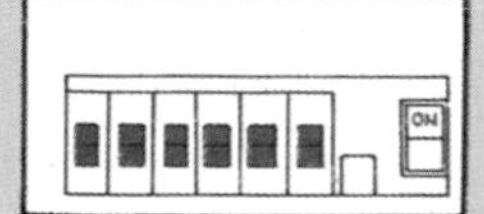

METER
Standard meters have a series of clock-like dials. To read the meter, ignore the red dial and read the remainder from left to right. If the pointer is between two numbers, take the lower one. A modern meter has a digital counter which gives a read-out in numbers, just like a pocket calculator. The meter measures the number of units used, and your electricity bill will be based on a standing charge and a set amount for each unit. You can change to Economy 7 tariff — you will pay a slightly higher standing charge and perhaps a slightly higher day-time unit rate, but the cost of night-time electricity will be much lower. Your electrical installation will have to be changed. There will be a dual-rate meter to replace your present meter, and a time switch which at night allows electricity to pass to the equipment in use.

WIRING A PLUG

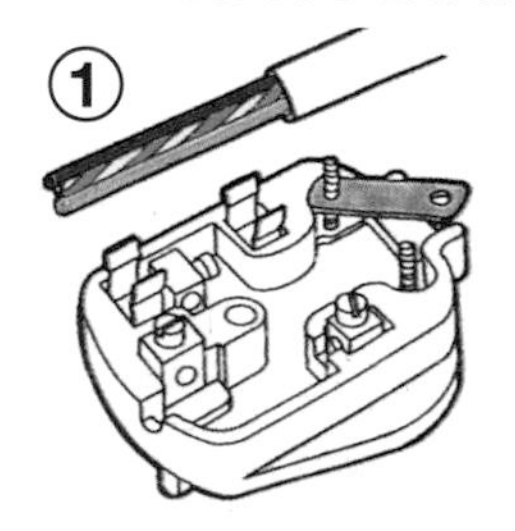

Remove the plug cover and fuse. Remove one flex clamp and screw. Loosen the other one — move the flex clamp aside. Carefully cut away flex outer sheath to length of plug (5 cm). Use a sharp knife.

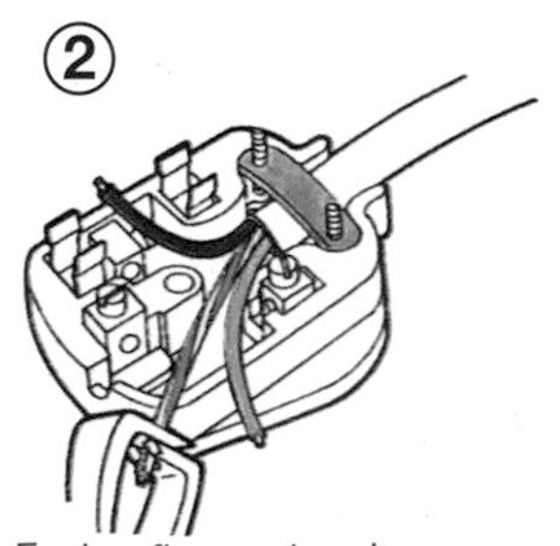

Fasten flex under clamp as shown. Cut wires to reach 1 cm beyond appropriate screw — use wire strippers to remove about 0.5 cm of insulation. Make sure the wires are directed to the correct terminals.

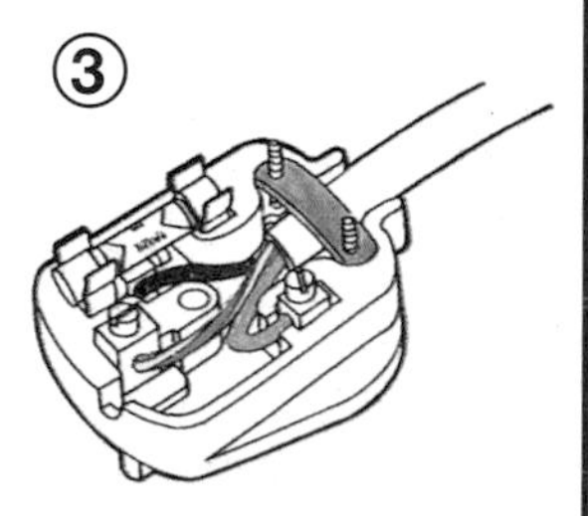

With each wire twist the strands of metal and place in fixing hole or wind clockwise around the terminal. Check that there are no loose strands. Tighten the screws, and fit correct fuse in holder. Replace the plug cover.

SYMBOLS

NICEIC
The National Inspection Council for Electrical Installation Contracting (0207 582 7746) will supply you with a list of Approved Contractors.

DOUBLE INSULATION MARK
This label on equipment indicates that it is double insulated — it can be used with 2-core flex.

WHAT THE WORDS MEAN

LIVE wire or conductor supplies electric current to the appliance or fitting. Attach to the terminal marked L

EARTH wire or conductor provides a safe escape to earth for the electric current if a fault develops. Attach to the terminal marked E or ⏚

NEUTRAL wire or conductor supplies electric current away from the appliance or fitting. Attach to the terminal marked N or P

The **Pressure** which drives the current through the wire is measured in **VOLTS** (V). The pressure in the U.K is 240 V. This pressure occasionally falls in winter if there is a sudden surge in demand — if this drop in voltage is large enough you will find that the TV picture shrinks and fluorescent lighting may not switch on.

The **Power** required by an appliance is measured in **WATTS** (W). This is what you pay for — the more watts used, the higher your bill will be. Some appliances require little electric power, such as a radio or refrigerator, but others have a high power requirement — a large cooker requires 3000 - 4000 watts.

1000 watts = 1 kW (1 kilowatt)

The **Amount** of current flowing through the circuit is measured in **AMPS** (A). As the power requirement is increased (watts), so is the amount of current flowing through the circuit (amps). Fuse wire is measured in amps.

Watts ÷ Volts = Amps

Your electricity bill will tell you the price of 1 unit. A **UNIT** is the amount of electricity used by a 1000 watt (1 kW) appliance in an hour.

Appliance	Watts	Time you get for 1 Unit
BLANKET	100	10 hours
CLOCK	1	1000 hours
DISHWASHER	3000	20 minutes
FAN HEATER	3000 - 1000	20 minutes - 1 hour
FOOD MIXER	200	5 hours
FREEZER	80	12 hours
HAIR DRYER	1500	40 minutes
HOT PLATE	4000 - 3000	15 - 20 minutes
IMMERSION HEATER	3000	20 minutes
IRON	500	2 hours
KETTLE	2000	30 minutes
LIGHT BULB	150 - 40	7 - 25 hours
OVEN	4000 - 3000	15 - 20 minutes
POWER DRILL	250	4 hours
RADIANT HEATER	3000 - 1000	20 minutes - 1 hour
RADIO	30	35 hours
REFRIGERATOR	100	10 hours
TOWEL RAIL	250	4 hours
TUMBLE DRIER	2000	30 minutes
TV - Colour	350	3 hours
VACUUM CLEANER	250	4 hours
WASHING MACHINE	3000	20 minutes

CABLE

Carries electricity from the consumer unit to sockets, switches and ceiling roses.

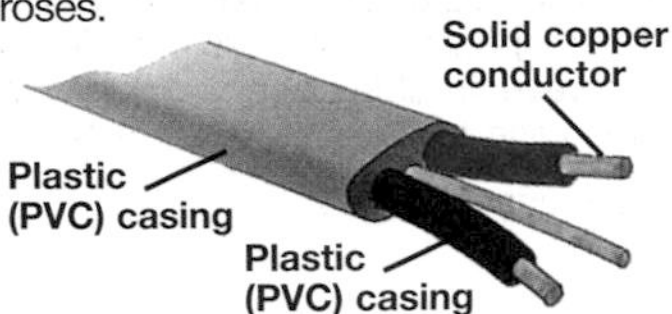

TWIN-CORE-AND-EARTH
1 sq.mm grade is used for lighting, 2.5 sq.mm for ring circuits

FLEX (Flexible cord)

Carries electricity from a socket to an appliance and from a ceiling rose to light fitting.

Core of copper threads
Plastic (PVC) casing
Plastic (PVC) casing

THREE-CORE SHEATHED
Standard flex for most purposes. Various grades (0.5 - 4 sq.mm) — the higher the wattage, the higher the grade number

THREE-CORE BRAIDED
Cotton braid surrounds wires covered by synthetic rubber. Good insulation — used for kettles and irons

TWO-CORE SHEATHED
Used for plastic lampholders and double-insulated appliances

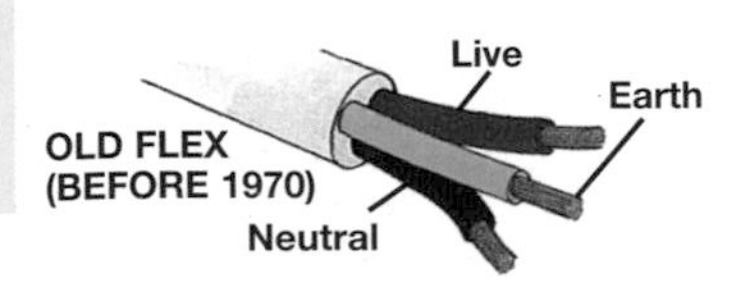

OLD FLEX (BEFORE 1970)

FUSES

A fuse is a weak point which is deliberately inserted in the circuit. The fuse 'blows' by melting if there is an overload.

PLUG FUSES

Use for equipment rated at less than 750 W. Never use a 3 A fuse for heating or cooking appliances

Use for equipment rated at more than 750 W

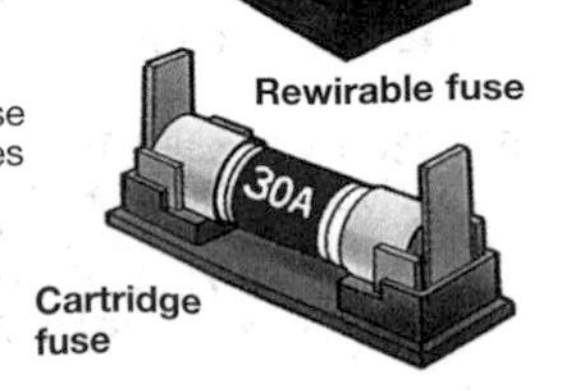

MAINS FUSES

An old-style consumer unit contains a row of **Rewirable fuses** — a length of fuse wire held between 2 screws. **Cartridge fuses** are easier to change — simply remove the blown cartridge and slip in a new one.

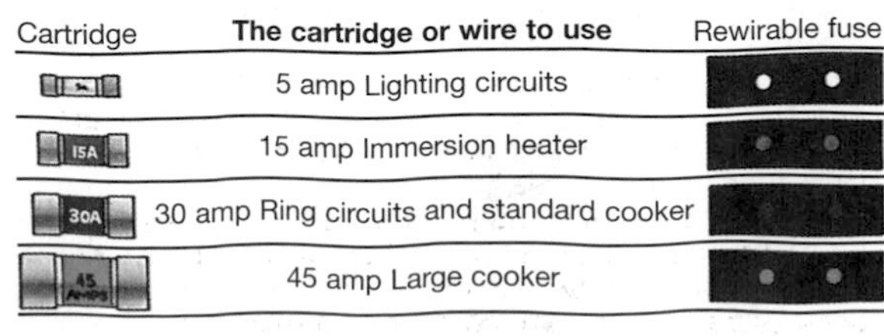

Cartridge	The cartridge or wire to use	Rewirable fuse
	5 amp Lighting circuits	
15A	15 amp Immersion heater	
30A	30 amp Ring circuits and standard cooker	
45 AMPS	45 amp Large cooker	

HOW TO AVOID ELECTRICAL PROBLEMS

- **KEEP AN ELECTRICITY TOOL KIT HANDY**

Few special tools are needed for electrical repairs. However trouble can strike quickly and without warning, so it is wise to keep the essential equipment together.

The essential kit:

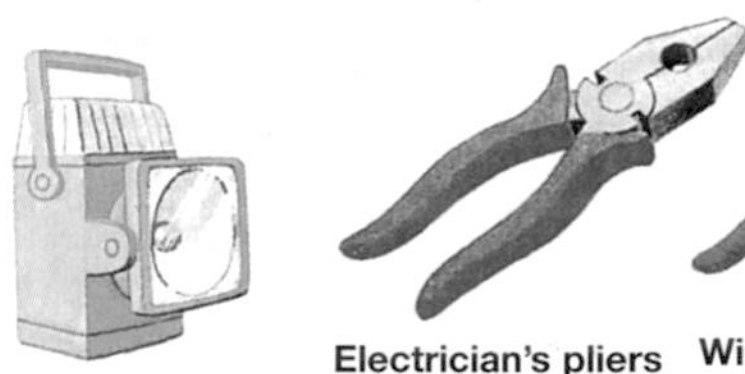

Torch
A free-standing one will leave your hands free

Electrician's pliers
Insulated handles; jaws for shaping and cutting wire

Wire strippers
Used to cut through insulation without cutting through the wire

Fuse wire or cartridges
The type of consumer unit determines whether wire or cartridges will be required

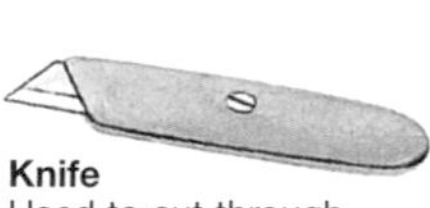

Knife
Used to cut through PVC sheathing

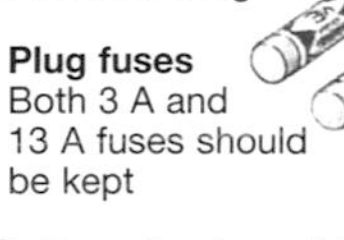

Plug fuses
Both 3 A and 13 A fuses should be kept

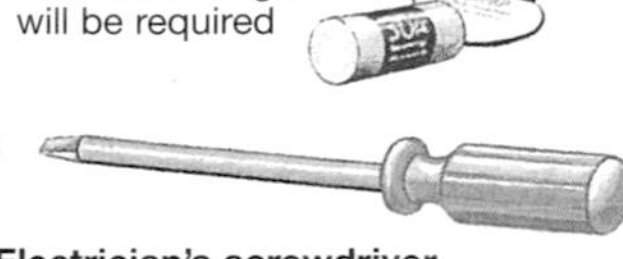

Electrician's screwdriver
Insulated handle; parallel-sided tip

Optional extras: Mains tester (a screwdriver with a neon bulb which lights when the blade touches a live connection). Connector strips for joining flex. Multimeter for testing circuits and batteries. Long-nosed pliers. Diagonal cutters for cutting cables. Cable clips for attaching cables to supports.

- **LABEL FUSES IN THE CONSUMER UNIT**

Make a list of the role of the fuses in the consumer unit. This list is usually written on the inside of the fuse unit cover, but it can be placed alongside or on adhesive strips stuck on the face of the consumer unit. Such a list will enable you to pull out the right fuse when one has blown.

- **CONSIDER REPLACING THE WIRING**

If your house was built before the mid 1950s, the electric cables will be sheathed in rubber. This will have started to deteriorate, and there is a chance that wires may be exposed. If you overload such a system there is the possibility of the copper conductors becoming hot and a fire may result. Look for the danger signs — round-pin plugs, old-fashioned switches, fuses blowing frequently, a smell of burning or sparks from sockets.

- **DON'T OVERLOAD THE CIRCUIT**

It is a great temptation these days to overload the circuit. There are so many new pieces of equipment, but the capacity of the domestic installation has not increased.

The maximum loading for a ring circuit is about 7 kW (7000 watts). At 10 kW the cartridge fuse in the mains will blow — if the fuse system uses wire it will not blow until 14 kW is being used. If blown fuses due to overloading are a recurring problem, cut down the load or have an additional ring circuit installed.

The standard 13 A plug has a maximum loading of 3 kW. You can put in an adaptor to run two appliances instead of one from the socket, but it is better to have twin sockets as a permanent home for the two plugs.

- **FOLLOW THE SAFETY RULES WHEN DEALING WITH APPLIANCES**

It is essential that you should use the appropriate plug, fuse and flex size when installing a piece of equipment. Use a 3-pin plug if an earth wire is present. Buy an unbreakable plug if it is to be regularly pushed in and pulled out of sockets. Do not pull out a plug by tugging the flex, and keep the flex well away from a source of heat.

Do not touch metal appliances with wet hands and do not immerse kitchen implements such as food mixers, electrical carving knives, etc in water. Never stand a vase of cut flowers on the TV. Whenever practical switch off equipment at the socket and remove the plug. Once a year check the flex and plug for wear and tear, and have large items such as washing machines, dishwashers and microwave ovens serviced regularly. The time interval between services will depend on the appliance.

- **FOLLOW THE SAFETY RULES WHEN DEALING WITH CABLES AND FLEX**

Unless there is an emergency, plan to work in daylight. Before you start, switch off the supply at the mains and remove the appropriate fuse. Put it in your pocket and do not replace it until the task is finished.

Never use ordinary staples to attach cables or flex to joists or skirting boards. Use insulated cable clips. Do not try to mend damaged flex with insulation tape — replace it with new flex of the correct type.

The length between the plug and the appliance should be kept as short as possible. Trailing flexes are a hazard, and flexes placed under a carpet can lead to a fire. Above all, never attempt to tackle a major task unless you know what you are doing.

- **FOLLOW THE SAFETY RULES IN THE BATHROOM**

Electricity and water are a hazardous mixture, so there are special rules for bathrooms. With the exception of a shaver point, you should not fix a socket in a bathroom. Furthermore you should make sure that all switches within the bathroom are of the cord-operated type.

Do not bring in portable equipment such as a hairdryer and make sure that all lampholders are out of reach of anyone standing in the bath or shower.

- **FIX AN RCD IF USING ELECTRICAL EQUIPMENT OUTDOORS**

A residual current device (RCD — see page 7) instead of a mains switch is a good idea if you are using an electrical hedgetrimmer or lawnmower in the garden or a power drill around the house. If the consumer unit does not have an RCD, you can buy a plug fitted with one and so you can protect yourself against shocks when using the socket.

- **EMPLOY A PROFESSIONAL ELECTRICIAN FOR OUTDOOR WIRING**

Although approval is not required for house wiring, the situation is different for wiring to provide lighting around the garden or to operate a pump in the pond. Here a contractor on the roll of the NICEIC (page 7) should be employed. Your electricity supply company will connect and then test the circuit.

- **INSTALL SUITABLE EQUIPMENT**

The standard voltage in the U.K is 240 V — equipment is generally marked 200 - 250 V AC (alternating current) or 200 - 250 V AC/DC. Equipment which is marked only DC (direct current) is not suitable.

HOW TO DEAL WITH ELECTRICAL PROBLEMS

APPLIANCE FAILURE

If an appliance fails to work when switched on, check that the other pieces of equipment on the circuit are working. If so, the most likely cause is a blown fuse in the plug.

Switch off and remove the plug. Check the wire connections — if all is in order remove the fuse. Test the fuse with a multimeter or an ordinary metal torch — see below.

Screw off the base of a metal torch. Hold the metal part of the fuse against the torch casing and the other end of the fuse on the base of the battery. Switch on. If the torch lights the fuse is sound

Replace the fuse if necessary and refit plug cover. If the appliance still fails and if the flex is sound, the fault is in the equipment and should be repaired by an electrician.

CIRCUIT FAILURE

If all the lights or sockets on a circuit are dead, then the most likely problem is a blown fuse in the consumer unit. You may have overloaded the circuit, or there may be a fault at one of the outlet points. If the circuit wasn't overloaded, you should switch off all the appliances or lights and then repair the fuse or reset the MCB (see page 7). Now switch on the lights or appliances one by one — if the fuse blows again you will have isolated the trouble spot. Check for loose connections — if you can't find the cause of the problem you should call in an electrician.

HOUSE SYSTEM FAILURE

If the whole electricity system fails, check with your neighbours. When you find that the district and not just your house is affected there is a power cut and there is nothing you can do about it. If your neighbours are not affected, you have house system failure. Check the fuses in the consumer unit — if they have not blown then you will most probably have a fault in the sealed fuse unit. Call your electricity supplier immediately.

POWER CUT

When you are first plunged into darkness, switch off appliances and most lights. Pull out the TV plug but do not switch off the refrigerator or the freezer. The freezer can be a problem, although the food will remain frozen for up to 12 hours during a power cut. Do not open the refrigerator or freezer doors until power is restored.

FLEX EXTENSION

It is sometimes necessary to extend a length of flex when an appliance is moved to a new position. You should never wind the wire ends together and bind the join with tape.

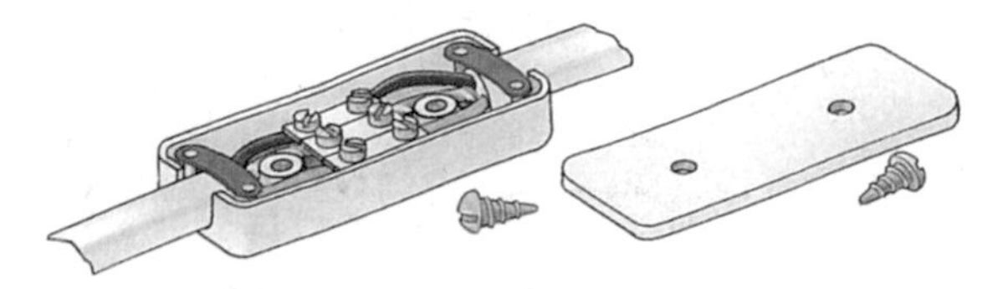

You can use an extension lead, but it is better to join an extra length of flex to the appliance wiring by means of a connector. Several types are available — the most straightforward is the one-part connector shown above.

LIGHT BULB FAILURE

If an ordinary tungsten filament bulb fails to light when switched on, check other lights on the circuit. If the problem is an isolated one, the most likely cause is a dead light bulb. You will need a new bulb.

Switch off, remove the bulb and replace. Remember to push the bulb firmly into the lampholder before twisting anti-clockwise to remove. If the bulb is broken in the socket, switch off at the mains and then push a cork into the broken base of the lamp bulb. Press and twist.

If the new bulb fails to light when switched on, the lampholder may be at fault. One of the metal plungers may have stuck or the holder may need rewiring.

Failure of a fluorescent tube to light may indicate a blown tube, but there are also several other possible causes — a defective starter switch, poor contact between the tube pins and the lampholder, a drop in voltage, a defective ballast, or a marked change in temperature.

UNPLEASANT SMELL

A type of plastic which was once used in the manufacture of light fittings emits a fishy smell when hot. Fortunately these fittings are no longer made and the only answer to the problem is to replace the unit or lampholder.

An acrid smell of burning rubber or wood is much more worrying. Check equipment quickly — if an appliance is causing the problem you must switch off and unplug it. Inspect sockets and plugs — if one is hot then take out the appropriate fuse and call an electrician immediately. If you cannot trace the fault then seek expert advice as soon as you can.

BLOWN FUSE

When a fault develops in a piece of equipment, it is the plug fuse which generally blows. If there is a fault in the flex or cable, or if the ring circuit has been overloaded, the fuse in the consumer unit blows. In a lighting circuit the cause of a blown fuse lies in either the bulb or the wiring.

If the fuse has blown because of overloading, the answer is simple. Repair the fuse and cut down the loading on that circuit. If, however, the fuse keeps blowing even when the circuit is not heavily loaded, you should call an electrician. What you must never do is to fit heavier wire in an attempt to resist blowing. Stop it blowing when there is a problem and you can have burnt-out wiring (or worse) on your hands.

To repair a rewirable fuse, turn off the main switch and remove the fuse carrier. You will find that the wire is broken and there may be scorch marks — loosen the two screws and remove all of the old wire. Wind a length of new wire of the correct rating (see page 8) round one screw and pass enough wire through the fuse to enable you to wind the end around the second terminal. Tighten the screws, cut off the excess wire, replace the fuse and switch on the current.

With a cartridge fuse insert a new cartridge between the two metal holders on the fuse carrier. With an MCB flick the switch or press the button to reset.

OVERHEATED PLUG OR SOCKET

If a plug feels warm, remove the top and see if a connection is loose or broken. Repair the fault and replace the plug cover. If a socket is warm or sparking, seek professional advice.

GAS

Although electricity has a virtual monopoly in the lighting of homes, gas still remains the main source of domestic energy. The type of gas has changed — the poisonous town gas obtained from coal has been replaced by natural gas extracted from below the North Sea and elsewhere.

Although no longer highly poisonous it should never be regarded as risk-free. The chance of an explosion remains if it is used carelessly and danger signs ignored. If incorrectly burnt the poisonous gas carbon monoxide is produced.

There are laws to protect you and your neighbour — ignore them and you could be fined. It is illegal to either install or service a piece of gas-burning equipment unless you are competent, and that means using a fitter who is registered with CORGI (see below). Gas installation is not for the DIY enthusiast.

You are also obliged not to use any equipment which you know to be faulty and you must take action if there is a gas leak. This calls for turning off the main gas tap, informing Transco (see page 12) and leaving the supply turned off until the fault has been repaired.

Gas is an excellent source of energy — easily controllable for cooking and highly versatile for heating. You now have a choice of suppliers which means that you may be able to find a cheaper source, but study the quotation carefully rather than just listening to the salesperson.

You must treat gas with respect and have your equipment serviced regularly. Make sure that any new item bears the CE mark — this denotes that the manufacturer guarantees that the appliance complies with the appropriate EEC directives, but it does not mean that it has been tested by an independent body. As a general rule do not buy a second-hand appliance unless the supplier is known to be reputable — remember that most faulty equipment accidents involve second-hand appliances.

LIGHTING THE GAS

In the old days a match was the only way to light gas appliances. Battery-operated spark guns were introduced to keep fingers away, and the pilot light was a great step forward. This small flame, however, has to be relit each time the appliance is switched off at the main tap and then switched on again. It can also go out in some appliances when the pressure drops, and so modern gas appliances have piezo ignition. This provides an instant spark when the control knob is turned or the ignition button is pressed.

CORGI

A CORGI registered engineer has been accepted by the Council for Registered Gas Installers. Competence is checked before an engineer is registered and competence is re-assessed every five years. An identity card is provided.

THE BALANCED FLUE

The exhaust fumes from a gas appliance must be allowed to escape — an old chimney must be carefully checked and cleaned before a gas appliance is attached to it. If there is no chimney a Balanced Flue system can be installed. This is attached to an outside wall and both the fresh air intake and flue outlet are sealed from the room.

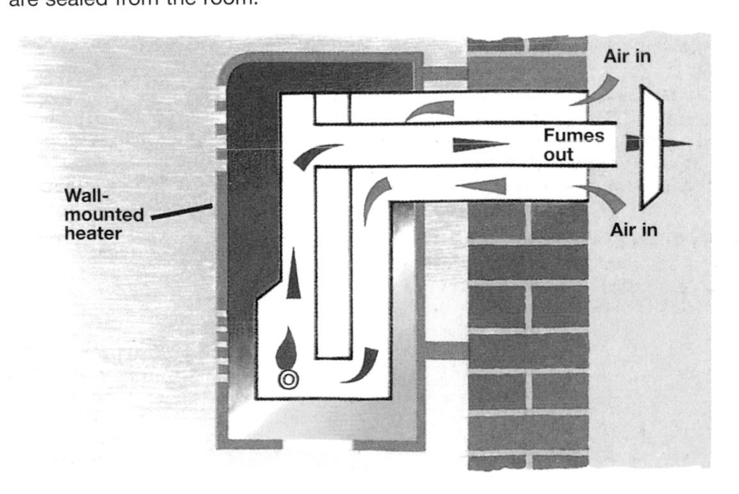

The Balanced Flue system is ideal for both wall-mounted room heaters and boilers and Ascot-type water heaters, but access to an outside wall is necessary. An alternative is the Instaduct system in which a flue duct is taken above the roof and is hidden within the house by a prefabricated chimney breast.

HOW TO AVOID GAS PROBLEMS

- **LOCATE AND TEST THE MAIN GAS TAP**
  Look for the main gas tap — it is generally located close to the meter. Test the handle — if it is stiff, call your gas supplier. Never try to force the handle or attempt to fix it yourself.

- **SWEEP THE CHIMNEY BEFORE FITTING AN APPLIANCE**
  A blocked chimney will not allow fumes to escape — the air in the room will be polluted. It is therefore essential to have the chimney swept before fitting a fire or other fixed appliance.

- **DO NOT BLOCK A VENTILATOR**
  Ventilators provide a constant stream of fresh air, and this allows natural gas to burn efficiently. Blocking a ventilator to cut down draughts or for some other reason can have harmful or even fatal results.

- **HAVE APPLIANCES SERVICED REGULARLY**
  Central heating and fires should be serviced annually — other appliances every 1 - 2 years. Do not attempt to service or repair equipment or appliances — use a CORGI registered engineer. It is a good idea to have a regular servicing contract — your gas supplier may offer this service.

- **CONSIDER INSTALLING A GAS DETECTOR**
  It is not usually necessary to install a detector to warn you if natural gas is escaping — your nose should be able to let you know if there is a problem. However a mains-operated unit fitted close to the ceiling may be a good idea if you have an impaired sense of smell.

- **CONSIDER SWITCHING OFF THE SUPPLY IF YOU ARE GOING AWAY**
  Before leaving on a long holiday you should switch off the main gas tap — check that there is no food in a gas-operated refrigerator or freezer. The situation is different if you are going away for a week or two in winter and your home is heated by gas central heating or if you have a gas water heater. Leave the gas on to avoid burst pipes, but turn the thermostat down.

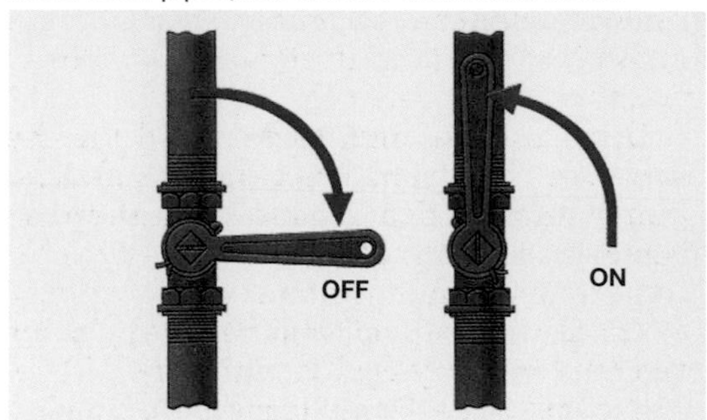

Turn off all appliance taps and pilot lights before turning the handle of the main gas tap to the OFF position. To restore the supply, move the handle to the ON position and relight the pilot lights immediately.

- **CONSIDER INSTALLING A CARBON MONOXIDE DETECTOR**
  It is more usual to have a carbon monoxide detector than one for natural gas as carbon monoxide is both odourless and highly poisonous.

HOW TO DEAL WITH GAS PROBLEMS

- **A SMELL OF GAS**
  Act immediately:
  1. Put out all naked flames. Do not smoke.
  2. Do not operate any electrical switches.
  3. Open doors and windows to allow the gas to escape. Do not close them until the problem has been solved.
  4. The most likely cause of a gas escape is a pilot light which has gone out or a tap which has been turned on but not lit. Relight, allow the smell to disappear and then close the doors and windows.
  5. If you cannot locate and remove the cause of the problem, turn off the main gas tap — see the illustration above.
  6. Call Transco's 24-hour year-round emergency service (0800 111 999). A fitter will call and stop the leak. This service is free, and so is the first 30 minutes of any minor repairs which may be necessary. Of course, if the fault is on the street side of the meter then no charge whatever is made for its repair.

  If the smell of gas is only slight and localised near a pipe joint, you can test for a leak by brushing soapy water over the area. The appearance of bubbles tells you that gas is escaping — turn off the main gas tap and call Transco.

  If you smell gas outside the house or when walking along the street, call Transco at once.

- **BROWN MARKS AROUND APPLIANCES**
  If brown or sooty marks appear above a gas fire or around the top of a water heater, the fumes are not escaping properly and you must have the installation inspected immediately.

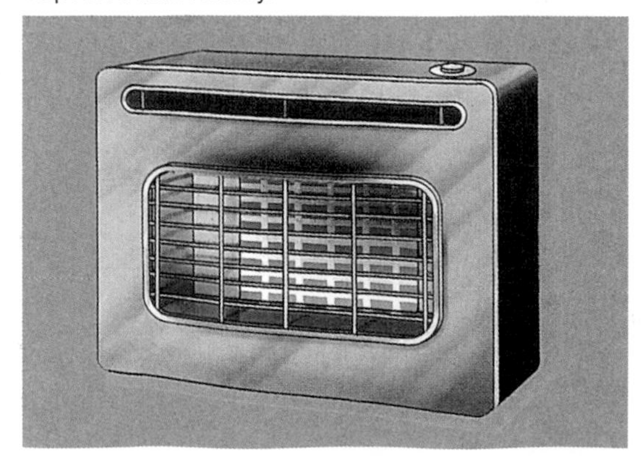

A blocked chimney is the usual cause of the trouble, and staining is only one of the by-products of faulty fume escape. The flame is usually yellow rather than blue, and carbon monoxide may build up in the room. This gas is poisonous — the main symptoms are headaches, drowsiness and weakness.

SOLID FUEL

Wood and then coal were once our most widely used fuels, but not any more. Gas and then electricity made solid fuels seem so time-consuming. Storage had to be provided and the fire required to be fed every few hours. There were ashes to remove, sparks to guard against and automatic heat control was not always possible.

Despite these drawbacks, solid fuel has staged a comeback. There is the satisfaction of an open fire in winter and there has been a revolution in appliance design. You can buy multi-fuel heaters which will burn wood as well as coal, and some appliances can use ordinary coal in Smokeless Zones. There are types with trays which hold a week's ash and others with hoppers which feed the fire with fuel. Coal is sold under all sorts of names. There is house coal — cheap but not smokeless and sold in various grades. Anthracite and Welsh dry steam coal are natural smokeless coals — there are in addition numerous brands of manufactured smokeless fuels. Ask your coal merchant for advice on the right type to buy for your appliance.

Wood is popular in areas where it is free for the taking, but use it with care. It should have been left to dry, for at least a year if possible, and the chimney must be properly lined. Sweeping will be necessary once a month if you burn wood every day.

It is illegal to emit smoke from your chimney if you live in a Smoke Control Area (Smokeless Zone). You must use a smokeless fuel or an exempted appliance burning coal or wood.

SOLID FUEL ASSOCIATION

Ring 0845 601 4406 for advice

	OPEN FIRE	ROOM HEATER	BOILER	COOKER
Heating the room	✓	✓		✓ An advantage in winter, but drawback in summer
Providing domestic hot water	✓ If a back boiler is fitted	✓ If a back boiler is fitted	✓	✓ If a boiler is fitted
Notes	You can choose from a standard open firegrate or a freestanding fire. Underfloor draught fires increase the range of suitable fuels and give greater control	The fire is enclosed in a glass-fronted firebox. This gives greater safety and much better heat control. Both radiant and convected heat is supplied	Small boilers heat the domestic water supply — large ones run the central heating as well. Gravity-feed ones need refuelling only once a day	There are usually 2 ovens — a 'hot' one for roasting and a 'cold' one for warming dishes. Cookers are available in a range of colours and sizes

HOW TO AVOID SOLID FUEL PROBLEMS

- **KEEP THE SYSTEM CLEAN**
  Decoke the parts where soot and ash build up — do this every month or as often as the makers advise. Have the chimney swept at least once a year. Consider fitting a carbon monoxide detector — see page 12.

- **AVOID THE RISK OF FIRE**
  Use a fireguard at all times when the fire is lit — it should be attached to the wall if small children are present. Do not hang clothes on a fireguard. Never use paraffin to start the fire and never bank it up with fuel to a dangerous level. Never use a sheet of newspaper to draw a coal fire.

- **ACT QUICKLY IF SOMETHING IS WRONG**
  Call the fire brigade immediately if the chimney catches fire or if the chimney breast suddenly gets too hot to touch. The opposite may happen — the fire burns very slowly and there is a strong smell of fumes. Let the fire go out and thoroughly clean the appliance. Call the Solid Fuel Association if the fumes persist — do not continue to use the fire.

- **LIGHT THE FIRE PROPERLY**
  You can use the traditional newspaper and firewood if you do not live in a Smoke Control Area — if you do then you will have to use white firelighters or an electric firelighter.

LIQUID FUEL

The two basic forms of liquid fuel are paraffin and bottled gas. Paraffin is stored in ordinary cans but bottled gas requires special steel canisters — it is gaseous fuel which has been liquefied and is kept in this form by the strength of the container. When the valve is opened the fuel escapes as a gas into the appliance.

Neither paraffin nor bottled gas needs a flue, and this makes them suitable for portable space heaters. They are used where there is neither mains electricity nor a natural gas supply — these heaters are sometimes also employed to provide extra warmth in winter or standby heat in case of a power cut.

They are efficient as none of the heat is lost up the flue as with a gas fire or oil boiler. But these liquid fuel appliances pose a number of problems. Good ventilation is essential if condensation is to be avoided. Thermostatic control is not available, although bottled gas heaters have several settings. Accidents do happen so follow the manufacturer's instructions. Some models get very hot so site appliances away from the line of traffic.

Paraffin has a limited range of uses — these days it is almost entirely restricted to space heaters. Bottled gas is quite different — the appliance is attached to a canister or storage tank from which gas passes to the burner. Here it behaves just like natural gas — it can be used for fixed fires, cookers, central heating systems and patio heaters.

PARAFFIN

Paraffin is a grade of kerosene, coloured pink or blue for identification. It is generally bought in small amounts for convector and/or radiant heaters — such models are usually portable but fixed versions are available. A modern paraffin stove is a useful standby if the basic source of heat fails — such heaters will have a fail-safe device which extinguishes the flame if the appliance is knocked over. Paraffin has a limited range of uses — it is not used for central heating. Regular attention is necessary if smells are to be avoided. Compared with electricity or gas, there is too much work involved. Cans have to be brought home, tanks have to be filled and wicks have to be trimmed. Furthermore, automatic control is not available.

BOTTLED GAS (LPG)

Bottled gas is the popular name for LPG — liquefied petroleum gas. Two types are available — the canisters of butane and propane are painted differently to avoid confusion. Do not use a butane canister for propane or vice versa — the two liquefied gases work at different pressures. Canisters are available in various sizes. The usual one for a portable space heater is 15 kg — this weighs 30 kg when full so bottled gas is cumbersome to handle. You will have to pay a hire charge for each canister and at least two will be required — one in use and the other to replace it when empty. LPG can be kept outdoors in a special storage tank. Supplies are obtained from a tanker and this is the most economical way to use LPG. It will fuel a central heating system just like natural gas but it will be appreciably more expensive. Unlike natural gas, bottled gas is heavier than air when it leaves the canister. Escaped gas will not disperse if you open a window — it collects at floor level.

Propane

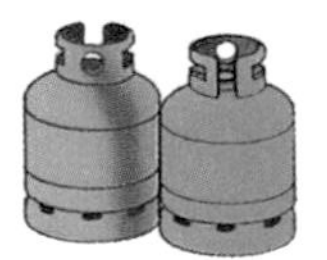
Butane

HOW TO AVOID LIQUID FUEL PROBLEMS

- **STORE THE FUEL PROPERLY**
  Paraffin should not be stored in the house. Bottled gas canisters should be stored outdoors wherever possible. If the canisters have been stored in a room or shed, make sure that the area is ventilated by opening the door before you strike a match or switch on the light. The storage area should be cool but an underground room such as a cellar should be avoided. Fixed storage tanks for bottled gas should be sited well away from the house.

- **HAVE EQUIPMENT SERVICED REGULARLY**
  Large pieces of equipment such as central heating and cookers using bottled gas should be serviced each year. Hoses connecting cylinders to appliances should be checked regularly for leaks. This is done by brushing soapy water over them — the appearance of bubbles indicates a leak.

- **HANDLE BOTTLED GAS CANISTERS WITH CARE**
  Extinguish all naked flames when changing canisters.

- **VENTILATE THE ROOM**
  Good ventilation is essential. Open a window slightly if the doors are draught-proofed — failure to do so will result in excessive condensation. Ventilation is necessary, but direct draughts must be avoided.

- **HANDLE APPLIANCES WITH CARE**
  Never fill a paraffin heater when it is still lit. Try to fill it outdoors and make sure the cap is properly secured after filling. Wipe the outside of the tank. Never move a heater when it is lit. Keep it away from curtains, furniture etc and face the appliance towards the centre of the room. Keep it out of the path of children and animals.

WATER

The provision of hot and cold water is the most vital and for many the most mysterious of the services which come into the house. With the help of a bewildering array of pipes, taps, valves, sanitary ware, basins, cylinders, boilers and so on we lead comfortable lives, but every now and again things go wrong or we decide to alter things by installing a new piece of equipment.

For most people this is the time to call in the professional, and unless you really know what you are doing it is the right decision. Repairing metal pipes or changing a sink calls for the right tools and experience. Make sure you choose a competent plumber. You can call the Institute of Plumbing for the name of a local member, but the best plan is to use someone who has done a satisfactory job for you in the past or ask a friend or neighbour for the name of someone they can recommend.

You can't leave everything to the plumber, and that's where this book can help. Frozen or burst pipes call for immediate action by you, so get to know how your system works, where the stopcocks and valves are, what to do in the case of an emergency and how to carry out simple repairs.

For the more adventurous you will find push-fit plastic pipes and a wide range of how-to-do-it leaflets at your DIY store. Do remember that there are numerous water by-laws which must be followed. Before undertaking any major work you must get in touch with your water supplier to check whether an inspection will be necessary.

TAPS & VALVES

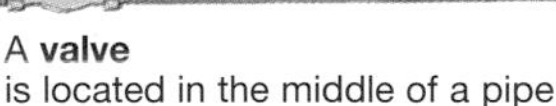
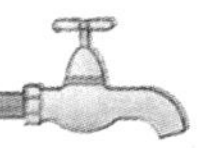

VALVES

STOPCOCK (stop valve)
Used when water is at mains pressure. Most have a single bar handle.

GATE VALVE
Used when water is at less than mains pressure (e.g water supply from cistern). Most have a wheel handle.

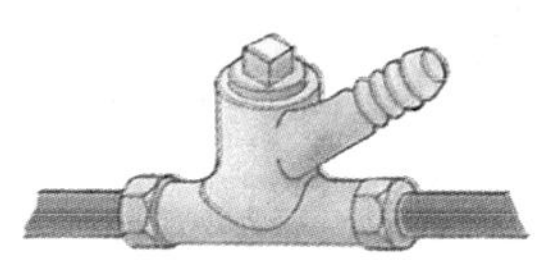

DRAINCOCK (drain valve)
Unlike others, it is usually kept closed. Used to drain water away. Most have a square nut instead of a handle.

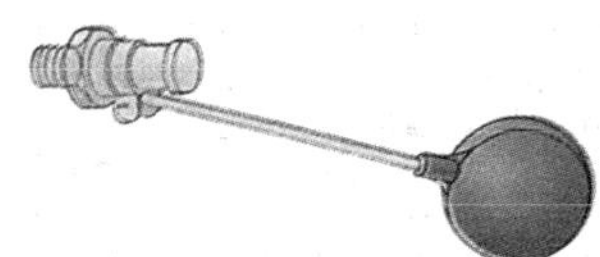

BALL VALVE
Technically a 'tap', not a valve. Used in a cistern or tank to prevent water rising above a pre-set level.

TAPS

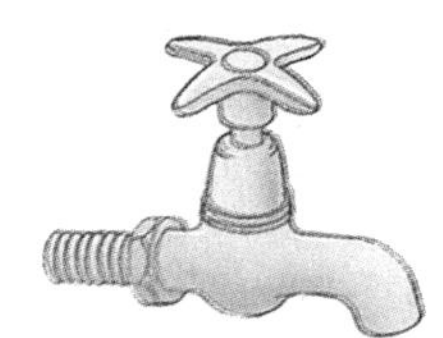

BIB TAP
Water enters horizontally. Handle is usually a crutch (single bar) or a capstan (cross bars). Securing screw is visible.

PILLAR TAP
Water enters vertically. Handle is usually a shrouded head, made of metal or plastic. Securing screw is under the plate at the top.

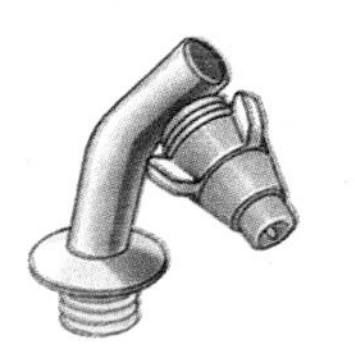

SUPATAP
Water enters vertically. A variation of the pillar tap — washer can be changed without having to turn off the water supply.

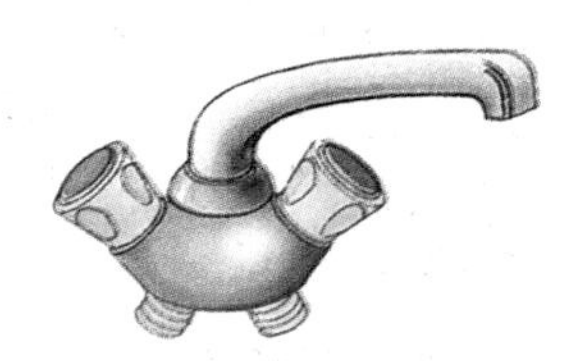

MIXER TAP
Water enters horizontally or vertically. Kitchen types have a movable spout — bathroom types may have a shower attachment.

THE PLUMBING SYSTEM

A service pipe leading from the water main in the road brings water to you and there are two basic ways in which cold water may be carried around the house. Some older houses have a **DIRECT PLUMBING SYSTEM** in which all the cold taps and WCs are fed from the rising main. It is a cheaper and simpler system than the indirect one, and you can obtain drinking water from any tap. But there are several drawbacks and these are serious enough for some councils to forbid the installation of the direct system in a new house.

These problems are avoided in the much more popular **INDIRECT PLUMBING SYSTEM** illustrated below. Here the rising main feeds the cold water cistern and the kitchen tap. The cistern is located in the attic or loft, and all other taps and units obtain their water from it. Excessive noise due to the high pressure in direct plumbing pipework is avoided and so is the danger of contaminating the mains supply by dirty water siphoning back along the pipework. In addition the water in the cistern allows WCs to be flushed when the system is temporarily closed down.

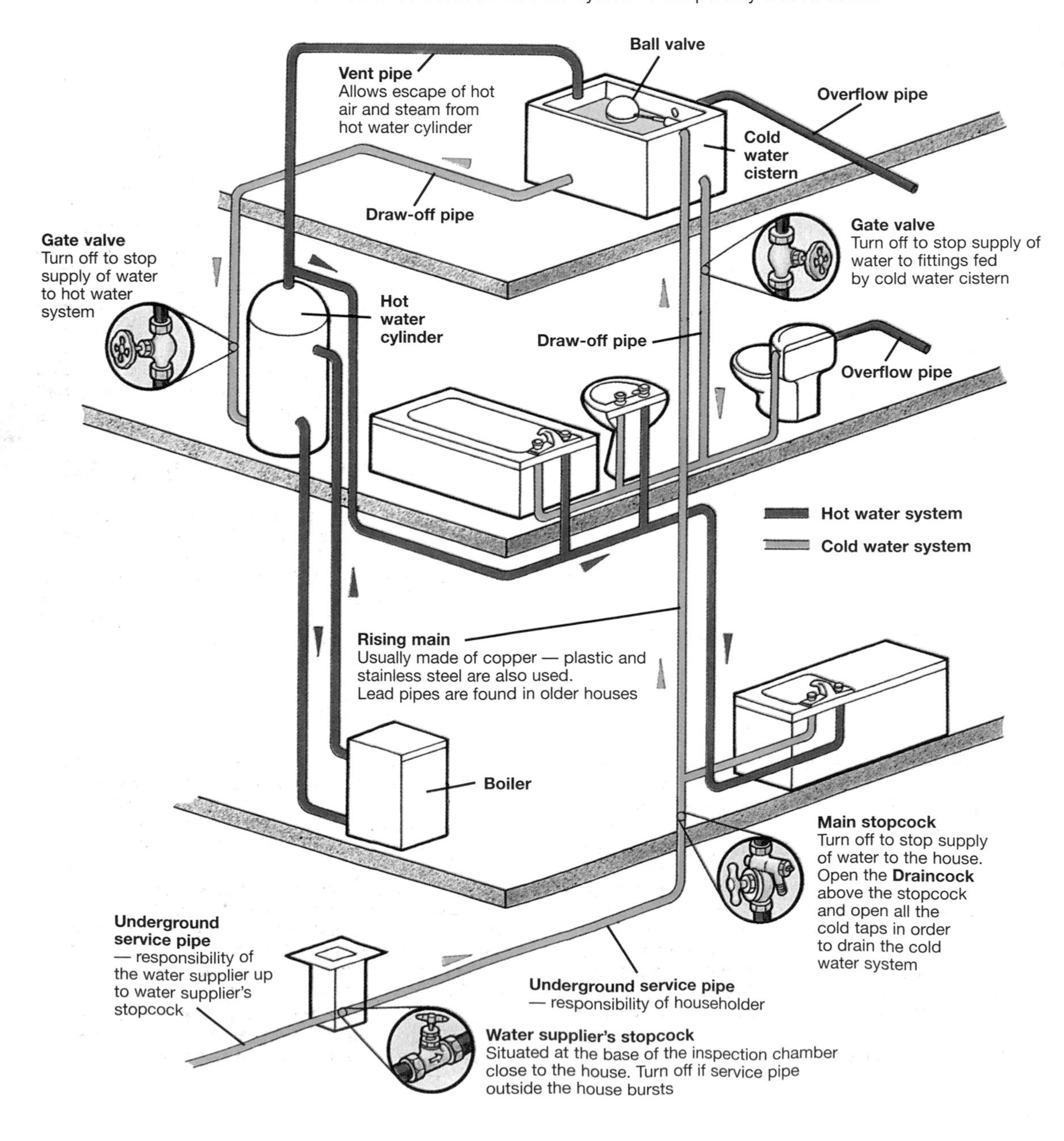

THE HOT WATER SYSTEM

INDIRECT SYSTEM

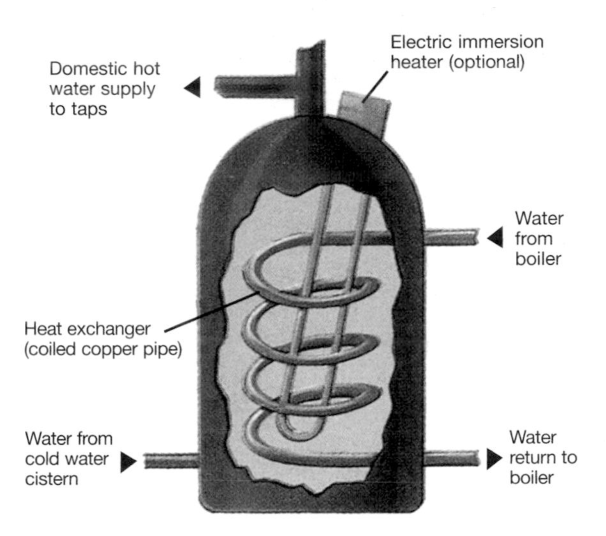

This system uses a boiler to heat both the domestic water supply and the central heating system. The primary circuit from the boiler heats the coiled pipes in the cylinder and also the radiators which make up the central heating system. This primary circuit is supplied with water from a feed-and-expansion cistern fitted in the roof space — in some houses self-priming indirect cylinders are installed which do not need a feed-and-expansion cistern. The secondary circuit, fed by the cold water cistern, supplies the hot water taps around the house. An electric immersion heater fitted in the cylinder will heat the domestic water supply when the boiler is switched off during the summer months. This open-vented wet system is the most popular form of central heating — for details of boilers, controls, pipework etc see pages 26-27. Some DIY books show how you can convert a direct into an indirect system, but this job should never be undertaken if you have no plumbing experience — it really is a job for the professional. It is your job, however, to learn how to use and maintain the system properly.

DIRECT SYSTEM

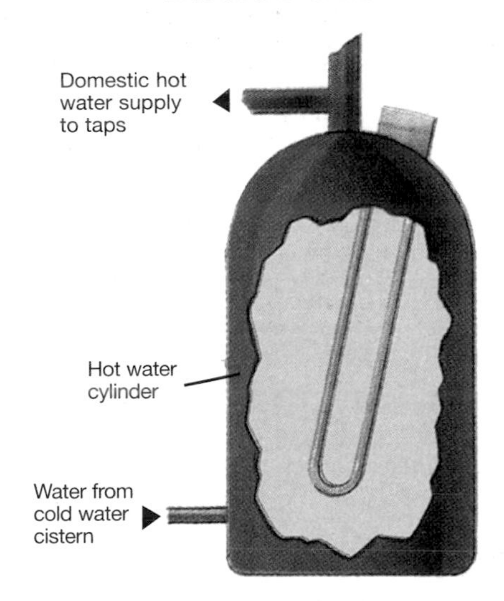

The water in the cylinder is heated by an immersion heater and is carried by the pipework to the hot water taps. It is less expensive and easier to install than the indirect system, but it is not suitable for linking to a central heating system. Scaling and corrosion are more of a problem and so the direct system should therefore not be used in a hard water area. Both top entry and side entry immersion heaters are available. The most economical type is the double-element heater.

INSTANTANEOUS SYSTEM

The Ascot style of water heater can be attached directly to the rising main. The gas jets or electric elements are activated by the water flow when the unit is switched on. There is no storage capacity, but heaters of this type are economical and can be installed in situations where a water storage system would not be possible or practical.

DRAINING THE SYSTEM

There are times when it is necessary to drain all or part of the plumbing system. A pipe may have burst, a washer may have to be fitted or a new piece of equipment installed.

Collect some water in the bath for flushing the toilet with a bucket and fill some pans to provide drinking water. Turn off the central heating. If the problem can be isolated then close the appropriate stopcock or gate valve — otherwise it will be necessary to turn off the main stopcock to close down the whole system. If the main stopcock cannot be turned it will be necessary to try to turn off the water supplier's stopcock (see page 16) — if you cannot do this then call the company immediately for assistance.

With the water supply from the mains turned off you should now open all the cold taps to drain the pipes and cistern as quickly as possible. If the problem is an upstairs leak and water is coming through the ceiling, switch off the lights and work with a torch. Make one or more holes with a nail at the spot where the water is dripping.

Drain the hot water system by opening the hot water taps and the draincock situated close to the cylinder. The central heating system can be drained by opening the valve which is situated at the lowest point of the system but do not drain the central heating system if it is not part of the problem.

It will be necessary to refill the plumbing system once the problem is over. Turn off all the taps and draincocks and then turn on the main stopcock.

HOW TO AVOID WATER PROBLEMS

- **LOCATE AND TEST THE VALVES**
Look for the various valves in your water system — don't wait for an emergency. Label if necessary. Turn the handles off and on once a year to make sure that they are working properly.

- **KEEP A ROLL OF WATERPROOF SELF-ADHESIVE TAPE**
This material can be used to make a temporary repair to a leaking joint or a burst pipe.

- **CHECK THE COLD WATER CISTERN OCCASIONALLY**
Make sure the lid fits properly — it should keep out light, flies and spiders but it should not be airtight. Look for corrosion both inside and outside the tank — consult a plumber if there are brown patches on the outside of a metal cistern.

- **TAKE PRECAUTIONS BEFORE A WINTER HOLIDAY**
There is a high risk of water freezing in the pipes if a house is left unoccupied and unheated for 2 or 3 weeks in winter. To avoid problems, leave the central heating on at a low level and open internal doors. If this seems costly or there is no central heating, drain both the cold and hot water systems. On your return, remember to refill the system before turning on the heat.

- **USE THE COLD TAP IN THE KITCHEN FOR DRINKING WATER**
The water reaching the rising main in your house is tested regularly by your water company. Some suppliers add fluoride to reduce the incidence of tooth decay in children. The purest water will be obtained from the cold tap in the kitchen. If lead piping is present in your home and you live in a soft water area, run the water for about 30 seconds before use in the morning or after a holiday.
Water drawn from the cold water cistern is best avoided for drinking purposes unless you know that the tank is clean and free from corrosion. Never use water from the hot water system for filling the kettle.

- **DEAL WITH HARD WATER**
Most of the water in the southern and eastern counties is hard. The cause is the presence of dissolved salts of calcium and magnesium — in the presence of soap a curd or scum is formed. Bathroom fixtures are stained, washed woollens are matted and soap does not lather properly.
The serious problem starts when the water is heated above 60°C. Kettles develop fur and hot water pipes develop scale. This scaling results in noisy pipes, increasing the cost of running the system and both the boiler and immersion heaters may be damaged.
Proprietary descalers are available for cleaning kettles and the heat exchanger in the hot water cylinder can be descaled by adding a lime-removing chemical to the feed-and-expansion cistern. This chemical must be flushed out after treatment — follow the manufacturer's instructions. Install an indirect cylinder (see page 17) to replace a direct one, and avoid setting the thermostat at above 60°C.
There are electromagnetic water conditioners which can be fitted to pipework very easily and these keep the calcium from settling on the pipework or shower-head, but the most satisfactory solution is to fit a water softener on the rising main above the cold water tap in the kitchen. This works on the ion exchange principle, sodium being added to the water in exchange for the system-damaging calcium and magnesium. It is necessary to top up the salt level at regular intervals.

- **CHECK THE WASHING MACHINE PIPES OCCASIONALLY**
The hoses on washing machines occasionally work loose and split. Examine them carefully every few months — refit or replace if necessary.

- **LAG THE TANKS AND PIPES**
The purpose of lagging the hot water system is to keep the heat in, thereby reducing the fuel bill. The role of lagging the cold water system is to keep the cold out in winter, which reduces the risk of freezing. Loft insulation to keep the house warmer has become popular in recent years, but it can spell danger. The cistern and associated pipes above the insulation will be colder than before and so some protection is necessary. Do not cover the area below the cistern when insulating the loft, and lag both the cistern and pipes. Remember to lag the overflow pipe as well as those carrying water.

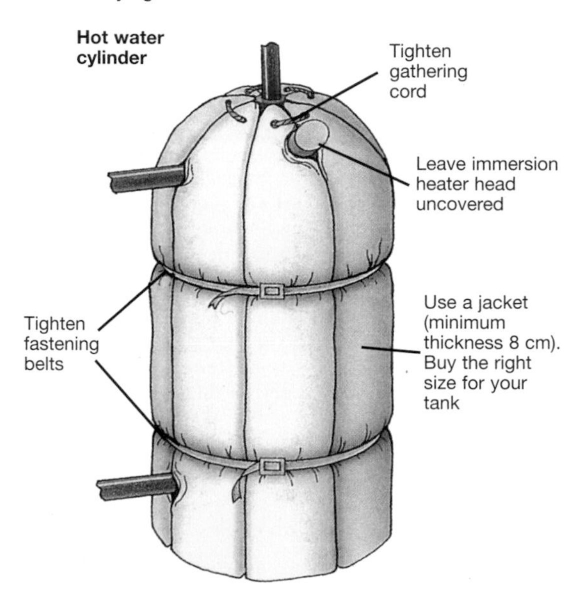

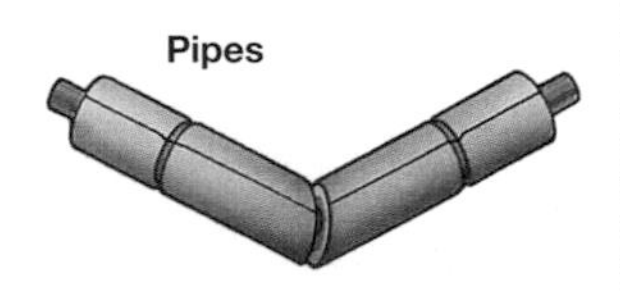

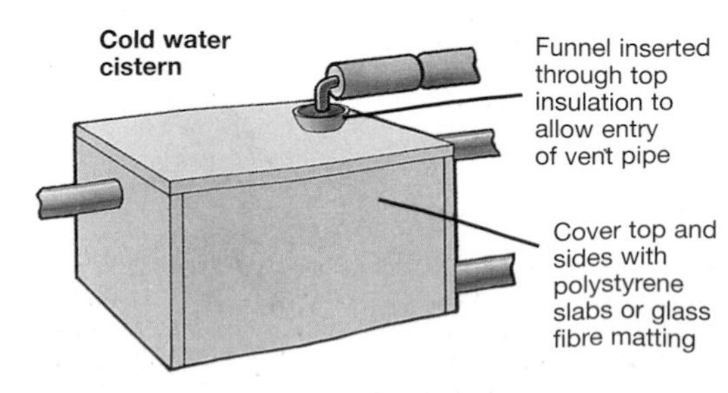

HOW TO DEAL WITH WATER PROBLEMS

- **DRIPPING TAP**
A tap which drips when closed usually needs a new washer. Turn off the water supply and leave the tap open. With a capstan head tap (see page 15) unscrew the shield below the handle. It is a little trickier with a modern shrouded head tap — you will need to prise up the cover to find a small retaining screw which must be released. Pull off the head.

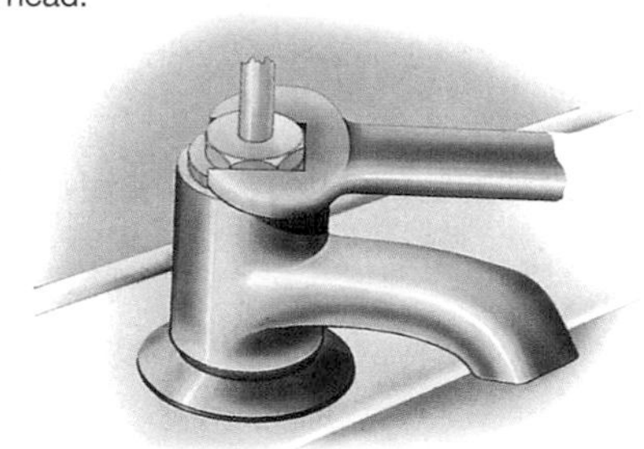

Use a spanner to undo the hexagonal nut which is revealed — lift out the top half of the tap. At the base of this assembly you will find a washer secured with a small nut. Remove this nut and fit a replacement rubber or nylon washer of the same diameter. Reassemble the tap and then restore the water supply. If the tap continues to leak after fitting a new washer, the tap seating requires refacing. Consult a plumber.

- **SEEPING TAP**
If water seeps out round the spindle, there is a fault in the gland unit. Buy a repair kit from your local DIY shop or consult a plumber.

- **NOISY PIPES**
It is normal for pipes carrying hot water to creak or knock occasionally as they expand. Insert plastic foam below the problem area if you are able to locate it. The presence of scale in the pipes is a common cause of noisy pipes in hard water areas (see page 18). A loud banging and vibration in the pipes is a water hammer, caused by the flow of water being shut off too quickly. The culprit is a worn washer or a faulty gland unit in a tap or an unsuitable ball valve in the cistern.

- **LEAKING PIPES**
There are several possible causes — a hole caused by a nail being driven into the pipe or a fracture due to corrosion or freezing. Immediate action is necessary to prevent damage to carpets, wall coverings etc. Turn off the water supply and dry the affected pipe area. For a small hole, drive in the point of a pencil and then break it off. Tightly bind the area with waterproof tape. If the trouble is a split rather than a hole, bind the fracture with waterproof tape. If the split is large, spread an epoxy glue over and around the fracture before binding with tape. After carrying out the temporary repair, restore the water supply and call a plumber to replace the pipe section.

- **FROZEN PIPES**
Inspect the pipes — if there is a fracture turn off the main stopcock and drain the system. Apply a temporary repair (see above) and then partly open the stopcock. To thaw a pipe, open the tap and apply heat, moving from the tap gradually backwards along the pipe. Never use a naked flame — employ a hair dryer or a hot-air paint stripper.

- **LEAKING JOINTS**
Where nuts are present (compression joint) tighten by a series of quarter turns. If this does not stop the leak or if the joint is a soldered one (capillary joint), treat as for a leaking pipe using waterproof tape or an epoxy glue plus tape.

- **DRIPPING OVERFLOW PIPE**
Carefully bend the lever arm of the ball valve downwards slightly to ensure cut off before the overflow level is reached.

- **POURING OVERFLOW PIPE**
There are several possible causes. Raise the ball float gently and see if the water flow ceases. If it does, the ball is faulty and needs replacing. To change a ball float, close the valve by tying the lever arm to a piece of wood across the top of the cistern. Empty the tank and unscrew the ball. Buy a plastic replacement and attach to the lever arm. If the water continues to flow when the ball is raised, the cause is a defective valve which will need to be replaced.

- **NOISY CISTERN**
A problem with old-fashioned cisterns. Replace the present ball valve with a modern one.

- **DIRTY WATER**
The usual cause is an inadequate cover on the cold water cistern. Drain the system, bale out remaining water in the cistern and clean the tank thoroughly. Restore water supply and fit a satisfactory cover.

- **RUSTY WATER**
If the cold water system is affected, then corrosion has occurred in the cistern. Rusty water is much more usual from the hot tap after a large volume of water has been drawn off. This indicates that the boiler has corroded — consult a plumber who will probably advise the installation of a new indirect system (page 17).

- **LITTLE OR NO WATER WHEN THE TAP IS OPEN**
If the mains water is running and the cold water cistern is full, the cause in the cold water system is a frozen pipe — see FROZEN PIPES on this page. In the hot water system the cause is an airlock — the symptoms are a spluttering noise and little or no water from the tap.

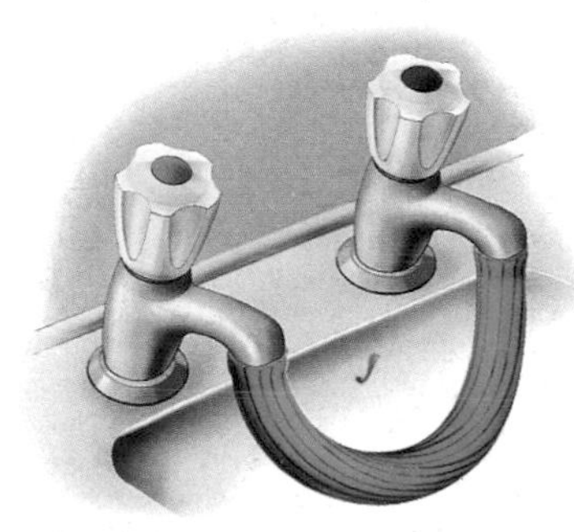

Attach a piece of hose between the hot and cold tap in the kitchen. Open the hot taps in the bathroom and then open the kitchen taps. The pressure of the mains water should drive out the air bubble — consult a plumber if the airlock is not removed as there may be a fault in the system.

DRAINAGE

Three distinct types of drainage water have to be carried away from the house. There is the soapy waste water from sinks, basins and bath plus the foul soil water from the WC. In addition there is rain-water collected by the gutters on the roof.

It was once thought that it was essential to keep waste water and soil water apart, which meant that different pipes were installed — the standard two pipe system. In modern houses, however, there is a single main stack into which the water from the upstairs WC, bath and basins flows — the one pipe system.

Before making any changes to your drainage system you will need to obtain permission from your local council. Permission is also required if you plan to erect an extension, garage or shed over a manhole cover.

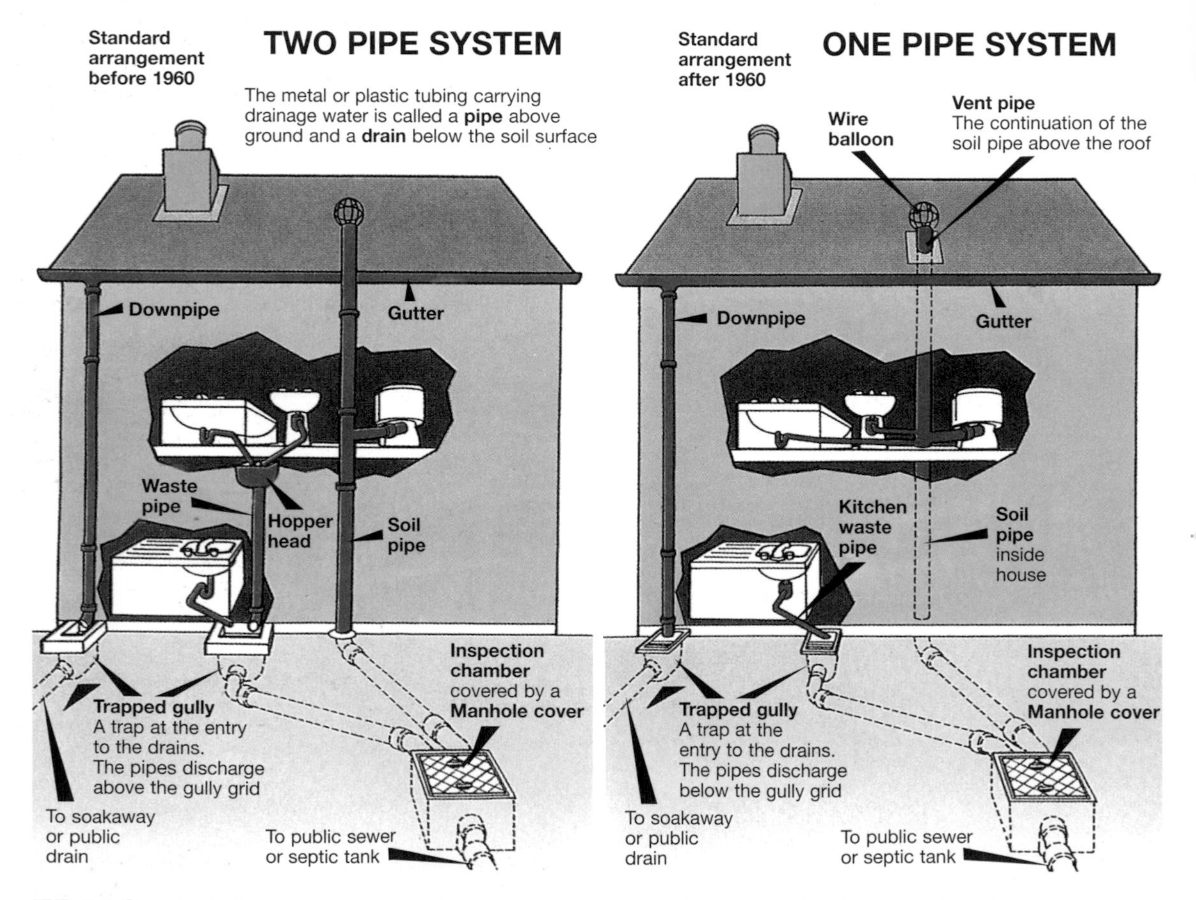

TRAPS

A trap is a water-filled pipe or device which prevents foul air entering the house from the drains. It is generally attached to the outlet pipe, but with a WC it is part of the fitting.

U TRAP
The old-fashioned trap on metal pipes. The trap is emptied by unscrewing the access plug at the base.

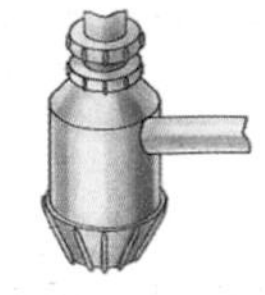

BOTTLE TRAP
A chromium-plated trap — popular where pipework is exposed. Main drawback is that it can slow down the flow rate.

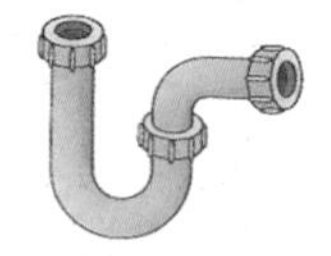

P TRAP
A plastic trap which can be unscrewed for clearing. The type to choose for a horizontal exit pipe.

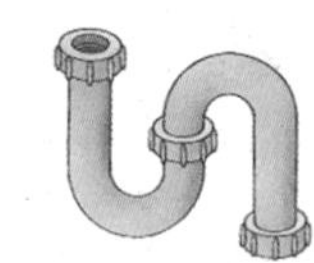

S TRAP
A plastic trap which can be unscrewed for clearing. The type to choose for a vertical exit pipe.

HOW TO AVOID DRAINAGE PROBLEMS

- **KEEP THE GUTTERS CLEAR**
A cake of dead leaves, bird droppings and other debris collects in gutters. The space for water is reduced and this can cause overflowing during heavy rain. Once a year remove this rubbish with a trowel — put it into a bucket and not down the pipe. Cover the mouth of the downpipe with a ball of wire netting.

- **KEEP THE WASTE PIPES CLEAR**
Do not put peelings, tea leaves, melted fat etc into the kitchen sink — keep the grille clean. You can install a waste disposal unit to wash away kitchen waste. Washing soda in hot water will remove grease from the pipework. If blockage has been a problem, use a plunger about once a year to prevent trouble.

HOW TO DEAL WITH DRAINAGE PROBLEMS

- **BLOCKED PIPEWORK**
There are several symptoms of this distressing and often difficult problem. Several fittings may refuse to drain or one fitting may fill up when another is emptied. There may be an unpleasant smell or a gully may overflow. Cleaning out a blocked hopper or gully is often a relatively simple job, but for nearly everyone a blocked soil pipe or drain is a job to leave to a specialist drainage company. If you do decide to tackle the job you should put on old clothes, an overall and gloves.

- **BLOCKED OR LEAKING DOWNPIPE/GUTTER**
See page 80 for details.

- **BLOCKED HOPPER**
Using your gloved hands remove debris from inside the hopper and then use a cane or draining rod to push down any blocking material in the pipe. Make sure the bottom of the pipe is free and then pour water into the hopper to ensure that the pipe is working properly.

- **BLOCKED GULLY**
Remove any rubbish which may be covering the grid before removing this protective cover. Use a stick to break up compacted debris within the trap and remove as much solid material as you can with your rubber-gloved hands. Flush with a hosepipe when water starts to run away freely. If the water is still not running through the gully then you have a drain problem.

- **BLOCKED DRAIN**
The best advice is to leave it to a drainage company. If you wish to try to clear the blockage yourself, the first task is to remove the manhole cover over the inspection chamber. Take care — lever it up carefully and have someone to help you. Next screw several lengths of draining rods together and fit a corkscrew or rubber plunger to the end. Push the rods into the drain and turn clockwise to free the blockage. Pull out the rods and flush the drain with a hose. Replace the manhole cover.

- **BLOCKED SOIL PIPE**
Call in a drainage company if the vent on the roof is the only access point. With a modern plastic soil pipe there will be a clearing eye along its length, and here you can try this unpleasant job yourself if you are a keen DIY person. Cover the surrounding area with plastic sheets and rags, and have buckets handy for the flooding. Undo the retaining screw, standing to one side as you open up the inspection hole. A flexible augur hired from a local supplier is used to clear the blockage. Close the clearing eye, after which the taps are turned on and the WC flushed several times to wash the inside of the pipe. Disinfect the area around the pipe.

- **BLOCKED WC**
The most likely cause is a blocked trap. Buy or hire a special WC plunger — this is larger than the standard sink model and has a metal disc around the base of the suction cap. Alternatively, use a mop with a polythene bag tied over the head. Bale out some of the water so that the bowl is about half full. Move the plunger or mop up and down rapidly about a dozen times. A gurgling sound will tell you that the trap is cleared — flush the cistern several times. Thoroughly wash and then disinfect the plunger before storing or returning it to the hire company.

- **BLOCKED SINK, BASIN OR BATH**
First of all, check that only one sink, basin or other fitting is affected. If more than one is blocked, your problem is in the soil pipe or a drain — see the appropriate section on this page.

A frozen trap in winter will prevent water from draining away. Thaw gently with a hair dryer or use rags soaked in hot water. If ice is not the problem, suspect a trap blocked with kitchen waste, hair or other household debris. The first step is to use a plunger. Press it down firmly and pump up and down rapidly about a dozen times. Pull off to break the seal and then repeat the pumping action until the water empties.

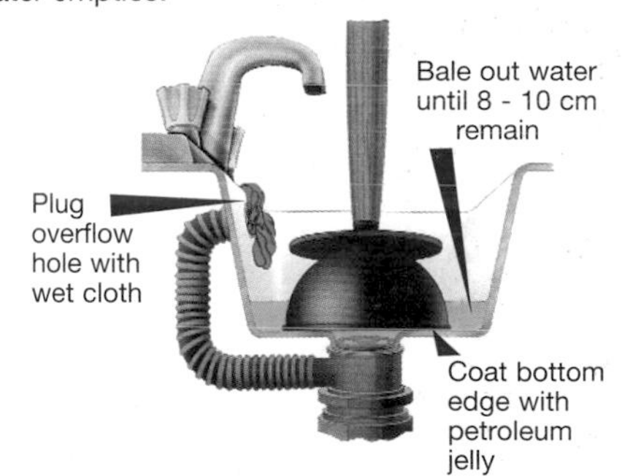

If using the plunger fails to unblock the sink or basin, remove the trap or open the access plug. Make sure a large bucket is in place under the outlet pipe before opening the trap, and use a piece of wire or cane to clear the pipes on either side of the trap. Thoroughly wash the pipe trap or bottle trap and then replace.

Run the taps. If waste does not drain away then the blockage must be beyond the trap. Use a flexible metal 'snake' or clearing rods hired from your local shop. In most cases, however, it is advisable to call a specialist drain-cleaning company at this stage.

You can buy drain-clearing chemicals. Caustic soda should be avoided — you can try washing soda in hot water or you can use a biological cleaner. These materials are useful in improving the flow through sluggish pipes, but should not be used if there is a complete blockage.

WASTE DISPOSAL

We collect a surprising amount of rubbish in our homes, and so regular disposal is essential. Since the end of World War II there has been a decline in the amount of ash and cinders, but the weight of refuse collected each week has risen.

There are several reasons for this increase. The steady rise in incomes and the greater range of goods in the shops have meant that we buy appreciably more these days. The amount of packaging material has grown dramatically, and deposits are no longer charged on beverage bottles. In addition, one day's newspaper is often bulkier than a whole week's collection of papers 50 years ago.

The disposal of refuse is basically a matter of putting kitchen and other waste into a suitable container for weekly collection by the council. Recyclable material should be taken to a 'bring bank' if kerbside collection is not available.

DOMESTIC WASTE

Your local council has a statutory duty to collect normal household refuse from you on a regular basis. The cleansing department may ask for your co-operation in various ways (emptying medicine bottles, excluding broken glass etc) and they have a right to impose their own set of rules. Clinical, hazardous and toxic waste should not be put into the dustbin — wrap sharp objects before disposal.

You must use the type of container which is specified by the council — dustbins, wheelie-bins or polythene bags. They also have the right to specify the number you can use — exceed the number or leave out rubbish in non-authorised containers and the council has the right to leave them or charge for their disposal.

You must leave the rubbish at the pick-up point they dictate. This may be at the back of the house or at the front of your property. It is an offence to leave it in the street. Make sure you close the top of the container to keep out prying animals. Look in your local paper for collection arrangements close to Bank Holidays.

KITCHEN WASTE

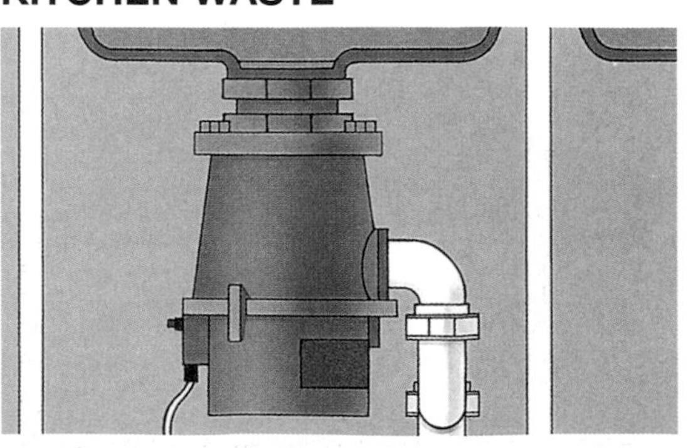

The usual plan is to place kitchen waste (peelings, bones, scraps etc) inside a plastic liner held in a polythene bin. Moving the filled liners to the dustbin is a chore in winter and a source of flies and smells in summer. If you are remodelling your kitchen, it's a good idea to fit a waste disposal unit. There are two types — the batch feed unit (waste has to be fed into the unit as a series of separate loads) and the more popular continuous feed unit (waste can be fed into the unit continually). Check that the model has reverse action and an overload cut-out.

RECYCLABLE WASTE

Throughout the country you will find bring banks (recycling collection points) in car parks, close to supermarkets and at waste sites. Once there were just bottle banks, but now you will find receptacles for items such as aluminium cans, paper, plastic bottles, textiles, cardboard, clear glass, green glass and brown glass.

GETTING RID OF LARGE ITEMS

Occasionally you will be faced with the problem of getting rid of a bulky item, such as an old carpet, cooker, fridge, a piece of furniture or a mattress. You must not dump it on waste land — abandoning a car carries a maximum £2500 fine. You should also refrain from burning old chairs, carpets etc — the smoke is a nuisance and some modern plastics emit poisonous fumes.

Consider whether the item would be useful to a local charity. If not, the right thing to do is either to ask the council to take the large item away for you or to transport it to the nearest household waste site. To get rid of an old car, report it to the local authority — the charge for disposal depends on whether the car is driven to the appointed scrap yard or if it has to be collected. Some councils will take away other large objects for nothing, but many impose a charge. Ask for a quotation before requesting the cleansing department to collect — they may not charge you if you are a senior citizen or out of work.

Your local council has a statutory duty to provide household waste sites, usually referred to as tips or dumps. Some councils impose a small fee for this use of their property, and at the entrance there will be a list of items which they will not accept. Examples of restricted objects are dead animals and asbestos. Ask advice from your local council before disposing of an old fridge or freezer.

CHAPTER 3

USING THE SERVICES

HEATING

Warmth is essential for comfort — even the most superbly furnished house is a miserable place without adequate heat in winter. This means that you are bound to have some form of basic heating, and it is useful to have a topping-up facility for abnormally cold weather.

The vast range of heaters and heating systems is bewildering, and there is no 'right' choice for everyone. If you live in a flat and go to work all day, central heating could well be unnecessary, but for most people central heating is the correct choice. There is, of course, a high initial outlay but this is more than offset by the comfort, convenience and the opportunity to use an economical source of fuel.

COMFORT LEVELS

BATHROOM	BEDROOM	BEDROOM
18°C	15°C For young babies it should be 21°C	15°C For the elderly it must be above 10°C
DINING ROOM 21°C	KITCHEN 18°C	LIVING ROOM 21°C

TYPES OF HEAT

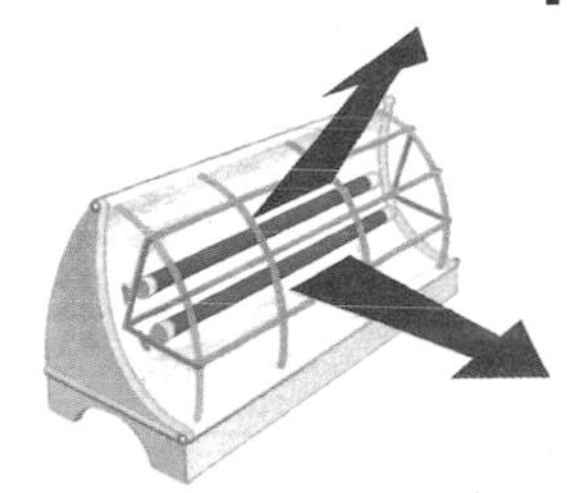

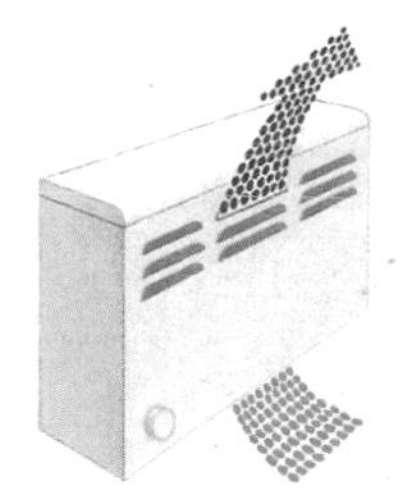

RADIANT HEAT

Radiant heat is a form of energy which moves away (radiates) from a very hot object. The source is usually 'red' heat — glowing coals, burning wood, red-hot electric elements etc. This type of heat does not warm the air in the room — it warms objects which the rays touch. These rays move in straight lines, so the back of an object is not warmed.

There are several advantages — electric and gas radiant fires are generally less expensive than convectors and there is an instant warming effect. The fire emits a cheerful glow and you can heat just part of a room if required. But there are drawbacks — when first lit or switched on there is the well-known 'hot front, cold back' effect and there is also the hazard of a very hot heating element. In addition, effective thermostatic control is not really practical.

Despite these drawbacks the use of radiant fires remains popular. The 'hot front, cold back' effect declines or disappears after a few hours — as the objects in the room are warmed they emit convected heat and so the temperature of the air in the room rises steadily.

CONVECTED HEAT

Convected heat consists of air currents which have been warmed by contact with a warm or hot object. The heated air rises upwards as it moves away from the source of heat. In convector heaters the source does not need to glow. It is generally 'black' heat — hot metal panels, hot wire filaments etc. With this type of heat it is the warm air and not direct rays which warm you.

There are several advantages — the heating elements are well guarded and the heating can be thermostatically controlled. There is all-over warmth, which means that temperature variations around the room are not large. But there are drawbacks — there is no cheerful glow and a specific area cannot be quickly warmed.

The drawbacks can be overcome by using a modification of the standard convector heater. A fan-assisted convector (fan heater) will provide instant warmth as the hot air is forcibly driven into the room, and a radiant/convector heater provides visible radiant heat as well as warm air.

SOURCES OF HEAT

INDIVIDUAL ROOM HEATING: PORTABLE EQUIPMENT
A self-contained heater which warms all or part of a room and can be moved without great effort from one room to another. Portable heaters are relatively inexpensive to buy but are expensive to run, having to rely on full-rate electricity, paraffin or bottled gas. It is useful to have at least one to use when other sources of heat break down or when extra warmth is required for a short time.

INDIVIDUAL ROOM HEATING: FIXED EQUIPMENT
A self-contained heater which warms all or part of a room and is either fixed to the floor or wall, or is too cumbersome to move from room to room. Fixed heaters are generally cheaper to run than portable ones, as they can use cheaper fuels such as gas and off-peak electricity. Note carefully that some types are much more efficient than others. A back boiler can sometimes be fitted to provide hot water or partial central heating.

CENTRAL HEATING
A system which has a central heat source from which warmth is distributed to some or all of the rooms in the house. The heart of the system is generally a boiler. The source of heat in each room is one or more radiators or convector heaters warmed by hot water or a duct emitting warm air. Gas is the most popular fuel.

FREE HEATING
A supply of heat derived from a piece of equipment which is not designed as a heater. An important factor in kitchens (cooker, refrigerator, washing machine etc) but less so in other rooms. Lights and people supply heat — up to one quarter of the total winter requirement is supplied as 'free' heat.

INDIVIDUAL ROOM HEATING: PORTABLE EQUIPMENT

ELECTRIC RADIANT FIRE
Now out of favour because of risk — buy a fan heater instead. One, two or three bars are present, each with an output of 0.6 - 1 kW. The heating effect is both visible and rapid, but thermostatic control is not possible. Heat is reduced by turning off one or more of the bars. A wire guard must be present. Even so, take care

ELECTRIC FAN HEATER
Hot air is blown out horizontally. This is the best of the electric portables — safe, thermostatically controlled and capable of warming a large area very quickly. Ceramic heaters have become popular because of their smaller size and lower operating temperature than traditional heated-wire types

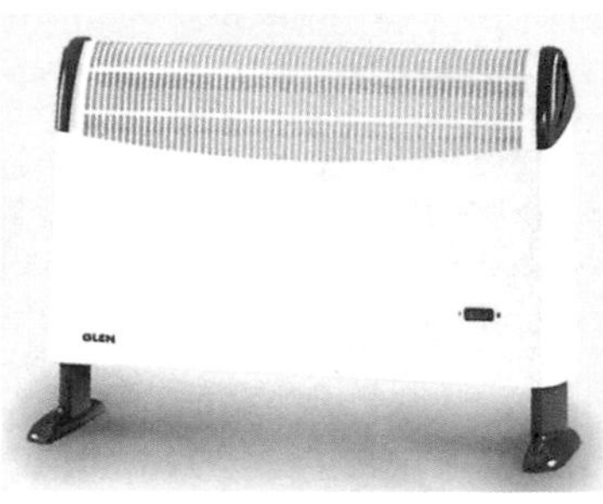

ELECTRIC CONVECTOR HEATER
Useful for providing background heat where central heating is absent or in a room where there isn't a radiator. It may take several hours for the air to warm to a satisfactory level, but there is thermostatic control, no noise and no obvious hazards. Make sure the model is not too heavy if you plan to move it from room to room

ELECTRIC OIL-FILLED RADIATOR
Portable versions of the fixed electric radiator are available. These types are single-panelled and free-standing, and are light enough to be moved about the house. Useful for providing background heat in a normally unheated room during a cold snap. There are usually several settings plus thermostatic control

PARAFFIN STOVE
Modern versions of the old standby show several improvements, including improved efficiency and automatic cut-out if it falls over. But all the major drawbacks remain — smell, need for regular refuelling, lack of thermostatic control and troublesome condensation in the absence of adequate ventilation. Still, a life-saver during a power cut

LPG HEATER
LPG (bottled gas) heaters produce both radiant and convected warmth — no chimney is needed and large areas can be quickly warmed. But there are drawbacks — lack of thermostatic control and troublesome condensation in the absence of adequate ventilation. Cylinders have to be replaced regularly but efficiency is equal to natural gas

INDIVIDUAL ROOM HEATING: FIXED EQUIPMENT

ELECTRIC RADIANT FIRE

There are types for mounting on the wall or standing in the fireplace. Some are quite plain, consisting of 2 or 3 heating bars like the standard portable model, but you can buy radiant/ convector types which emit heated air into the room, and there are also artificial coal and artificial log models

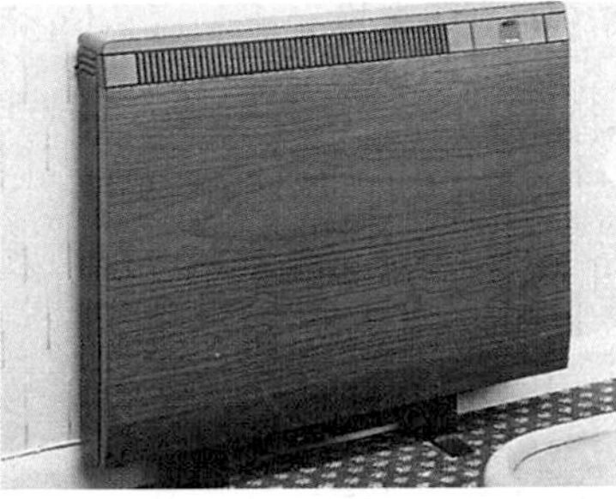

ELECTRIC STORAGE HEATER

The most economical electric heater. It is programmed to use cheap-rate electricity at night — the heat stored in the solid core is then released during the day. One of the problems has been the danger of the heat being exhausted by the end of the day — modern models have a booster control

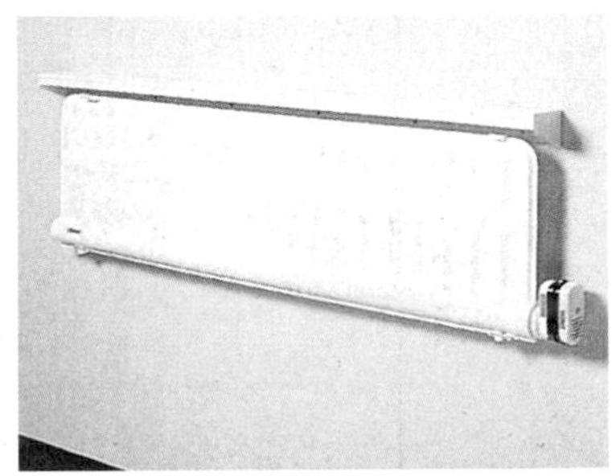

ELECTRIC OIL-FILLED RADIATOR

The large panels or tubes contain oil which is heated by the electric elements contained within. Floor-standing and wall models are available — the heating action is identical to a radiator in a central heating system. The room is warmed evenly. Expensive — full-rate electricity is used

ELECTRIC UNDERFLOOR HEATER

The underground version of the electric storage heater. Uses cheap-rate electricity at night. The stored heat is released during the day. The heat is evenly distributed all round the room. Obviously it is usually installed when the house is being built, but it is possible to put in an underfloor heating system in an existing home

GAS RADIANT FIRE

The traditional type of gas fire bears a series of elements which glow when heated by a series of gas jets. There is rapid visible warmth, but it is better to buy a radiant/convector heater which warms the air as well as the objects in front of it. There are glass-fronted models with heating elements in the form of 'logs' or 'coals'

GAS CONVECTOR HEATER

It is slightly more efficient to turn gas energy into convected rather than radiant heat, but a gas convector lacks a cheery glow. There are no hot elements to guard against and so the convector heater is the closest gas-fired equivalent to a standard radiator in the absence of central heating. Buy a thermostatically-controlled model

GAS LOG-EFFECT FIRE

There are gas fires which produce real flames above a bed of artificial logs or glowing coals — the cheeriness of a 'real' fire without the mess and trouble of coal or wood. There is a major drawback — such fires are thermally inefficient as most of the heat goes up the chimney. They are also a hazard like any open fire

SOLID FUEL OPEN FIRE

In the past this was the only type of heater, and even today it is regarded by many as an essential feature. Guard against the dangers of flying sparks and naked flames. There are several modern improvements — throat restriction, fan assistance and underfloor ventilation. The chores of refuelling and regular cleaning remain

SOLID FUEL ROOM HEATER

An improvement on the open fire — it is both safer and more efficient but partly hides the 'real' fire effect. The heat passes into the room through glass doors — buy one which needs refuelling only once a day, bears convector grilles and has a damper which automatically closes down when the burning rate is too high

CENTRAL HEATING

Putting in central heating is not cheap — mistakes in design or installation can be frustrating and costly. DIY central heating is possible, but never undertake such a venture unless you have already tackled several large-scale plumbing jobs. For nearly everyone it is much better to employ a qualified heating engineer. It will be up to you to decide which fuel to use and the number of rooms to be heated — it will be up to him to recommend a suitable system and its components. The size of the boiler will depend on the number of radiators required, and it is most unwise to skimp at this stage. It really isn't worthwhile installing a system for just two or three radiators. The installer will quote for a standard layout and may also recommend several optional extras such as thermostatic radiator valves, convectors and independently controlled hot water and heating systems. Some of the extras are worthwhile, but make sure you understand what is being offered before saying yes or no.

WET SYSTEM
Water is heated in a boiler and then circulated through pipework to the heaters, which are radiators or convectors. Here the water loses some of its heat and returns to the boiler for reheating

DRY SYSTEM
Much less popular than the Wet system. Heated air is blown from the boiler through ducts into the rooms. This system is installed when the house is being built and has several drawbacks, such as noise and grime around the ducts

GRAVITY FLOW
Rarely used nowadays. The flow is created by the natural tendency of hot water to rise and for cold water to fall. Large bore pipes are needed

PUMPED FLOW
The standard domestic system. A pump is used to send the water around the pipework and through the radiators. Small or microbore pipes are used

OPEN-VENTED TYPE
The standard U.K type of Wet system. There is a feed-and-expansion cistern which keeps the water topped up. It also allows steam and excess water to escape

SEALED TYPE
Popular in the U.S — now becoming more widely used in the U.K. A closed expansion vessel takes the place of the feed-and-expansion cistern. Not all boilers are suitable

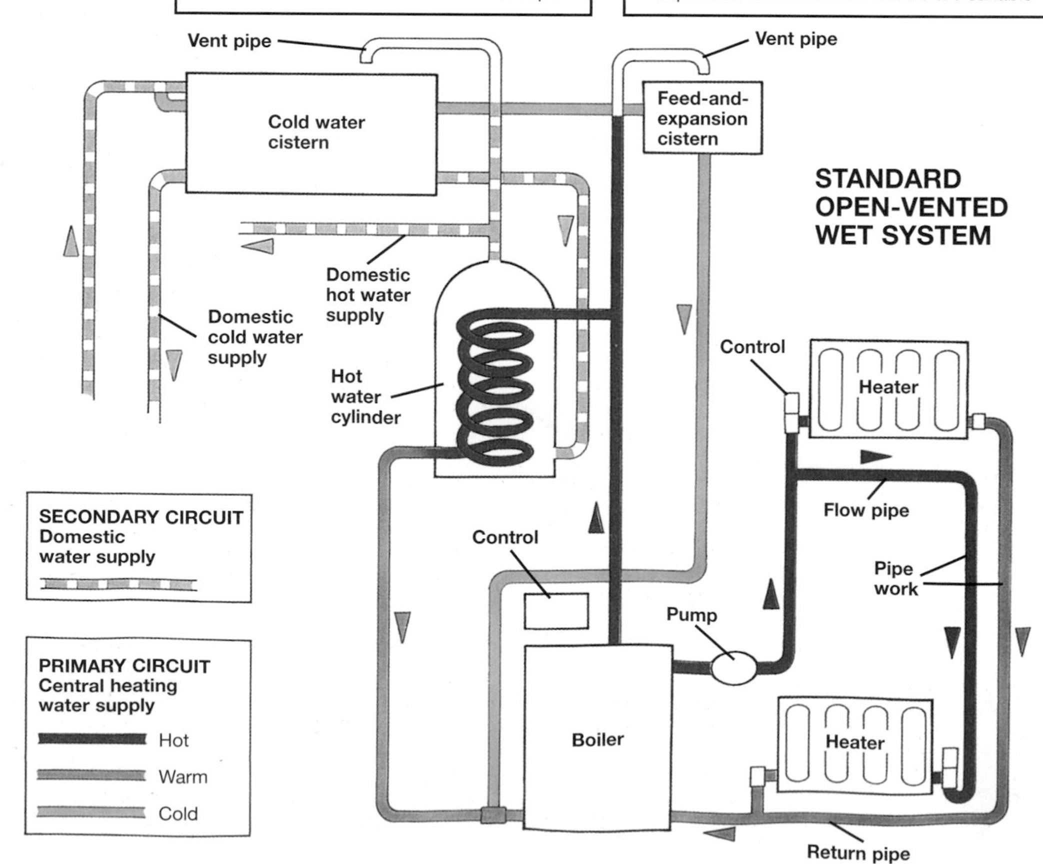

BASIC COMPONENTS

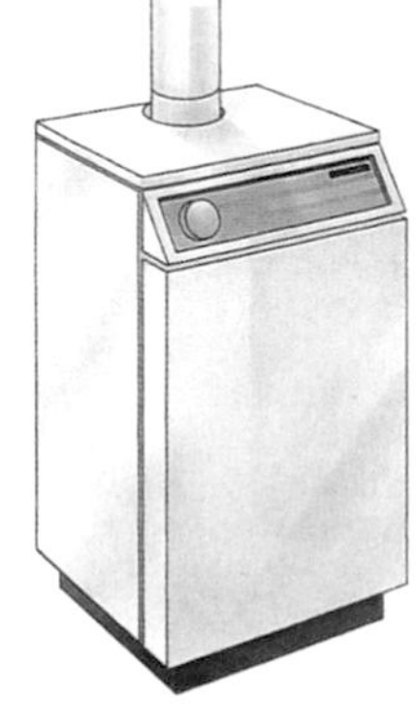

BOILER The centre of the system — it produces the heat

The boiler should be large enough to provide the desired level of warmth in the rooms to be heated when the outside temperature is 0°C. If it is too small it will not warm the rooms sufficiently in mid winter. If it is too large it will be inefficient — boilers need to run at near full capacity.

There are a number of decisions to make. First of all, the fuel to use. The usual choice is between oil and gas, and most people these days pick gas — it is clean, requires no storage and can be accurately controlled. Even within a single fuel type there may be a wide choice of models — free-standing boilers, wall-mounted boilers and back boilers for placing behind a fire or heater. Correct siting calls for a strong floor, easy access for servicing and adequate ventilation if the fuel is gas, oil or coal.

Gas boiler Choose carefully. There are types which can be fitted to a conventional chimney and there are balanced flue models — see page 11. The most efficient one is the condensing gas boiler, but it is more expensive than the standard type. There is also the combination boiler which combines a central heating boiler with a hot water cylinder. LPG boilers are available.

Oil boiler There are both floor-standing and wall-mounted models. Pressure-jet boilers have improved in recent years but they are still noisier than the vaporizing types.

Solid fuel boiler The hopper-fed boiler needs refuelling only once or twice a day and the boilers fitted with combustion air fans can give a degree of heat control which was quite impossible with simple, hand-fed boilers.

PUMP The heart of the system — it circulates the water round the pipes

It was the development of the near-silent and highly efficient pump which allowed the change-over from the gravity system to the pump system. This meant that during the 1950s domestic central heating using small bore pipes became a practical proposition.

At first the pump was connected only to the primary circuit which supplied the radiators — the domestic hot water system (secondary circuit) relied on gravity. Nowadays the pump usually moves the water in both circuits.

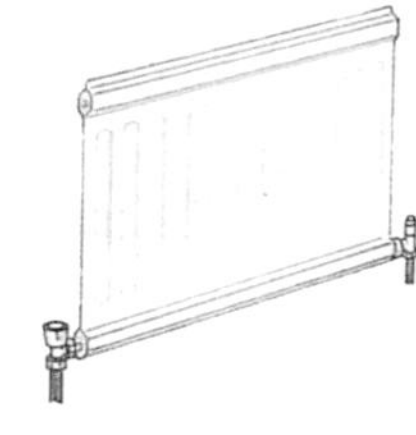

HEATERS The purpose of the system — they supply warmth in the rooms

The old cast iron, heavy radiator is a thing of the past — the modern standard heater is the steel panel radiator. Its surface is usually corrugated to increase the efficiency and there may be one, two or three panels on each radiator. The convector radiator has a series of fins. Site a radiator under a window whenever possible. Do not cover with curtains at night. A shelf above a radiator deflects heat into the room and prevents unsightly wall stains.

The word 'radiator' is misleading — most of the heat is convected and not radiated (see page 23). You can buy convector heaters where all the warmth is obtained by convection. A fan-assisted model allows you to warm a room very quickly. A skirting-board model allows you to reduce draughts and improve the evenness of the heat around the room.

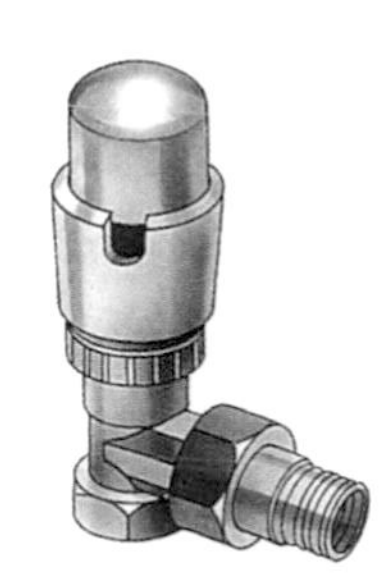

CONTROLS The brains of the system — they make it do what you want

The purpose of controls is to allow the system to go on and off automatically at pre-set times and to maintain the desired air temperature in the heated rooms. Timers and programmers come in all shapes and sizes — their job is to switch the system on and off. The simplest just switches off the heating circuit at a desired time and then switches it on as required in a 24 hour cycle. The sophisticated ones have independent controls for heating and domestic hot water and have a wide range of settings. Make sure that you install a programmer which has an override switch and battery back-up.

Thermostats switch off part or all of the system when a desired temperature is reached and not at a pre-set time. The boiler thermostat stops the water leaving at an undesirably high temperature — it also ensures that the return water is not too cool as this can lead to corrosion. A room thermostat in the living room switches off the system when the required temperature is reached. This can mean that other rooms may be too hot or too cold — it is better to have a thermostatic radiator valve (TRV) fitted to each heater. A frost thermostat is installed outside the house and switches on the system when the temperature falls below zero. This control is not necessary unless you plan to leave the house unoccupied for a long time in winter.

PIPEWORK The veins and arteries of the system — they transport the water

In the standard system small bore pipe is used — this is mainly 15 mm tubing with one or more runs of 22 mm tubing. Mild steel is inexpensive, but copper is preferable as it is less likely to corrode. In this system there is the two-pipe circuit — one set of pipes taking the hot water to the radiators and another set returning it to the boiler.

You can buy microbore pipe — 8 mm, 10 mm or 12 mm. The advantages are obvious — the piping can be bent and pushed between joists like electric cable. But there are drawbacks — it needs to be joined very carefully and blockages can occur. Installing microbore central heating is definitely a job for the professional.

HOW TO AVOID CENTRAL HEATING PROBLEMS

- **BLEED RADIATORS TWICE A YEAR**

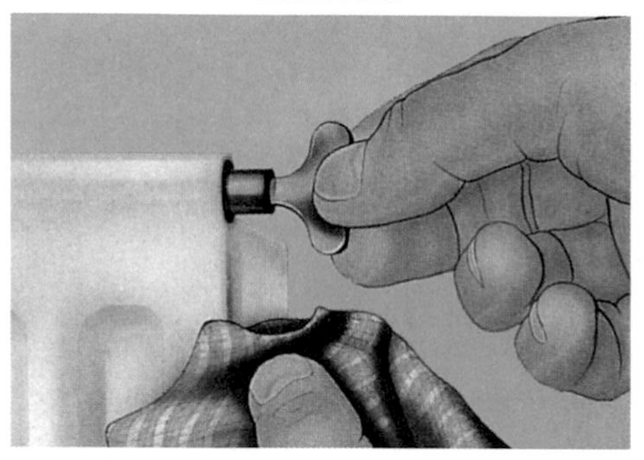

It is inevitable that some air will get into the system, and it is essential for it to be removed. A small amount of air will move into one of the radiators and cause it to be cool at the top — a large amount can seriously restrict the flow of water and so cut off heat to several radiators. Even worse, air will encourage corrosion and the by-products are hydrogen gas and rust in the radiators and black sludge throughout the system. Remove air and gas from the radiators as a matter of routine. Switch down the thermostat. Insert the radiator key into the valve nut and turn anti-clockwise. Hold a cloth under the key and close the valve as soon as water starts to escape. A hissing sound before this stage indicates that air was present. If a radiator feels cold at the top or if there is a gurgling sound within, bleed it immediately and don't wait for the routine treatment.

- **SET THE THERMOSTATS AND TIMERS CORRECTLY**
There is no point in wasting heat when you are not around but it is often false economy to switch the system off on cold nights. It usually saves fuel in the long run to keep the house at a minimum of 10°C, and this means running the system with the thermostats at a low setting during mid winter nights. Make sure the boiler thermostat is at the recommended setting — the boiler will be damaged if the return water is too cool.

- **OPERATE THE PUMP IN SUMMER**
It is the pump and not the boiler which is the weakest part of the system. If not in use during the summer, run the pump for a few minutes at least once a month. Failure to do so can result in a build-up of sludge which may cause it to cease to operate.

- **HAVE THE SYSTEM SERVICED REGULARLY**
Never wait for trouble to occur before calling in a heating engineer. Have a regular service contract with a firm you can trust and this will give you the protection of a detailed examination plus any necessary repair work at least once a year. If something goes seriously wrong call for help immediately. Dangers to watch for are serious overheating accompanied by loud knocking or a hissing sound, and also water leaking from pipes or valves. In the case of a leaking radiator joint, try to tighten the nuts with two spanners before calling for help.

- **USE A CORROSION INHIBITOR**
If sludge and rust are present in the pipes and radiators it will be necessary to drain the system by opening the lowest draincock in the system. The system is then flushed with water until all the deposit has gone and the water from the draincock runs clear. Make sure that a proprietary corrosion inhibitor is added to the feed-and-expansion cistern when it is refilled.

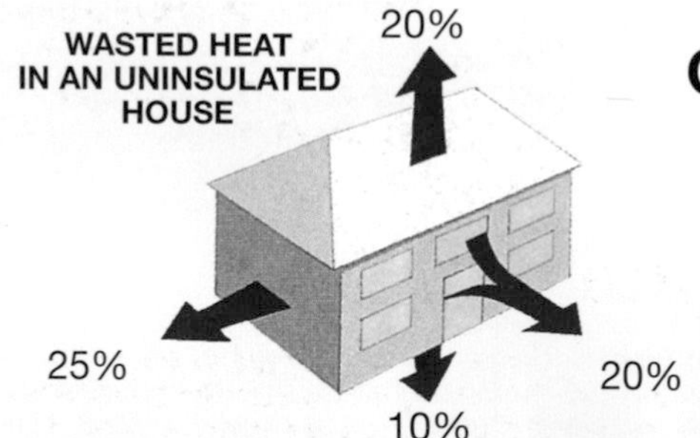

CUTTING HEATING BILLS

Expenditure on fuel is a major item in your household budget, and most of the money goes in heating the air and water. Sadly you only receive the benefit of part of the energy you pay for — most of the heat is lost through walls, doors, roof etc. In a poorly insulated house about three-quarters of the heat is wasted in this way. This loss is not inevitable — it is possible to halve the cost of heating. To do this you must carry out measures which either reduce heat loss or increase the efficiency of the fuel you use.

MONEY-SAVING MEASURE	TYPE OF SAVING	DETAILS	VALUE FOR MONEY SPENT
DRAUGHT PROOFING	More heat retained	See page 113	★★★
HOT WATER CYLINDER & LOFT INSULATION	More heat retained	See pages 18 and 113	★★★
CAVITY WALL INSULATION	More heat retained	See page 113	★★
DOUBLE GLAZING	More heat retained	See page 67	★★
IMPROVED HEAT CONTROL & USE	Less fuel used	Set thermostats no higher than necessary — turning the setting down by 1°C can cut the fuel bill by 10%. Set the hot water cylinder thermostat at 60°C. Fit foil behind radiators. Draw curtains at night. Make sure that the heating system and the hot water system can be controlled separately. Fit time switches on room heaters if area is used for only part of the day	★★★★
BETTER BUYING OF FUEL	Less money spent	Use Economy 7 instead of full-rate electricity whenever possible. Compare prices from different fuel suppliers. Keep watch for off-season special offers	★★★★

★★★★ Most value
★ Least value

LIGHTING

Lighting can do much more than enable you to see at night. When properly used it will dramatically improve the appearance of the room as well as being able to provide a decorative feature in its own right. In addition, lighting can be used to deter burglars and to reduce the risk of home accidents by illuminating danger spots.

Unfortunately most homeowners use lighting in a purely practical way and far too often the sole source of illumination in a room is a single pendent fitting hanging from the ceiling. It is a much better idea to have multi-point lighting which enhances the beauty of attractive features and shades uninteresting parts.

There are three different types of illumination. First of all, there is **diffuse illumination** which spreads upwards, sideways and downwards. Such fittings (paper lamp shades, fluorescent tubes etc) are used to produce general lighting. At the other extreme there is **directional illumination** which is a wide or narrow beam of light. A spotlight is the classical example and such sources of illumination are used for all sorts of dramatic lighting schemes. The standard lamp shade is an example of the third type of light source — **semi-directional illumination**. Most of the light is directed downwards but some spreads outwards and upwards.

TYPES OF LIGHTING

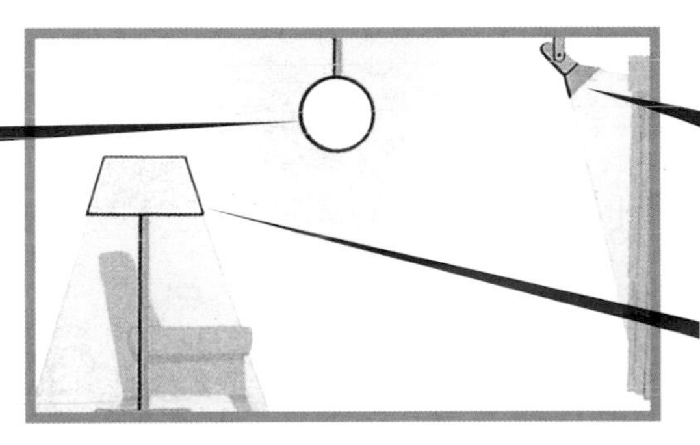

GENERAL LIGHTING illuminates the room — it is sometimes called background lighting. Aim for 20 watts per sq.m of floor with tungsten lamps, 10 watts per sq.m with fluorescent lamps

EFFECT LIGHTING illuminates a particular area for decorative purposes (e.g spotlight over curtains). Best combined with general lighting

SPECIFIC LIGHTING illuminates a particular area for practical purposes (e.g standard light by armchair). Best combined with general lighting

USING LIGHTING PROPERLY

Begin outside the house. Bright lighting at the front and back doors will increase security against burglars and will provide a welcome to visitors.

The hall needs warm but not over-bright general lighting. Remove dark shadows from stairs with carefully placed directional illumination. The rules for the kitchen are quite different — here you require strong general lighting. Choose diffuser-covered fluorescent tubes, downlighters or a ceiling made of illuminated panels. Miniature fluorescent tubes are effective when placed under wall units.

A popular light fitting for the dining room is a rise-and-fall pendent over the table — for maximum effect install a dimmer switch. The living room needs more care in design and a greater variety of lighting than other areas. First of all there should be a source of general lighting operated from a switch close to the door. Pendent lights and wall lights are suitable for this purpose. You will also need specific lighting for reading, watching TV etc plus effect lighting to add interest to curtains, pictures, house plants etc.

Bathrooms need a safe source of general lighting — a closed ceiling-mounted fitting is the usual choice. Illumination is needed for the shaving/make-up mirror — make sure that the light shines on your face and not on the glass. Switches within the room must be of the pullcord type. Bedroom lighting is very much a matter of personal taste. Bedside lamps are essential if you read in bed — choose a narrow spotlight if your partner is not to be disturbed. Some general and dressing table lighting is required.

The light requirement depends on the colour of the surface to be lit. A dark wall may require four times the wattage of a light one to produce adequate brightness. Use fluorescent lighting with care. It is excellent for kitchens and some other areas, but the light tends to be 'cold'.

To make a high ceiling look lower, direct the light downwards. Use downlighters or a shade on a pendent light which permits little or no light to shine upwards. To make a low ceiling look higher, direct the light upwards. Use a pendent shade which diffuses the light or employ wall lights which shine upwards as well as downwards. Avoid placing pendent lights in the line of traffic if there is a chance of bumping your head.

BULBS & TUBES

TYPE OF LAMP	DETAILS	EXAMPLE	NOTES
TUNGSTEN BULB Other names — Filament bulb, Incandescent bulb The thin metal filament within the bulb is heated by the current and glows brightly	**General Lighting Service (GLS)**. By far the most popular form of electric lamp — pear-shaped, clear or pearl and a range of outputs from 8 to 150 W. There are many variations. The white mushroom is better than the pear type for shallow light fittings. Shapes and types include pygmy, candle, globe and flickering flame		Life expectancy: Standard bulb 1000 hours Long-life bulb 2000 hours Bulb choice: 8 - 10 W Night light 40 - 60 W Bedside light 60 W Wall light 60 - 150 W Pendent light 75 - 100 W Table lamp 100 - 150 W Standard lamp Output: Long-life bulbs give 10% less light than standard bulbs
	Crown Silvered (CS). The front of the bulb is silvered so that the light is reflected backwards to the reflector which then produces an intense narrow beam. The bulb to use if you want to light up a single object	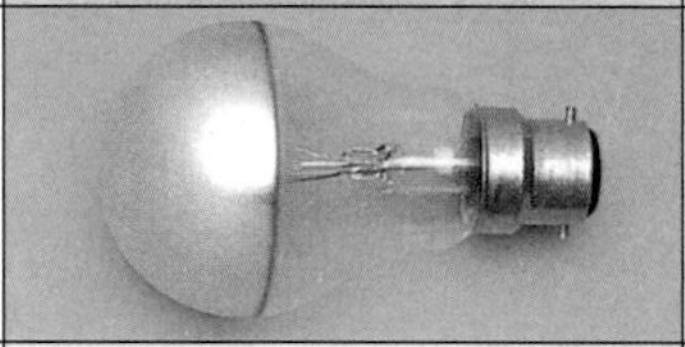	A special spotlight fitting with a dish reflector is essential for use with this bulb. Usual cap is an Edison screw — Bayonet cap type is available in some sizes 40 - 100 W
	Internal Silvered Lamp (ISL) is the standard medium and wide beam bulb for indoor use — Bayonet cap and Edison screw cap are available. **Parabolic Aluminised Reflector (PAR 38)** is made in toughened glass for both indoor and outdoor use	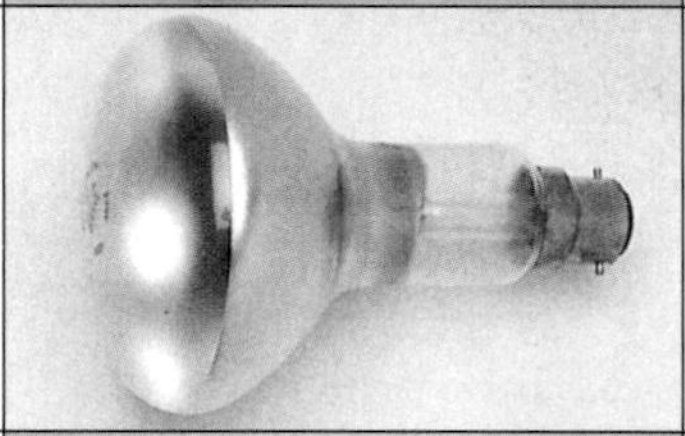	The glass front of the spotlight is clear — the rest is silvered to produce the beam ISL: 25 - 100 W PAR 38: 60 - 120 W No special type of fitting is required — these bulbs have their own built-in reflector
ARCHITECTURAL TUBE Other name — Strip light	An inexpensive alternative to the fluorescent tube for attaching to furniture and for picture lighting, but not where heat can be a problem	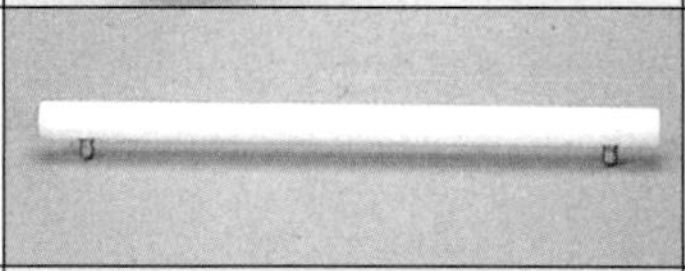	Available with Bayonet cap, Peg cap and Double cap fittings
FLUORESCENT TUBE The particles which coat the inside of the tube glow brightly (fluoresce) when the current is switched on	Available in various lengths (45 cm - 2.4 m) and 2 diameters (26 or 38 mm). Miniature fluorescent tubes are 15 - 52 cm long and 16 mm across. Usual fitting is the 2 Pin type. An adaptor is available to allow use in a Bayonet cap holder. Several colour types are available — choose with care. Circular as well as straight tubes are available	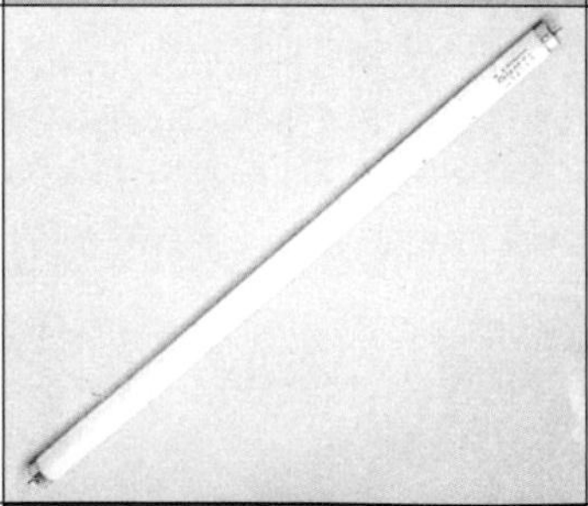	Life expectancy: 6000 - 7000 hours Fluorescent lamps are cheaper to run than tungsten ones, but only if they are not switched on and off at frequent intervals Failure to light — Firmly push starter into fitting. If it still fails, replace starter Light shimmering or dull — Change tube
LOW ENERGY BULB	Available in many shapes. Some look like regular tungsten bulbs — the more usual type is a narrow U-shaped fluorescent tube. Range of fittings is Bayonet cap, Edison screw, 2 and 4 Pin	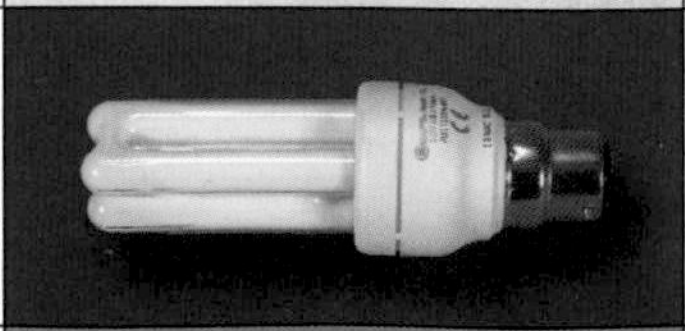	Expensive — but they are cheaper in the long run These bulbs last 5 - 10 times longer than an ordinary tungsten bulb, and only 25% of the electricity is required
HALOGEN BULB The tungsten filament is housed in a bulb which is filled with halogen gas. The light is clearer and whiter than an ordinary tungsten bulb	240 V standard-size spotlights for ordinary lamp fittings are available, but the usual halogen bulb is a 12 V miniature measuring 35 mm or 50 mm across. Popular for recessed lighting. The bulb has a built in reflector and both glass-fronted and open-fronted types are available		Life expectancy: 2000 - 4000 hours More expensive than a tungsten bulb, but cheaper in the long run as electricity consumption is in the 20 - 50 W range. The fitting is either Twist & lock or 2 Pin

LIGHTING AROUND THE ROOM

CEILING-MOUNTED LIGHTING The fitting containing the holder for the lamp or bulb is attached to the ceiling. This type of light fitting is popular both in kitchens and bathrooms, and is also used where lack of height would make a pendent fitting a source of danger. The standard fluorescent tube fitting belongs here — so do the plastic and glass milky globes for tungsten bulbs. They tend to be utilitarian rather than highly decorative, but they still have a vital part to play in the lighting scene.

SPOTLIGHTING The fitting containing the bulb holder can be turned so that the beam produced is directed on to an object or area as required. The width of the beam depends on the fitting and the bulb — use a CS bulb for a narrow intense beam or an ISL or PAR 38 bulb for a medium or wide beam. A spotlight cluster can be used to replace a central pendent light fitting.

DOWNLIGHTING The fitting is fully recessed, partly recessed or mounted on to the ceiling, all of the light being directed downwards. Reflector lights of the ISL type or ordinary tungsten bulbs are used — the most versatile lamp is the eyeball spot which can be moved like a spotlight to illuminate a particular object or area. A series of downlights provides an effective means of general lighting in a modern setting. A dimmer switch is essential in a living room.

PENDENT LIGHTING The fitting containing the bulb holder is separated from the ceiling attachment by flex or a tube containing flex. The simplest form is a glass, plastic, fabric or paper shade covering a tungsten bulb — the illumination is diffuse and in most houses pendent fittings provide the basic source of general lighting. The range is enormous. There may be one or several bulb holders attached to the flex — styles vary from Tudor to Futuristic.

TRACK LIGHTING The fitting consists of a metal or plastic channel which is screwed on to the ceiling or wall. Flex is carried within this channel and several spotlights are plugged into the track. The spotlights can produce beams of different colours and widths or can be used with ordinary bulbs so that a great deal of variety can be produced in the lighting scheme. Track lighting is useful in the kitchen to illuminate various surfaces and in the modern living room to add dramatic touches. Always angle spotlights away from direct view.

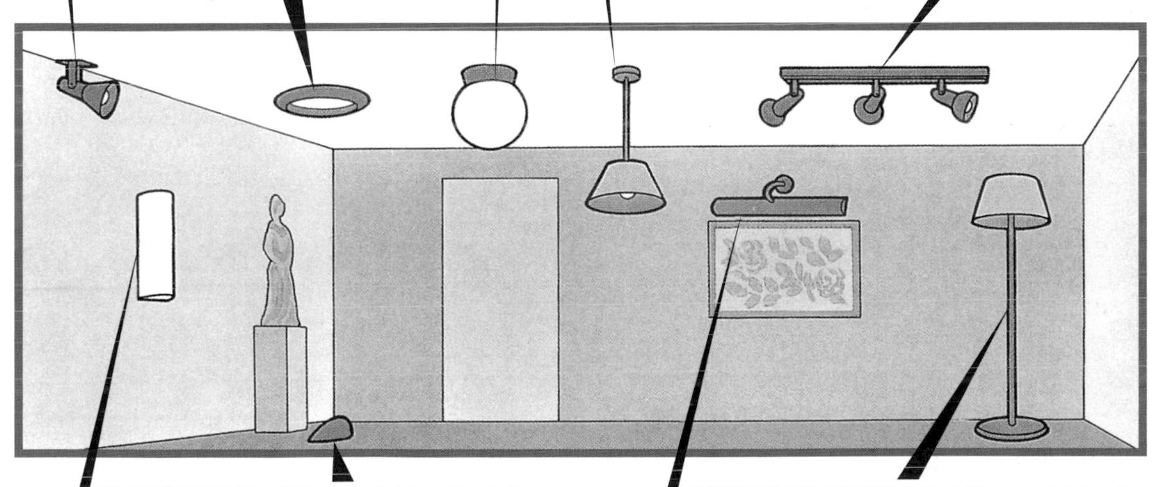

UPLIGHTING The fitting containing the bulb or tube holder is set on the floor or wall and all of the light is directed upwards. Uplighting is not commonly used, but the effect can be extremely dramatic. An uplight set at the base of an object such as a statuette or a specimen house plant will bring the details of the object into sharp relief — alter the angle and position of the light for maximum effect. Place the uplight behind the object for a quite different effect — the figure or plant is now seen in silhouette.

PORTABLE LIGHTING The fitting containing the bulb or tube holder is not attached to any surface and can be moved from place to place. Table and floor-standing (standard) lamps are the most popular examples — the illumination may be diffuse or directional. Models range from plain to highly ornate, and you should certainly think about a piece of furniture and not just a source of light when making your choice. The bulb in a table lamp should be about 1 m above the ground.

WALL LIGHTING The fitting is attached to the wall and can be used in a surprisingly large number of ways. The usual approach is to attach bracket fixtures to produce diffuse or semi-directional illumination. You can instead fix individual spotlights or track lighting, or you can install fittings which bathe the wall in light — a technique known as wallwashing.

STRIP LIGHTING The fitting containing the tube holder is attached to a suitable surface so that the light is directed as required. Fluorescent or tungsten tubes can be used — examples of strip lighting are picture lights, cupboard lights, lights inside pelmets and above kitchen work surfaces and lights within living room wall units. Purely functional and with no decorative value when switched off, strip lighting can be extremely effective when switched on.

COOKING

If you plan to install a new cooker don't buy the first one you see in the showroom on the basis that 'they must all be the same'. There are basic differences and you should consider the points below before making your choice.

The first step is to decide on the type of fuel, and the choice is nearly always between gas and electricity. Both have advantages and disadvantages with the market divided about equally between them. Electric cookers provide clean heat and the distribution of this heat in the oven is generally thought to be superior to the gas version. On the other hand gas cookers are less expensive to run and the burners on the hob respond immediately to the turn of a switch. These traditional differences have tended to disappear — fan-assisted gas ovens have evenly-distributed heat and electric halogen hobs have instant controllability. For many the ideal is an electric oven with a gas hob, and this arrangement is available.

Free-standing cookers are still the most popular choice from the simplest models to large ranges with two or more ovens and several hobs. Built-in hobs and ovens can be sited together or separated (split level) to give a fully-fitted look to the kitchen. Alternatively you can buy a built-under oven to fit below a work surface or a slot-in cooker made with the width, depth and height of standard kitchen units.

CHOOSING A COOKER

Grill

Is it in the right position? The grill may be at eye or waist level — if you choose an eye-level one, make sure that you can see the contents of the grill pan without having to take it out. **Is the grill in the oven?** This is the standard arrangement in most cookers, but it does mean that you cannot use the oven when grilling. A second oven/grill chamber is desirable but expensive. **Is there a safety stop on the grill pan?** A useful safety measure

Hob

Are the rings or burners efficient? The advent of red dot solid plates and halogen hobs have improved the efficiency of electric hobs, but they have also added to the cost. **Is the hob easy to clean?** Radiant rings can be a problem — make sure that spillage bowls can be readily removed for cleaning. The ceramic hob is the ideal — just wipe the top like any other work surface. With gas cookers look for sealed burners. **Is there a lid?** Check that it can be used as a work surface

FLOOR-STANDING COOKER
A wide choice is available. Economical — no extra fitting is required

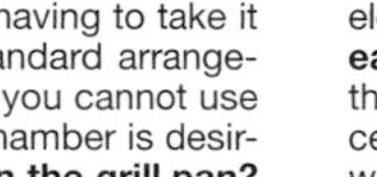

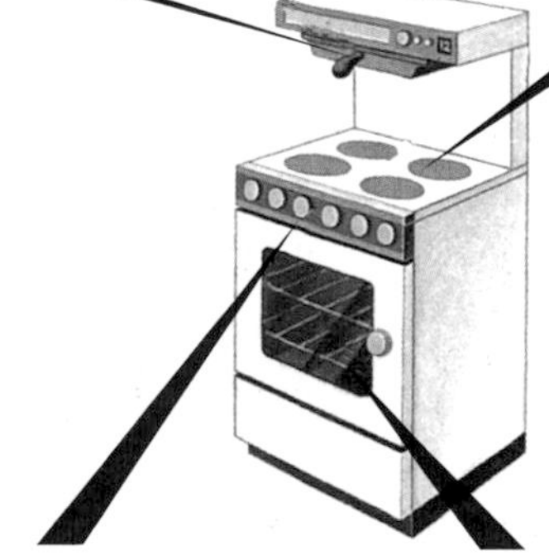

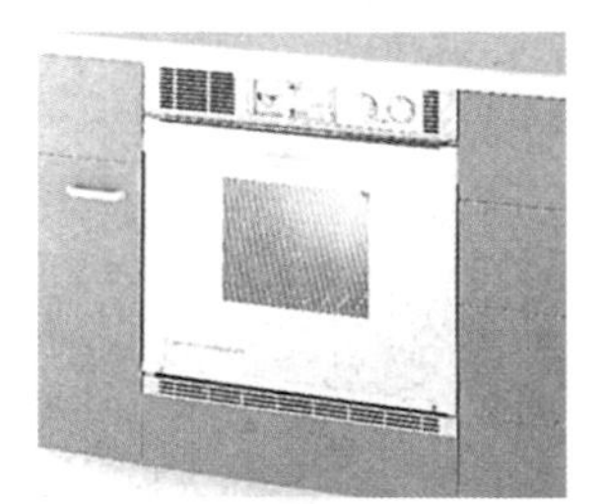

BUILT-UNDER OVEN
Most useful where space is limited — the oven slides under a standard worktop

BUILT-IN COOKER
No dust traps behind the hob and oven. Smart in appearance, but there is the extra cost plus housing and fitting

Controls

Do I need all the knobs and dials? Many clever automated features are now available — meat probes to switch off the current at a pre-set temperature, thermostatically controlled rings and burners, variable heat programmers for roasting, and so on. But all these aids add to the cost — don't pay for more than you need. A clock and timer are generally part of the standard equipment on a modern cooker — an autotimer which switches itself on and then off again at pre-set times is useful if you work during the day

Oven

Is it at the right height? Most of us are used to stooping down to reach the oven, but an eye-level model is a great boon for the not-so-young. **Can you see inside?** It is most useful to have a glass door and a strong light within. **Are there two ovens?** It is often very handy to have a small oven as well as the standard family-sized one. **Is it fan-assisted?** This modern innovation is a boon for the keen cook — see page 33. **Is it self-cleaning?** Many cookers now have this built-in feature

SLOT-IN COOKER
Perhaps the best of both worlds for many — a free-standing model which fits between kitchen units for a fully fitted look

ELECTRIC COOKER

HOB

Radiant Ring Formerly the basic type of boiling ring. The heating element is encased in a metal sheath and there is rapid heating up and cooling down. The major drawback is the amount of work necessary to clean up spillages.

Sealed Plate A flat metal disc sealed into the hob. It takes longer to heat up and cool down than a radiant ring but it takes less time to clean. Thermostatically controlled versions are available. Red-centred types take less time to heat.

Ceramic Hob A major advance in cooker design — the hob is a smooth sheet of heat-resisting glass below which are installed the boiling rings. Their position is marked by etched designs which glow when in use. Attractive but also practical — the heat control is precise and cleaning after use merely calls for a rub-down with a cloth. The hob can serve as a work surface when the rings are switched off. Make sure a 'hot hob' light is present.

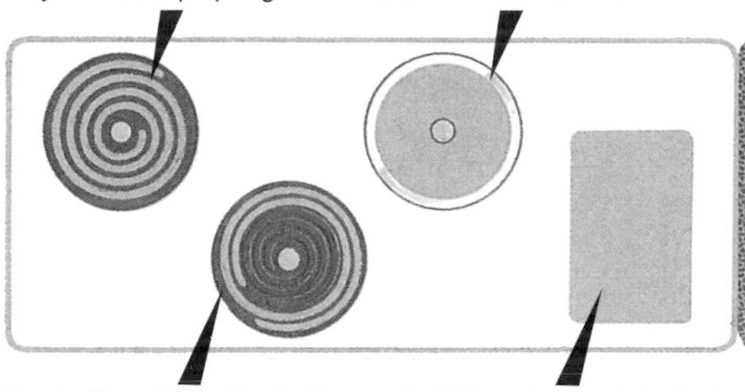

Dual Circuit Radiant Ring Sometimes found in modern hobs — an energy-saving advance on the radiant ring. Heating can be restricted to the centre if a small pan is being used. The basic advantage and disadvantage of the radiant ring remain.

Griddle A useful but uncommon feature — a large rectangular metal plate which is controlled and fitted like a sealed plate. Some foods, such as hamburgers and griddle cakes, can be cooked directly on its surface.

Magnetic Induction Hob An advance in ceramic hob design. Instead of having to switch on or switch off with a knob, you merely lift the metal pan on or off the ceramic hob surface. Useful for forgetful people, perhaps, but not often seen on domestic cookers.

Halogen Ring An advance in ceramic hob design with an important benefit. The standard element below the glass surface is replaced by a tungsten halogen lamp. As with gas, response to the control knob is instantaneous.

OVEN

Conventional Oven The heating elements are on the sides or at the top and bottom. This produces zoned heat — the top of the oven is about 10°C hotter than the bottom. Many models now have a grill situated at the top of the oven and some of these have a rotating motor-driven spit for joints, poultry, kebabs etc. This indoor barbecue method is thought to give a moister result with an attractive crisp exterior. Most modern ovens are self-cleaning although it may still be necessary to clean the bottom plates and racks. The basic cleaning system is the catalytic surface. The pyrolytic surface is more expensive and less popular — deposits are burnt off at a very high temperature.

Fan Oven In a fan-assisted oven there is a fan at the back which circulates the hot air. There are several advantages — the oven heats up more quickly, you don't have to take care to avoid hot spots and the food is cooked rather more quickly and at a slightly lower temperature than is needed in a conventional oven. A further development is the fan-ducted (convection) oven which is more expensive and much less common. Here there is a central heating element and the fan drives the hot air into the oven through ducts. Large cookers usually have separate conventional and fan ovens. Smaller ones may have a **multifunctional oven** — grill, conventional and fan-assisted all in one unit.

GAS COOKER

The instant response to turning up or turning down the heat is perhaps the main attraction, but gas is also slightly cheaper to use than electricity.

The modern gas cooker bears little similarity to the robust spartan models of earlier times. **Ignition:** The match or spark-maker has gone — choose between automatic ignition (flame appears when the gas-supply knob is turned) or semi-automatic ignition (flame appears when ignition button is pressed). **Hob:** Make sure there is a good range of burner sizes. **Grill:** Eye-level grills are more popular on gas cookers than electric ones. Some models allow you to choose between full-grill and half-grill operation. **Oven:** In the traditional gas oven the upper part is slightly hotter and the bottom slightly cooler than the gas mark setting. The new fan-assisted gas ovens have even heat distribution throughout the oven. Models with self-cleaning linings are available.

°F	°C equivalent	GAS MARK	DESCRIPTION
225	105	1/4	VERY SLOW
250	120	1/2	
275	135	1	SLOW
300	150	2	
325	165	3	MODERATE
350	175	4	
375	190	5	MODERATELY HOT
400	205	6	
425	220	7	HOT
450	230	8	
475	245	9	VERY HOT

MICROWAVE OVEN

Microwave ovens have several advantages compared with an ordinary oven, but one feature is dominant — speed of cooking. A meal can be reheated in about 4 minutes without fear of drying out and with many dishes it takes between one quarter and one half of the normal cooking time. Linked with speed is the saving in electricity and cooking smells are virtually eliminated.

There are drawbacks. A microwave oven does not brown food. There are browning dishes for sausages, hamburgers etc but the only really satisfactory answer is to buy a model with some form of browning element — see the section on Buying a Microwave. Uneven cooking is another problem with cheaper microwave ovens. Turning the food at regular intervals during cooking is a tiresome task — buy a model with some form of microwave distribution such as a turntable.

The final problem is that it is difficult to adapt a standard recipe from a cookery book. The microwave cooking time depends on the wattage of oven, the quality and the moisture content of the ingredients etc.

COOKING WITH A MICROWAVE

Never use metal or metal-decorated containers. There are specially made utensils, but you can use any non-metal dish which stays cool after cooking.

Cover dishes with film recommended for microwave use. Prick the film before placing the dish in the oven.

Standing (or equalisation) time is essential. This is the period when the microwave is switched off and the heat is allowed to move inwards. Follow the directions on the packet exactly.

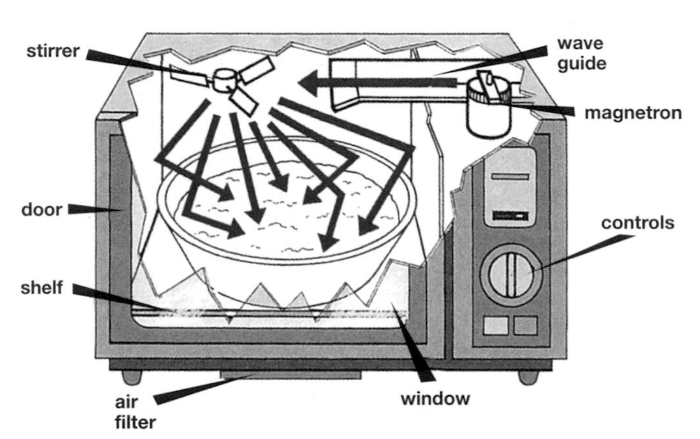

The magnetron at the top of the oven produces electro-magnetic waves (microwaves). These pass along a wave guide to a rotating stirrer which distributes them into the body of the oven. The microwaves bounce off the walls and into the food, in which the heating-up process starts.

The water molecules in the top 4 cm of food start to move violently and this rapidly raises the temperature. The more moisture present in the food, the quicker the heating-up process. With dry ingredients and suitable containers there is little or no heat generated.

BUYING A MICROWAVE

The simplest and cheapest models work solely by microwave activity. That is all you need if you want an oven just to defrost frozen food and to heat made-up dishes from the fridge or freezer. The basic problem with a microwave-only oven is that it does not brown the surface of chicken, meat etc — if you want some of the cooked food to have a crisp surface then buy a microwave/grill oven.

For maximum versatility choose a combination oven — microwave, grill and conventional convection oven all in one. There are automated models which choose the best method of cooking the dish and then switch off the power when it is cooked.

PLUG-IN COOKER

MULTI-COOKER
An excellent piece of equipment where space is limited and the cooking need is small — alternatively it can be used as an extra cooker in a large household. The base looks like a frying pan — use it for frying by removing the lid. Put the lid back on for roasting, steaming or braising — the temperature is thermostatically controlled

CONTACT GRILL
The food (bacon, steaks, chops, sausages etc) is held between two aluminium plates. Grilling takes place when the current is switched on, and there are advantages compared with ordinary grilling. Both sides are cooked at the same time and the surface is rapidly sealed by infra-red heat. Meat can go directly from freezer to grill

SANDWICH MAKER
A popular adaptation of the contact grill. The non-stick aluminium plates are patterned to decorate and cut the sandwiches, and the edges of the plates are flanged in order to seal the sides of the bread. All sorts of fillings can be used to make toasted sandwiches — remember to butter the bread on the outside

DEEP FAT FRYER
Despite all the appeals to cut down on fatty food consumption your family may be addicted to chips, fried fish, fried chicken etc. If so, the best way to ensure crispy food with a minimum of inner grease is to use a deep fat fryer. The secret is the depth of oil and the constant temperature maintained by the thermostat

CLEANING

Electrically-powered machines can make the task of cleaning much easier. This is universally accepted for floors — almost every home owns a vacuum cleaner. Floor coverings are kept cleaner and last longer, but it is necessary to empty the cleaner and change the filter as recommended.

The attitude towards washing dishes is different — many British homes do not possess a dishwasher. Shortage of space can be a problem and so can concern about noise, but the basic cause is the view that a dishwasher is a non-vital luxury and washing is more thorough (it isn't!) by hand.

THE VACUUM CLEANER

There have been a number of developments during the past 10 years. Bagless upright and cylinder models are available and so are vacuum cleaners with washable permanent filters. The cyclone system has become popular and there are HEPA filters which retain much more dust than the standard type. There are wet/dry cylinder and hand-held models for liquid spills as well as dry waste, and there are models specially designed for houses with pets.

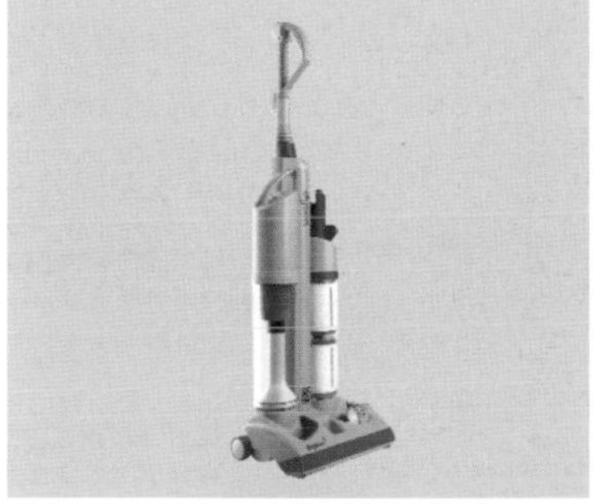

UPRIGHT
It is not necessarily a good idea to buy the largest model you can afford — lightweight cleaners are much easier to carry upstairs and are more manoeuvrable. Uprights generally clean more quickly than cylinder models and all sorts of refinements have appeared in recent years

CYLINDER
The great virtue of the cylinder cleaner is its versatility. Reaching under low objects is no problem and the attachments supplied allow you to clean soft furnishings, etc. Many refinements are available these days — power brushes, telescopic tubing, automatic cable rewind etc

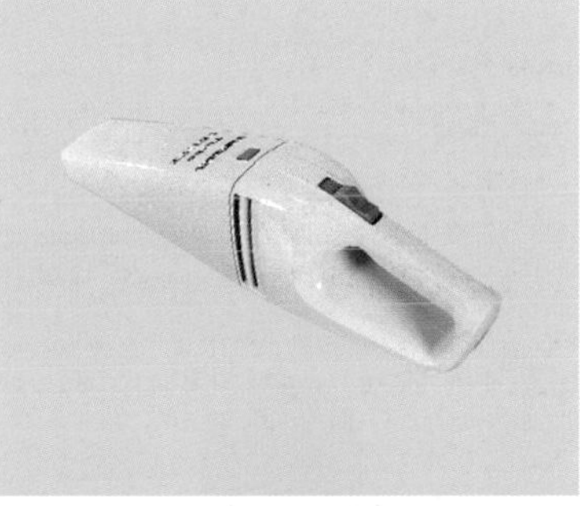

HAND-HELD
The hand vac became popular during the 1990s. The rechargeable battery model is useful for taking up spills and for cleaning difficult areas such as the car interior. Running time is short — mains-operated versions are available and so are models which use the car cigarette lighter fitting

THE DISHWASHER

If you have a large family or entertain frequently, a dishwasher is a near-essential piece of equipment. Washing-up in the average home takes an hour a day, and the scalding hot water used in a machine ensures cleaner and more hygienic dishes. Dirty crockery and cutlery can be put away immediately, which means a cleaner kitchen. The usual size is 12 place settings (a place setting is the amount of cutlery and crockery required for a 3 course dinner). The machine will have to be plumbed into the water supply. The features of the models available vary widely — study a range of leaflets before you buy. Most standard dishwashers are fitted under the work surface. For smaller kitchens you can buy a slimline model (8 - 9 place settings) or a table-top dishwasher (4 - 5 place settings).

It is up to you to choose the most suitable routine. A popular plan is to fill the machine with dishes, pans, cutlery etc during the day and then switch it on at bedtime.

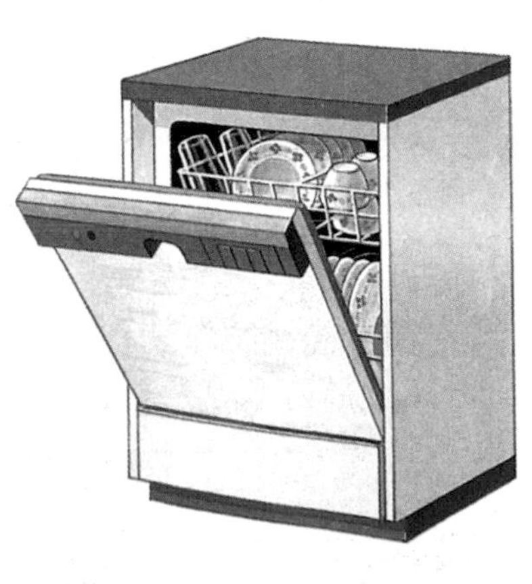

You will have to use a special dishwasher detergent. Don't use an ordinary detergent — it is not designed to break up food deposits. You will also need a rinse-aid to prevent water marks forming on glasses and dishes. Many dishwashers have a built-in water softener — top up with salt as recommended by the manufacturer. Alternatively you can buy 3-in-1 tablets, containing detergent, rinse-aid and water softener.

Not suitable for dishwashing
- Lead crystal glasses
- Fine or hand-painted china
- Gold- or silver-decorated china
- Wooden-, plastic- or bone-handled cutlery and pans
- Polythene dishes and utensils

LAUNDERING

For nearly everyone a washing machine is regarded as an essential item and the basic choice these days is between a separate washer and tumble-drier or a combined washer/drier. The range of machines on offer is bewildering and you should study the leaflets or labels carefully before deciding what to buy. At one end of the scale are simple machines with just a few controls — at the other end of the scale are the 'fuzzy logic' models which measure the amount of water necessary for the load in the drum. All sorts of programmes and refinements are available — quick-wash and half-load settings, delay timers, anti-crease and stain removal programmes, economy-wash buttons and so on. Most but not all models can be plumbed into either the hot or cold water system. All machines should have a label showing the Energy Efficiency and Work Efficiency rating on a scale from A (best) to G (worst).

Choose the right washing powder, liquid or tablet. Some but not all are suitable for woollens and silks. People with sensitive skin usually use a non-biological detergent. Follow the washing instructions on the label. With a mixed load use the programme for the most delicate items — see the table on page 37.

THE WASHER & DRIER

FRONT-LOADING WASHER
By far the most popular type of washer in the U.K. The door of the machine opens directly into one end of the horizontal drum, which rotates for washing and spinning. It can be placed under a worktop or used to carry a tumble-drier on top. Standard load is 5 - 6 kg (cottons) or 2.5 kg (synthetic fabrics) for standard front-loading washers

TOP-LOADING WASHER
Not popular, but updated models continue to appear. There are several advantages including slimline body which takes a standard load and filling/emptying without having to crouch down. There are drawbacks — it cannot be housed under a worktop and they are generally not as efficient as a top-grade front-loading machine

TUMBLE-DRIER
The damp clothes from the washer are tumbled in warm air and then in cold air for a brief spell. Once there were only vented types which needed a hose leading through the wall or window to the outside — now there are also condenser models which collect the condensed water in a tray. Clean the filter after use

WASHER-DRIER
The all-in-one machine — washer, spin-drier and tumble-drier. At first glance the perfect answer — dirty clothes in, clean and dry clothes out. Not perfect, however — you cannot wash and dry at the same time and performance is not quite as good as top-grade separate washer and tumble-drier units

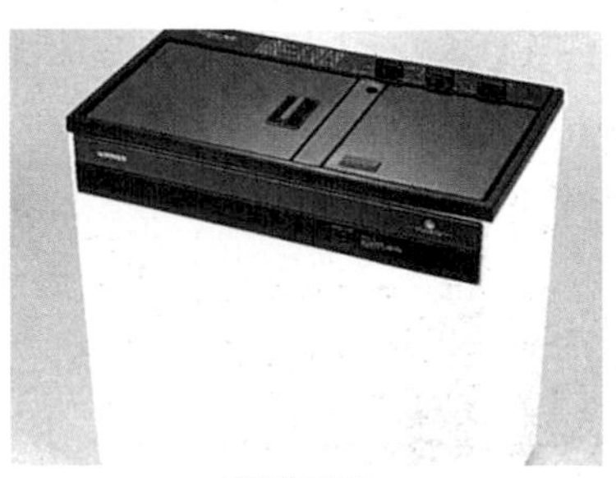

TWIN-TUB
You will no longer find twin-tubs at your local showroom but you will find them in many homes throughout Britain. Clothes are washed and spun ready for drying in quick time, but the lifting, watching and lack of controls made them unpopular. Specially-formulated twin-tub washing powder is available

AIRER-DRIER
The principle is simple — damp laundry from your washer is hung on racks near a heater. There are free-standing and wall-mounted models — inexpensive compared with a tumble-drier but it is slow with limited capacity. It is, however, a useful piece of equipment for items not suitable for tumble drying

THE IRON

The simple flat iron is a thing of the past — the modern steam iron allows you to press garments without spraying or using a damp cloth. Look for a water level indicator, safety cut-out and a self-cleaning feature which allows you to use tap water in a hard water area.

The steam/spray produces a fine spray of water at the touch of a button — further advances include irons which produce a shot of steam or a vertical jet of steam for ironing hanging curtains. Corded and cordless versions are available and so are advanced irons which allow you to use steam without dripping at low temperatures for delicate fabrics.

Choose an iron which is comfortable to hold — don't be influenced by the weight as a light iron will do just as well as a heavy one if the temperature and dampness are correct.

Choose an ironing board with care. Place an iron on it — the handle should be the same height as your elbow. Buy a tie-on board cover — choose one lined with milium to ensure heat retention.

THE CARE LABEL

At the neck, waist or side seam of a garment you will find a Care Label — this bears symbols which are part of the International Textile Care Labelling Code. The basic symbol is the Washing Code — arrange your wash into piles of similar symbols.

WASHING CODE

See below

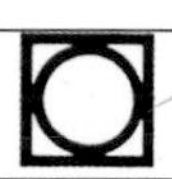

DRYING CODE

Tumble drying is beneficial

Do not tumble dry

BLEACHING CODE

Household (chlorine) bleach can be used

Household (chlorine) bleach must not be used

IRONING CODE

Cool (120°C) Acrylic, nylon, acetate, silk, polyester

Warm (160°C) Polyester mixtures, wool

Hot (210°C) Cotton, linen, viscose or modified viscose

Do not iron

DRY CLEANING CODE

(A) Any solvent may be used

(P) Perchloroethylene, white spirit, Solvent 11 & 113 may be used

(F) White spirit and Solvent 113 may be used

Do not dry clean

WASHING CODE

SYMBOL	MACHINE PROGRAMME	FABRICS	WASHING TEMPERATURE MACHINE	WASHING TEMPERATURE HAND	AGITATION	RINSE	SPINNING/ WRINGING
95	Cotton cycle	**White Cotton programme** For white cotton and linen without special finishes. The most vigorous washing conditions are provided — the results are maximum whiteness and stain removal	Very hot (95°C) to boil	Hand-hot (50°C)	Maximum	Normal	Normal
60	Cotton cycle	**Colourfast Cotton programme** For coloured cotton, linen and viscose without special finishes — colours fast at 60°C. Vigorous washing takes place at a temperature which maintains the colours	Hot (60°C)	Hand-hot (50°C)	Maximum	Normal	Normal
50	Synthetics cycle	**Synthetics programme** For nylon, polyester, cotton and viscose with special finishes, acrylic + cotton, polyester + cotton. Water is cooler than the programmes above to safeguard colours and finish	Hand-hot (50°C)	Hand-hot (50°C)	Medium	Cold	Short spin or drip dry
40	Cotton cycle	**Non-colourfast Cotton programme** For coloured cotton, linen and viscose — colours fast at 40°C but not at 60°C. Agitation, rinsing and spinning as Colourfast Cotton programme, but lower temperature to safeguard colours	Warm (40°C)	Warm (40°C)	Maximum	Normal	Normal
40	Synthetics cycle	**Acrylic and Wool + Synthetics programme** For acrylics, acetate and triacetate (with or without wool) and polyester + wool. A gentle programme to preserve colour and shape and to minimise creasing	Warm (40°C)	Warm (40°C)	Minimum	Cold	Short spin
40	Wool cycle	**Wool and Silk programme** For wool and wool mixtures with cotton or viscose, and for silk with colours fast at 40°C. Low wash temperature, minimum agitation plus normal rinsing and spinning preserve colours, size and handle (the feel of the fabric)	Warm (40°C)	Warm (40°C)	Minimum (do not rub)	Normal	Normal spin — do not wring
	—	Do not machine wash — hand wash only		Warm (40°C)			
	—	Do not wash					

WASHING

In your home there are a number of receptacles designed to hold water from the hot and cold taps, releasing this water to the drainage system once the plug has been removed. Sinks hold water for kitchen use, basins bring water to our bodies while baths bring our bodies to the water.

Occasionally it is necessary to replace an old installation or to put in a new one. A major plumbed-in structure is often expected to last for decades, so think ahead. Make sure that the hand grips on or near a new bath would help someone at least ten years older than you are now!

THE BATH

The standard bath is rectangular — 1.7 m long x 70 cm wide x 50 - 55 cm high. This may not suit you. Choose a longer one if you are tall and have the space, or a shorter one if the bathroom is small. A 90 cm sit-in hip bath is an option for the infirm or if the room is tiny. If you want to be different there are baths in many weird and wonderful shapes.

The usual choice is a vitreous-enamelled pressed steel or an acrylic bath — the acrylic type is the favourite one for the DIY enthusiast. Break up an old cast-iron tub in the bathroom to facilitate removal — cover with a cloth, wear goggles and take care. For many, a sunken bath sounds like real luxury but it is difficult to install. A better idea is to raise the floor to the rim of the tub, with steps leading to the bath of your dreams. However, you will need a bathroom with a high ceiling to make it possible.

PORCELAIN-ENAMELLED CAST IRON
The traditional type, as solid and as heavy as a rock. It resists flames, scratches and is extremely hard wearing, but the drawbacks are many. It is expensive, troublesome to install, liable to chip and it is cold to the touch. For most people this is a bath for taking out rather than putting in

VITREOUS-ENAMELLED PRESSED STEEL
A modern version of the old cast-iron bath — cheaper and half the weight. It has the same virtues but also some of the same faults — it is liable to chip and the range of colours and designs is limited. Heat is lost through the metal by conduction

ACRYLIC PLASTIC
The popular modern choice — lightweight, warm to the touch and available in a wide range of shapes, colours and sizes. Even inexpensive models may have dipped rims, backrests, side handles etc. It resists chipping but scratches easily. The bath is sold with a supporting cradle — this must be erected carefully if the bath is not to warp

GLASS-REINFORCED PLASTIC (GRP)
Like acrylic plastic in many ways but with a major additional virtue — GRP is rigid and so the need for careful cradling is removed. Chipping is not a problem but deep scratches reveal a different colour below the surface. Luxury baths are moulded from GRP — textured surfaces, gold inlays and so on

THE SHOWER

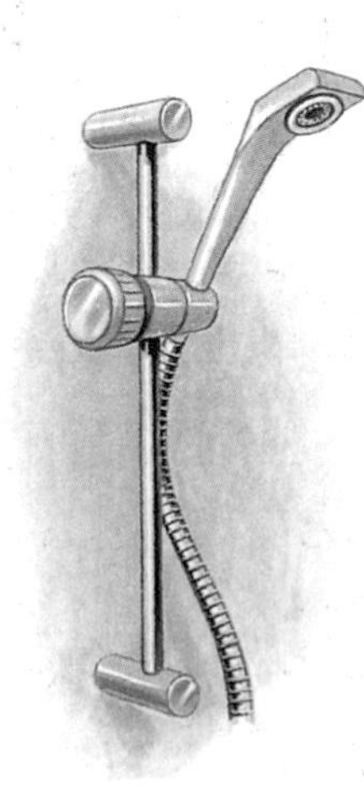

A shower has none of the lazy indulgence of a hot bath, but it has many other advantages. It takes only 20 per cent of the hot water, it is often safer for elderly and handicapped people, and it is quicker, more hygienic and invigorating.

The simplest type of shower is fitted over the bath — the base of the bath under the shower head should have a non-slip surface. You can use a Y-shaped flexible hosepipe which pushes on to the taps, but it is much more satisfactory to install a bath/shower mixer in place of the existing taps — a flick of the lever and the water is diverted from the bath to the shower.

There are problems with these simple arrangements. If someone turns on a tap elsewhere in the house there is a drop in pressure and a change in water temperature which can be dangerous. In addition, the force of the spray will be inadequate if the distance between the shower head and the bottom of the cold water cistern is less than 1 m.

A good answer to these problems is to install an instant electric shower. There is a temperature stabiliser to ensure no cooling or overheating when a tap is switched on, and there is no low pressure problem. Power showers are now popular.

A wide range of shower cubicles is available. An excellent addition to any home — look for a thermostatic shower mixer, tight-fitting doors and a shower tray which is non-slip and at least 15 cm high and more than 75 cm square.

THE BASIN

Basins for bathrooms and bedrooms are available in a wide range of colours and shapes. The traditional washbasin was a rectangle — 60 cm wide and 40 cm deep, but today you will find ovals, circles, quarter-circles, scallop shells and so on. Materials as well as shapes have been extended. Once all basins were made of vitreous china, and this type of bowl remains the most popular. It is heavy and hard wearing, easy to clean and resistant to scratches, but it can be chipped or cracked. The increasing popularity of vanity units has resulted in the production of both enamelled pressed steel and plastic basins.

PEDESTAL BASIN

A popular form of basin — the unsightly pipes are hidden from the front by the hollow leg. This pedestal takes some of the weight of the bowl, but it must never be the sole means of support. A firm wall fixing is necessary. There are one or two drawbacks — the height of the bowl rim is fixed at about 80 cm, which may be too high or too low for your family. Another disadvantage is the need to cut the floor covering around a somewhat difficult shape

WALL-HUNG BASIN

Many types are available in addition to the standard rectangular pattern which is hung on brackets fixed to the wall. There are corner units and semi-recessed types which are partly set into the wall. Both save space, and so do the 30 cm deep mini-basins used in cloakrooms. With wall-hung basins there is no pedestal to clean and there is unimpeded foot room, but the plumbing is exposed unless the pipes are taken through the wall

VANITY BASIN

A vanity unit is a low cupboard with a basin set in or on the upper surface. This structure is generally more expensive than buying a simple bowl, but there are several advantages over an ordinary basin — storage space, an extended work surface, a built-in look and hidden plumbing. In the lay-on type the basin unit forms the whole of the top surface — in the inset type the basin is mounted in a hole cut in the top of the unit

THE SINK

A feature of the pre-war British kitchen was the Belfast sink. Its stout white-glazed body was borne on large brackets and on the wall behind were the bib taps. On one side was a wooden draining board.

About 55 years ago the age of the sink unit began. The unit provides drawer space as well as storage space below. In nearly all cases it is placed under the window. The key point is that it should be close to the cooker. The sink is nearly always stainless steel or vitreous-enamelled pressed steel. Stainless steel is often dearer and it may show water marks after draining dishes. There are no attractive colours from which to choose, but stainless steel is still a popular choice. The modern enamelled pressed steel sink is much less liable to chip than the early ones. There are plastic sinks available, but damage by hot utensils can be a problem.

LAY-ON SINK

This is the standard stainless steel 'sink top' — the sink fits over the top of the base unit and so provides the whole of the work surface. The lay-on sink is generally the least expensive, but it is also the most limited in versatility and range of designs. Depending on the space, you can choose a single- or a double-bowl model with a single or double drainer. The bowl depth is usually 18 cm

INSET SINK

Here the sink is set into a hole cut in the work surface — take care to make the seal between the sink and worktop watertight. Many designs are available, and there is no need to seal between the unit and the wall. Round, square or rectangular bowls, deep or shallow, stainless steel, enamel or plastic — go to a DIY superstore to see the large range which is now offered. A waste disposal unit will need a wide outlet

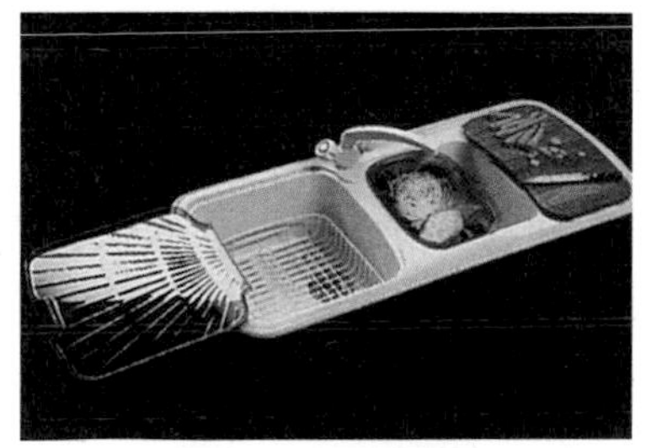

WORK CENTRE SINK

A development of the ordinary inset sink — the dividing line between the two is rather vague. A work centre always has more than a standard bowl and a drainer — the usual additions are an extra shallow bowl and drainer basket for washing up, plus a cutting board cover for the bowl. There are also half bowls for waste disposal, cutlery holders, washing-up brushes and so on. Clearly the sink of the future

COOLING & FREEZING

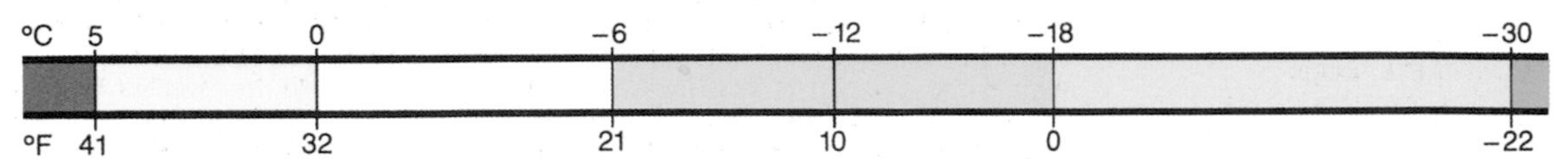

REFRIGERATOR
An appliance which keeps perishable food fresh and safe to eat for a limited period

Don't guess the temperature — keep a thermometer in the refrigerator and the deep freeze

ICEBOX
An appliance fitted in a standard refrigerator which makes ice cubes and preserves shop-bought frozen food for a limited period. The length of this period is denoted by a star rating — see below

FREEZER
An appliance which preserves shop-bought frozen food up to the 'best before' date printed on the container. It can also be used to freeze and store fresh and kitchen-prepared food — see page 41

THE REFRIGERATOR

Buy as large a refrigerator as your pocket and space will allow. Check that the door swings the right way for your needs and make sure that tall bottles can be housed. All models now have an Energy Efficiency rating from A (best) to C (worst).

Set the refrigerator 5 - 10 cm away from the wall so that heat can escape. If placed under a work surface, there must be a space on either side. Set it away from the cooker or other source of heat and make sure that it is level.

Do not put hot food into the refrigerator — always cover dishes to prevent the transfer of smells and flavours. Space out the items to allow cold air to circulate. Do not open the door more than necessary.

Defrost every few months. Turn off, empty the shelves and place a bowl of hot water inside. When all the ice has melted, empty the drip tray and switch on. A semi-automatic defroster operates by pushing a button, but you still have to empty the drip tray. With an automatic defroster you have to do nothing at all.

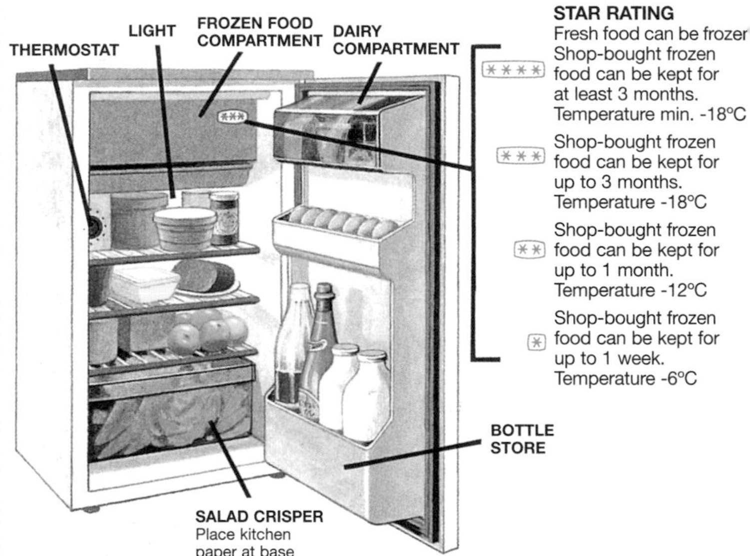

STANDARD REFRIGERATOR
The main body of the refrigerator stores perishable items at above-freezing temperature. The thermostat is used to maintain the temperature in the 0° - 5°C range — a different setting will be needed in summer compared to winter. At the top there is a frozen food compartment (icebox) which is maintained below freezing point — the temperature is indicated by the star rating on the front flap

LARDER REFRIGERATOR
In homes where there is a freezer as well as a standard refrigerator it is often found that the refrigerator section is filled to capacity whereas the icebox section is hardly used. In such cases it is sensible to buy a larder refrigerator when the standard model has to be replaced. There is no icebox, which means that all the capacity is used to store perishable items at above-freezing temperature

FRIDGE-FREEZER
The ideal answer where you haven't the space or need for a separate refrigerator and freezer. With a single control model the temperature of one unit can affect the efficiency and running costs of the other. It is better to buy the more expensive but also more satisfactory dual control type — here the fridge and freezer run independently. The freezer is generally at the bottom

THE FREEZER

DEEP FREEZE MARK
This star rating indicates that the appliance is a true freezer. It is capable of storing shop-bought frozen food and at the same time freezing both fresh and kitchen-prepared food

In a large store you will find models with capacities ranging from 75 to 250 litres. Buy a small model if your needs are modest — packs of frozen foods from the shops, a loaf or two for emergencies and meat or fish for the weekend. Before deciding on a small freezer you should think about the other jobs a freezer can do. Vegetables from the garden and from the shops when prices are low can be stored, meat and fish can be purchased in bulk and dishes can be cooked in large quantities and then stored in meal-sized portions for later use. Check the details of the model before you buy it. Some but not all freezers are suitable for housing in the garage or other unheated building. Look at the Energy Efficiency rating — the range is from A (best) to C or E (worst). A frost-free model will save you the tiresome job of regular defrosting.

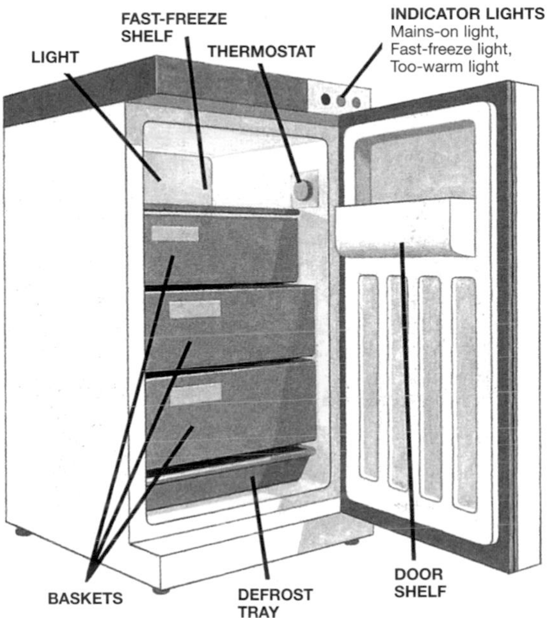

A freezer works by keeping food at a minimum of -18°C (0°F) — at this temperature both harmful and spoiling bacteria are dormant and food-spoiling enzymes in the food are deactivated. Most models have a fast-freezing section — to freeze fresh food and made-up dishes, place the items in this section and press the fast-freeze button. Your instruction book may recommend that this button is pressed 24 hours before putting in the food. After 4 - 24 hours (depending on the quantity of food being frozen) switch off the fast-freeze button and place the food in one of the baskets or trays.

FREEZING TIPS

- Use suitable containers such as heavy gauge polythene bags, waxed containers, plastic boxes with lids, aluminium foil and foil dishes. Drive out as much air as possible with solid foods before sealing — liquids should have a 2 cm head space. Double-wrap such items as bread, meat, fish and poultry.
- Freeze food at peak freshness — fish should be frozen on the day of purchase. Slightly undercook and underseason food which is to be frozen. Cool all food to room temperature or below before placing in the freezer. Label and date all packages and keep the freezer reasonably full.
- Food removed from the freezer should be allowed to thaw and then be eaten at once, cooked or placed in the refrigerator. Thawed food which has been kept at room temperature for an hour or two should not be refrozen.
- Defrost once or twice a year when stocks are low. Remove and wrap food in newspaper — place in a cool spot. Switch off and place newspapers on the floor. Remove the excess ice with a wooden or plastic scraper and leave the door open. Place a basin at the base to catch the water. When all the ice has gone, remove food stains with bicarbonate of soda solution. Wipe the inside, reconnect and set at the lowest temperature. Replace food and alter the thermostat to the normal setting.
- Do not open the door if a power cut occurs. The food inside will stay frozen for up to 12 hours — a full freezer will remain cold for much longer than a half empty one. Once power is restored put on fast-freeze for 6 hours.

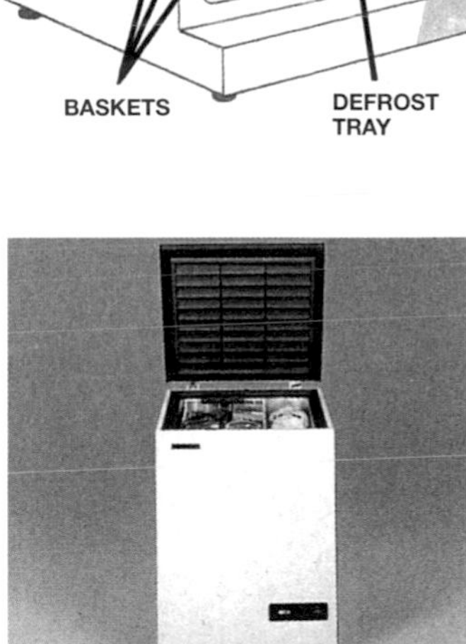

CHEST FREEZER
Space is the main problem — chest freezers are often placed in garages or outbuildings as kitchens are generally too small. There is also the problem of arranging the various food items and then readily locating them when required — organising packages vertically is more difficult than horizontally. But there are advantages — chest freezers are less expensive to buy and run, and less cold air is lost when the door is opened. Large items such as turkeys and sides of beef are easier to store

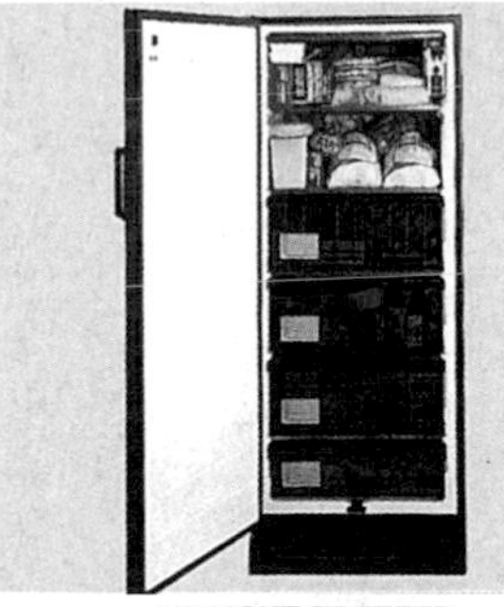

UPRIGHT FREEZER
More popular than the chest freezer. It takes up no more floor space than an ordinary refrigerator — in fact, it is sometimes possible to place one on top of the other. The front-loading arrangement makes frozen items much easier to arrange and locate, and the top can serve as a work surface. The main problem is that a bulky object such as a large joint or turkey cannot be housed unless one or more of the shelves are removed. In addition cooling down occurs more rapidly if the power supply fails

NOT FOR FREEZING

Whole eggs in shells • Single cream • Bananas • Avocados • Salad vegetables • Stuffed poultry • Cooked potatoes • Jelly • Cream cheese • Whole strawberries.

CHAPTER 4

INSIDE THE HOUSE

In each room of your home there is a basic framework — floor below, ceiling above and walls, windows and doors in between. Their size and surface coverings largely determine the overall feel and character of the room — furnishings can enhance the effect, but they cannot fully compensate for deficiencies which exist in this framework.

There will be times when changes will be necessary. Minor maintenance jobs have to be done — hinges oiled, sinks unblocked, taps re-washered, shelves erected and so on. These are simple jobs which anyone can tackle by following the instructions in this book. But redecoration calls for time, equipment and a degree of expertise — only you can decide whether to tackle the job yourself or to call in a professional. The DIY boom continues and about nine in every ten households do at least some decorating for themselves. There is, of course, nothing wrong with this — but the situation is different if a major structural change is planned or a complex repair problem has arisen. In most cases it is wise to seek outside help — moving walls or installing new pipes can lead to disaster if you do not know what you are doing.

WHAT THE WORDS MEAN

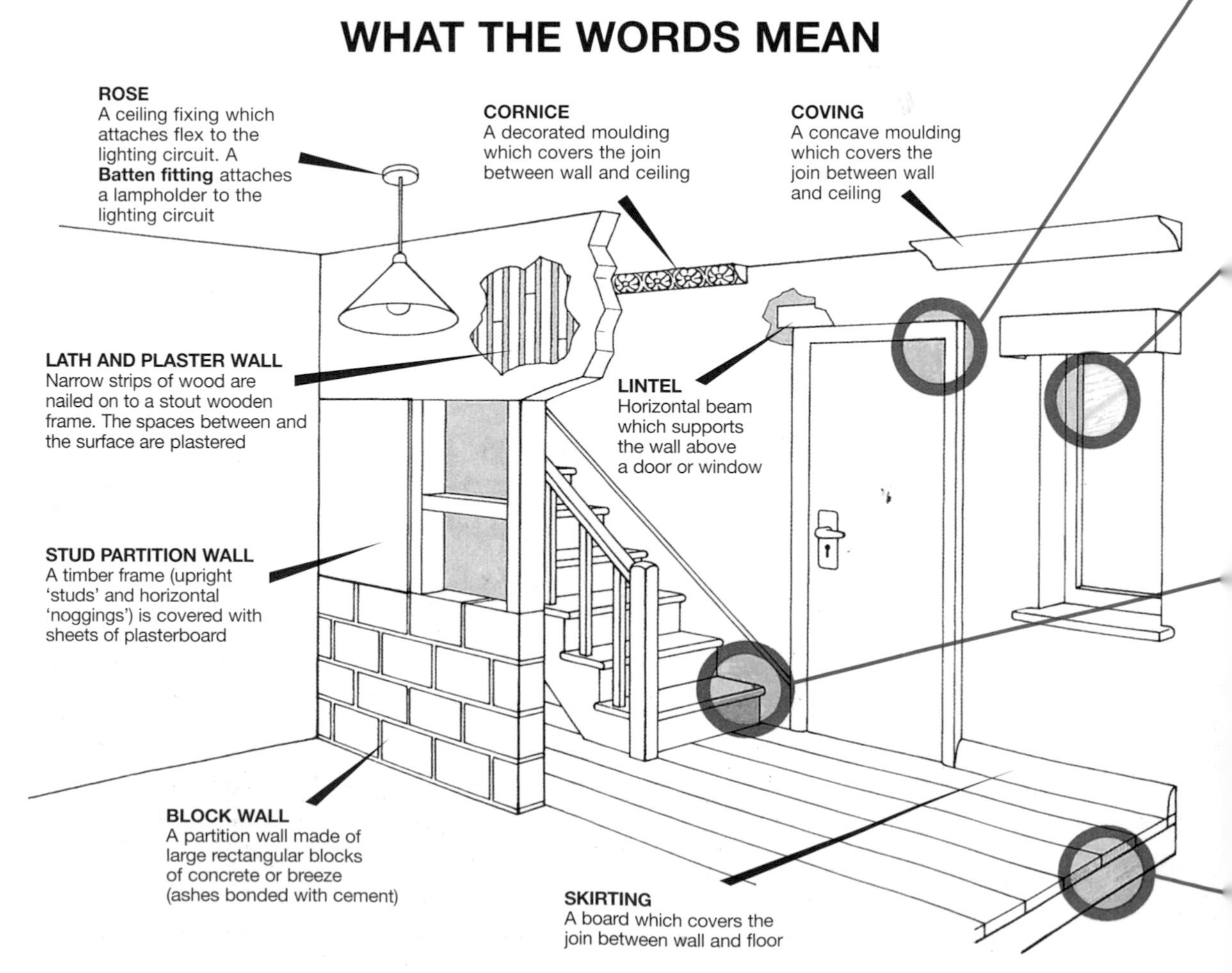

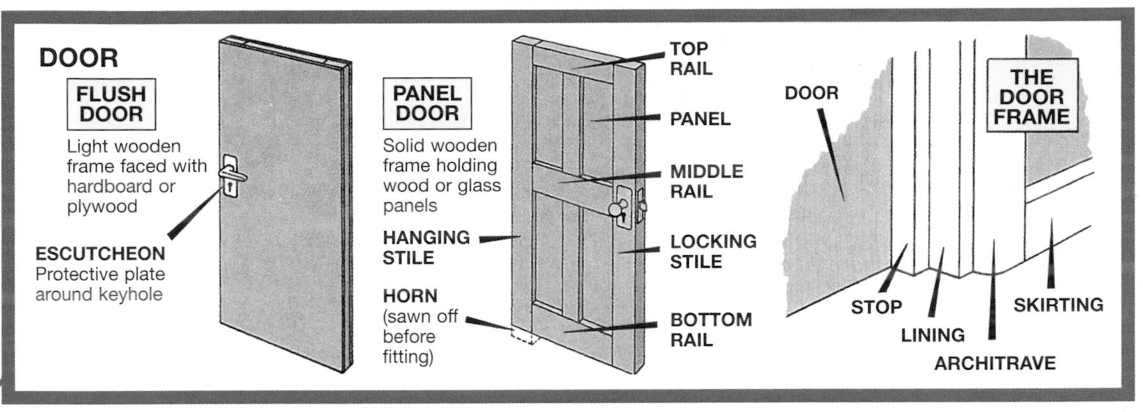
DOOR
FLUSH DOOR
Light wooden frame faced with hardboard or plywood
ESCUTCHEON
Protective plate around keyhole
PANEL DOOR
Solid wooden frame holding wood or glass panels
HANGING STILE
HORN
(sawn off before fitting)
TOP RAIL
PANEL
MIDDLE RAIL
LOCKING STILE
BOTTOM RAIL
DOOR
THE DOOR FRAME
STOP
LINING
ARCHITRAVE
SKIRTING

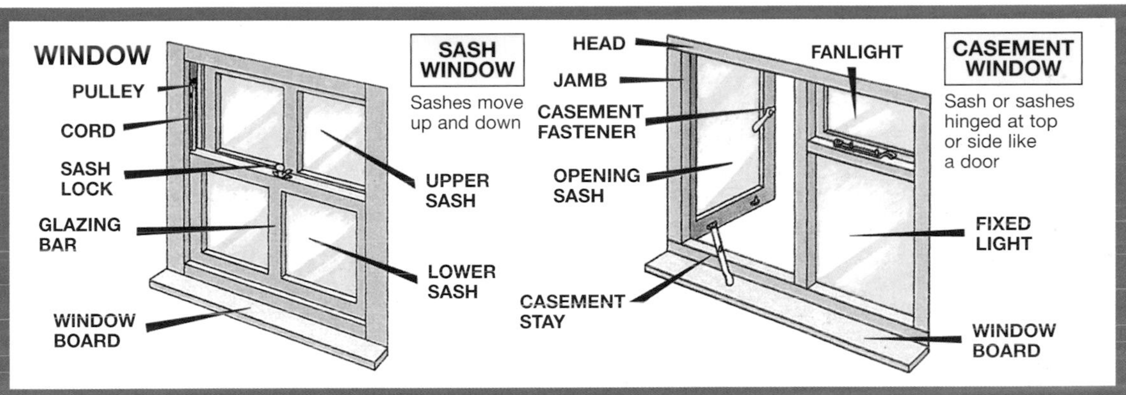
WINDOW
PULLEY
CORD
SASH LOCK
GLAZING BAR
WINDOW BOARD
SASH WINDOW
Sashes move up and down
UPPER SASH
LOWER SASH
HEAD
JAMB
CASEMENT FASTENER
OPENING SASH
CASEMENT STAY
FANLIGHT
CASEMENT WINDOW
Sash or sashes hinged at top or side like a door
FIXED LIGHT
WINDOW BOARD

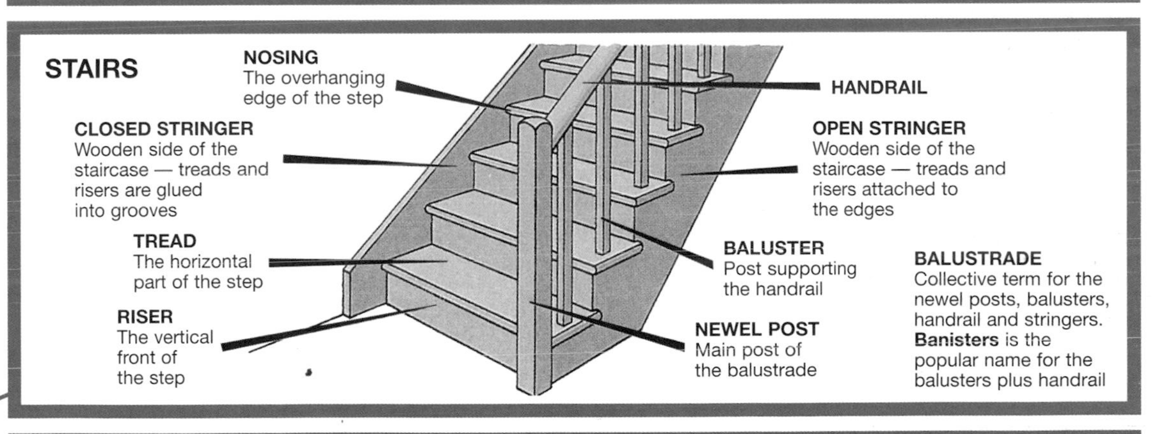
STAIRS
NOSING
The overhanging edge of the step
CLOSED STRINGER
Wooden side of the staircase — treads and risers are glued into grooves
TREAD
The horizontal part of the step
RISER
The vertical front of the step
HANDRAIL
OPEN STRINGER
Wooden side of the staircase — treads and risers attached to the edges
BALUSTER
Post supporting the handrail
NEWEL POST
Main post of the balustrade
BALUSTRADE
Collective term for the newel posts, balusters, handrail and stringers. Banisters is the popular name for the balusters plus handrail

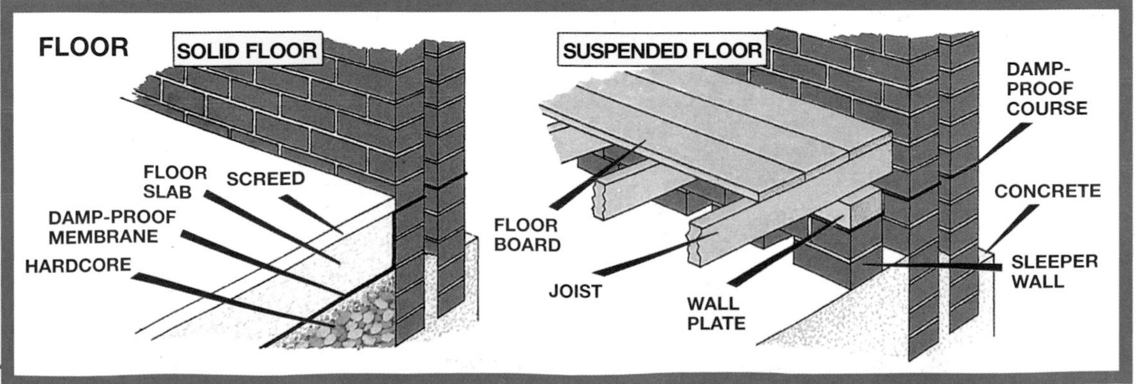
FLOOR
SOLID FLOOR
FLOOR SLAB
SCREED
DAMP-PROOF MEMBRANE
HARDCORE
SUSPENDED FLOOR
FLOOR BOARD
JOIST
WALL PLATE
DAMP-PROOF COURSE
CONCRETE
SLEEPER WALL

FLOORS

Before the start of World War II both downstairs and upstairs floors were of the **suspended** type. Floorboards were laid on stout wooden joists set about 40 cm apart — on the ground floor these joists were stood on an open brickwork wall (sleeper wall). Since the war the standard ground floor has been of the **solid** type — a block of concrete laid directly on the ground, and upstairs floors are often made of chipboard or plywood rather than floorboards.

In nearly all cases it is desirable to cover this wood or concrete with flooring material. Sixty years and more ago it was all so simple — stained floorboards with a carpet square for the living and entertaining rooms, bodywidth carpet up the stairs and lino sheeting in the kitchen. Now it is not so simple. There is a staggering variety of flooring materials, ranging from the very cheap to the amazingly expensive and from the practical to the distinctly delicate.

The advantages and disadvantages of the six basic types are set out on page 47. There are additional types, such as vegetable matting, rubber tiles, slate, terrazzo tiles and bricks. In making your choice the aim must be to balance an attractive appearance with several practical considerations. Use the check-list below:

Appearance: Personal likes and dislikes play a strong role — some people cannot stand patterned floorings whereas others find plain surfaces far too dull. The flooring type should be in keeping with the style of the room.

Comfort and safety: Warmth and quietness are highly desirable in the living room, bedrooms and playroom. Even in working areas such as the kitchen it is worth considering high-density flocked carpet or cushion-backed vinyl rather than a solid vinyl. Safety is an important factor if there are old people and small children around — pick a non-slip surface and look for a 'soft' flooring material which has a good deal of resilience.

Durability: Areas near outside doors must be able to withstand dirt and grit. Kitchen coverings must not be damaged by fat-laden spills, and bathroom flooring must stand up to moisture-laden air and wet patches. Hard wear is bound to occur in living rooms and kitchens — durable coverings are essential here.

Ease of laying: See page 50.

THE UNCOVERED FLOOR

TURN IT INTO A SUITABLE SUB-FLOOR

A sub-floor is the basic floor structure on which a decorative flooring material such as carpet, vinyl or parquet blocks is laid. There are three basic requirements — this sub-floor must be level, dry and firm. If it is not level the imperfections may be an eyesore and the flooring material may either crack or wear badly. A weak sub-floor will creak and sag — it is either difficult or impossible to tackle this problem once the flooring has been laid. Finally, the sub-floor must be dry — dampness will make adhesion difficult and can lead to the destruction of most floor coverings.

Wood sub-floor: Rot, woodworm or damp must be cured before you start. Fix all loose floorboards and cure creaks — fill gaps and drive in protruding nails. The main problem is to obtain a level surface — old floorboards are often bowed, and hollows may appear here and there. Sanding is the answer if the surface of the sub-floor is basically smooth — if it is markedly uneven then a covering with hardboard is the answer (see page 46).

Solid sub-floor: Call in a builder to relay the floor if it is wet — you can deal with slight dampness by painting with damp-proofing material or laying down a sheet of building paper. Hollows in a solid sub-floor can be cured with a self-levelling compound (see page 45), but if the surface is badly pitted and cracked you will need to have the floor re-screeded by a builder.

TURN IT INTO A DECORATIVE FLOOR

It is not always necessary to cover the floorboards in order to produce a decorative floor. Stained and polished floorboards in the dining room can be a most attractive feature.

The boards will have to be sound, reasonably level and free from unsightly holes and gaps. Don't worry about old stain or grime — this will be removed by the first step of the operation. Sanding is the essential start, and you will need to hire the proper equipment (see page 46) rather than trying to use a hand sander.

After sanding all dust must be removed. When the surfaces have been thoroughly cleaned it is time to stain the floor, if staining is necessary. Treat small test areas to find the right colour — choose spots which will be hidden by rugs or furniture.

Apply the first coat of a polyurethane varnish when the stain has dried. This will seal the surface and should be put on as soon as possible before dust gets into the grain. Use a cotton pad for this first coat of varnish — rub it well into the wood and leave it to dry for a day. Rub down the surface with fine steel wool, then dust and apply a second coat with a good quality paint brush. When dry apply a third and final coat.

HOW TO DEAL WITH FLOOR PROBLEMS

LIFTING A FLOORBOARD

There are several reasons why it may be necessary to lift a floorboard. It may be damaged by disease or insects, it may have become warped due to water damage or it may be necessary to get to pipes or cables below. Mark the area of board which is to be lifted — this must run from joist to joist. The first job is to saw across the floorboard. The nails denote the middle of a joist — cut to one side with a jigsaw or small handsaw and repeat at the other end of the marked area. Be careful not to push the saw in too deeply if there are cables or pipes below. It is a good idea to test the area with a metal/cable detector before you start — switch off the electricity supply until you have finished if there are cables below. After cutting through the floorboard remove any screws which are present.

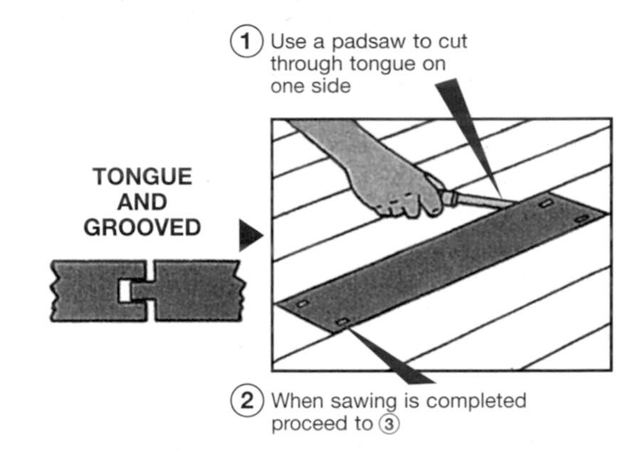

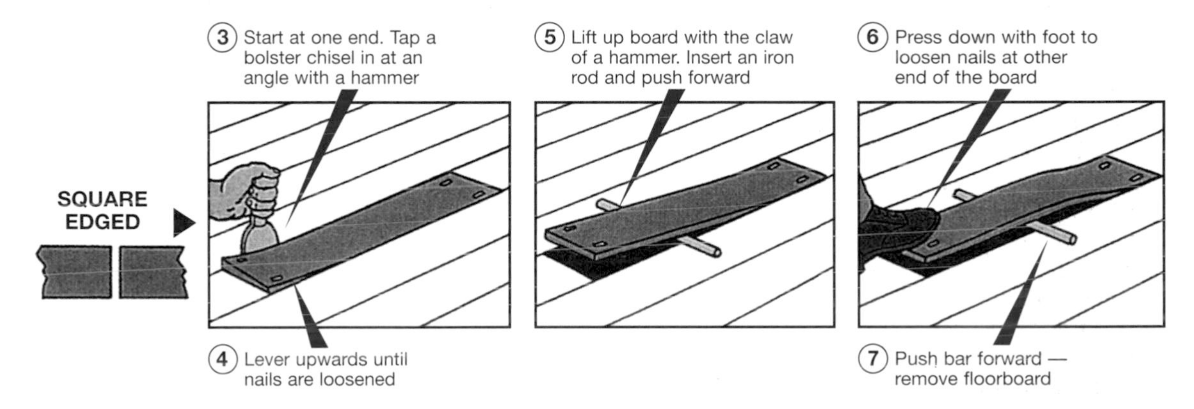

LEVELLING A SOLID FLOOR

Test the surface for hollow areas. Use the torch technique described for levelling a wood floor — see page 46. Solid floors can be made smooth by using a self-levelling screeding compound. It is mixed with water and the first batch should be used to fill minor depressions. When the compound has set the whole floor can be treated. Dampen a fairly small area and pour on the compound — smooth the surface with a trowel or float. The compound will settle to form a smooth and level surface — continue until all the floor is covered. This technique is not suitable for wood floors.

REMOVING OLD FLOORING MATERIAL

Most types of flooring material should be removed before new floor covering is laid. The best way to remove most materials is to slide a spade between the vinyl, linoleum etc and the floor — lever upwards and pull up the sheet or remove the broken tiles. Quarry and ceramic tiles are best left in place and used as a base for the new covering.

TREATING A CONCRETE FLOOR

Solid floors are not attractive in the uncovered state but for the garage or workroom you may not wish to go to the expense and trouble of laying a flooring material. The application of a couple of coats of a suitable floor paint is the answer — the epoxy and polyurethane ones are the longest-lasting. The most economical are the water-based acrylic floor paints — easy to apply but not capable of standing up to heavy traffic.

REPAIRING LOOSE AND SQUEAKING FLOORBOARDS

A squeak is caused by one floorboard rubbing against its neighbours when you stand on it. Tightening the board so that it doesn't move is an obvious answer — screw the board on to the joists in the offending area or add extra brads as shown below.

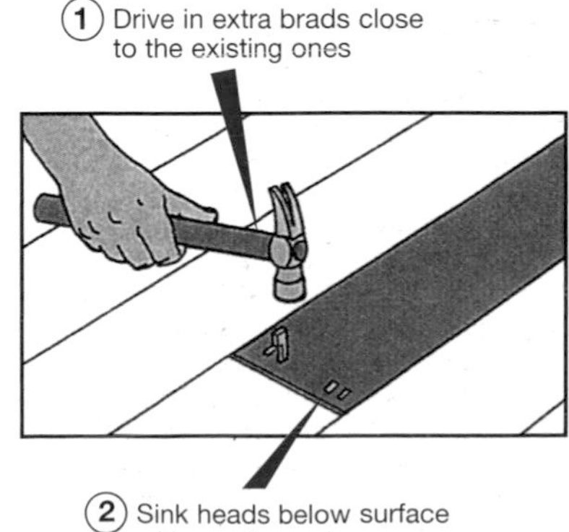

If squeaking persists, dust talcum powder into the cracks. If all else fails, drive thin wooden wedges into the cracks between the floorboard and its neighbours — make sure that the wedge tops are no higher than the floor surface when you have finished.

HOW TO DEAL WITH FLOOR PROBLEMS contd.

- **FILLING GAPS BETWEEN FLOORBOARDS**

There are several reasons why gaps appear between floorboards. Shrinkage is a common cause — so is splintering due to pest or disease attack. If the wood is diseased, replace the board with a new one. Where the boards are healthy, there are several ways of dealing with the problem.

Tiny gaps Fill with wood filler. Smooth surface with sandpaper when dry.

Small gaps Fill with papier-mache (shredded newspaper pulped with thick wallpaper paste, plus appropriate stain if boards are exposed). Smooth surface with sandpaper when dry.

Large gaps If there are just a few gaps, drive in strips of wood — tap down until level with the surface. Sometimes gaps are numerous, making the floor quite unsuitable for covering. The perfectionist lifts all the floorboards and relays them, but it is easier to cover the surface with hardboard.

- **REPAIRING A WEAKENED JOIST**

When walking over the floor you may find that some of the floorboards are springy — a linked problem is sagging joists when a new piece of furniture is introduced. The usual answer is to strengthen or replace the joists.

If you are not a handyman, call in a reputable builder. The joist may be broken or rotten, or the sleeper wall (see page 43) may have cracked. Serious problems are generally best left to the professional, but if you are a DIY enthusiast it is worth looking under the floorboards to see if you can tackle the problem. Remove the sagging or springy floorboard using the technique described on page 45 (Lifting a floorboard). You may find that although the joists are free from insect or fungus attack there is one which is not firm and can be moved up and down by standing on it. Fix a strengthener to it — a stout piece of wood which is securely bolted to the side of the weakened joist. Make sure that the top of this strengthener is no higher than the top of the joist.

- **LEVELLING A WOOD FLOOR**

To check if the floor is level place a batten across the floorboards and switch on a torch behind it. Light coming through below the batten indicates that the surface is uneven. It may be that nailing down a few loose boards or replacing a warped floorboard is all that is required, but you may find that the whole surface has to be levelled before putting on a floor covering such as vinyl tiles, or parquet blocks. There are two alternative methods — sanding if the unevenness is slight and sheeting if the raised areas are obviously too high to consider sanding them away.

Sanding

Hire a floor sander with a 20 cm drum, and also an edge sander. You will also need to obtain goggles and a face mask. Prepare the floor carefully before you begin to use the sander. Remove all bits of metal, protruding tacks etc and then drive all floorboard nails below the surface.

1. To begin, tilt the floor sander backwards and switch on. Gently lower on to the floor and allow to move forward slowly. Never allow the machine to operate without moving
2. Begin with medium-grade paper — finish with fine-grade paper

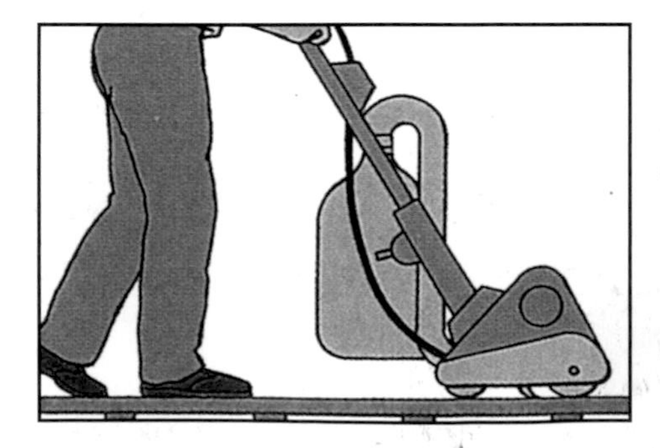

3. Work along the length of the floorboards, never along the line of the joists. Keep the cable over your shoulder. If the floor is rough or the boards are warped, begin at 45° to the floorboards and finish parallel to them as noted above
4. Use the edge sander close to the skirting boards. Once again work parallel to and never across the floorboards
5. When finished, clean up thoroughly with a vacuum cleaner and then with a dry cloth

Sheeting

Buy 3 mm thick hardboard — the standard size is 8 ft x 4 ft (244 cm x 122 cm) but smaller sizes are available and are more convenient for taking home from the DIY store. Condition the board for use by sprinkling the rough (mesh) side with water and leaving the sheets spread out in the room for a couple of days. Prepare the floor carefully before laying the hardboard. Remove all bits of metal, protruding tacks etc and drive all floorboard nails below the surface.

1. Cut large boards into 4 ft x 4 ft (122 cm x 122 cm) and 4 ft x 2 ft (122 cm x 61 cm) pieces. Lay the cut boards rough side uppermost. Start at the centre of the room — press the edges together and stagger the joins as shown below

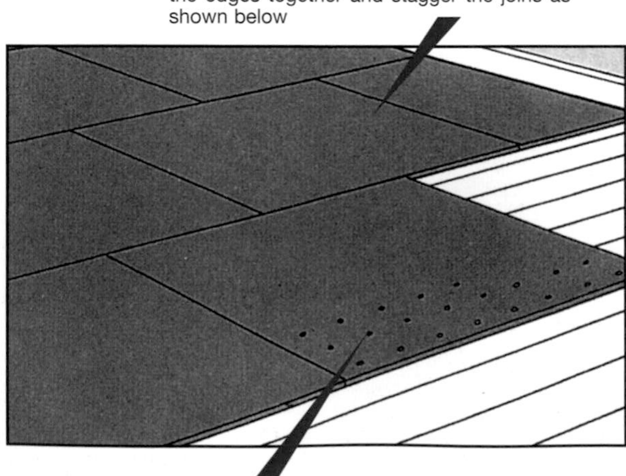

2. Nail down the boards using 20 mm pins at 15 cm intervals. Drive the heads below the surface of the boards

FLOORING MATERIALS

TYPE OF FLOORING	DETAILS
CARPET	Carpeting is the popular choice for living areas, bedrooms and stairs. In dining rooms it competes with wood and rugs — in bathrooms and kitchens it is rivalled by vinyl tiles. The variety of colours, patterns and surfaces is enormous — the prices range from fairly cheap to very expensive and the wide assortment of fibres now available means that there are carpets which are ideal for every room in the house. Carpeting materials include wool, synthetics, cotton, coir, sisal, jute, rush and seagrass. Deciding which one to buy is difficult — read pages 48 - 49 before making your choice.
LINOLEUM	The ingredients of linoleum are cork, wood-flour and linseed oil with a hessian backing. Once the darling of the kitchen and bathroom but now a thing of the past. Although now only made for the industrial market, linoleum in both sheet and tile form is still to be found in homes scattered about the country. This flooring material had several good points — it was inexpensive, easy to clean, hard-wearing and fairly resilient. But now vinyl tiles have taken over completely from their former rival for kitchens and bathrooms — they are softer than linoleum tiles and they do not readily curl up at the edges when water gets into the seams.
VINYL	A popular covering for kitchens and bathrooms, but regarded as rather austere for living rooms, bedrooms and stairs. Vinyl sheet is not easy to lay, but tiles are straightforward. Printed vinyl is popular and colourful, but the 'wear layer' is thin and so signs of wear occur after a few years. Cushioned vinyl is softer to walk on and will also take up minor floor irregularities, but again it lacks durability. If you want a vinyl which will last for many years, then solid vinyl tiles are the answer but they can be slippery when wet. Vinyl asbestos tiles were long-lasting, inexpensive and tolerant of slightly damp floors, but they were also liable to crack and are no longer available.
WOOD	In the right setting polished wood has an elegance and richness which nothing can match. It can be noisy, expensive and sometimes tricky to lay, but it is also extremely durable and a good investment. If you are lucky you may be able to sand and polish the existing floorboards (see page 44), although you are much more likely to have to buy either strips, blocks or mosaic panels. Wood strips are high-quality narrow floorboards which are laid at right angles to the floorboards. Wood blocks are laid in a parquet pattern. Mosaic panels are popular — a basket weave of miniature strips of wood on a backing. These tile-like panels may be hardwood or veneered, unfinished or surface-coated. All wood floors must be sealed after laying.
CORK	Cork is nearly always bought as tiles rather than in sheet form. These tiles are not difficult to lay and are suitable for both wooden and solid floors. You are most likely to find them in the bathroom or playroom, where their warmth, softness and quietness are highly desirable features. The drawbacks of cork are few — it is not as durable as hardwood and can be marked and dented by sharp objects. Direct sunlight can cause bleaching but the main disadvantage is the very restricted range of colours. Two types are available — unsealed and plastic-coated. Coated tiles can be slippery — where this could be a problem it is better to lay unsealed tiles. Treat later, if necessary, with a polyurethane sealer.
CLAY & STONE	Quarry tiles have long been popular for porches, their waterproof, stone-like and easy-to-clean surface providing an excellent bridge between the outdoors and inside. Made by baking unrefined, silica-rich clay, these tiles are unglazed and nearly always 15 cm squares in reds or browns. Most people cannot see the appeal of quarry tiles indoors, as they are cold, noisy and completely unresilient. Yet they do have their adherents for kitchens, bathrooms and hallways. Their more glamorous cousins, the ceramic tiles, are available in a wide range of colours and shapes and can be used to provide a shiny, exotic look to rooms. Marble is the most luxurious (and expensive) stone tile — all these 'hard' tiles can be used on solid (not wood) floors fitted with underfloor heating.

CARPETING

All of the flooring materials described in this chapter have a part to play in the modern home, but carpeting has a charm which nothing else can match. There is a feeling of warmth and comfort, and after 1950 the carpet square was steadily replaced by the fitted carpet.

Carpets are available in various widths. There is **broadloom** (1.8 - 4 m wide) for fitted carpets, **bodywidth** (up to 90 cm wide) for hallways and stairs, **squares** of various widths to cover part but not all of a room and **tiles** (30 - 60 cm wide) for kitchens and bathrooms. These tiles are often made of hair rather than natural or synthetic fibres.

Many different fibres are used these days and their nature helps to determine the suitability of the carpet for the room in question. The way the fibres are put together will also influence the properties of the carpet.

Your new carpet will shed fluff for a few weeks — this is nothing to worry about. Vacuum carefully. With all-wool or velvet carpets use a hand brush during this period and snip off any 'shooting' tufts (groups of fibres which are standing above the surface). After about a month you can vacuum in the normal way. To prevent localised wear try to move chairs and tables about from time to time.

Rugs and matting are close relatives to carpeting. Rugs are small carpets which can be readily moved from one spot to another — make sure that there is a non-slip underlay on a slippery surface. Matting is generally rough on the feet but kind on the pocket — woven vegetable fibre such as sisal, coir and seagrass is used in passageways and spare bedrooms.

BUYING — WHAT TO LOOK FOR

Department stores and flooring specialists offer an enormous range of colours and qualities, but many of the carpets will not be right for your room.

Before you go shopping, think of the amount of wear and the amount of dirt which the carpet will have to suffer. Also write down the amount you can afford to pay. At the store, check for labels which will suit your purpose — a moderate domestic grade would not be good enough for a living room filled with children. For a kitchen you will need a carpet which has been treated with a stain protector.

Now it's down to money. If your budget is strictly limited then there is no point in looking at all-wool woven carpets — you will have to choose something cheaper. Do remember that most of the wear grades come in a wide range of prices. The general rule is to buy a carpet which is as densely packed with tufts as you can afford. The more tufts, the dearer the carpet as denseness is a key feature of quality. Bend a sample of the carpet back on itself — if the base is easily seen then the pile is not very dense.

Finally there are colour and pattern, and nobody can help you here. Choose the style which makes you happy, but remember that pale colours without a pattern make a room look larger but patterns and bright colours are better at hiding dirt and minor imperfections. Try to obtain a sample to take home — it may look quite different next to your curtains and in your lighting. Remember to buy underlay. If fitting is extra, get a written quotation.

LOOKING AT THE LABEL

There is no universally accepted system for the labelling of carpets — British manufacturers generally follow a similar code but about half our carpets are imported. However, you should find most if not all the following information on the label. **Design** or **Pattern Number** (the name of the carpet), **Colour**, **Pile** (the fibre/s used), **Construction** (see page 49), **Width** (feet or metres), **Backing**, **Pattern Repeat** (distance between top and bottom of the pattern), **Suitability** (see table below), **Treatment** (moth-proofing, stain protection etc) and **Recommended use** (room-by-room suitability). The Carpet Foundation Quality Mark is a guarantee of the durability stated on the label.

VERY HEAVY DOMESTIC	The most durable domestic grade — for stairs and much-used living rooms
HEAVY DOMESTIC	The standard grade for busy areas at home — living rooms, main hallways etc
GENERAL DOMESTIC	The grade for average wear — dining rooms, entertaining rooms etc
MEDIUM DOMESTIC	The bedroom grade, suitable for rooms which get used for only part of the day
LIGHT DOMESTIC	The grade for rooms which are used only occasionally, such as the spare bedroom

UNDERLAY

Some carpets have a built-in underlay, but these foam-backed types are not meant for heavy-duty wear. Put down lining paper before laying a foam-backed carpet. With all other carpets you should always use a separate underlay — softness is increased, insulation is improved and life expectancy is extended. The most resilient underlay is the crumb rubber type — sponge and foam rubber products are also available. Match the grade to the quality of the carpet. Never use old underlay or old carpeting — uneven wearing of the carpet is bound to result

SHADING

Shading is a peculiar phenomenon. Light and dark areas appear due to the tufts leaning in different directions, and the effect on a plain carpet can be an eyesore. It is a feature of cut pile carpets with straight fine-textured yarns — velvet piles are most affected. It is more noticeable on plain carpets than patterned ones and the effect is heightened by pastel shades rather than strong colours. Pressure marking is easy to understand — the area along traffic lanes tends to be affected by shading. But true shading remains a mystery — in some (but not all) velvet carpets an irregular-shaped patch will suddenly appear to turn a darker shade as the tufts change direction, and nobody seems to know why it happens

COATINGS

Stain protectors: Scotchgard protector is available as an aerosol for treating new or shampooed carpets. The coated fibres do not absorb stains and dirt penetration is inhibited. The need for frequent cleaning is reduced, and the protective film will withstand several shampooings.

Anti-static sprays: Most synthetic fibres generate static electricity in a dry atmosphere, and the result is a mild shock when a metal object is touched. This can be unpleasant — increase the humidity of the room or spray on an anti-static product which contains metal particles which earth the fibres

CARPET CONSTRUCTION

The traditional method of making carpets is to weave them. Two methods are involved — Axminster and Wilton, which are types of weaving and not brand names nor indications of quality. Tufted carpets are a modern and less expensive alternative to weaving, and so are bonded carpets. Needleloom carpets do not have a standard pile — fibres are punched into the backing and secured with an adhesive.

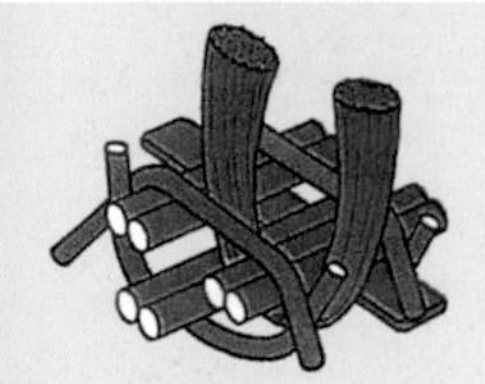

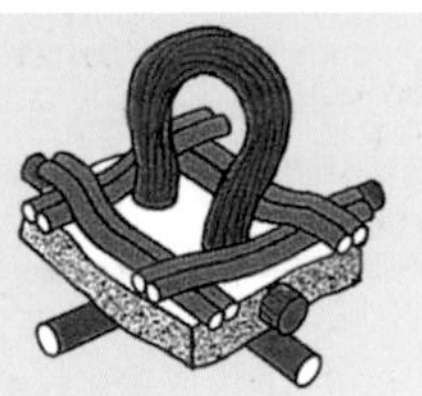

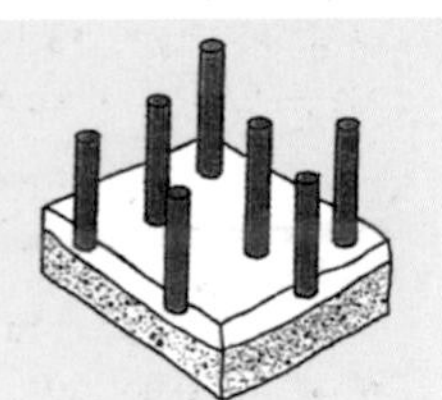

AXMINSTER
The pile is woven in as a series of tufts, the tufts being cut during the weaving process. The main features are a wide variety of colours and patterns with a smooth cut pile. Multi-coloured luxury carpets are Axminster — backing is jute or plastic yarn

WILTON
The pile is woven in as a continuous length rather than as a series of tufts. The main features are a carpet with 1 - 5 colours and an absence of complex patterns. The pile is nearly always looped, but may occasionally be cut

TUFTED
The pile is stitched into the primary backing, coated with latex and then secured with a second backing. The main features are a vast range of colours and patterns with either a cut or looped pile

BONDED
The pile is stuck on to the backing with an adhesive, producing a surface ranging from an almost flat pile to a soft and velvety one. Loops may be cut or uncut. The main features are plain colours and absence of fraying when cut

FLOCKED
A form of bonded carpet — the short fibres (usually nylon) are electrostatically fixed into the adhesive on the backing. A flocked carpet does not fray when cut. High-density flocking produces kitchen-grade carpets

CUT PILE
Each tuft is cut off at the top so that the pile is made of single and not looped fibres. Standard cut pile is neither velvety nor shaggy

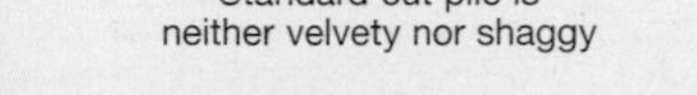

LOOPED PILE
Each tuft contains loops of fibres which are left uncut. The looped tufts are less likely than cut pile to crush down under pressure, but they are more difficult to clean

CUT & LOOPED PILE
Both cut and looped tufts are present

VELVET PILE Carpet with short and densely packed fibres. More likely to show shading and tracking than other types — note that all strips must be laid the same way. The velvety effect is less pronounced in Velour, Plush and Saxony carpets

TWIST PILE Carpet with tufts made from tightly twisted yarn. These tufts lie at various angles — less likely to show shading and tracking than straight pile

SHAG PILE Carpet with tufts at least 3 cm long. Luxurious, but the pile is not dense and so mats down very quickly with heavy traffic. Needs regular cleaning and combing

STRAIGHT PILE Carpets with tufts made from untwisted yarn. Less 'pebbly' than twisted yarn, but increased tracking is the cost of this smoother look

BRUSSELS PILE Carpet with long loops — a Wilton carpet

CORD Carpet with very short loops — a Wilton carpet. Woolcord is made from sheep's wool — haircord is produced from the hair of goats, pigs or horses. Cords are hard-wearing — cheaper cords are bonded (not woven) carpets

BERBER Carpet with a number of distinctive features — thick yarn, dense pile, looped tufts and 'natural' colours such as cream or grey. Wool is the usual fibre

SCULPTURED PILE Carpet with areas of cut and looped tufts giving a distinct pattern. The terms 'figured pile' and 'embossed pile' are used to describe this effect, although the sculptured look can be obtained by combining straight and twisted yarns or by using tufts of different lengths

CARPET FIBRES

FIBRE	PROPERTIES
WOOL	The traditional carpet fibre with many advantages — unequalled appearance and feel, excellent resistance to flattening, static electricity and staining plus the ability to dye well. It cleans easily and is flame resistant, but there are three basic drawbacks. It is expensive, it requires moth-proofing and it is not as durable as nylon. As a result blends are very popular — see below
ACRYLIC	This is the man-made fibre which looks and feels rather like wool. It is easy to clean and stains can be removed very simply. Unfortunately it does flatten although it is hard-wearing
NYLON	This is the hardest-wearing fibre, easily cleaned and with good stain resistance. With ordinary nylons there is none of the soft feel of wool and there can be both static and cigarette-burn problems. Newer nylons such as Antron and Timbrelle are rather wool-like and resist flattening
POLYESTER	Soft and easy to clean, but with the usual static and cigarette-burn problems. Its resilience is not good — blending with other materials is necessary to produce a hard-wearing carpet
POLYPROPYLENE	A hard-wearing synthetic fibre which is used in blends. On its own it crushes easily and has a harsh feel, but it is waterproof and inexpensive. The range of colours is limited
VISCOSE & MODIFIED VISCOSE	A cheap fibre which was once the standard blend with more expensive materials. It does not wear well and it is not particularly resilient
BLENDS	Blends of fibres are popular — synthetics can reduce the price of wool and also add other features. The classic blend is 80 per cent wool/20 per cent nylon, but there are many other types

LAYING FLOORING MATERIALS

LAYING SOFT TILES (cork, carpet, wood and vinyl)

1. Stretch chalked string across centre of room from wall to wall — stretch another chalked string at right angles (check with a set square)
3. Place a tile where the 2 lines cross — set out other tiles from all 4 sides to reach walls
5. Tiles may be self-adhesive or need glue. Work out from centre line in pyramid fashion. If using glue, stick down about 6 at a time
7. Place second tile on top of loose tile close to wall. Place third tile and cut as shown

2. Pull up strings and then release to leave chalk lines. Remove strings
4. If gap between wall and last tile is very narrow, adjust chalk lines to aim for at least 1/3 tile width as the space at the end of each arm
6. Do not stick down tile row closest to wall

   Key: loose tile (white); stuck-down tile (grey)
8. Then fix this filler tile in gap formed when the bottom tile is moved and fixed against the wall. Note: with wood blocks and panels leave narrow expansion strip at wall edge — fill with cork strip

HINTS & TIPS

- Buy about 5 per cent more than the measured area of the room — increase this amount if the flooring material has a large pattern.
- Some floorings (vinyl, cork, wood etc) should be conditioned before laying. This calls for spreading them out in the room for about two days before starting work.
- Not all floorings are suitable in rooms with underfloor heating. Insulators (rubber, foam-backed carpets etc) and thermoplastic tiles are out of the question — seek advice before making up your mind.
- Do not attempt a job which is beyond your capabilities. Quarry tiles and stone floors should be laid by a flooring contractor, and laying fitted carpets calls for a good deal of experience as well as the right tools.

SHEET OR TILE?

A number of floorings are available in both large sheet (up to 4 m/13 ft width) and small tile form. Each has its own advantages and disadvantages.

Sheet: The great advantage here is that there are few joins, so there is no network of narrow spaces to spoil the luxury appearance (an important point with carpets) or to absorb water, dirt and spills (an important point in kitchens and bathrooms). But sheet is awkward to handle and even more awkward to lay. Waste is inevitable, especially in irregular-shaped rooms.

Tile: The great advantage here is that the basic material is easy to handle and easy to lay even by the inexperienced do-it-yourselfer. There is little waste and a mistake is not costly — all you have to do is to cut another tile. Worn areas are quite easily replaced, but there are drawbacks. Carpet tiles do not have quite the same overall fitted appearance of broadloom carpeting, and the choice of colours and patterns is more limited.

LAYING VINYL SHEETS

1. Place sheet about 5 cm from side wall — leave 8 cm overlap at ends
2. Then run scriber (wooden block with a protruding nail) along side wall to mark the surface. Cut along the line
3. Push sheet against side wall — fit should be exact. Leave overlap against end wall
4. Then mark side of sheet 20 cm from end wall
5. Pull sheet back so it is about 5 cm from end wall. Keep sheet flush against side wall
6. Then make a second mark 20 cm in front of the first. Move sheet so that scriber point is on this second mark
7. Run scriber along end wall from the second mark. Cut along the scratch mark
8. Then push sheet forward to fit end wall. Stick down sheet according to instructions

WALLS

One painted or papered wall may look very much like another, but the structure behind them can be quite different. There are times when it is necessary to know the make-up of the inner walls — when you are putting up shelves or repairing holes prior to papering etc. It is essential to know the wall structure if you plan to make any structural alterations — it may be a loadbearing wall, supporting the roof or some other structure upstairs. In that case, you will have to obtain planning permission from your local council before starting work.

The outer walls of your house may be constructed in various ways, depending on its age and style. Once it was just a matter of brick, stone or wood, but in modern houses you will usually find either a supporting wall of bricks with an inner skin of concrete blocks, or a supporting frame of timber with an outer skin of bricks (see page 78). In all cases, both outer and internal walls carry inner linings which form the rooms of the house.

This lining is nearly always plaster or plasterboard, providing fire insulation, heat insulation and noise reduction as well as a smooth surface for decorating. The range of coverings these days is enormous, but wallpaper remains the usual choice.

PLASTER

Plastering the walls of rooms has been going on for thousands of years, but there have been many advances in recent years to make the job easier and more successful for the amateur. Old-fashioned cement plaster is still widely used for rendering outside walls or damp walls inside, but for standard work gypsum-based plasters are a much better choice. They are easily worked, set quickly and produce a smooth finish.

Don't buy more than you need — gypsum plaster quickly deteriorates when stored. Choose the correct grade — this will depend on the surface to be plastered and the job the plaster has to do. An **undercoat** plaster is applied quite thickly to remove the unevenness of the surface. This coat has several alternative names — undercoat, base coat, browning coat, backing coat or floating coat. **Finish** plaster is finer-grained and is applied as a 3 mm layer over undercoat plaster or as a 5 mm layer over plasterboard. This layer is carefully smoothed to produce a surface which can be papered or painted.

For the DIY enthusiast there are **one-coat** plasters which can be used for both the undercoat and finish layers. More convenient, but also more expensive.

INNER WALL TYPES

SOLID WALL

Plaster on masonry (brick, stone, concrete, blocks etc). A common form of lining on the walls of old houses — bricks are covered with two or three coats of plaster. Such walls are the easiest in which to secure fixings.

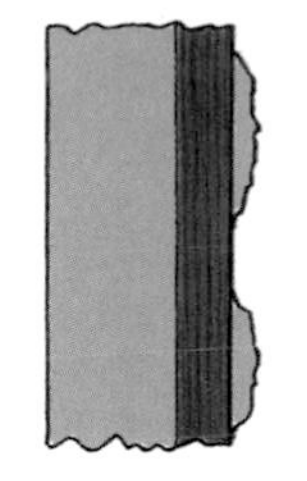

LATH AND PLASTER WALL

A common form of lining on the walls and ceilings of houses until about 70 years ago. Plaster was laid on a framework of narrow wooden laths — such walls are difficult to attach heavy objects to and are often uneven.

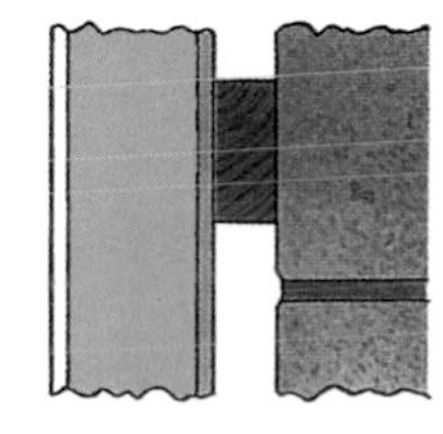

DRYLINED WALL

Plasterboard on masonry. Plasterboard began replacing plaster about 80 years ago — today it is the standard wall lining. It is easier and quicker to use than plaster. Fixing battens may or may not be present.

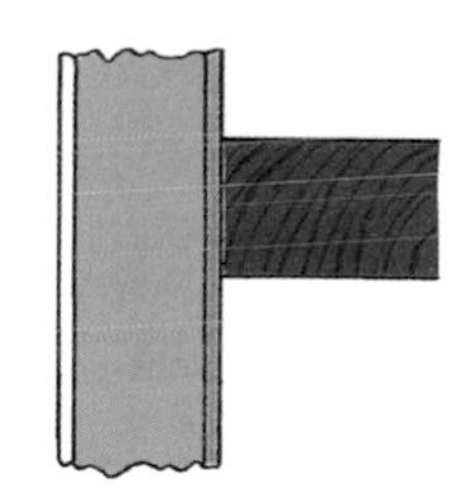

PARTITION WALL

Plasterboard on stud. Wooden frames of upright studs and horizontal noggings are used for both external and internal walls in modern houses. The frame is covered with plasterboard — the wall is hollow.

IDENTIFYING YOUR WALL TYPE

The first step is to tell whether it is a hollow partition wall or if there is a backing of wood or masonry behind the plaster or plasterboard. The usual advice is to tap the wall and see if there is a hollow sound, but this can be deceptive — some concrete block walls sound hollow when tapped. Undoubtedly the best way is to drill a small test hole in an inconspicuous place — if there is white dust, little resistance to the bit and the drill soon shoots forward, you are dealing with a partition wall. Wood dust in the bit would suggest a lath and plaster wall.

With more solid walls examine the bit after drilling — this will tell you the material behind the plaster or plasterboard. Brick gives red dust and only moderate resistance to the drill. Breeze blocks produce dark grey dust. Strong resistance to the drill plus light grey or cream dust reveals concrete or stone.

HOW TO DEAL WITH WALL PROBLEMS

- **SMALL HOLES & CRACKS IN PLASTER**

(1) Remove all loose plaster with a filling knife. Sides of the damaged area must be sound

(2) Undercut edges, if possible, so filler can key into plaster

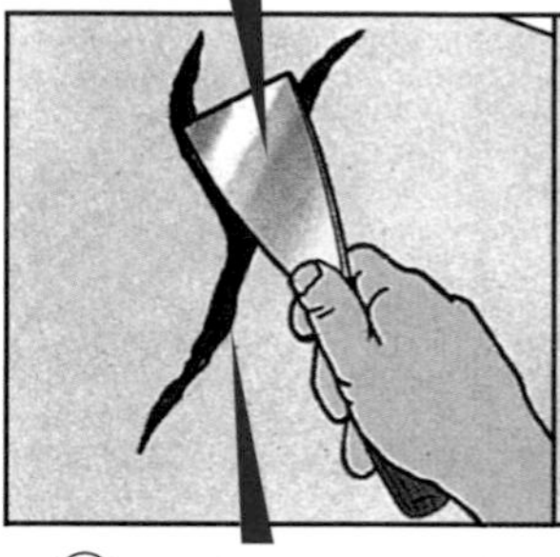

(3) Brush away all dust from the damaged area

(4) Dampen the sides of the crack or hole with a paintbrush

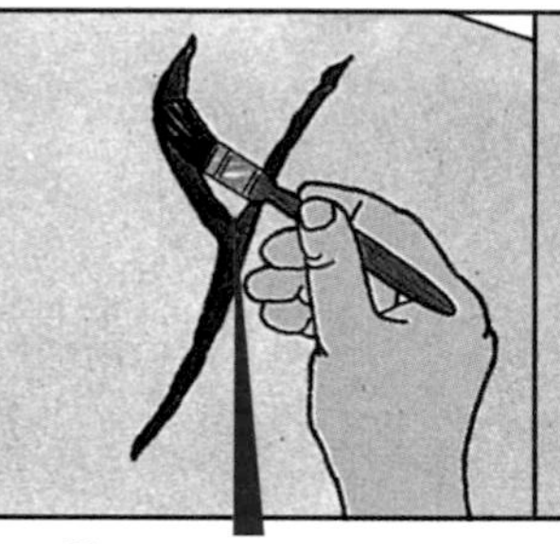

(5) Press the filler into the damaged area, moving the knife at right angles to the crack

(6) Remove excess filler by drawing the knife along the crack

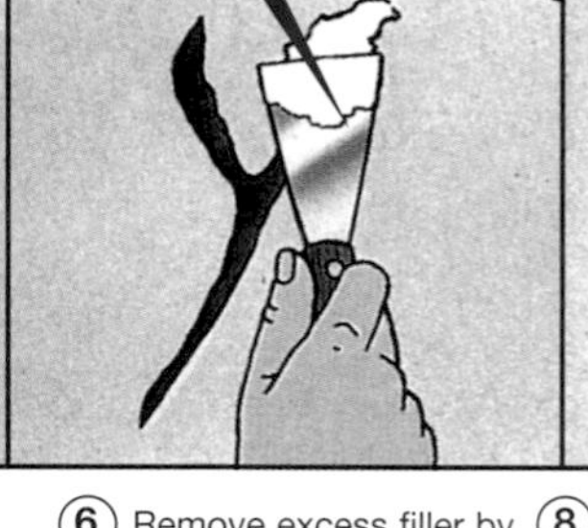

(7) With deep cracks it may be necessary to apply two separate layers to fill the hole

(8) When dry the surface should be sanded with fine glasspaper to produce a flush finish

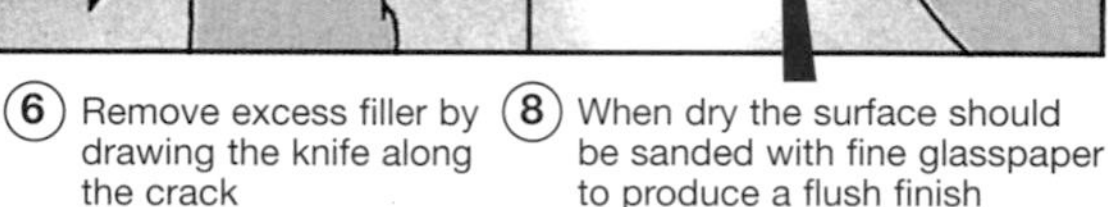

- **HAIRLINE CRACKS IN WALLS AND CEILINGS**
These are caused by the movement of plasterboards and are extremely difficult to fill — filler soon drops out. You can widen the crack to provide a more satisfactory key, but it is better to cover the affected ceiling or walls with a textured paper.

- **GAPS BETWEEN CEILING AND WALLS**
These are caused by movements of the house, and there is no point in trying to fill them. Cover with a coving to bridge the gap.

- **LONG AND WIDE VERTICAL CRACKS**
These may indicate a serious structural fault such as subsidence. Seek professional advice.

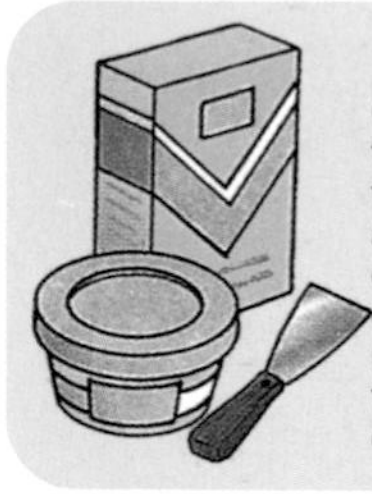

FILLERS

Cellulose fillers are available in both powder form for mixing with water and in ready-to-use form. The advantage of a powder product is the ability to produce different consistencies. Deep cracks and wide holes need a stiff paste — fine cracks call for a cream-like mix. Add the recommended amount of water and stir thoroughly — an uneven mixture will produce disappointing results

- **HOLES IN PLASTERBOARD**
Small holes can be repaired with scrim (see below) and plaster, but it is more usual to fix a patch. The damaged board is cut away to the joists or studs. A new piece is fitted and the edges covered with scrim and plaster before applying a thin layer of plaster over the whole area.

- **LARGE HOLES IN PLASTER**
When a piece of plaster falls away, tap the wall. If it sounds hollow call in a builder to replaster. If the wall is sound and a limited area is affected, you can try patching.

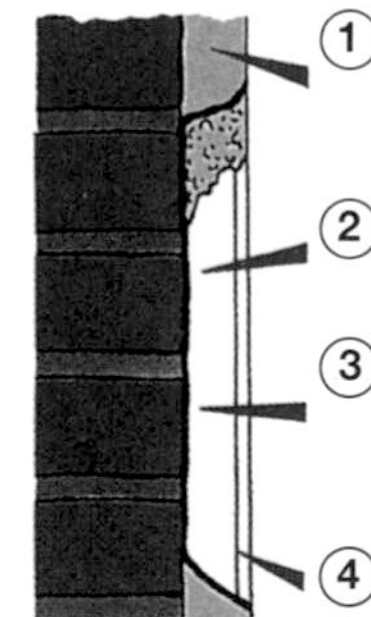

(1) Cut back to sound plaster and down to the masonry if necessary. Remove all loose plaster and dust

(2) Paint the hole with PVA bonding agent if the masonry below is absorbent

(3) Fill the hole with undercoat plaster. Smooth off by drawing a straight board across the plaster. Score the surface with a nail. Leave to dry

(4) Apply a thin layer of finish plaster

PLASTERBOARD

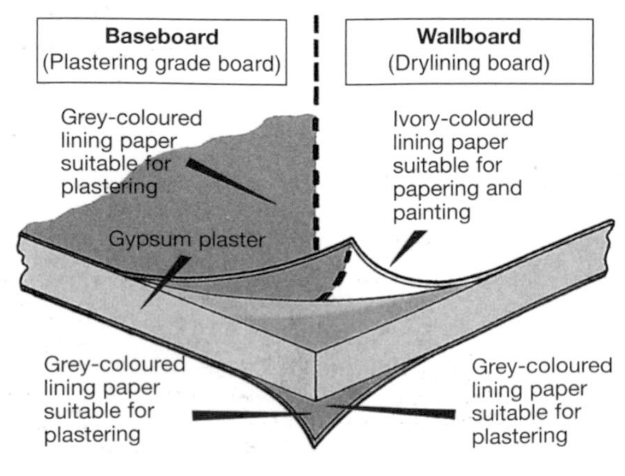

- Wallboards are the most popular material for lining rooms. They can be stuck directly on to masonry with an adhesive or nailed with plasterboard nails on to the studs and noggings of a partition wall or on to wooden battens fixed on a masonry wall.
- The usual sizes are 8 ft x 4 ft (244 cm x 122 cm) and 6 ft x 3 ft (183 cm x 91 cm) — the thicknesses are $^1/_2$ in. and $^3/_8$ in. Store boards flat but carry them upright. The best type to use for decorating have tapered edges. The slight hollows left between boards after erecting are filled with plaster in which scrim (bandage-like fine hessian) is embedded.
- Use a fine-toothed saw for cutting wallboard — work from the ivory side. Support the board to prevent cracking. Non-standard types are available — these have an improved feature such as fire resistance, water resistance, noise suppression or heat insulation.

WALL FIXINGS

There always seems to be something which has to be fixed to a wall. If the wall is a solid one you have no problem — there are satisfactory fittings for any weight from small pictures to cupboards. But lath and plaster walls do pose a problem — a heavy-duty fixing is not possible here. The answer is to locate a support (usually wooden but occasionally metal) behind the plaster or plasterboard and then screw or bolt into it

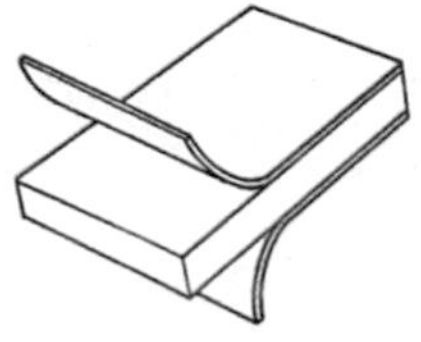

SELF-ADHESIVE PAD
Double-sided, self-adhesive pads made of PVC foam can be used on a clean and non-fibrous surface to hold lightweight pictures. Adhesion is strong, but the fixing is no stronger than the bond of the paper or paint to the wall

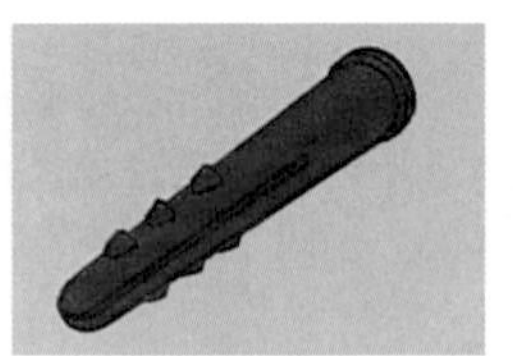

WALL PLUG
The plug should be large enough to go to the back of the hole and wide enough to fit the hole tightly. As the screw is driven in the plug expands to grip the hole. Plastic wall plugs have largely replaced the fibre ones

PICTURE HOOK
Brass picture hooks can be used for hanging framed pictures and small mirrors to solid walls. There will be 1, 2 or 3 hardened pins — use a pin hammer to drive them in. Picture hooks are not suitable for heavy frames

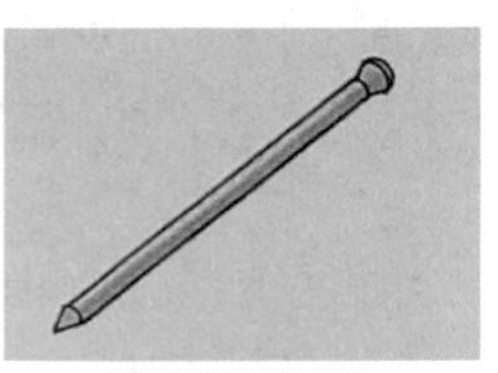

MASONRY NAIL
These extra-hard nails are driven directly into masonry — there should be at least 3 cm penetration into the brick, block etc behind the plaster or plaster-board. Drive in with a series of light taps. Wear goggles

PLASTIC FILLER
Sometimes a hole becomes too large and ragged to hold a plug. Widen the hole at the back and then moisten filler. Ram into the hole and insert the screw. Do not tighten fully until the filler has hardened

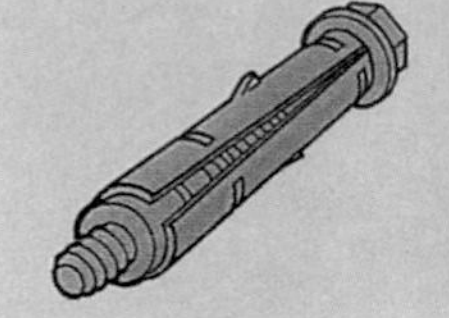

WALL ANCHOR
This is the fitting for heavy-duty work in solid walls, especially if there are any doubts about the strength of the masonry behind. As the bolt is tightened, the metal 'wings' open to grip the sides of the hole

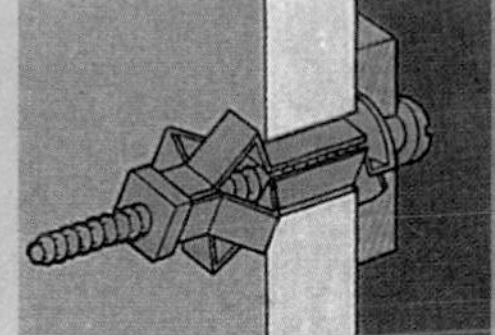

HOLLOW-WALL PLUG
A fixing for hollow walls. As the screw is tightened, the metal, plastic or rubber casing inside the cavity flattens against the inside surface, thereby forming a firm anchor. Turn the screw gradually

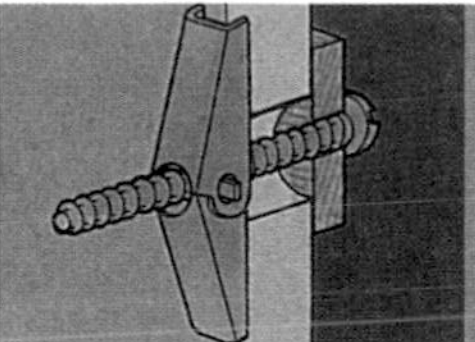

SPRING TOGGLE BOLT
A fixing for ceilings and hollow walls. Two spring-loaded wings open when the bolt has been inserted — these wings grip the inside surface. Make sure there is enough space for the wings to operate

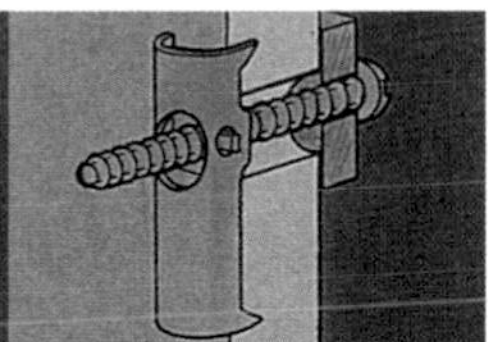

GRAVITY TOGGLE BOLT
A fixing for hollow walls. A bar drops down when the bolt has been inserted — this bar grips the inside surface as the screw is tightened. Make sure there is space for the bar to operate

CHOOSING THE RIGHT FIXING

	LIGHT LOAD eg Pictures Skirting boards Plaques	MEDIUM LOAD eg Large mirrors Shelves for plates Small wall units	HEAVY LOAD eg Cupboards Shelves for books Large wall units
SOLID WALL	Masonry nail *or* Picture hook *or* Wall plug	Wall plug (Use a cellular block plug if masonry behind is breeze block or aerated concrete block)	Wall anchor *or* No. 10 or 12 wall plug if masonry behind is brick or concrete
LATH AND PLASTER WALL	Toggle bolt *or* Nail or screw into stud or joist behind plaster	Toggle bolt *or* Screw into stud or joist behind plaster	Screw into stud or joist behind plaster
DRYLINED WALL	Masonry nail *or* Wall plug (Make sure the nail or plug goes into masonry behind plasterboard)	Wall plug (Make sure the plug goes at least 3 cm into masonry behind plasterboard)	Wall anchor (Make sure the wall anchor goes 3 - 5 cm into masonry behind plasterboard)
PARTITION WALL	Hollow-wall plug *or* Nail or screw into stud or joist behind plasterboard	Hollow-wall plug *or* Toggle bolt *or* Screw into stud or joist behind plasterboard	Screw into stud or joist behind plasterboard

LOCATING WOODEN SUPPORTS

If you plan to put up a heavy object on a lath and plaster or partition wall or a ceiling you will have to find a wooden support which can bear the retaining screws. The simplest way is to tap the wall with the handle of a screwdriver — a change in sound to a dull thud indicates that a wooden joist, stud or nogging has been reached. Sounds simple, but it doesn't always work. To make sure, check with a battery-operated metal/cable/wood frame detector.

BORING THE HOLE

Use a masonry bit for boring into walls — an 8 - 12 mm bit is suitable for most jobs. Use a slow speed, removing the bit occasionally to let it cool and to remove dust. When making this withdrawal do not switch off or the bit may jam in the hole. Aim to make a hole which is 3 - 5 cm deep in the masonry — do not let it wander or a conical hole will result. For concrete walls use a hammer-action drill. Check with a metal detector that there are no cables or pipes behind the plaster.

WALL COVERINGS

WALL COVERINGS

ROLLS

TYPE	DETAILS
LINING PAPER for painting or papering over	It is not generally necessary to line the walls before papering or painting, but a plain lining paper is sometimes needed to provide a smooth and even surface. Lining is essential if you plan to paper a painted wall. Rolls are usually longer and wider than standard wallpaper — the strips of paper are laid horizontally. Buy **Medium Grade** to hide cracks and other imperfections — lightweight grade tends to stretch when pasted. **Linen-backed Lining Paper** The best choice if the wall is subject to movement and cracking. **Extra-white Lining Paper** The best choice if the surface is to be painted rather than papered.
RELIEF COVERING	If the surface is uneven and somewhat bumpy, it is often better to use a paper which has a raised rather than a plain surface. There are numerous types — they are generally easy to hang but are difficult to remove. **'Anaglypta'** Two layers of paper embossed with a low-relief pattern. Many types available. **'Lincrusta'** Clay-like high-relief pattern on paper. Lasts longer than ordinary relief papers. **'Vinaglypta'** Paper with a vinyl surface, embossed with a high-relief pattern. Hard-wearing and scrubbable. **Foamed Vinyl** The raised pattern is spongy and not embossed — the paper backing is flat. There is no danger of squashing the pattern when hanging. Expensive. **Woodchip Paper** Paper in which wood chips and sawdust have been included to produce an oatmeal-like surface. Inexpensive.
STANDARD WALLPAPER	Despite all the innovations of recent years, standard wallpaper in 10 m x 52 cm (33 ft x 20½ in.) rolls remains by far the most popular type of wall covering. The paper bears a printed pattern and the surface is either smooth or embossed. Choose an embossed paper if the wall is uneven. The advantages of standard wallpapers are economy and the enormous range of colours and patterns. However, they are not resistant to scuffing or soiling, and they cannot be washed. Look at paper quality and not just colour and pattern when buying. Cheap and lightweight papers tend to stretch and tear easily when wet with paste. To avoid problems choose a medium- or heavy-weight paper. **Ordinary Wallpaper** is machine-printed. **Hand-printed Wallpaper** is made by block- or screen-printing — the result is exclusive, expensive and often in non-standard roll sizes.
WASHABLE WALLPAPER	A thin plastic coating is placed on standard wallpaper during manufacture — the result is a surface which has good stain resistance and can be wiped clean with a damp cloth. It is not as easy to hang as standard wallpaper and is also more difficult to strip.
VINYL	Vinyls (also called **Paper-backed Vinyls**) are an excellent choice for kitchens, bathrooms and children's rooms. A thick layer of PVC which contains the pattern is fused on to a paper backing. Vinyls are waterproof, scrubbable and easy to hang. They are also dry-strippable (the plastic layer can be easily pulled away from the backing paper which remains as a lining paper for redecoration). They are stain- and scuff-resistant, but they are also expensive. **Smooth Vinyl** is available in many colours and patterns — **Relief Vinyl** is embossed and many tile-like designs are available.
FLOCK PAPER	Plastic fibres or silk ones are stuck on to a wallpaper or vinyl base. The result is a wall covering with a velvet-like pile. For ease of hanging and upkeep, buy a ready-pasted type with a vinyl base.
FOIL PAPER	Patterned and coloured foil is attached to a paper backing to give an unusual and light-reflecting wall covering. There are more problems than advantages — it is difficult to hang and expensive to buy, and small imperfections on the wall surface are highlighted. Foils should not be used in bathrooms or behind light fixtures.
READY-PASTED COVERING	Removes the need for a pasting table. The back of the paper is coated with dry adhesive — this turns into paste when the ready-pasted wall covering is drawn through water in a trough. A number of the wall coverings described on this page are available in ready-pasted form.
FOAMED POLYETHYLENE	Removes the need for a pasting table. The wall is pasted, not the wall covering. You work straight from the roll — a sheet of lightweight plastic which is textured and patterned. **'Novamura'** is easy to hang and strip, feels warm to the touch and can be sponged down.
FABRIC & CORK	A variety of luxury papers is available in which either a thin layer of **Cork** or a fabric is bonded on to backing paper. **Hessian** is the cheapest — unbacked hessian is even less expensive but it is more difficult to hang. **Grasscloth** and **Silk** are difficult to handle and with all of them it is better to get a professional to do the work unless you have the skill and experience. The rolls are wider than wallpaper and it is usual to paste the wall rather than the paper.

TILES

TYPE	DETAILS
CERAMIC	The basic tile, made of clay which is coloured, glazed and fired. The surface may be plain or patterned, smooth or textured, shiny or semi-matt. The tiles are durable, stain- and water-resistant, making them a good choice for kitchens and bathrooms. Choose heat-resistant tiles for fixing around a fireplace, boiler or cooker. Squares are the most popular type, and the basic sizes are 100 mm x 100 mm and 150 mm x 150 mm. Other sizes up to 330 mm x 330 mm are available. Ordinary tiles have square edges and you will need to use spacers between adjacent tiles so that there will be narrow gaps for grouting. Tiles with one or two rounded and glazed edges for finishing off sides and corners are no longer available. If you are new to tiling you may prefer to use universal tiles rather than the square edge sort. The edges are bevelled so that you don't have to leave a space between adjacent tiles when fixing.
MOSAIC	Smooth ceramic tiles are mounted on a sheet — this paper or mesh may be on the back of the tiles or on their face, depending on the manufacturer. Mosaic tiles are fixed in the usual way (see pages 60 - 61) — remove surface sheeting (if present) when the adhesive is dry. Grout between the tiles as with ordinary ceramics. Quite expensive, but useful for tiling small or awkwardly-shaped areas.
PLASTIC	Once popular but no longer available. These tiles were made to look like ceramic ones but with several advantages — they are warm to the touch, can be cut with scissors and bent round corners, and could be attached with double-sided, self-adhesive pads. Standard sizes were 4¼ in. x 4¼ in., 6 in. x 6 in. and 12 in. x 12 in. Good for the not-so-handy, but they had serious drawbacks — poor durability, no scratch-resistance and inflammability.
METAL	Attractive in the right situation — gold, silver or copper with a shiny or matt surface. They are easily fixed and can be cut with scissors, but do not fix them under light fittings and never use an abrasive cleaner.
MIRROR	Squares of silvered glass, which may be clear or tinted, are attached to walls with double-sided, self-adhesive pads. A good way of increasing the apparent depth of an alcove, but the wall must be perfectly flat or the distorted reflection will be unsightly.
BRICK & STONE	Thin slices of real or simulated brick or stone can be used to provide a real-wall effect. More realistic than brick or stone wallpaper or vinyl, but you can't remove them with ease if you later change your mind. Make sure that you buy a suitable adhesive for the brick or stone tiles you have chosen.
CORK	Sheets of cork in a variety of shades, usually 300 mm x 300 mm. Cork provides good heat and noise insulation and is warm to the touch, but do buy a steam-proof grade if you intend to use them in the bathroom. Seal cork tiles with a polyurethane varnish after fixing.
CEILING	**Polystyrene Tiles** are the cheapest and the most popular. Lightweight, easy to fix and available in both smooth and embossed forms, they do pose a fire risk in certain situations. Don't use them in the kitchen and do not cover with an oil-based paint. **Fibre Tiles** are thicker and have better insulating properties. Edges are usually tongue-and-grooved so that you can pin an interlaced sheet to the ceiling joists. The usual sizes for ceiling tiles are 300 mm x 300 mm and 500 mm x 500 mm.

WOODEN PANELS

TYPE	DETAILS
CLADDING	Tongue-and-grooved or shiplap boards provide a warm and durable wall surface with a touch of luxury. Whitewood (for staining) and knotty pine are the least expensive — hard-wood boards such as mahogany are the dearest. The standard board size is 2.4 m x 95 mm, but there are smaller sizes available.
SHEET	Decorative-faced sheets of plywood or hardboard can be used to cover walls quickly — the standard sheet size is 2400 mm x 1200 mm, but smaller sizes are available. Panels with an embossed grain can be especially effective. There is a wide range of prices. At one end of the scale are sheets faced with luxury hardwood veneers such as rosewood — at the other end are sheets of thin plywood faced with printed plastic or paper.

WALLPAPERING

BUYING

- **MAKE SURE THE TYPE AND DESIGN SUIT THE ROOM**
  The type you choose should be right for the room — washables where steam or stains can be a problem, embossed or woodchip papers for poor-quality walls and so on. The choice of colour and pattern should also be influenced by the room. Choose a plain or small-patterned, light-coloured paper to create a feeling of space. Dark colours and large patterns will make a room look smaller. Horizontal stripes will make a wall look longer — vertical stripes will make a ceiling look higher.

- **BUY THE RIGHT TYPE FOR YOUR SKILL**
  Avoid thin papers, foils, flocks and fabrics if you are inexperienced and plan to do the work yourself.

- **FIND OUT HOW MANY ROLLS YOU WILL NEED**
  Cut a piece of wood or string to provide a 52 cm measure. Working round the room use this to find out the number of full-length strips you will need. Now work out how many strips you will get from each roll — measure the length from ceiling to skirting, add 10 cm and divide this length into 10 m. You can now calculate the answer — for example, you will need 7 rolls if the total number of strips required is 28 and you can get 4 strips from each roll. Buy extra if you have chosen a patterned paper.

- **BUY WISELY**
  Check that the batch number on each roll is the same. Also beware of the label 'Shade before hanging' — it means that there can be colour variations in the same batch.

PREPARING

- **GET THE ROOM READY**
  Remove as much furniture as possible. Roll back or cover the carpet with newspaper. Cover chairs, tables etc with dustsheets as wall preparation can be messy work.

- **GET THE WALLS READY**
  The basic objective is to obtain a clean, dry and flat surface. This surface must be rough enough ('keyed') to grip both paste and paper, and firm enough not to move away from the undersurface after wallpapering. It must also be impervious enough not to soak up the paste. Holes and cracks must be filled. Mark screw holes by inserting matchsticks into them.
  Wallpaper: Paper over it only if it is smooth paper (not plastic) and firmly attached to the wall. Otherwise it will have to be stripped — a long and difficult job. Soak with a solution of a proprietary stripper in warm water. Remove paper with a stripping knife held at an angle to the wall — avoid gouging out holes. Rub off remaining scraps with a glasspaper block. Washable and painted papers are very difficult to remove — score with a serrated scraper before soaking. For large areas hire a steam stripper.
  Plaster: You should leave at least 6 months between plastering and papering. New plaster should be treated with a primer/sealer — use size on old plaster.
  Plasterboard: Treat with primer/sealer.
  Paint: Wash down emulsion paint — if some washes off you will have to remove all of it. Rub down gloss paint with coarse glasspaper — get rid of all blisters and use lining paper if the prepared surface is uneven and the chosen paper is smooth-surfaced.

EQUIPMENT

SCISSORS
Small household scissors are useful for cutting around light fittings, but for cutting and trimming strips you need 25 cm long paperhanging scissors

HANGING BRUSH
Used for smoothing the paper on to the wall. Professionals choose a brush with natural bristles

PENCIL

TAPE RULE
A flexible steel tape is useful for measuring wall and ceiling distances

PLUMBLINE
A small weight attached to a piece of string — the string is chalked to mark a vertical line on the wall. A long spirit level can be used as an alternative

PASTING TABLE
A 2 m x 60 cm fold-up pasting table can be bought quite cheaply — much more satisfactory than the kitchen table or a board on the dining room one

CLOTH & SPONGE
Useful items for removing excess paste or pressing down paper

SEAM ROLLER
The professional's tool for pressing down edges — never use on embossed paper. For DIY work a soft cloth can be used instead of a seam roller

PASTE BRUSH
Buy a 15 cm distemper brush

BUCKET OF PASTE
Choose the right paste. Fungicidal grade is essential for vinyls, washables, foils and foamed polyethylene. For wallpaper use universal grade for all types or pick a specific type (lightweight, heavy duty etc) to match the weight of the paper. Tie a piece of string across the handle lugs to support the brush

TRIMMING KNIFE
Required for cutting edges if plastics or fabrics are being hung

STRAIGHT EDGE
A wooden or steel rule is used for measuring and marking out strips before cutting

Illustrated here are the major tools used when paper hanging — not illustrated are stepladders, scaffoldboards for ceilings etc

(1) Start at one side of the largest window in the room and work towards the door

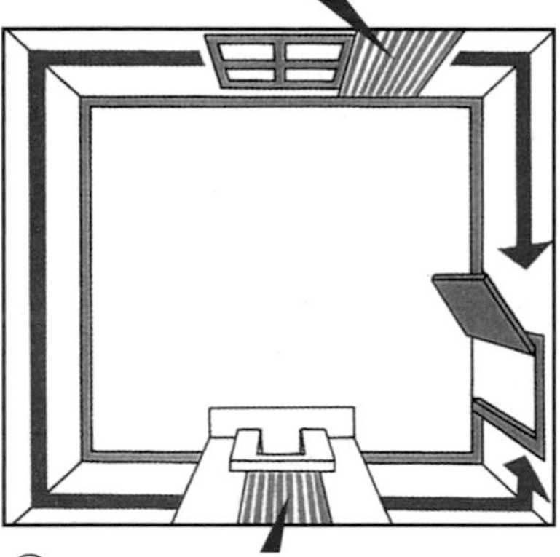

(2) Exception: Start at the centre of the chimney breast if the paper has a large pattern

(3) Use a plumbline to mark a true vertical. Chalk the string. Pin end to top of wall one roll width less 2 cm from window frame

(4) Let weight come to rest. Hold string against the wall and then pluck to leave chalk line

(5) Measure the height from ceiling to the skirting board

(6) Unroll paper on the pasting table and mark out this length plus 10 cm. Cut at right angles to the edge

(7) Paste the paper: Cover one half at a time — paste strip A first, then paste out to B and C. Make sure edge overlaps table when pasting

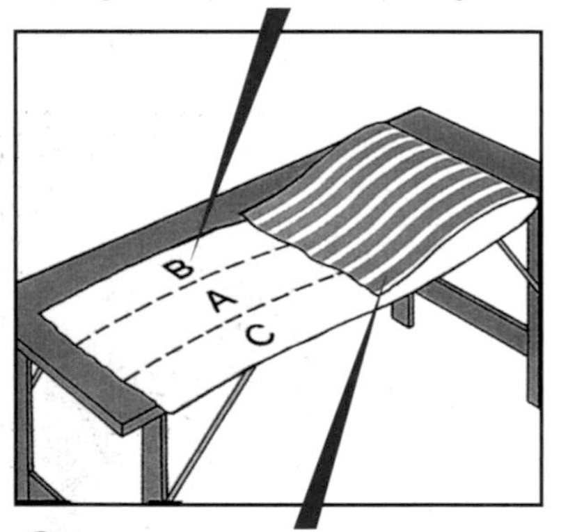

(8) Fold pasted half of paper as shown — then paste second half. Wipe off any which has got on to the table

(9) Leave paper to soak for time recommended on package. Make sure all strips are left to soak for the same time

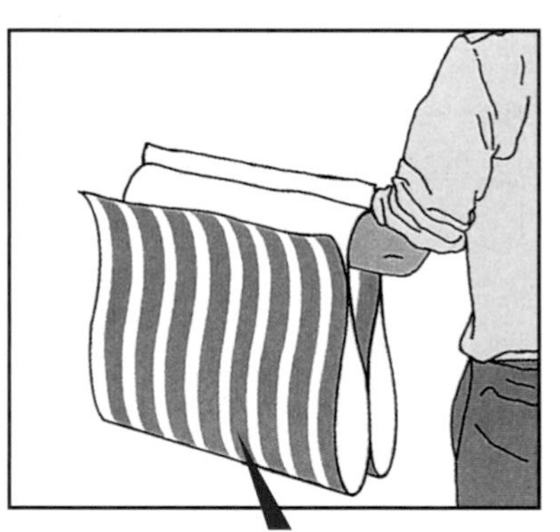

(10) Carry the strip to the wall, as shown. With experience, you can have one strip pasted and soaking whilst hanging a previous one

(11) Open top half. Holding both edges place the paper so that it touches the chalk line and overlaps ceiling join by about 5 cm

(12) With the palm of one hand move the paper so that the edge lies along the chalk line

(13) Brush down the middle holding the paper slightly away from the wall

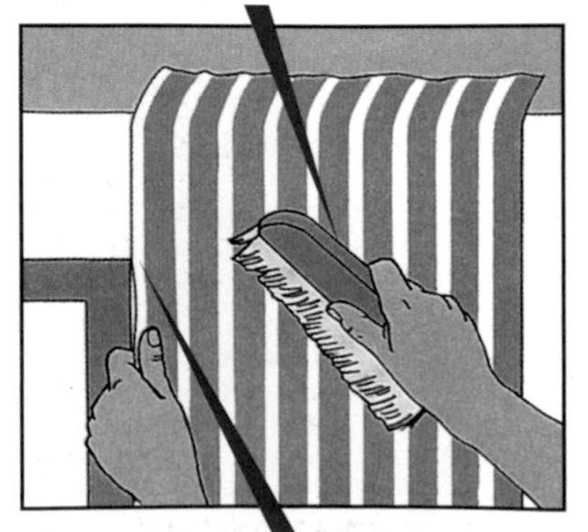

(14) Then work towards the edges, brushing well into corners. Wipe the brush frequently

(15) Crease the paper along the edge, using the tip of the scissors

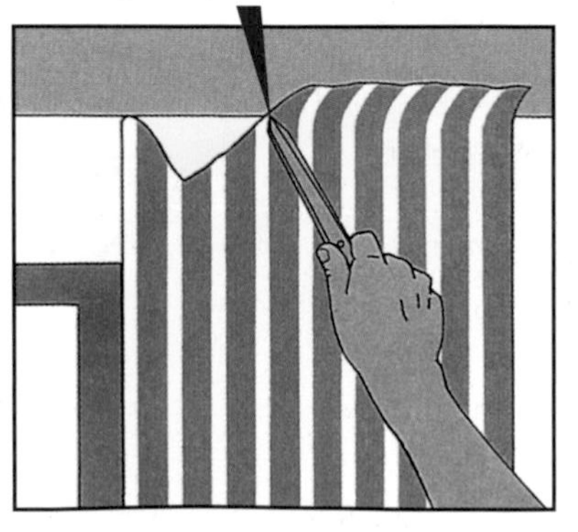

(16) Pull the paper back gently. Cut along the crease and then brush back in place

(17) Unfold the bottom half of the strip. Smooth down with the hanging brush

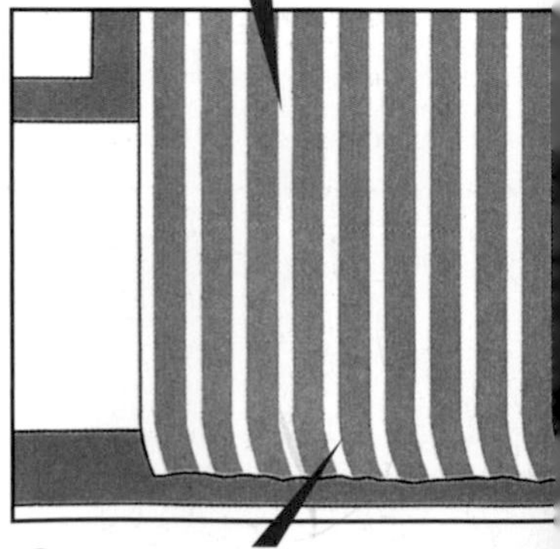

(18) Carry out stages **15** and **16**. Wipe off any paste on the ceiling and skirting board

19 Lay the roll on the floor and measure out the next strip. Make sure the pattern matches and that there is at least a 5 cm overlap at the top and bottom

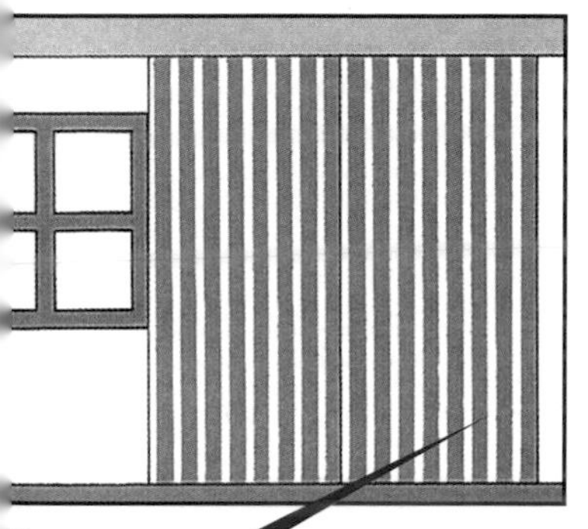

20 Carry out stages **7** to **18**. This second strip should butt neatly and tightly against the first one

21 **Room corner:** Cut the last strip vertically so that there will be a 2 cm overlap on the unpapered wall. Keep the offcut

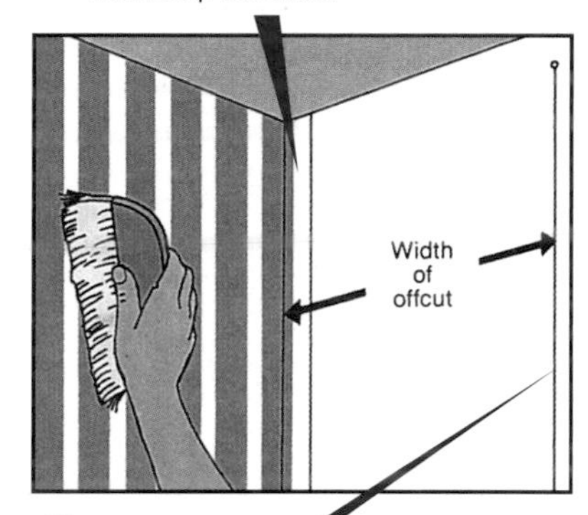

22 Follow stages **3** and **4** to make a vertical chalk line. Hang the offcut to the chalk line — lifting up or down to match pattern

23 **Protruding corner:** Cut the last strip vertically so that there will be a 3 cm overlap on the unpapered wall. Keep the offcut

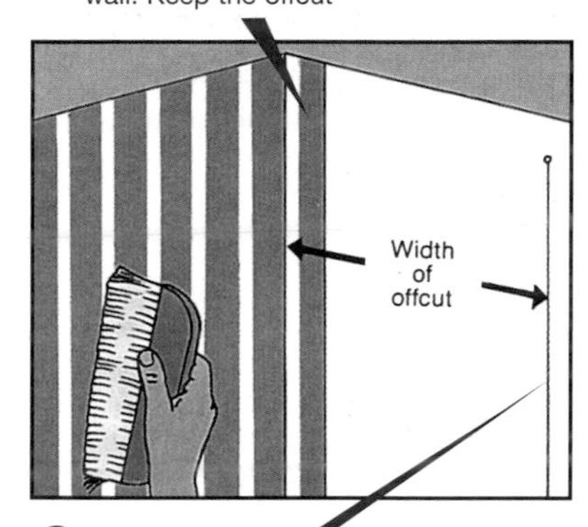

24 Follow stages **3** and **4** to make a vertical chalk line. Hang the offcut to the chalk line — lifting up or down to match pattern

25 Light fittings: Switch off at mains. Unscrew fitting and pull forward — trim, leaving a narrow margin inside the area covered by the plate

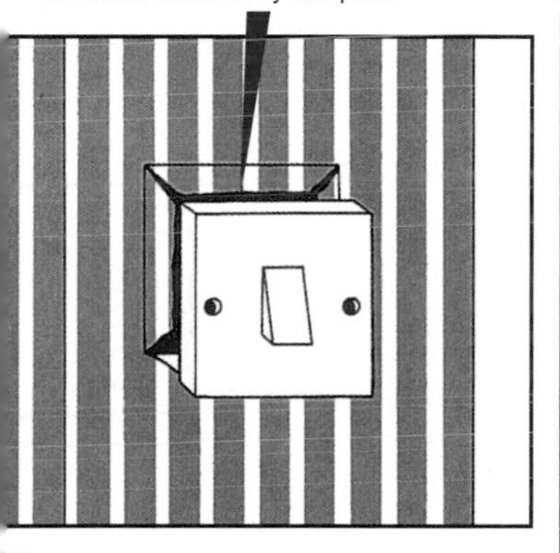

26 Where the cover cannot be removed, make a series of triangular cuts around the fitting and trim back neatly

Ceiling: Paper ceiling before walls. The techniques for measuring, pasting and trimming are basically the same as for wall hanging, but the work is more tiring. You will probably need someone to help. Erect a stout platform using 2 ladders and a board directly under where you will have to work. Begin at the window and work inwards

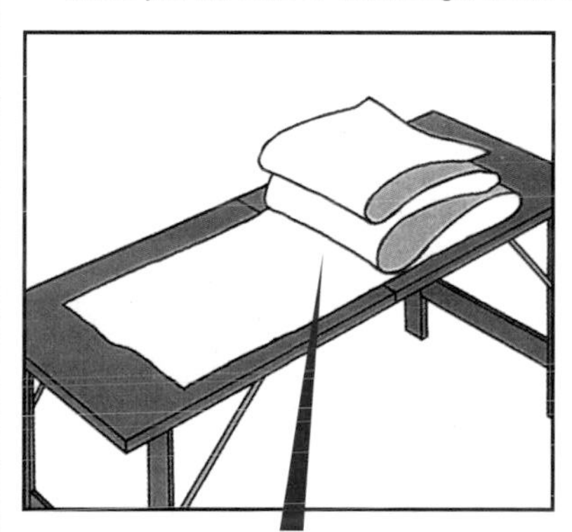

Paste paper as stage **7**, but fold the pasted portions into concertina-like pleats about 45 cm long

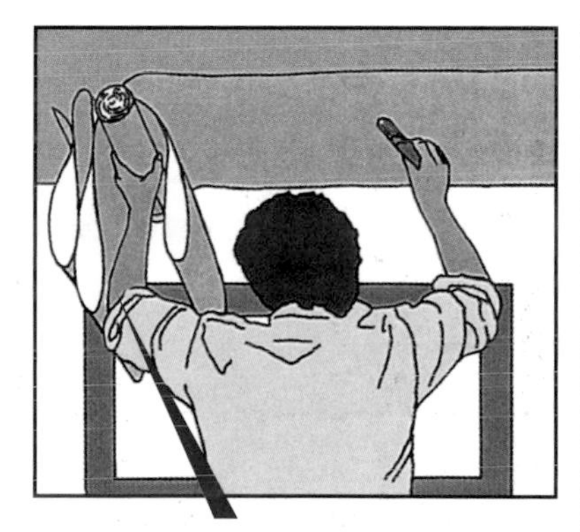

Overlap walls by about 2 cm. Hold up all folds with a spare roll of wallpaper — brush into place as you move along the platform

Ready-pasted paper: Cut each strip to the required length (see stages **6** and **19**) and roll loosely with pattern inside. Leave paper immersed in the trough for recommended time

Raise paper gradually and place in position. Smooth down with a sponge, working from the centre to the edges

HOW TO DEAL WITH WALLPAPERING PROBLEMS

- **BUBBLES**
  The usual cause is careless brushing out — areas are allowed to stick to the wall before all the air behind them has been removed. Bubbles can also be caused by lumpy paste and insufficient soaking time. If the paste is still wet, lift the paper and smooth out properly. If the paste has dried, cut a cross at the centre of the bubble and then stick down the flaps.
- **BUMPS**
  Unlike bubbles, there is no air within. The cause is poor preparation.
- **TEARS**
  Usual causes are poor-quality paper, careless handling and/or leaving the paper to soak for longer than necessary.
- **PAPER NOT ADHERING**
  There are numerous causes, such as damp walls, untreated porous walls and too little paste.
- **EDGES NOT ADHERING**
  The usual cause is either too little paste applied to the edges or drying out due to spending too much time over stages **13** and **14**. Remember to press edges with a seam roller or cloth.
- **PATTERN NOT MATCHING**
  The usual cause is irregular stretching due to strips being allowed to soak for varying times. Do not allow part of a long length to drop suddenly when hanging.

TILING

BUYING

- **MAKE SURE THE MATERIALS SUIT THE ROOM**
  A vast range is available from cheap, mass-produced tiles to expensive, hand-painted ones. There are other variations — a glazed surface is essential if the surface is to be regularly washed and heat-resistant tiles should be used for the area around a boiler or cooker. You must also pick a suitable adhesive — a water-resistant grade for kitchen or bathroom or a heat-resistant grade where high temperatures will be a problem.

- **BUY WISELY**
  It is more economical to purchase tiles by the box rather than singly. It is always wise to buy a few extra ones, and a few very cheap tiles in order to practice cutting. Always check for breakages and imperfections before leaving the shop and buy the required number of plastic spacers if you are not going to use universal tiles (see page 56).

SETTING OUT

At this vital first step the tiling pattern is carefully worked out before fixing begins. The purpose is to find both the correct starting point and the correct level for the first row. This ensures that the lines between the tiles will be truly horizontal and vertical. In addition, the aim is to have the body of the tiled area and the top row made up entirely of whole tiles. This means that the cut tiles will be at the sides and the lowest level. A gauge stick and spirit level are used for setting out. The standard pattern is to have the first row of tiles at one tile's length (or less) above the skirting board, and equal-sized cut tiles at both sides.

PREPARING

- **GET THE WALL READY**
  The surface to be tiled must be dry, level and free from grease. In addition it must be rigid and must also be capable of carrying the weight of the tiles.
  Plaster: A suitable tiling surface provided it is at least 6 weeks old and has a finish coating (see page 51). Fill cracks and holes, remove bumps and then paint with a plaster primer. Tiling can begin when this is dry.
  Paint: Check carefully. With gloss paint, test that it is firmly bonded on to the wall by pulling at the surface with a strip of adhesive tape. If the paint pulls away, the surface will have to be removed or covered with plywood before tiling. If the paint is sound, remove any loose patches or blisters with a scraper and apply primer to any bare areas. Wash down and rub with coarse glasspaper. Emulsion paint should be removed before tiling.
  Wallpaper: Wallpaper and other wall coverings must be removed before tiling. It is necessary to get down to the plaster or plasterboard. Wash down with water after stripping.
  Wood: Narrow panels are not really suitable for tiling, but wood sheeting, plywood, hardboard and chipboard sheets can be tiled provided they are firmly attached to the wall. Use a flexible tile adhesive.
  Brick: This surface can be tiled as long as it is smooth and dry. Brick walls are, however, usually too rough for tiling — it is generally necessary to line with plywood.
  Tiles: Tiles make a satisfactory base. Fix any loose tiles and rub down with a suitable abrasive paper to provide a key. Wash down thoroughly before tiling begins.

EQUIPMENT

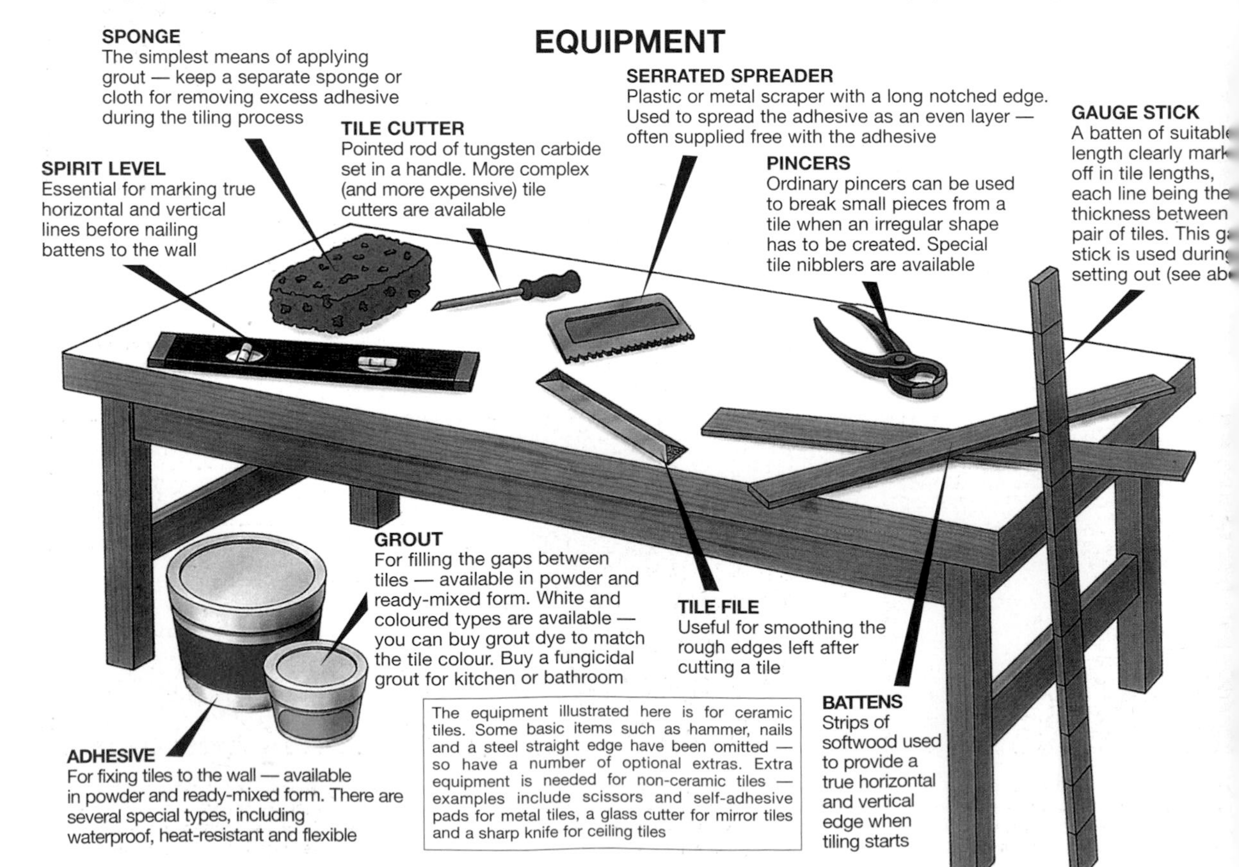

The equipment illustrated here is for ceramic tiles. Some basic items such as hammer, nails and a steel straight edge have been omitted — so have a number of optional extras. Extra equipment is needed for non-ceramic tiles — examples include scissors and self-adhesive pads for metal tiles, a glass cutter for mirror tiles and a sharp knife for ceiling tiles

Nail a batten along the wall to form the horizontal support for the first row. Check with spirit level

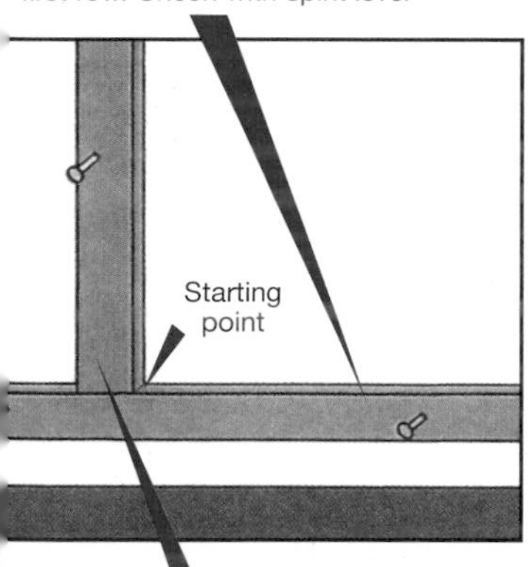

Nail second batten on top of this horizontal batten. Check that it is truly vertical

Check occasionally that rows are truly horizontal. Remove battens and spacers when all whole tiles have been laid and the adhesive has set (12 - 24 hours)

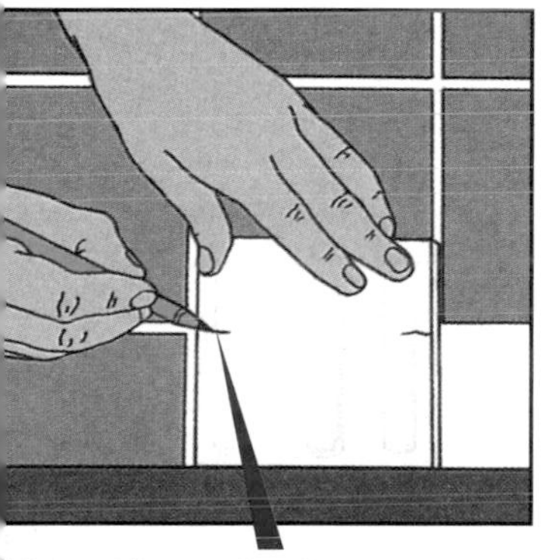

Cut and fit remaining tiles as required. Hold the tile to be cut back to front in the space to be fitted. Mark the edges with a pencil

Rub grout into the spaces with a sponge once all the tiles have been laid and the adhesive has set

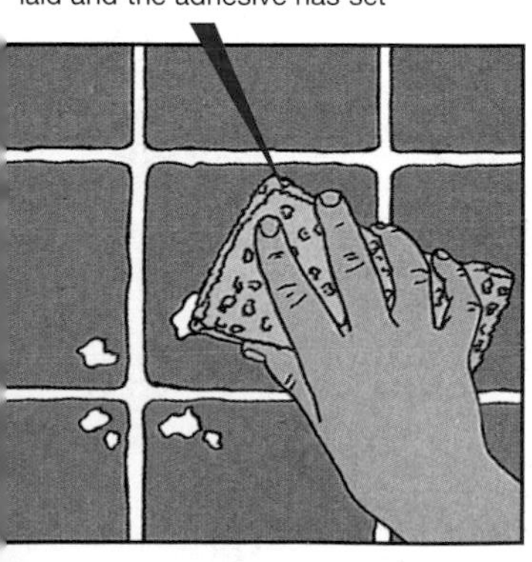

Run a rounded stick or wet finger along the lines to produce a smooth finish. Rub the surface briskly with a soft cloth when the grout is dry

(3) Spread adhesive as a 3 mm layer over an area of about 1 sq.m. Use a serrated spreader

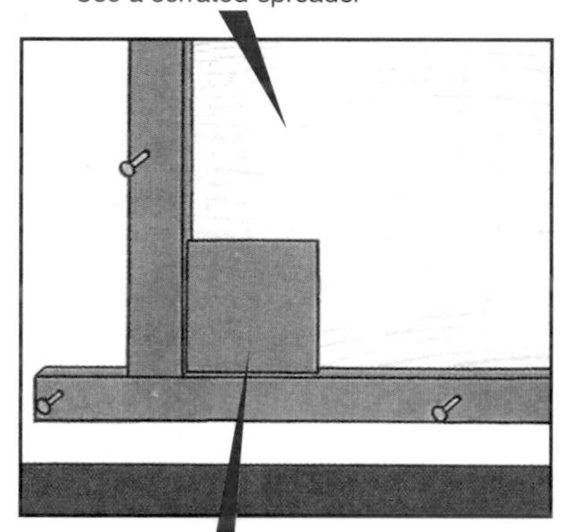

(4) Place first tile in position. Press against adhesive

(9) Reverse the tile and mark the front. Firmly score the tile with the tile cutter and a steel straight edge

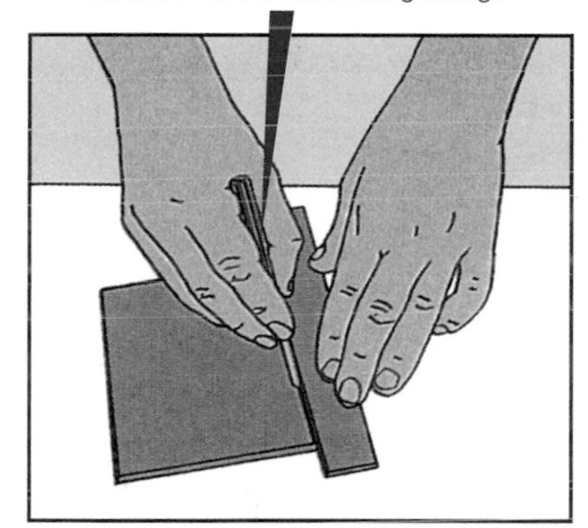

(10) Place a matchstick at both edges of the tile directly under the scored line. Press down on each side to snap the tile

Mirror tiles: A perfectly smooth surface is required. Fix with self-adhesive pads — never use ordinary tile adhesive

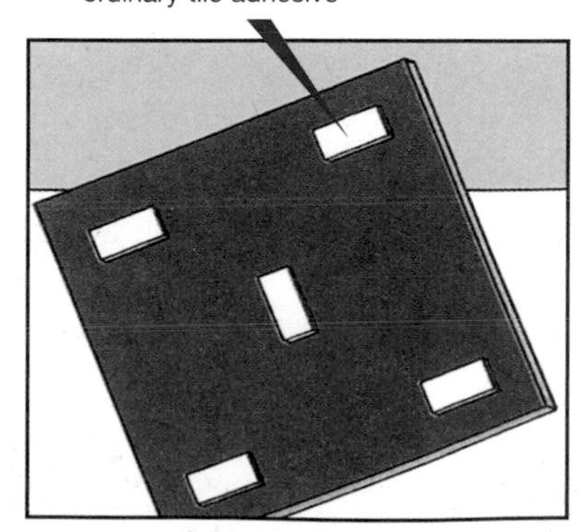

To cut tiles, follow stage **9** using a glass cutter in place of the tile cutter. Irregular-shaped cuts are very difficult to make

(5) Work in horizontal rows, pressing (not sliding) tiles into position. Wipe off adhesive which oozes to the surface

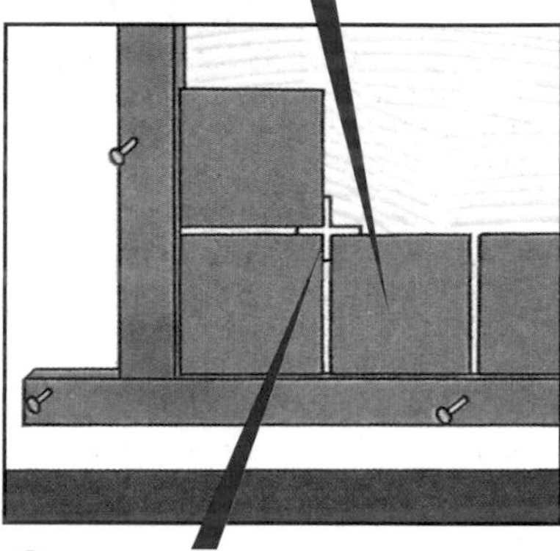

(6) Insert plastic spacers (or matchsticks). Not necessary if universal tiles are used

(11) L-shaped and irregular cuts require different treatment. Mark and then score the area to be removed. Make extra score lines

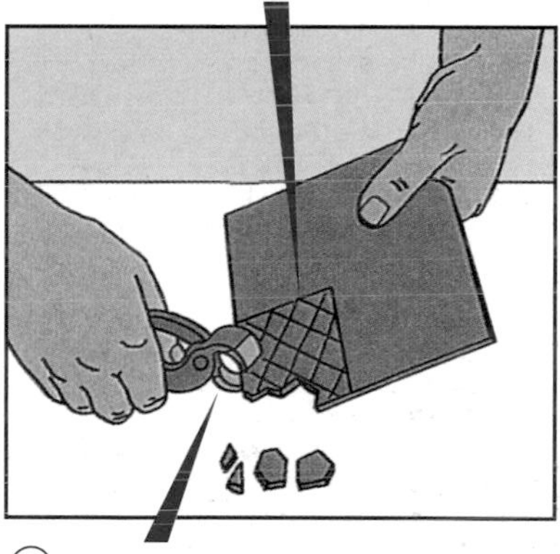

(12) Use pincers to 'nibble' (remove small pieces of tile) until the line is reached. Clean edge with the tile file

Polystyrene ceiling tiles: Mark the ceiling with 2 chalk lines, crossing at right angles near the centre

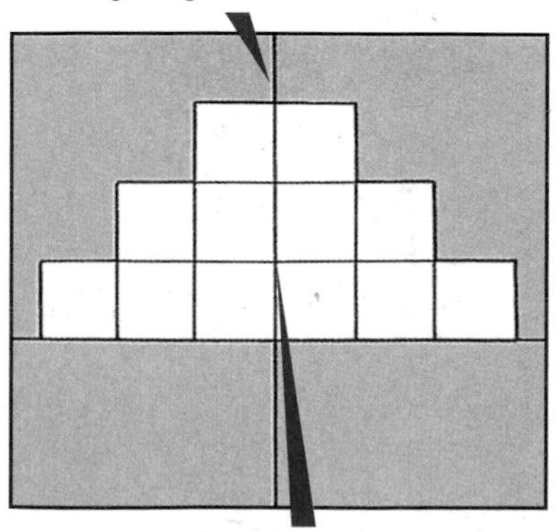

Spread polystyrene adhesive on the back of each tile, going near to but not reaching the edges. Press into place. Work to the edges in pyramid fashion

WINDOWS

The basic purpose of a window is to let light into the room, and here you must strike a balance. Too little glass makes the room dingy — too large an expanse of unshaded glass results in soaring temperatures in summer. As a general rule the window area should be about 15 per cent of the floor area.

Windows also provide ventilation which is so vital for dispelling stale air, preventing mould, reducing condensation and so on. Here there are strict rules — the area of openable glass must be at least 5 per cent of the floor area if the room is to be lived in for part of the day.

A window cannot be simply lifted out and replaced like a cupboard. Despite the large amount of work and expense involved there are still times when it is necessary to have one or more replacement windows installed. The wooden frame may have rotted, you may wish to modernise your home or you may be tired of having to paint steel-framed windows every few years. It is, of course, sensible to install double-glazed replacement windows when such needs arise, but to put in double glazing solely to cut down on heating bills may not be worthwhile.

Consider all the factors before deciding to tear out your windows. If the house was built before the war then the windows will not be standard size and you won't be able to buy a replacement off the shelf. Pick a suitable style and construction material. Always insist on safety glass in any high-risk zone such as patio doors or child-high panes of glass. Many thousands go to hospital each year because this simple rule is often ignored. Before fitting a replacement window, check with the installer that the work will comply with the Building Regulations.

In addition to providing light and ventilation, windows give a view of the world outside. This means that during daylight hours a window is a focal point, and interior decorators spend a great deal of time thinking about this aspect. If the view is attractive then the window covering should do nothing to detract from the scene — if the view is an eyesore or open to public gaze then there are blinds, net curtains etc to make life more comfortable. See pages 68-70 for basic guidelines on blinds and curtains.

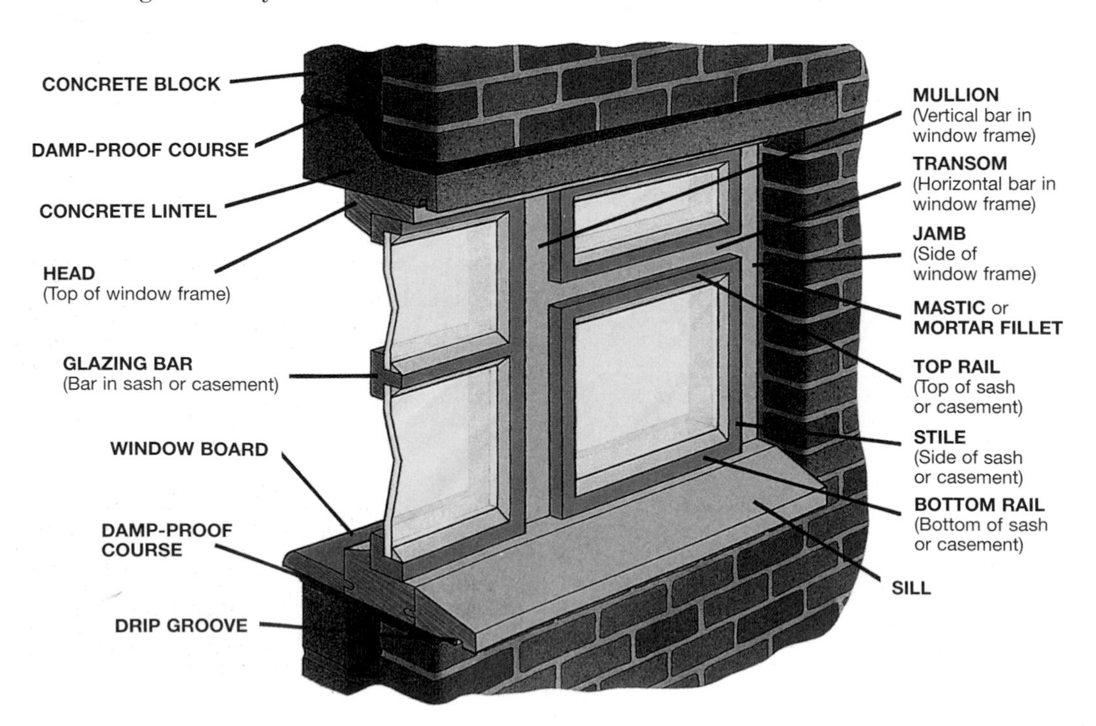

WINDOW TYPES

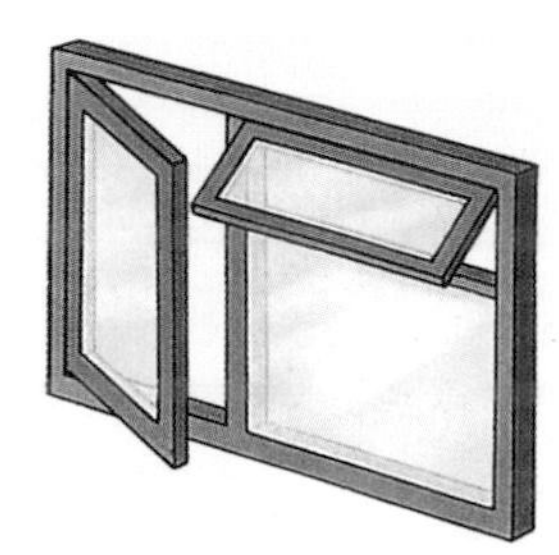

CASEMENT WINDOW

The casement window has taken over from the traditional sash window as the most popular type. A large number of styles and sizes are available — all have at least one hinged piece of framed glass (the casement) and the usual pattern is one side-hung casement plus a fixed pane of glass and a top-hung fanlight. Look for easy-clean hinges — they allow you to get behind the casement to clean the glass. For French windows see page 71

SASH WINDOW

Stout windows with two wooden sashes which slide up and down were once the basic type. There are advantages — good ventilation and it's relatively safe to open the top sash for ventilation when children are around. But there are problems — they can rattle, stick and sash cords can break. In modern windows spring sash balances have replaced the old system of cord-carried weights and pullies. Aluminium sash windows are available

PIVOT WINDOW

The answer to outside window cleaning — the window can be reversed for washing and such windows can be a boon where cleaning from outside would be impossible. Wood is the usual construction material and both horizontal and vertical pivot types are made. The pivot window can be attractive in a modern setting but has not become popular. When open part of it projects into the room and small children can easily crawl through

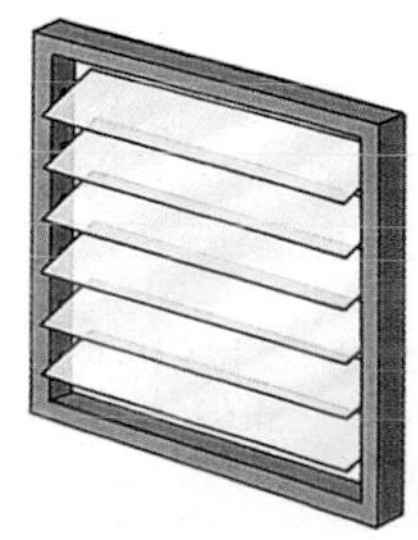

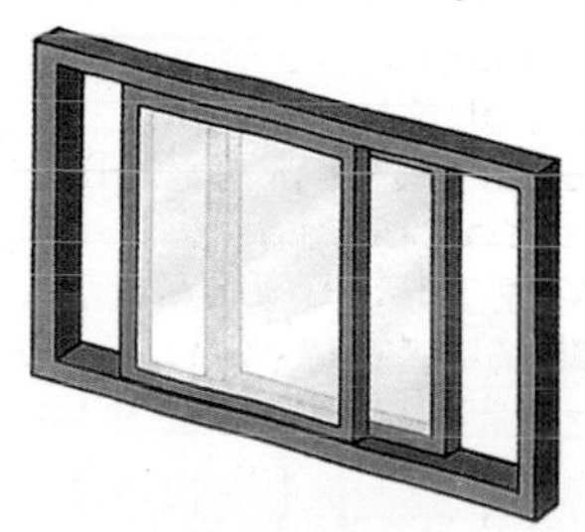

LOUVRE WINDOW

Strips of glass are fitted into a metal frame which contains an open-shut lever. When closed the glass panes press together — when open there is a large space with very little obstruction to the air outside. Not very popular — the view outdoors is obstructed and they can be draughty when closed. An added drawback is the security risk as panes can be removed. You can buy casement windows which have a louvred section instead of a fanlight

BAY WINDOW

A basic feature of the Victorian villa. Nowadays, however, the bay window has lost much of its appeal. There are several styles — square bays which are block shaped, splayed bays with sloping sides, curved bays etc. The roof above the bay may be flat or pitched, and the projection may involve one floor only or the whole height of the house. A Georgian variation is the bow window — a curved bay with many glazing bars

SLIDING WINDOW

Until the appearance of aluminium as a construction material, horizontal sash windows (Yorkshire lights) were not popular. Lightweight sliding windows are now seen everywhere — in office blocks, hotels and in houses. When open there is no projection either outside or inside, and there is good control of ventilation. Sliding windows are usually double glazed, and the patio door (the type giving access to the garden) is very popular

WOOD

Despite the introduction of aluminium and plastic, timber remains the most popular material for window construction. An off-the-shelf softwood window is the cheapest type and its insulation properties are excellent. Of course there is the problem of bulky frames and sections, and the much more serious drawback of regular maintenance. The rule is to choose carefully. Any softwood used in the construction should have been pressure-impregnated with a preservative. Choose a hardwood frame if you can afford it — at least make sure the sill is made of hardwood

STEEL

Galvanised steel windows were popular between the wars. They were fixed in a wooden subframe and adorned semi-detached villas everywhere, but the drawbacks have pushed them into bottom place for replacement windows. Regular maintenance is necessary to prevent rust, and heat insulation is poor. Condensation can be a problem and the wooden subframe will need occasional maintenance. The steel window did introduce one major advantage to window construction — slim sections in place of the stout frames of wooden windows

ALUMINIUM

The double-glazing boom increased the popularity of aluminium windows. They are available in anodised or acrylic colours as well as the traditional silvery-grey, and very little maintenance is needed — merely rub down with water and a little detergent twice a year. Some manufacturers fit a thermal break which reduces heat loss and condensation. Another way of reducing heat loss is to buy an aluminium/uPVC composite window. A hardwood subframe is nearly always needed for aluminium windows

uPVC

Unplasticised polyvinyl chloride frames were widely used on the Continent before the advantages of plastic frames became apparent in Britain. The white, grey or wood-effect frames and casements are rigid, require no maintenance and have the heat-insulating properties of wood. A timber subframe is not usually required and the cost of a made-to-measure window should be no more than for an aluminium one. Drawbacks are few — the surface can be scratched and it will be damaged by a naked flame

HOW TO DEAL WITH WINDOW PROBLEMS

● **GENERAL MAINTENANCE**
Wooden windows should be painted once every 4 - 5 years. Prepare carefully before you begin to paint — if rot is present, carry out remedial treatment (see page 107). Metal windows should also be painted regularly — if rust is present you should cure the problem as soon as possible (see page 114). Do not apply too much paint — avoid a build-up which can cause sashes or casements to stick or fail to close properly. Oil hinges regularly and tighten loose screws. The exception here is the pivot window — do not oil.

● **RATTLING WINDOWS**
This is a problem of ageing sash windows. Because of movement and shrinkage the beads (strips of wood between and in front of the sashes) no longer fit properly. Wind causes the sashes to move in the space and a rattle is the result. Wedges can be used to hold the sashes tight but this is not a satisfactory solution. It is better to fit nylon-pile draught excluder between the sash edges and the beads. If this fails then the beads will have to be moved — a job for a joiner or DIY enthusiast.

● **REPAIRING A BROKEN WINDOW**

(1) Wear gloves to remove broken glass. Use a screwdriver or chisel to get rid of all old putty. Remove any glazing sprigs, metal clips or beading and then brush away dirt and dust

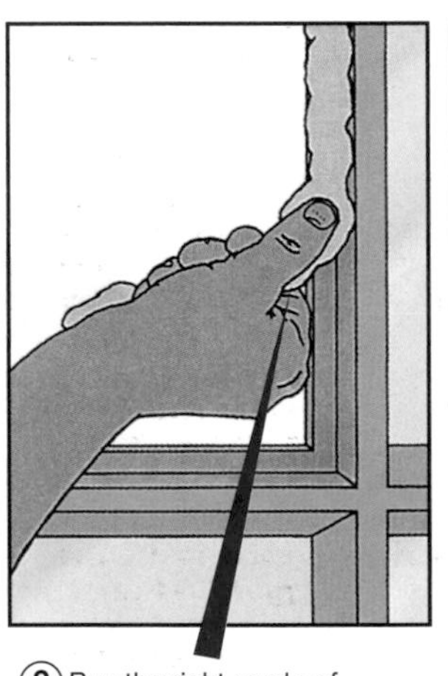

(2) Buy the right grade of putty — linseed oil putty for wood, and metal casement putty for metal. Mould the putty in your hands until it is soft — squeeze a 5 - 8 mm thick strip into the rebate

(3) The new pane should be 3 mm smaller than the minimum width and height of the opening. Make sure you buy the right grade and thickness — see pages 65 - 66 for details

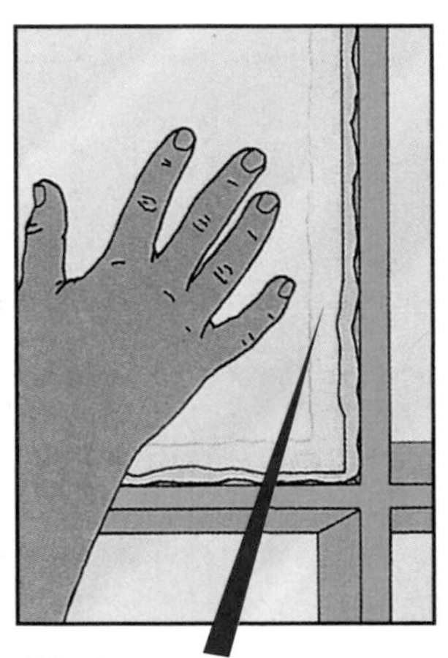

(4) Press the glass into the putty until it is firmly bedded in place. Put the bottom of the pane into position first and then press forward — always press the edges and never the middle of the glass

(5) Place new glazing sprigs in position if the frame is a wooden one. Knock the sprigs into the rebate with the side of an old chisel. Slide the blade along the surface of the glass — do not use a hammer

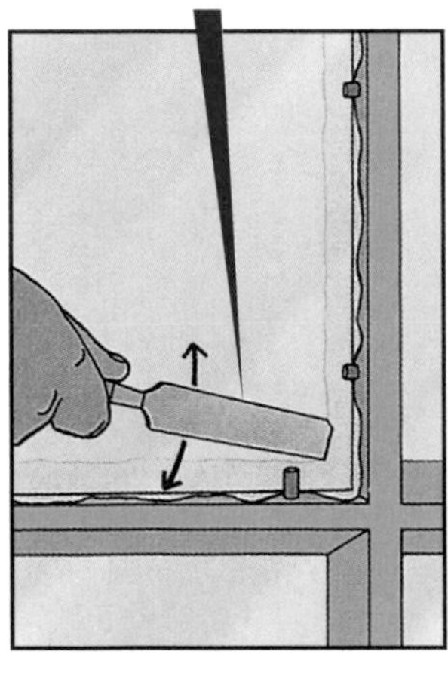

(6) In a metal window use glazing clips. Run another strip of putty in the angle between the new pane and the wooden frame. Only a small amount of putty will be needed if beading is to be fitted

(7) Use a putty knife to smooth the putty as a neat bevel. Mitre the corners and then remove all excess putty from glass surface and glazing bars

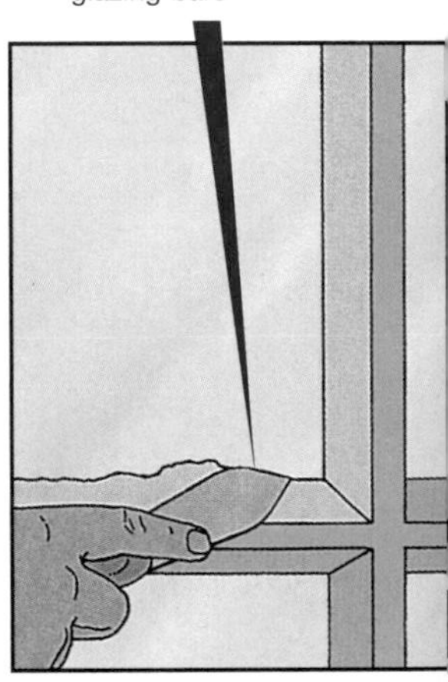

(8) Wipe off remaining traces of putty and fingerprints with a cloth soaked in methylated spirits. Run a moist brush along the putty surface and leave for 2 weeks. Paint, covering all putty

● **STICKING WINDOWS**
If a sash is shut tight and will not move, tape the glass so that it will not shatter. Then use a mallet to tap a block of wood placed against the wooden or metal rail or stile. Move the block all round the window until the seal is broken. Once opened, rub the inner channels with a block of beeswax or spray with a silicone lubricant. This simple technique may not succeed — the cause may be a build-up of paint, which calls for stripping and then repainting, or it may be due to swelling which requires planing down. The cause of sticking of a casement window may be quite simple — stiff hinges, loose hinges or too much paint. Check all these points.

Unfortunately the cause of sticking of both sash and casement windows may be more serious. The joints of the frame may be loose or the sash may have warped. Another possible reason is that the sash cords have broken, and in all of these cases you should call in a joiner unless you are a knowledgeable DIY enthusiast.

● **DRAUGHTS**
Hold a lighted candle close to the edges of the window — a flickering flame will reveal that you have a draught problem. The cause may be a break in the mortar fillet between the window frame and the wall — this should be filled with mastic sealer. It is much more likely, however, that the draught is due to a space between the sash or casement and the window frame. The answer with a casement window is usually quite simple — apply self-adhesive foam strip all the way round the rebate of the frame. Sash windows require plastic or nylon-pile draught excluders.

● **REPLACEMENT WINDOWS**
Numerous DIY books indicate that taking out old windows and installing new ones is a straightforward job provided the diagrams are followed. This advice is best avoided — either leave it to a builder or a replacement window company.

GLASS

For most of us panes of glass are things to be washed and not seen, but this desire for complete invisibility was not really satisfied until the early 1960s. Before that time **sheet glass** was used for house windows — smooth and clear but with varying thicknesses along the panes. The result was some distortion of the view outdoors — this could only be overcome by using **plate glass**. Unfortunately this was expensive and so was restricted to areas such as shop fronts. Both types have now largely been replaced by **float glass** which is perfectly flat, free from distortion and inexpensive enough to use for all windows.

In general we don't want to notice window glass, and yet it can be a material to add either decorative charm or personal tragedy. Patterned or decorated glass can enhance the appearance of a room, especially when used in internal doors or room dividers. But there is also the danger element — ordinary (or annealed) glass will shatter with razor-sharp pieces when broken. So when putting in new windows keep both the beauty and safety aspects in mind.

Thickness (Imperial)	Thickness (Metric)	Recommended uses
24 oz	3 mm	Only for very small windows — do not use in a high-risk zone Picture framing
32 oz	4 mm	The best choice for windows up to 1 sq.m in area — do not use in a high-risk zone
$^{3}/_{16}$ in.	5 mm	The best choice for windows 1 - 2 sq.m in area — do not use in a high-risk zone
$^{1}/_{4}$ in.	6 mm	The best choice for windows 2 - 3 sq.m in area — up to 2 sq.m in a high-risk zone Patio doors. Table tops
$^{3}/_{8}$ in.	10 mm	The best choice for very large windows — 2 - 3 sq.m in a high-risk zone Patio doors. Table tops

GLAZING FOR SAFETY

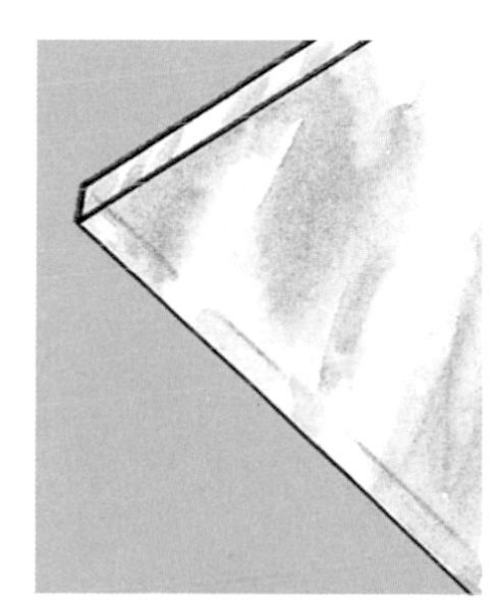

The rule of thumb is to use 4 mm window glass for small areas and 6 mm for larger areas — but this only applies for sites where there is negligible risk and where high winds are unlikely to be a problem. Where there is some risk of breakage or if the window is exposed to high winds, you should use thicker glass than standard — raise the rule of thumb to 6 mm and 10 mm glass.

In truly high-risk zones this is not enough. You should use some form of safety material — toughened glass, laminated glass or wired glass. Typical high-risk zones are doors with large panes of glass, large glass panels next to doors, glassed-in balustrades and shower screens. Always use safety glass if the glazed area extends below 80 cm from the floor and is likely to have children running nearby.

Of course, you may have a high-risk zone which has been glazed with ordinary window glass. One solution is to cover the existing glass with self-adhesive transparent film which will prevent the glass from shattering in case of an accident. Breakage is not the only problem — children (and the absent-minded) do walk into closed patio doors. One answer is to have some form of sticker or central strip on a large expanse of glass.

CUTTING GLASS

(1) Place the glass on a flat and even surface which has been covered with felt or layers of newspaper

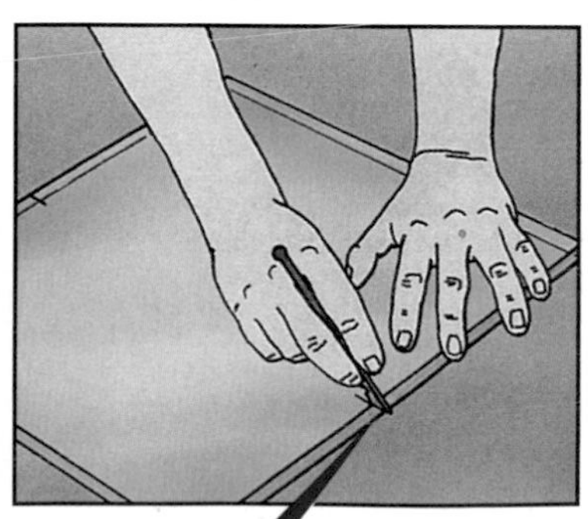

(2) Mark out the line to be cut by nicking both edges with the glass cutter. With patterned glass keep smooth side uppermost

(3) Clean the glass with turps and then place a straight edge between the 2 nicks

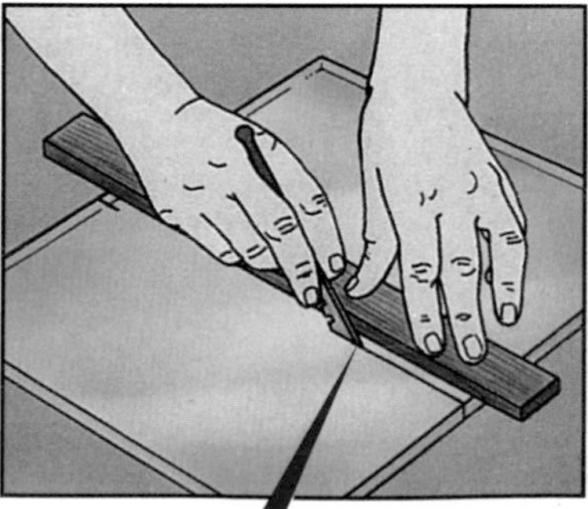

(4) Draw the glass cutter along the straight edge from one side to the other in a single motion, applying firm pressure

(5) Put the straight edge under the glass with one side along the scored line. Do this immediately after cutting

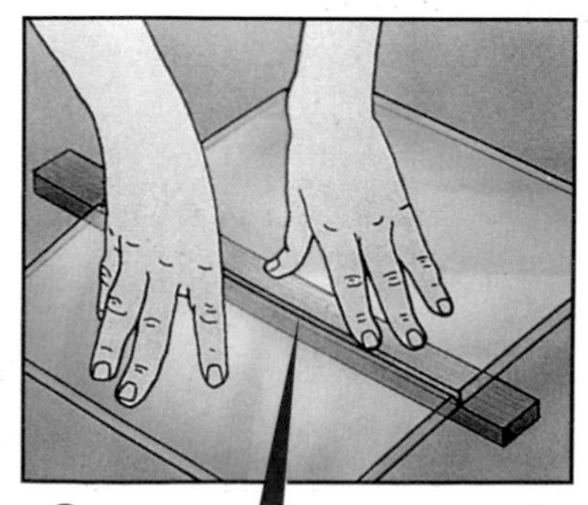

(6) Hold the glass firmly with both hands as shown above. Press down lightly until the glass breaks

GLASS TYPES

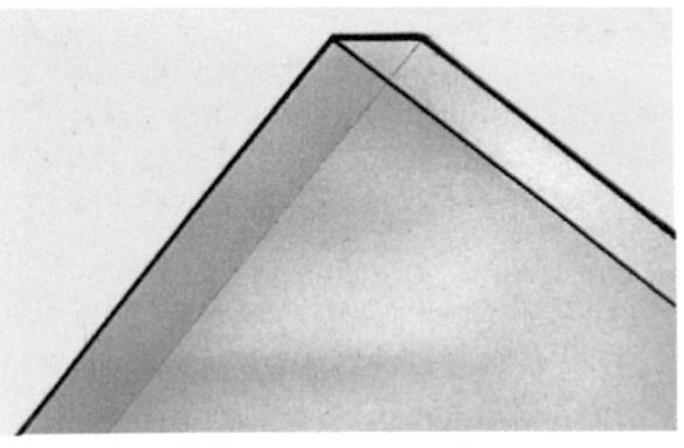

WINDOW GLASS
For most glazing purposes you will need ordinary window glass which is perfectly clear and distortion-free. The standard choice these days is float glass and the thickness may be 4 mm, 5 mm or 6 mm — see the table on the previous page. For some purposes you will need one of the special glasses shown on this page, but they will cost more than float glass. You can save money by ordering 3 mm glass for small windows which are well away from small children

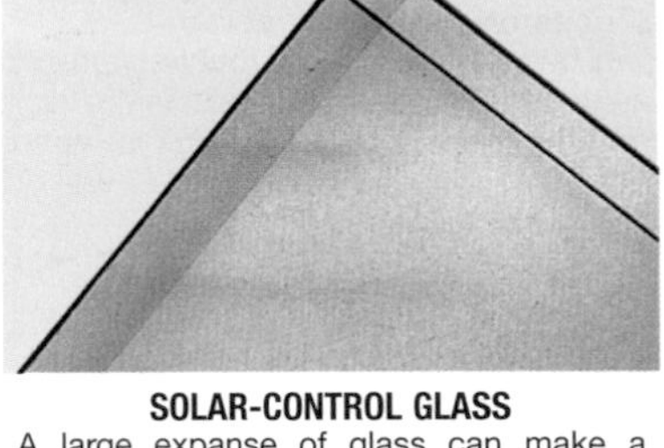

SOLAR-CONTROL GLASS
A large expanse of glass can make a room unbearably hot in summer — one answer is to use solar-control glass. With the most successful types the heat entering the room is cut by 80 per cent and glare is greatly reduced. Most brands are tinted bronze or grey and some can provide privacy by serving as a one-way mirror. Solar-control glass is available in all popular thicknesses and for doors there are both toughened and laminated grades

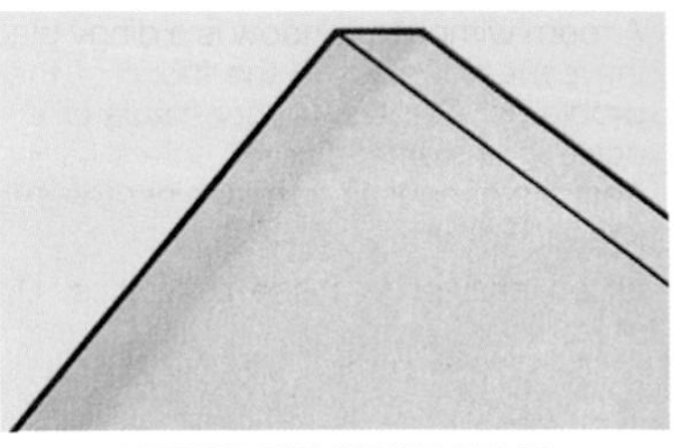

DIFFUSE-REFLECTION GLASS
Plain window glass has the annoying property of reflecting bright objects (lamp bulbs, sunny windows etc) when used for framing pictures. The answer is to use diffuse-reflection (popularly known as non-reflective) glass. The surface has a very slightly roughened texture which does not impair transparency to any noticeable extent. The roughened surface, however, has very poor reflective powers. The thickness is 2 mm

TOUGHENED GLASS
The strongest of the standard safety glasses — toughened (or tempered) glass has been subjected to a special heat treatment which makes it about five times stronger than ordinary window glass. When hit hard enough it crazes rather than shatters, and the tiny pieces are rounded granules rather than jagged spears. Good for doors and table tops — obscure and clear grades are available. It cannot be cut or drilled — you will have to order the size you want

LAMINATED GLASS
The panes sold as laminated glass are not toughened — they are just 2 ordinary sheets of glass which sandwich a sheet of tough plastic between them. The result is glass which may crack but will not shatter, and there are grades which are burglar-proof and even bullet-proof. The standard thickness is 5.4 mm and there are many variants — solar control, patterned surfaces, tinting and so on can be introduced. You will have to order the size required as it is difficult to cut

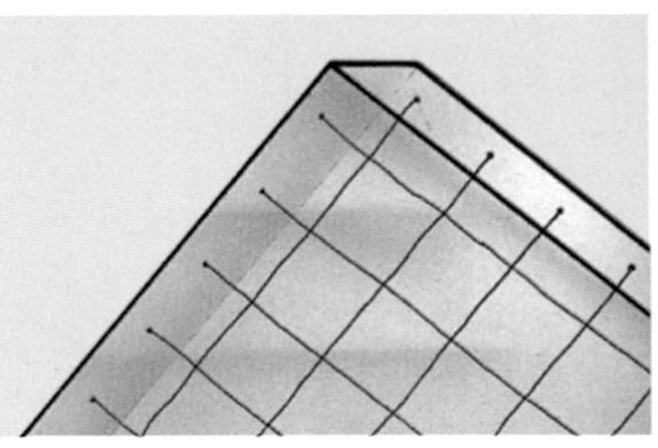

WIRED GLASS
The glass here is no stronger than the ordinary window grade — the safety factor is a welded wire mesh which is embedded within the pane. The square- or diamond-shaped pattern of wire holds the glass fragments together in case of breakage. Wired glass is widely used where a high degree of fire-resistance is required. Clear and translucent grades are available — the standard thickness is 6 mm. Use where safety is more important than appearance

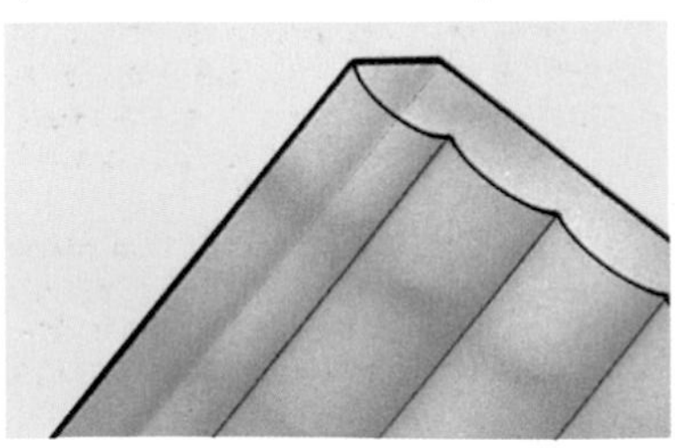

PATTERNED GLASS
One side has a textured pattern — the other side is plain. Patterned glass is chosen for either its decorative effect or ability to obscure the view. All too often it is chosen for the bathroom window only as a means of privacy, with no thought of the beauty it can provide. These days there are scores of patterns in clear or tinted glass, and you should look at a number of samples before making your choice. Both 4 mm and 6 mm grades are available — buy the toughened type for doors or shower screens

DECORATED GLASS
Included here are all the decorative effects other than patterned glass with a texture produced by a roller at the time of manufacture. Among the decorative glasses is stained glass, once decried as old fashioned but now staging a minor comeback. There are also sand-blasted glass with a variety of shaded effects, and engraved glass which is used to produce decorated screens. Most decorated glass is in the luxury class, but glass bearing a transparent transfer belongs here

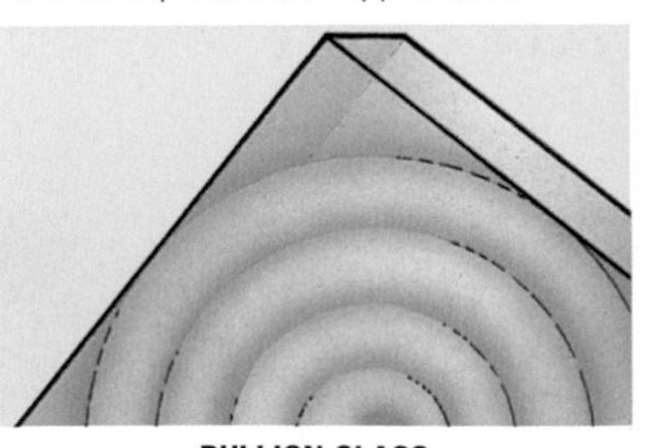

BULLION GLASS
A few panes of bullion glass are used in multi-pane windows to provide an old-world touch to neo-Georgian houses, and they do have a long history of decorating windows. Bullions were once made by a hand-spinning process — such authentic bullions are expensive. Modern bullions are made by rollers, like patterned glass, and both clear and amber-tinted types can be bought in a variety of sizes ranging from 15 cm x 15 cm to 70 cm x 45 cm. Don't overdo it — too many will mar the view

DOUBLE GLAZING

A room without a window is a dingy place indeed, but inserting panes of glass in the fabric of the wall does create its problems. Glass is a poor insulator — letting heat out and noise in. In winter cold air enters through faulty frames, and pockets of cool air form against the surface of the glass.

Double glazing has been heavily promoted in recent years as an answer to these difficulties. Double glazing simply means having two panes of glass instead of a single sheet of glass. It is the air between the panes and not the glass itself which acts as the insulator — this air should be dry, still and the space between the panes must be the correct width for the job which has to be done.

Installing double glazing is an expensive and disruptive business and you should think carefully before going ahead. As pointed out earlier, your motive should not be solely to cut down on fuel bills — it will take many, many years to pay for itself. You should only go ahead if at least some of the other advantages appeal to you — reduced draughts, reduced condensation, improved window appearance, increased security and so on.

- A single-glazed house loses about 20 per cent of its heat in winter through windows and the cracks around doors. Double glazing can reduce this by about a half, but only if it is efficiently constructed and installed, and if the panes are 5 - 25 mm apart. A smaller gap is less efficient in conserving heat — a wider gap is slightly less efficient.
- Double glazing can cut down noise from outside, but the glass should be thick and the gap between the panes has to be at least 10 cm wide.
- Double glazing makes entry and exit more difficult. Breaking and entering through two panes of glass is an effective burglar deterrent, but secondary windows can also prove to be a fatal barrier in case of fire. Make sure that the windows can be opened in an emergency and show each member of the family what to do if the need arises.
- You may qualify for a grant towards double glazing — ask your local authority. Make sure the installer is a member of the Glass and Glazing Federation.

SEALED UNIT

Two panes of glass are joined by an airtight seal. This unit is used **in place of** an existing pane

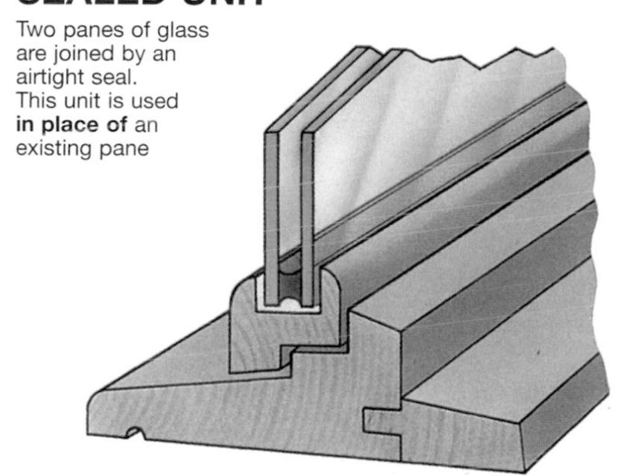

There are three advantages compared with secondary windows. Sealed units do not have a condensation problem between the panes, they are suitable for all types of window and they are unnoticeable. The gap between the panes is 8 - 15 mm, which means they will reduce heat loss but will do little to reduce noise.

If the rebate in the window is wide enough you should buy spaced units in which the two panes are the same size. In most cases you will have to use stepped units in which each outer pane is larger than the inner one and so fits outside the rebate.

Sealed units (sometimes called insulating glass) are available in many sizes and varieties. The glass may be as thin as 3 mm or as thick as 10 mm — it may be toughened, patterned or wired. Low E (low emissivity) glass improves insulation by reflecting heat back into the room and also cuts down the amount of ultra-violet light entering the room from outside.

SECONDARY WINDOW

A sheet of glass or plastic is placed inside (or sometimes outside) an existing window. This sheet is used **in addition to** an existing pane

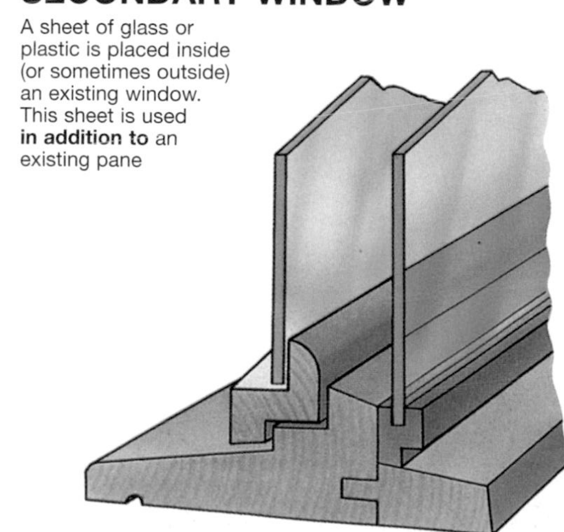

The simplest form of secondary window is a sheet of **plastic film** stretched over the window and fixed with self-adhesive tape. Condensation will be reduced or eliminated, but the insulating effect is often slight and the overall appearance is usually unsightly.

You can use acetate sheet in a simple frame, but the most satisfactory simple method is the **plastic channel** which contains a pane of 4 mm float glass and is attached to the sash or casement with clips. The window is opened and closed in the usual way.

With the **secondary sash** the second sheet of glass is fitted against the window frame and not against the sash or casement. This secondary sash is made of aluminium or plastic and may be fixed or hinged. The space between the original pane and the secondary one may be quite large, so this arrangement is suitable for noise insulation.

The basic secondary sash system described above is not difficult to fit but it does not make for easy opening. The sliding type with the glass moving in horizontal or vertical channels provides much easier access to the outside but it also increases the incidence of condensation between the panes.

CURTAINS

Not all windows have to be curtained. The experts tell us that windows by the stairs and areas of decorative glass are best left uncovered, and in some cases blinds may be a better choice. But for the vast majority of homeowners a window without a curtain is shamelessly undressed. Curtains are used to add both height and width to a window and also to add colour and perhaps a touch of luxury. Yet there is more to it than decoration — curtains keep heat in on winter nights and out during summer days, draughts are reduced and outside noise minimised. Undesirable views outside can be hidden and privacy inside can be preserved.

Buying new curtains means that several decisions have to be made. The curtain rail is probably already in position — if not, look at the pictures on this page. Tracks should have 12 gliders per metre — poles require 12 rings per metre. Length is an important consideration — full-length curtains are always elegant but are not always practical. They can overpower a tiny room, can cost the earth in an expensive fabric and there may be a radiator under the window. For most situations the choice is between sill- and apron-length — the experts frown on mid-length curtains which are half-way between sill and floor.

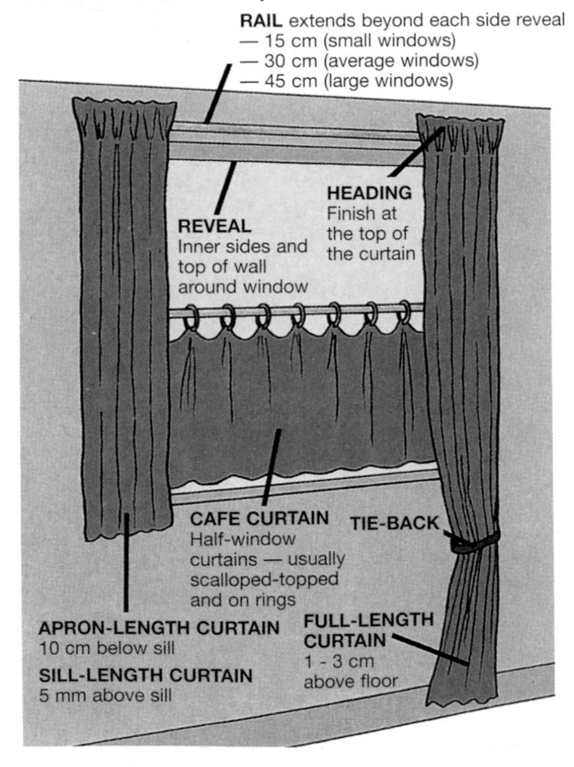

LINING

Lining may not be worthwhile for cheap curtains in some rooms, but it is needed for the main windows. Lined curtains hang better and the fabric is protected from the sun. Cotton sateen is the usual lining material. Heat insulation is improved and early morning light is kept out of bedrooms (use rubberised lining for top efficiency). Most linings are sewn to the curtain fabric but there are advantages in having loose linings which are attached to the heading tape and only tacked to the fabric — they can be washed separately.

RAILS & CORDING

Choose the curtain rail with care — if a pelmet or valance is not to be fitted then the face of the rail should be either decorative or not noticeable when the curtains are open or drawn. The usual choice of rail is a track rather than a pole, and the popular material is plastic. For heavy curtains, however, you should buy a metal track. Ceiling- and wall-brackets are available and there are brands of plastic track which can be bent around corners. For heavy curtains buy overlapping tracks which allow one curtain to pass about 15 cm in front of the other when drawn. A pull-cord to close the curtains will prevent wear and tear through handling — choose a ready-corded rail or fit a cording set to an existing track.

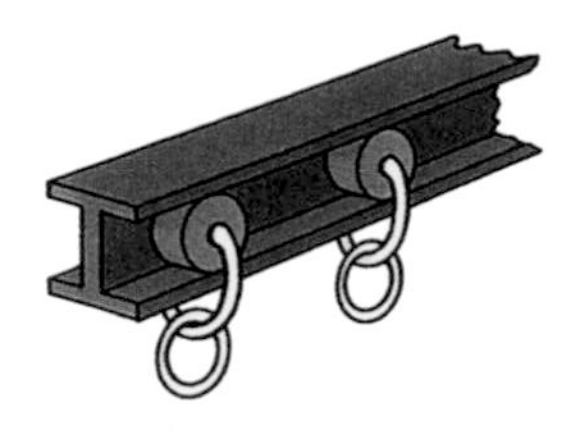

GIRDER TRACK
The traditional type of track, made of metal or plastic. The gliders run along the bottom of the girder — the track is usually exposed when the curtains are closed and so a pelmet is generally used

BOTTOM CHANNEL TRACK
The gliders run along the channel at the bottom of the track. Decorative-faced types can be used without a pelmet. Light-weight ceiling-mounted versions are available for fitting within the window recess

CONCEALED GLIDER TRACK
The gliders run along a channel at the back of the track. Very popular — Swish Deluxe, Luxa-flex etc. Decorative-faced types can be used without a pelmet

EXPOSED GLIDER TRACK
The gliders which run along the face of the track have built-in hooks at the front. At the base of each of these glider-hooks is a small ring which can be used to carry a separate lining

POLE
True poles are made of wood or metal with decorative finials at the ends. Large gliding rings carry small rings at their base which hold the curtain hooks. Imitation poles have gliders attached to the rings and these run along a track at the back

COVERED WIRE & ROD
Expandable wire is the traditional rail for net curtains. It is supported by means of hooks fitted into eyes which are screwed into either the wall or the window frame. Telescopic rods are very useful for putting up net curtains — the rod fits inside the window reveal

BUYING CURTAINS

Before buying or ordering curtains you must measure the exact length of the rail and also the drop from the hook rings on the pole or track to the length desired. You should also know the type of heading you want.

Buying ready-made curtains makes the job easy. There is a large range in a wide variety of widths, but the choice of lengths is strictly limited. There are advantages — you can see what you are getting and you know that the material is suitable as curtaining. But ready-made curtains are not always a practical choice. Custom-made curtains are often the answer. Get a detailed quote before placing your order. You can sew your own but making complex curtains is not a job for a beginner.

The golden rule when buying curtain material is to make sure that they will look full even when drawn. It is better to buy ample cheap material which will show off its folds than expensive curtaining which has to be pulled tight to close. Choose material carefully, and think of practical considerations as well as purely decorative ones. Pale curtains or ones which blend in with the wall will show off the view — bright fabrics and large patterns will show off the curtains. Thick curtains will effectively reduce outside noise — bedrooms will need properly lined curtains.

Take home a sample before ordering — the material may look quite different in your room. The choice of materials is enormous. Sheer and semi-sheer fabrics such as net, lace, openweave etc provide privacy without darkening the room. Cottons and linens are excellent but silk tends to disintegrate in sunlight. Velvets, brocades, moires, satins ... the choice of luxury fabrics is a wide one.

PELMETS & VALANCES

The purpose of a pelmet or valance is to hide the rail as well as the heading of the curtains. There are no strict rules for the correct depth — ⅛th of the length of floor-length curtains is the usual recommendation.

Pelmet A 10 cm wide pelmet board is fitted a few centimetres above and on either side of the curtains. This board is either faced with wood for staining, painting or polishing or covered with stiffened fabric. The lower edge may be straight, scalloped or curved

Pelmet board

Valance A short unstiffened curtain is gathered or pleated using standard heading tape. The material can match or contrast with the curtains and the lower edge may be straight or ruched. The valance is attached to a pelmet board or to a second rail in front of the curtain one

HEADING

Heading tape is usually but not always used — cased and scalloped curtains do not employ tape. But if you want a gathered or decorative heading then you will need to buy the appropriate tape for the style chosen. Drawstrings are present to produce the gathering or pleating and there are slits to carry the curtain hooks. Use deep heading tape (7.5 cm wide) for heavy fabrics and standard tape (2.5 cm wide) for light ones

HEADING TYPE	WIDTH OF FABRIC REQUIRED	NOTES
GATHERED	1½ - 2 times the length of the rail	Used on unlined curtains for small windows and/or in rooms not in regular use — also suitable where a pelmet or valance hides the curtain track. Buy standard heading tape — choose the lightweight grade for sheers such as net curtains.
PENCIL PLEAT	2¼ - 2½ times the length of the rail	Used on lightweight and medium weight fabrics — suitable for either track or pole. Straight and narrow pleats are produced along the whole length of the material — especially effective on full-length curtains. Decorative, but less so than pinched pleats.
PINCHED PLEAT	2 times the length of the rail	Used on all types of fabrics, ranging from fleecy nets to heavy velvets. Pinches of 2- or 3-fold French pleats are separated by smooth cloth. Suitable for either track or pole — buy deep heading tape for maximum effect; narrow tape for sheer fabrics.
CASED	1¼ - 1½ times the length of the rail	Unloved, often unmentioned, but still the basic type on lightweight and net curtains in millions of homes. A 5 cm hem is sewn at the top — this wide hem is divided by a row of stitching along the centre. The rod or wire is threaded through this open hem.
SCALLOPED	1¼ - 1½ times the length of the rail	Used on cafe curtains where a pole is used without a pelmet or valance so that the heading can be clearly seen. Economical — too much fullness would spoil the effect. Use firm material — do not line and attach curtain rings as shown on page 68.

BLINDS

Blinds have been used traditionally in bathrooms and kitchens where curtains may be inconvenient. They have also been used on tiny or sloping windows where curtains could be impractical, but blinds are not used where a highly decorative effect is required ...

You can forget these prejudices — blinds can be as luxurious as any curtain. There are all sorts of styles available, ranging from no-nonsense roller and Venetian blinds to billowing Austrian blinds with exaggerated flounces. Kits can be bought which require no special skill for construction — you can also buy made-to-measure blinds or fabric and the necessary accessories from your department store. The darling of the interior decorator is the curtain and blind combination. Dress (or non-closing) curtains are used to frame the window, and so there is a saving in fabric cost compared with standard curtains. The role of the blind is to provide privacy, light control and extra interest to the room.

Blinds are fitted either inside the window recess (especially when part of a curtain and blind combination) or outside on the ceiling or wall. Most are easy to install, but use a spirit level to make sure that the fall is perfectly vertical.

Choose the fabric for roller or Roman blinds with care. Avoid flimsy material which will stretch easily and also heavy fabric which will not roll or fold properly. Plastics and synthetic fibres are frequently used, but perhaps the best choice is stiffened cotton or cotton blends. You can buy specially prepared blind fabric, or you can treat ordinary closely-woven cloth with a liquid or aerosol stiffener. Fabric is not the only material for blinds — wood, metal, plastic and paper are all widely used. Illustrated here are the main varieties of blinds, but there are others. An example is the slatted blind — strips of wood or cane woven together with cotton. The colour range is not large, but then neither is the price.

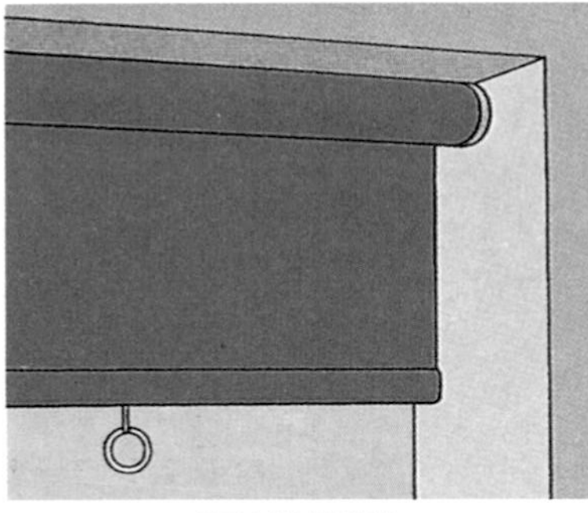

ROLLER BLIND
A roller blind kit consists of a spring-loaded roller (which can easily be cut to fit the exact space) plus a bar for the bottom of the blind. There are also brackets and a pull cord. The fabric can be chosen to match the wallpaper, curtains, carpet or any other feature, and the bottom edge can be plain, fringed, braided or shaped. Where money is no object, you can have the fabric hand-painted to match your room decoration

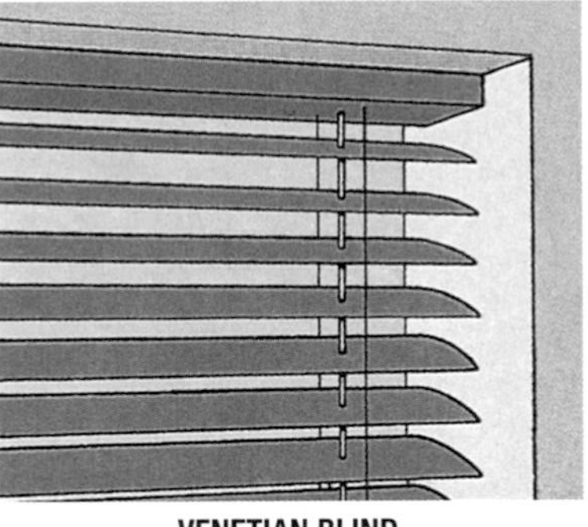

VENETIAN BLIND
Slats of plastic or metal are controlled on a 2-pulley system, one to tilt the slats and the other to move the blind up and down. Once associated with offices and public buildings, Venetian blinds are now widely used in the home. The colour range is large, and this style fits in well with a curtain and blind combination. There are no kits available — you must buy a standard model or have the blind made to measure

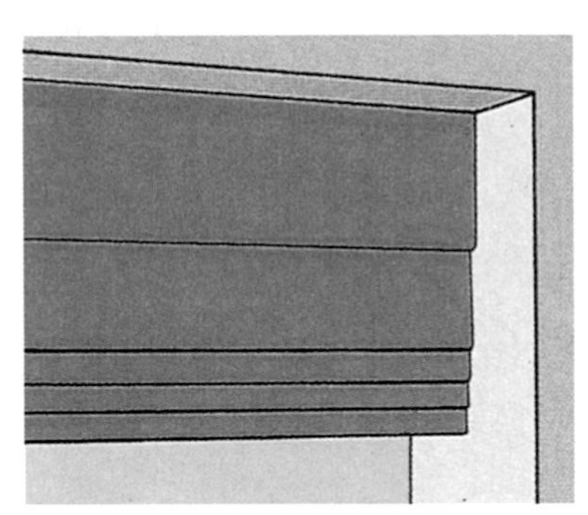

ROMAN BLIND
When fully extended a Roman blind looks somewhat like a roller blind. Pull the cord and the difference is seen immediately — the fabric rises up in a series of flat folds. The pleats are formed by horizontal wooden slats which are sewn in at intervals. When fully open the pleated fabric forms a pelmet. The fabric is always lined, which means that it keeps out light and cuts down on draughts better than a roller blind

AUSTRIAN BLIND
As the cording raises the lightweight fabric a series of ballooning swags appears at the base. With a festoon blind these swags are apparent even when the blind is fully closed. These blinds are at home in an ornate living room or bedroom where the billowy effect of the half-closed blind adds a welcome touch of luxury. Buy them ready-made or you can make your own by using a special track and Austrian blind heading-tape

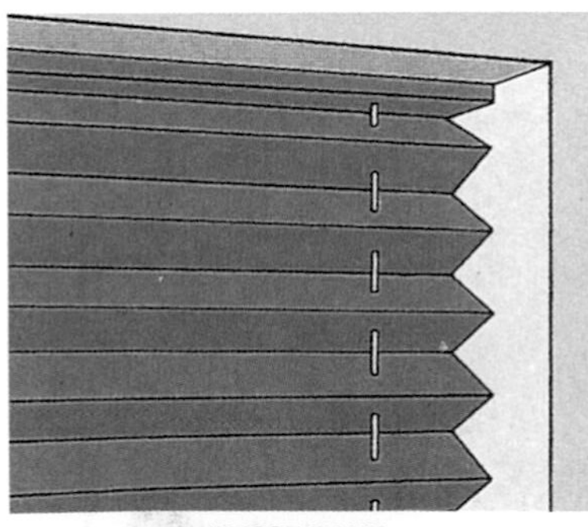

PLISSE BLIND
This type is at the other extreme from the Austrian blind. Thoroughly practical, limited in both style and colour, its purpose is to provide privacy whilst allowing some light to enter. The aluminium-backed version provides heat insulation. The plisse blind looks a little like a Venetian one, but is in fact a sheet of folded paper or stiff fabric which is raised by side cords which pass through punched holes

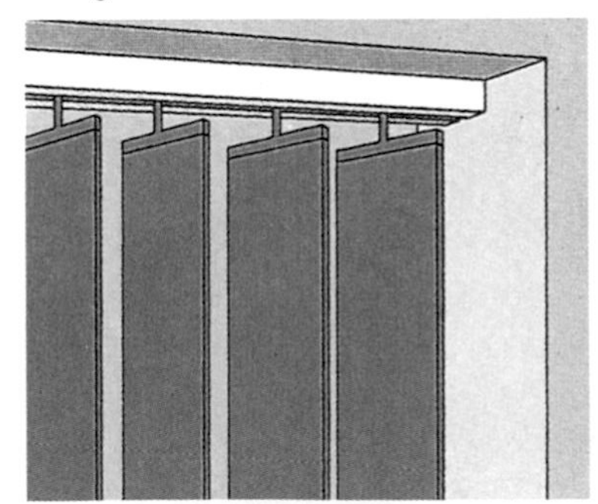

VERTICAL BLIND
Wide strips of stiffened fabric hang from the headrail — as with a Venetian blind the 'vanes' can be swivelled by one cord and the whole blind moved aside by means of another. The advantages over Venetian blinds include less dust on the strips and less interruption of the view, but they are expensive and the range is quite limited. The vertical louvre blind is highly recommended where a large picture window is to be clothed

DOORS

A stranger's first impression of your house is usually gained on the doorstep — a poor quality front door in need of decoration says a great deal about the occupants. This does not mean that you should buy the grandest front door you can afford — a highly ornamental door bedecked in brass would be out of place as the entrance to a cottage-style house. The golden rule is to make sure that the front door is regularly maintained and is in keeping with the style, surroundings and size of the house. Inside doors also have an important part to play in interior decoration, and so do the doors of wardrobes, cupboards etc. But doors also have a number of practical jobs to do and none more so than the front door. This must keep out weather, noise, intruders, insects, domestic animals, dust and draughts. Internal doors have a simpler job to do — they cut down the passage of noise and they provide a barrier for rooms where privacy is essential. Before fitting a replacement glazed door, check with the installer that the work will comply with the Building Regulations.

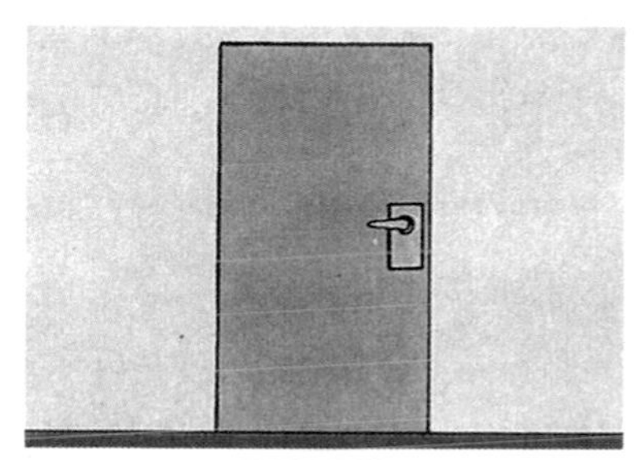

FLUSH DOOR

The most popular type of room door — unfinished or veneered facings cover a lightweight wooden frame. A recent innovation is the embossed flush door which looks like a panel one. The inner core may be empty or filled with cardboard, wood strips or plasterboard depending on the weight and purpose of the door. The edges of the door are covered (lipped) with thin strips of wood and the position to attach hinges and the lock is usually marked on the appropriate lip

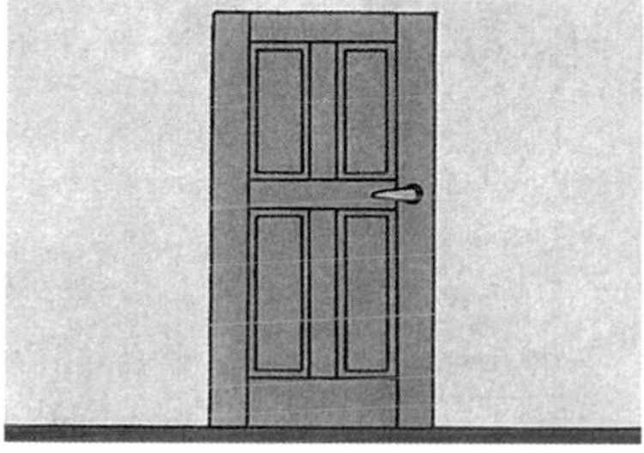

PANEL DOOR

The basic structure consists of two vertical wooden stiles with three or more horizontal rails. The open spaces are filled with wood, plywood or glass. Panelled doors are nearly always made of softwood when designed for indoor use, but front doors are usually constructed from hardwood so that they can be sealed and varnished rather than painted. If you buy a front door which has a softwood base, make sure that it has been treated with a preservative to prevent rotting

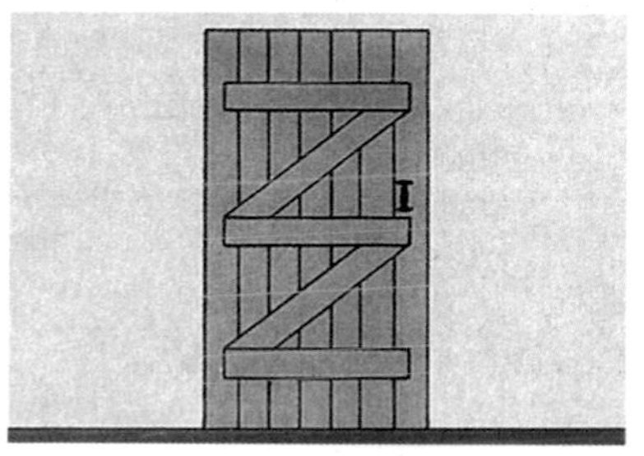

BOARDED DOOR

A sturdy door which belongs on a country cottage, shed or garage rather than an urban home. Strong but plain, the simplest version (ledged and braced) is made up of tongued and grooved boards held together by horizontal ledges and diagonal braces. The stable door version has an upper and lower section. The best type of boarded door is the framed, ledged and braced door. A stout frame constructed with mortise and tenon joints surrounds the boards. A mortise lock can be fitted

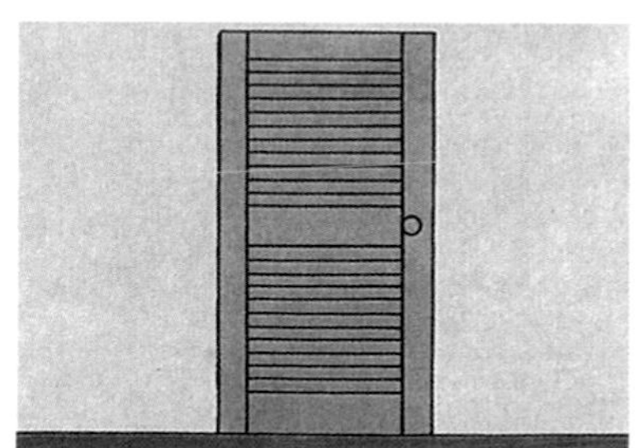

LOUVRED DOOR

A timber frame holds numerous wooden slats which are set at an angle. The number and the angle of the slats ensure that air passes freely through the door but the view is blocked. A wide range of sizes for cupboard and room doors is available — softwood is usually used and louvre doors are often sealed and varnished to preserve the natural wood appearance. Paired louvred doors are occasionally used to produce Western-style swing doors. Built-in wardrobe doors are often louvred

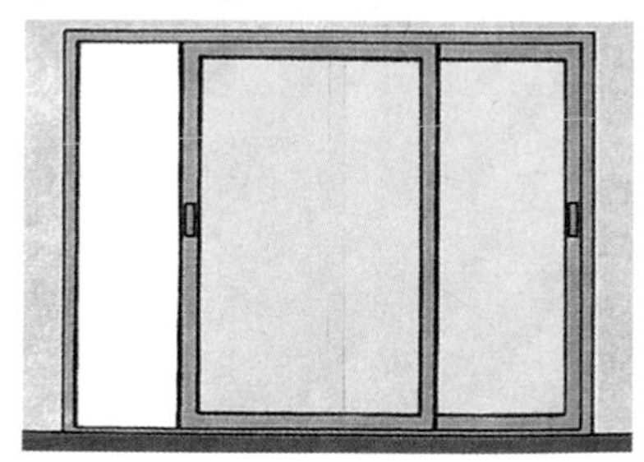

PATIO DOOR

Aluminium alloy is the usual frame material, although plastic and wooden versions are available. The fully glazed floor-to-ceiling panel or panels slide horizontally, bringing the living room and garden together in summer. For many people it is the favourite window, but it is also a favourite for burglars and accidents. Use safety glass for glazing (see page 65) and have some form of decoration on the glass to indicate that the window is not open. Fit high-security locks

FRENCH WINDOW

Glazed casement doors, fitted singly or in pairs, have long been the traditional way of stepping from the living room into the garden, but their role is now being steadily taken over by patio doors. Wooden French doors keep their place in period houses, although they tend to be draughtier than patio ones and stays must be fitted to keep them open. In addition they lack effective control over ventilation. Use safety glass for at least the lower panes and fit a mortise lock to ensure security

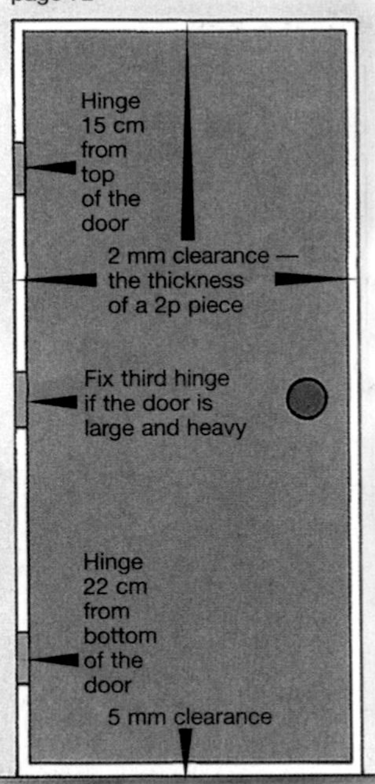

EXTERNAL DOOR

Make sure that the door you buy is constructed for exterior use. Aluminium and plastic (uPVC) doors are guaranteed to be weatherproof, but the usual choice is a wooden door. The popular one is a panelled door made from hardwood, or a softwood base covered with a hardwood veneer. The glue used will be exterior grade and the panels will be made of plywood (not hardboard) — the stiles should be at least 10 cm wide. Alternatively you can buy a flush door — make sure that it is for exterior and not interior use. This means that it will be more strongly built with facings of water-resistant plywood and a central block to hold the letter plate. Use brass or stainless steel hinges. At the bottom of the frame a door sill (or threshold) must be present to keep water away from the frame/wall join, and the door will have a weatherboard to keep rain out of the narrow gap between door and frame.

INTERNAL DOOR

The choice is much greater when you require a room door rather than an external one. Both softwood and hardwood panel doors are available for staining, although cheaper softwood types are generally painted. Flush doors for internal use range from cheap ones with hardboard facings and a hollow core to luxury ones with veneered facings and a wood-filled core. Before fitting a new door you should check the regulations with the local council if you live in a flat — it may be necessary to fit a fire-resisting door with a self-closing mechanism. Most internal doors are either panel or flush ones, but there are other types. Louvred doors are more popular for cupboards rather than as room doors, although they are used as pairs in folding form as room dividers. Another form of room divider is the concertina door — a folding door made up of numerous narrow sections which take up very little room when open. Sliding doors are an alternative where space is restricted.

LOCKS

A **catch** is a closure which can be simply released by pulling the knob or handle forward. A **latch** is more secure — a handle, knob or key has to be turned to open it, but the latch is not locked inside the striking plate — an intruder can force it open by inserting a credit card between the frame and the door. A **deadbolt** is the most secure of all — it is opened and closed by a key and cannot be forced when closed.

RIM LOCK A lock which is mounted on the inside face of the door.

NIGHTLATCH
Traditional front door lock — opened and closed from the inside by a knob and from the outside by a key which operates a cylinder-type lock. The latch is not deadlocked and so the security rating is not high

DEADLOCKING NIGHTLATCH
Basically similar to the ordinary nightlatch, but turning the key from either the inside or outside turns the latch into a deadbolt. The lock should be made to British Standard 3621

MORTISE LOCK A lock which is set within a mortise or slot cut into the door.

MORTISE DEADLOCK
The second security lock which is often fitted to the front door near to the nightlatch. It is a lever-type lock with a traditional-type key — make sure that there are at least 5 levers. A double-throw lock moves the bolt further forward with a second turn of the key

SASH LOCK
A combined lock for back doors. The latch is operated by a handle or knob and the deadbolt is closed by means of the key at night or when the house is unoccupied

CYLINDRICAL LOCK A lock which is installed through 2 holes bored into the door, one for the handle/lock and the other for the latch/bolt.

Easier to install than a mortise lock. The latch is reversible with an automatic deadlocking mechanism. The key operates a cylinder-type lock fitted inside the handle. The simpler latch-only version for interior use is known as a tubular lock

HINGES

Hinges are simple things, but you can easily buy the wrong sort if you don't take care. Tell the supplier the size, type and thickness of the door and the way it has to open. If there is no one to help, check the wording on the package carefully to make sure the set of hinges will be satisfactory. Several materials are used to make hinges — brass, stainless steel, cast steel, nylon etc. Screw the hinges first on to the door and then on to the frame.

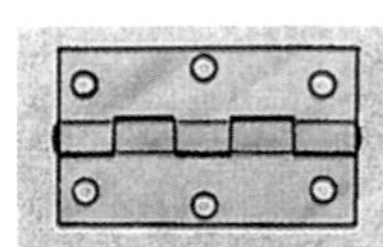

BUTT HINGE
The standard type for all sorts of doors except fire-resisting ones. The two leaves of an ordinary butt hinge cannot be separated, but you can buy loose-pin (or lift-off) hinges

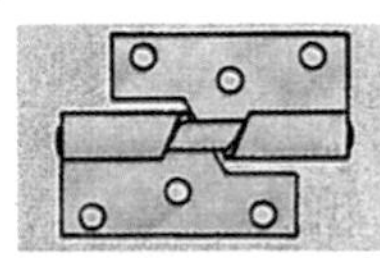

RISING BUTT HINGE
The door lifts when it is opened — not enough to notice but sufficient to carry it over a thick carpet. The top of the frame may have to be slightly chamfered. This type of hinge is often self-closing

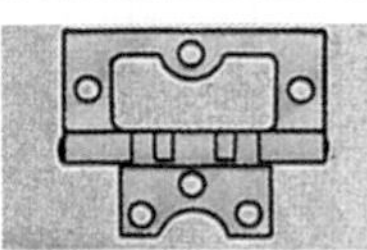

FLUSH HINGE
This hinge does not have to be recessed like a butt hinge. It is used for lightweight flush doors — simply screw on to the surface of the door and then on to the side of the door frame

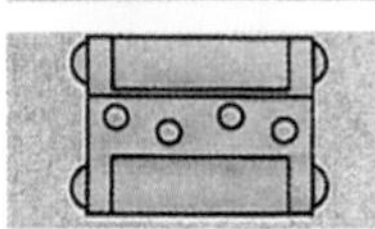

HELICAL SPRING HINGE
The spring loading of this hinge makes the door return to the closed position after it has been opened. Two-way spring hinges are often used on restaurant kitchen doors

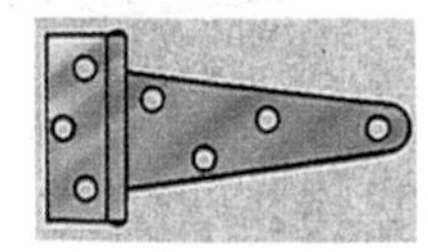

T HINGE
The standard type for boarded doors — practical but not decorative. They are made of galvanised or painted steel — for heavy doors a stronger version (hook and band hinge) is required

CONCEALED HINGE
This type of spring-loaded hinge is fitted inside a cabinet so that the set-in door can open and move in line with the side of the unit

HOW TO DEAL WITH DOOR PROBLEMS

SQUEAKING DOOR
The usual cause is hinge stiffness. Apply just a drop of light oil at the top of each metal hinge — wipe off excess oil immediately. Rising butt hinges should be oiled regularly but do not oil plastic hinges.

RATTLING DOOR
A rattling door indicates an improper fit. Fitting a self-adhesive foam strip may cure the problem, but not if the lock and the striking plate on the frame are out of position. It may be necessary to move the plate slightly.

HINGE-BOUND DOOR
A door is hinge-bound when either the door and frame or the hinge screws come together before the door is closed. Projecting screws can be the problem — drive them home firmly or use shorter screws

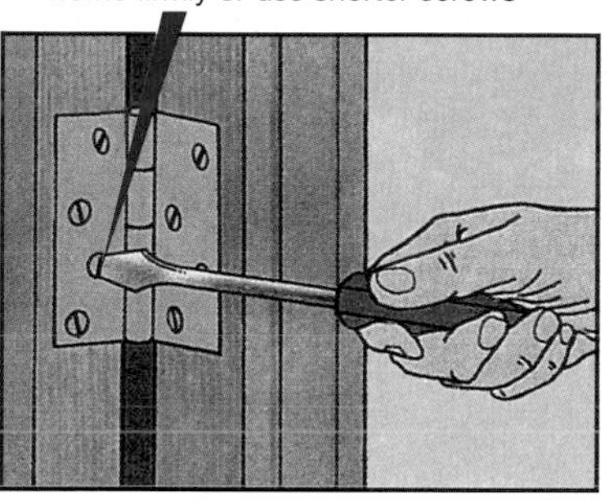

The cause may be that the hinge has been set too far into either the door or the frame. Unscrew hinge leaf and pack recess with a strip of cardboard. Rescrew. Pack out other side of hinge if still not cured

SIDE-STICKING DOOR
Doors can stick at the sides or top for a number of reasons. The point of sticking is sometimes obvious — if not, carry out carbon paper test. Hold paper at various points — black smudge reveals sticking area

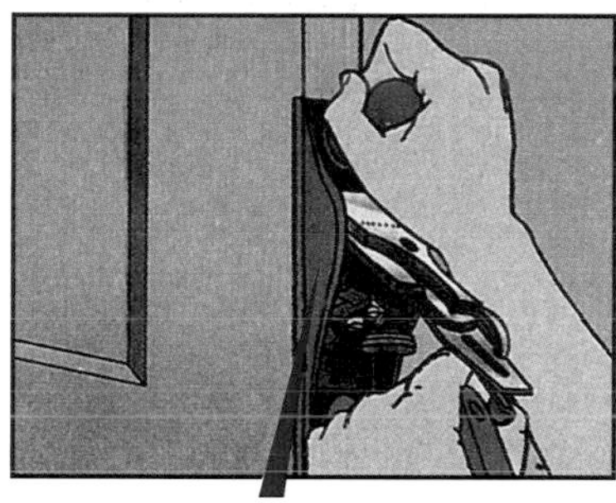

The cause may be too much paint — rub or plane off the excess.
In bathroom and outside doors the wood may have swollen. Plane sticking area on the door on a dry day.
Take care not to remove too much wood

BOTTOM-STICKING DOOR
If the problem is only slight, you might be able to remove excess wood by opening the door several times over coarse abrasive paper.
If the problem is more severe, remove door and plane bottom

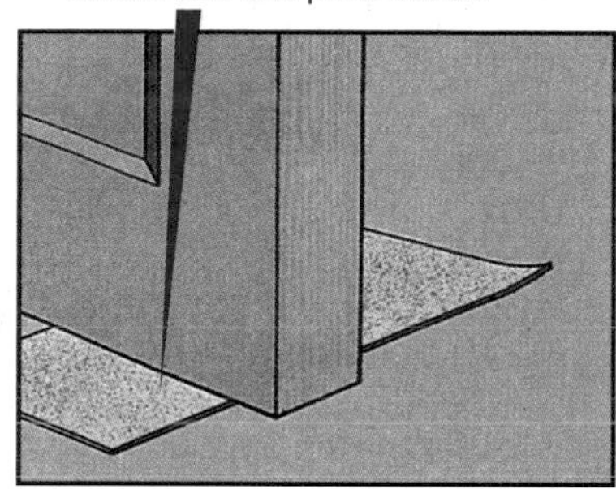

A common cause of bottom sticking is the introduction of a thick carpet in place of a thin one. Planing the bottom of the door may not be possible with a flush door. Cure the problem by using rising butt hinges

WARPED DOOR
Doors warp and twist for a number of reasons — radiator too close, unseasoned wood, marked heat difference on either side of the door etc. If the warp is at the top or bottom and the door can be kept closed, force back, close and insert small wedge between door and frame. Leave for 7 days

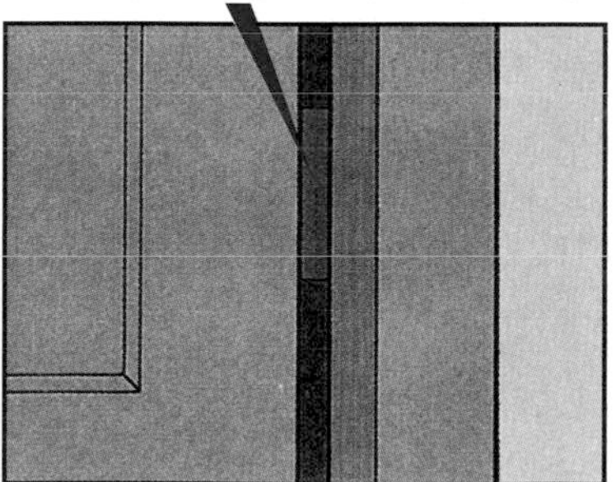

If centre of the door is bowed, remove door and straddle between chairs, with curve facing upwards. Place bricks at centre to press down wood — leave for 7 days. If the warp is at hinge side of door, fit additional hinge midway between existing hinges

DROPPED DOOR
There are several symptoms of a dropped or sagging door — squeaking, sticking and failure to close properly. Loose hinges are the usual cause — tighten screws. If this fails, use longer screws or insert dowels in holes before rescrewing

The trouble may be more serious.
In old panel doors the joints may have opened. The answer is to hire a sash clamp to pull the door back into shape. Strengthen by drilling holes at each joint and inserting pieces of dowel

LOOSE FRAME
The proper way to repair a loose frame is to remove the door and architrave, replace the packing between the frame and wall and then drill deep holes through the wood and into the masonry. The holes are plugged and then screws are fitted

If only one side of the frame is loose and the frame is truly vertical, you can try a much simpler remedy. Drill holes through the offending side and at least 5 cm into the masonry.
Plug and screw firmly

STIFF LOCK
Do not squeeze oil into the lock. With a cylinder-type lock such as a nightlatch, spread a little light oil over the latch and dust the key with powdered graphite. Turn the key several times. With a lever-type lock such as a mortise deadlock again add a little oil to the extended bolt but apply a little light oil and not graphite to the head of the key. Open and close the lock several times.

LOST KEY
You should be able to force back the latch of a nightlatch from the outside (see page 72) — you will certainly be able to open it from the inside. Outside or inside, you have a difficult problem with a bolted mortise lock if the key is lost. The only answer is to call in a locksmith. It is a wise precaution to have duplicates of all external door keys. Keep the spare in a safe place in case of an emergency — but not under the carpet or anywhere close to the door.

CHAPTER 5

OUTSIDE THE HOUSE

Most of the money spent on home decorating goes towards improving the appearance of the rooms inside, and yet it is the outside which the world at large sees. Maintenance of the outer fabric is necessary to give a good impression, but there is much more to it than that. Neglect a spare bedroom and nothing frightening happens — neglect the outside and small problems can quickly become major headaches. A small area of rot on a door frame can be easily dealt with if caught in time — ignore this and similar problems at your peril.

Neglect is usually due to the fact that working on the outside is often more difficult than working indoors, but do get into the routine of inspecting the outside each spring and after a gale. To do this properly you will need a ladder, and that calls for safety measures. The base should be at least a quarter of the height away from the house, and make sure that the foot of the ladder has a firm and level base. The ladder must be secure — place a heavy sack against the ladder or have someone hold the sides.

WHAT THE WORDS MEAN

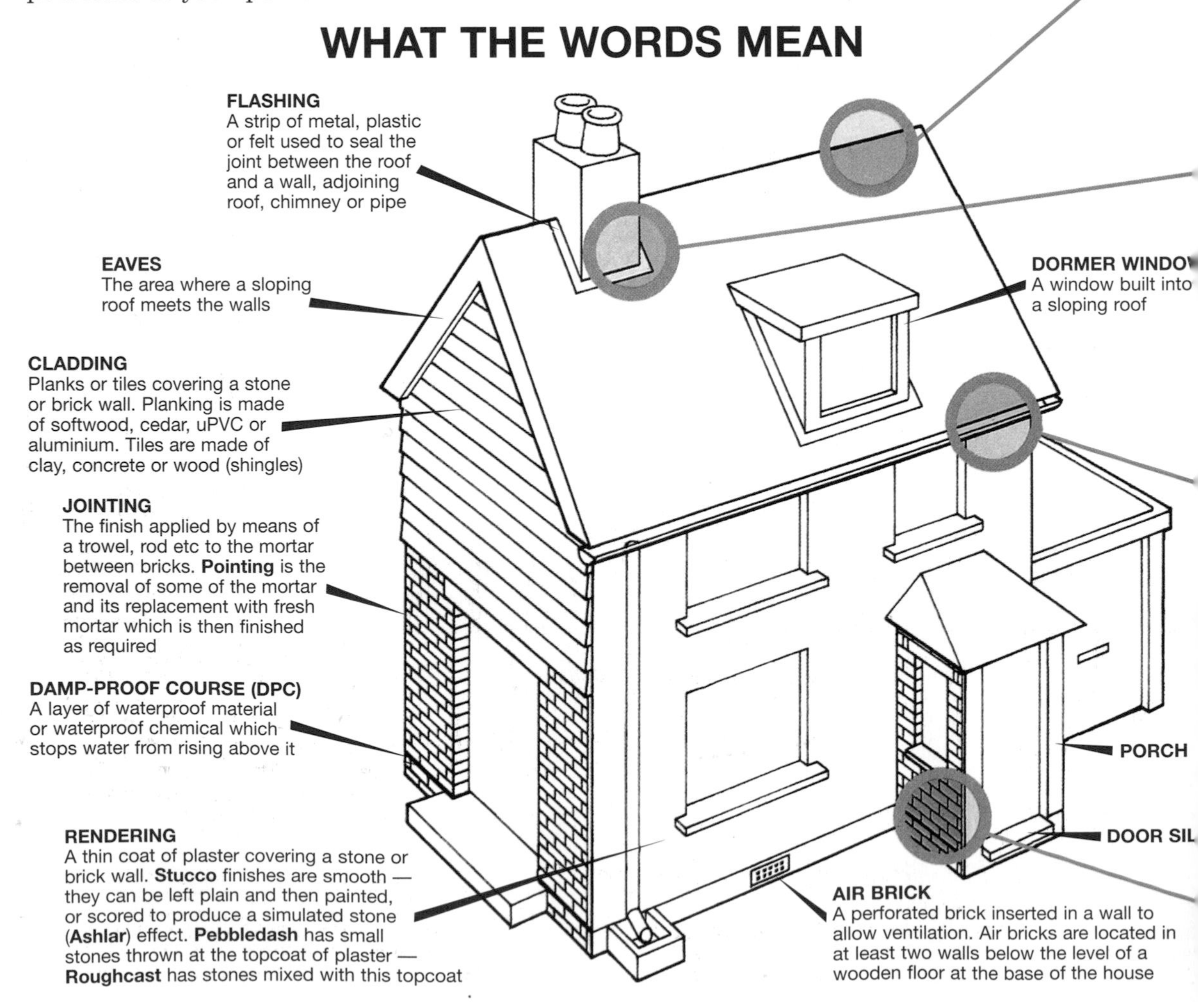

ROOF

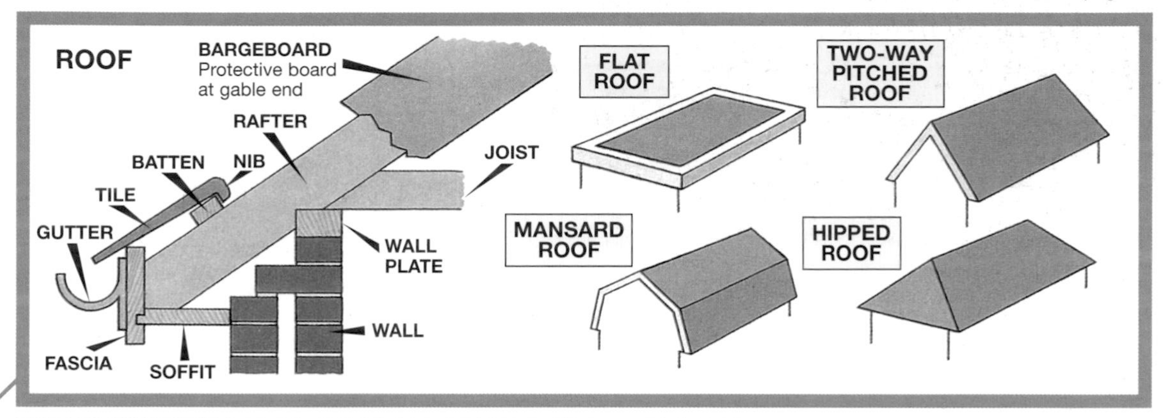

CHIMNEY

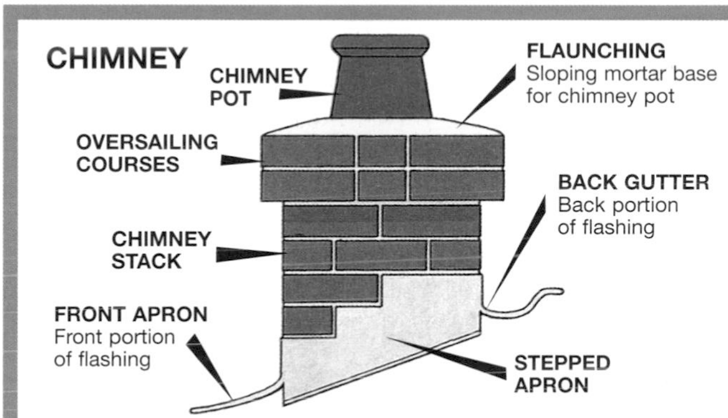

A **FLUE** is the passage through which smoke and gases escape into the atmosphere. A **CHIMNEY** is the structure which forms the flue

A **FLUE LINING** protects the body of the chimney from the hot and corrosive gases in the flue. Linings are usually made of fireclay or high alumina concrete

A **COWL** is a hooded structure which is installed at the top of a chimney to aid ventilation and prevent the entry of rain

GUTTERING

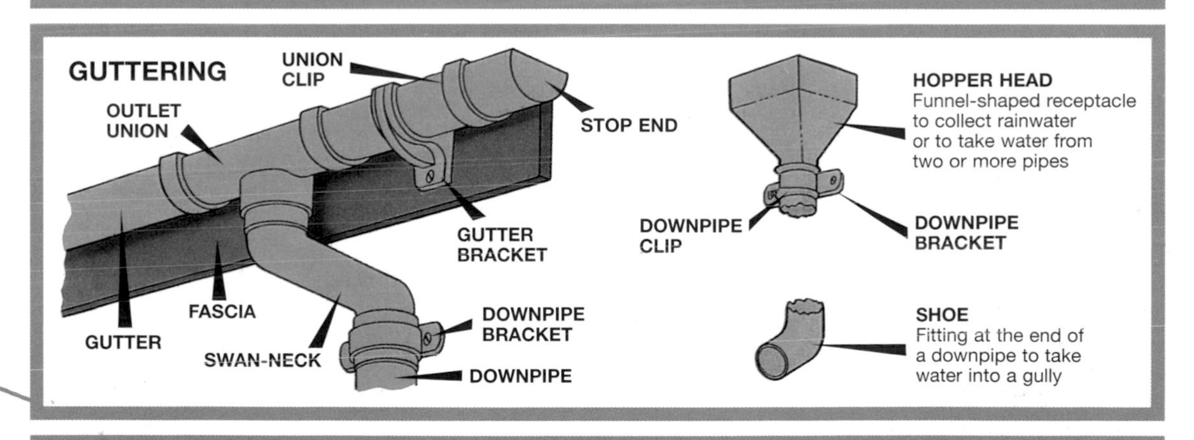

WALLS

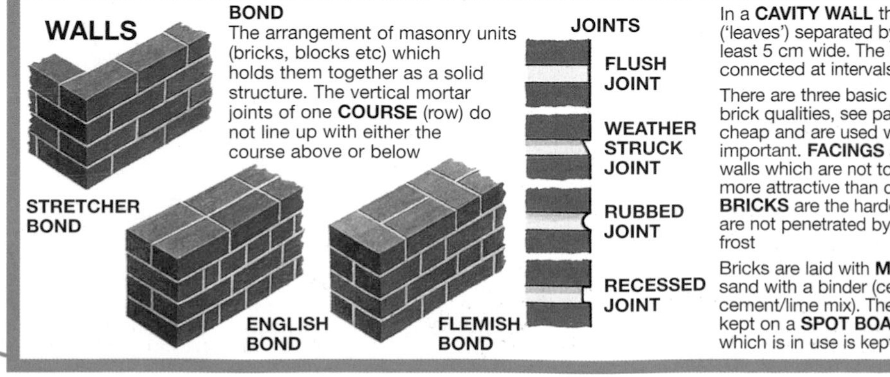

In a **CAVITY WALL** there are two parallel walls ('leaves') separated by an air gap which is at least 5 cm wide. The outer and inner walls are connected at intervals by metal **WALL TIES**

There are three basic brick types — for details of brick qualities, see page 78. **COMMONS** are cheap and are used where appearance is not important. **FACINGS** are the standard type for walls which are not to be covered — they are more attractive than commons. **ENGINEERING BRICKS** are the hardest and strongest — they are not penetrated by water nor damaged by frost

Bricks are laid with **MORTAR** — a mixture of sand with a binder (cement, lime or a cement/lime mix). The reserve of mortar is kept on a **SPOT BOARD** — the small quantity which is in use is kept on a hand-held **HAWK**

ROOFS

For most people, the roof is a no-go area. Routine inspections are not carried out, and the first sign of trouble is water dripping through a bedroom ceiling. This is worrying enough, but the hidden danger of a leaking roof is even worse — wet rot can take hold and ruin the roof timbers.

Despite the mystery, a pitched (sloping) roof is built on a simple principle. There is a series of parallel wooden triangles with rafters as the sides and joists at the base of each one. In all cases the triangles are joined by rows of horizontal battens which hold the roof covering. In traditional pitched roofs there is a stout ridge board joining all the triangles along the apex — in the modern trussed rafter roof there is no ridge.

Roofs do deteriorate with age and you should look at yours at least once a year. Look out from your neighbour's bedroom windows if you don't want to go up a ladder. Are the flaunching and chimney pots sound? Are there any cracks in the flashing? Can any broken slates or tiles be seen? Is the wood around the roof in need of painting? If there is a problem, tackle it at once. For major jobs call in a specialist roofing company — make sure that it is a member of the National Federation of Roofing Contractors or a similar association.

ROOF COVERING

The purpose of the roof covering is to prevent the entry of water and rapidly moving air despite the onslaught of heavy rain, driving snow and gales. It must last for many years despite bitter frosts and baking sun — roof replacement every 20 years is soon enough!

Many materials are used — thatch, wooden shingles, plastic corrugated sheeting, wired glass, copper sheeting etc, but by far the most popular coverings are slates and tiles for pitched roofs and bitumen felt for flat ones.

You will still find slate on older houses — it was the most popular roofing material in Victorian times. Take care when buying second-hand slates — avoid chipped edges, flaking surfaces and enlarged nail holes. Clay tiles took over the crown from slate in the last century, but since the war concrete has become the most important tiling material — it is less liable than clay to be damaged by frost.

Tiles are available in many colours and surface textures these days, and also many shapes — waved pantiles, semicircular Roman tiles, exotic Spanish tiles, flat-faced plain tiles and so on. In older houses the visible roof covering is the only line of defence against the elements — in new houses there is a layer of felt or even boarding under the battens holding the slates or tiles.

PLAIN TILE
Each tile bears two holes near the top, but there are usually two nibs (projections) at the back. The nibs are hooked over the battens and every fourth row is nailed down. There is a wide overlap (double lapping) and the tiles in each row are staggered

SLATE
Once very popular — now rarely used on new houses because of the price. Second-hand slates are often used for repairs. Slates come in many colour variations and sizes — check before buying. Each slate is nailed either along the upper edge or along the centre

INTERLOCKING TILE
Most interlocking tiles are fixed like plain tiles, the nibs hooking over battens and every third row being nailed down. Some types must be secured individually. Many 3-D shapes are available, and because of the tight fit between neighbouring tiles they are laid with little overlap

BITUMEN FELT
The standard material for flat roofs — the first layer is nailed to the wooden decking of the roof and the second layer is bonded to it with hot bitumen. A third layer of bitumen felt is bonded in similar fashion, and the surface is covered with stone chippings or reflective paint to reflect the sun's heat

HOW TO DEAL WITH ROOF PROBLEMS

- **WORKING ON THE ROOF**

A small roof job, such as replacing a broken tile, can be carried out by the homeowner provided the equipment and technique are satisfactory. Choose a still and dry day. Make sure the ladder against the roof is properly secured and at the correct angle — see page 74. Never lean it on the gutter — use a ladder stay and make sure that the ladder projects at least 60 cm above the gutter.

Few tools will be required for working on a sloping roof — make sure they are secured in some way and tie the top of the ladder to the wall or the fascia board by means of a rope through an eye-bolt. Put on rubber-soled shoes and you are ready to start work — provided the problem can be reached from the ladder. If you have to work on the roof itself, you will need a special roof ladder which can be hired. The hook at the top of this ladder is placed over the ridge. Never walk on the roof.

Flat roofs have their own rules. They are not designed to carry your weight which means that the surface should be protected. It is especially important not to walk across a chipping-covered roof in hot weather — the chippings will be pressed into the surface and damage will result.

For extensive roof repairs a scaffolding tower is necessary and many of the ladder rules apply — secure footing, fix to the wall with a rope through an eye-bolt, never stretch too far without moving the structure etc.

- **HIRING SOMEONE ELSE TO WORK ON THE ROOF**

Apart from the need to find the money, it would seem to be an easy job to employ a roofing contractor to do the work for you. But there are pitfalls for the unwary. Get two or three quotes if the work is more than replacing a few tiles. Get the quotes in writing — make sure that they contain the details you want. If the roof leaks after repair you will only have yourself to blame if you did not insist that the quotation bears the words — 'the roof to be watertight after completion of the repairs'. The contractor has no obligation to remove the rubbish if the quote did not mention the requirement.

Choosing the right roofer is not easy. The best course of action is to find someone who has had a roof repaired recently and is pleased with the work. If this is not possible, check that the contractor is a member of a reputable association.

- **REPAIRING A FLAT ROOF**

The first sign of trouble is usually a damp patch on an upstairs ceiling. Don't expect the trouble to be directly above — water often travels some way before finding a weak spot in the plasterboard. Small repairs can be quite easily carried out. If there is a bubble, make two cuts at right angles and fold back the flaps to dry out the area. As with a crack, remove the chippings and clean the surrounding region. When dry, coat with a bitumastic compound and fold back the flaps. Re-treat the area a day or two later and put back the chippings. Unfortunately the trouble may be more serious than a simple crack or bubble — the roof may have perished. You will then have to have it reroofed by a specialist contractor or you can use one of the synthetic rubber products which are now available in DIY shops for sealing roofs.

- **BLOCKING OFF A CHIMNEY**

About a quarter of chimneys designed for solid fuel are no longer in use. Leaving an open flue in a chimney which is never used can lead to problems — the simplest answer is to cap the top of the chimney pot with a half round tile. Rain is kept out but there is adequate ventilation.

- **REPLACING A BROKEN SLATE**

The slate will be nailed to a batten — it is necessary to break off these nails by using a slate ripper.

Hook one of the barbs under a nail and pull downwards. Repeat with the other nail and then remove the slate. Now fix a tingle (2 x 20 cm strip of copper or lead) between the two slates which lay under the broken one.

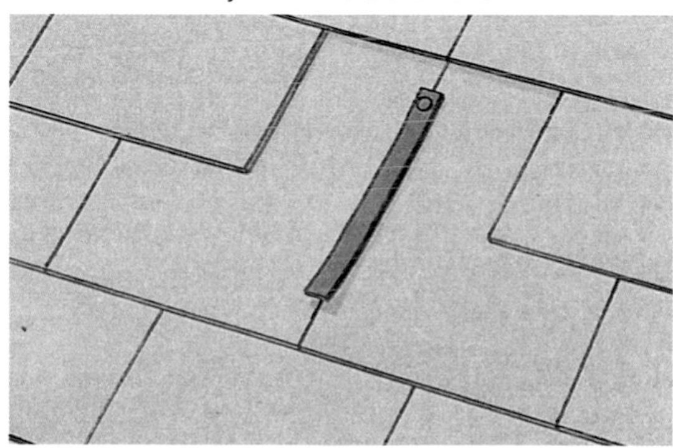

Push the new slate under the ones above. When it is aligned with the others on the same course, bend the bottom of the tingle upwards and then press down on to the lower edge of the new slate to form a firm hook.

- **REPLACING A BROKEN TILE**

It is usually easier to replace a tile than a slate. Lift up the tiles on the course above, which lie on either side of the broken one. Insert small wooden wedges below them and then lift out the one to be replaced by unhooking from the holding batten. You may need a large bricklayer's trowel.

Push the new tile under the ones above until the nibs hook over the batten. Remove the wedges. A loose tile should be reattached to the roof in the same way, but a nailed-down tile which is either broken or loose will have to be treated in the same way as a slate.

- **REPAIRING FLASHING**

Flashing may come away — scrape out old mortar, push the flashing into the gap and repoint the space between the bricks. If the flashing is torn, clean the affected area and then treat with flashing strip primer. Cover with self-adhesive flashing strip.

WALLS

A long car journey rather than a textbook will impress you with the wide range of wall types in this country — wood, stone, concrete, but above all brick. Brick walls have evolved over the years, as the illustrations below clearly show. Once they were all solid walls — one brick-length or a brick and a half wide. Heat loss was high and weather resistance low, so in many cases the outer surface was rendered by coating with a plaster mix or cladded with tiles or planks of timber. Double cavity walls were known in Victorian times, but if your brick house was built before 1914 it almost certainly has solid walls — if it was constructed after World War II then there are cavity walls. The cavity wall has continued to evolve. Once it was brick/brick but in the modern house it is either brick/concrete block or brick/timber (see below).

Whatever the construction the outside needs regular inspection and maintenance. Check the walls for cracks, dampness, flaking, missing mortar between the bricks and discoloration. Clear rubbish away from air bricks and damp-proof courses and look at the woodwork for signs of decay. Prod the bottom of the door and window frames — the standard danger points. If you are tired of your plain brick walls, you can clean, render or clad them ... but don't paint them.

WALL STRUCTURE

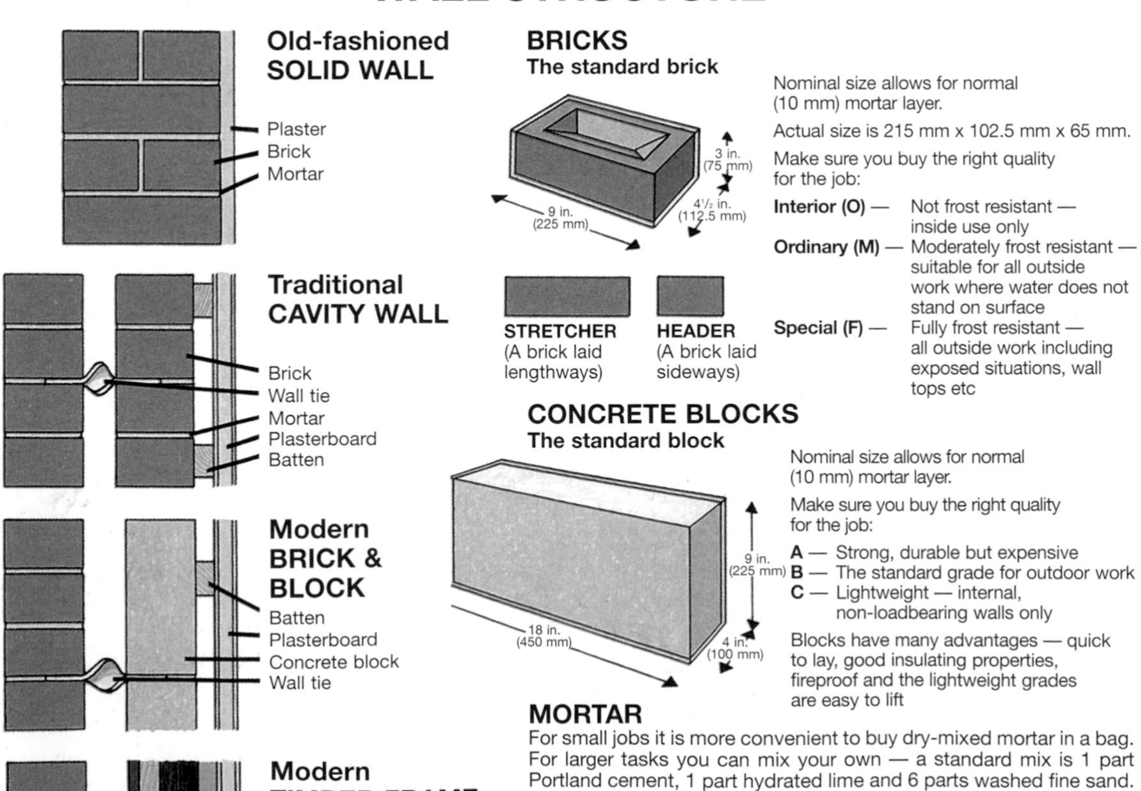

BRICKS
The standard brick

Nominal size allows for normal (10 mm) mortar layer.

Actual size is 215 mm x 102.5 mm x 65 mm.

Make sure you buy the right quality for the job:

Interior (O) — Not frost resistant — inside use only

Ordinary (M) — Moderately frost resistant — suitable for all outside work where water does not stand on surface

Special (F) — Fully frost resistant — all outside work including exposed situations, wall tops etc

CONCRETE BLOCKS
The standard block

Nominal size allows for normal (10 mm) mortar layer.

Make sure you buy the right quality for the job:

A — Strong, durable but expensive
B — The standard grade for outdoor work
C — Lightweight — internal, non-loadbearing walls only

Blocks have many advantages — quick to lay, good insulating properties, fireproof and the lightweight grades are easy to lift

MORTAR

For small jobs it is more convenient to buy dry-mixed mortar in a bag. For larger tasks you can mix your own — a standard mix is 1 part Portland cement, 1 part hydrated lime and 6 parts washed fine sand.

To mix mortar, turn over the dry ingredients until the mixture has an even colour. Flatten the heap and make a central crater with a spade or shovel. Pour water into this crater and slowly bring the outer wall into the centre. Mix and turn — add sprinklings of water until the pile is well mixed and thoroughly moist.

With regard to the craft of bricklaying itself, either watch a professional bricklayer at work or ask a skilled friend to show you how. It is not a craft you can acquire by reading a book.

HOW TO DEAL WITH WALL & WOODWORK PROBLEMS

CLEANING DIRTY WALLS

Examine the discoloration before you do anything. Moss and green slime often indicate dampness, which means that the basic problem must be put right or the trouble will return. White powder (efflorescence) is unsightly but is nothing to worry about — see page 103. There are several steps involved in cleaning rendered, exposed brick and stone walls. Begin by using a stiff brush. Next, scrub with plain water — never use soap or detergent. If algae, moss or mould is present a proprietary fungicide or household bleach should be added to the water (1 part bleach : 4 parts water) — leave for about a couple of days and then wash off with plain water. To renovate brickwork, rub the surface with a piece of similar brick. Stone should be treated with a stone 'sanding block' in the same way — keep the block wet at all times. A word of warning — wear goggles when using a brush or water containing an anti-slime chemical. Mortar as well as masonry may be discoloured. Use an acid-based stone cleaner.

RESTORING POOR QUALITY WOODWORK

If door or window frames are in poor condition, you must do something about it or the problem is bound to get worse. Flaking paint must be removed and the area sanded down to bare wood before repainting. Read the section on Paint (pages 89 - 96) before repainting outside woodwork.

You may find that part of the wood is rotten — there is little resistance to a steel point pushed into the surface. Treatment depends on the extent of the rot. If there is one large area, it will be necessary to cut out the rotten wood and replace with a section of new timber. The affected patch may be quite small — tackle the problem with a proprietary wood rot treatment as described on page 107. Unfortunately you may have waited too long and there are large areas of rot in several parts of the frame. Try one or other of the techniques above, but in the end you will probably have to replace the frame.

REPAIRING CRACKS

It is quite normal for a few fine cracks to appear as a new house settles — these cracks may be quite long. Fill with mortar when the movement stops.

Wall cracks can mean one of the most feared of all house problems — subsidence. Look for the danger signs — cracks running sideways from the corners of windows and doors, and cracks running downwards from the sides of windows or close to the corners of the house. Check by using the glass slide test.

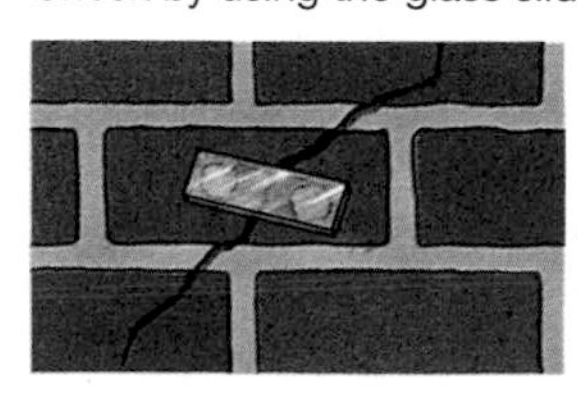

Glue a glass slide over the crack. Keep watch over the next few months. If it breaks you must consult a surveyor as quickly as possible as subsidence may be occurring — see page 106 for details.

REPAIRING SPALLING

Isolated bricks may allow water to penetrate and then freeze in winter. The surface breaks away, an effect known as spalling. Use a club hammer and cold chisel to remove the softened part. Cut a second-hand brick to fit the gap — mortar in place with a cement-rich mix (1 part cement : 3 parts sand). With a double cavity wall you can remove the whole brick — it is sometimes possible to reverse the brick and use it for refacing the wall. Do not allow mortar to drop into the cavity.

REPOINTING

Sooner or later the combined effect of wind, rain and frost will loosen some of the mortar between the bricks. The effect is unsightly and the weatherproofing property of the wall is reduced. Remove the loose mortar to a depth of about 1 cm with a screwdriver, a club hammer and cold chisel or an electric drill fitted with a chasing bit. Make up mortar as described on page 78 — never mix more than you can use in 1 - 2 hours. Brush away all bits and dust with a stiff brush and then thoroughly soak the bricks and underlying mortar with water.

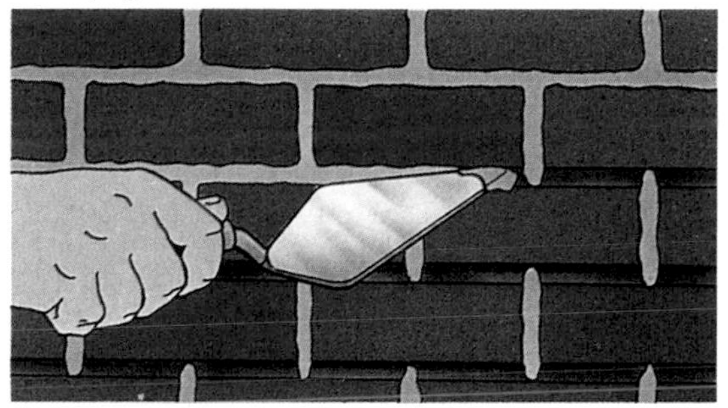

Use a pointing trowel to force the mortar into the gaps — start with the upright joints and then fill the horizontal ones. Now smooth the mortar — cut away the excess and follow the joint style (see page 75) which has been used on the wall. The final step is to brush off any traces of mortar when the repointed area is almost dry. It is a wise precaution to make up a small amount of mortar and repoint the gap between a brick or two before starting on the whole area. You may find that the mortar has quite a different colour to the rest of the jointing — colourants for mortar mixes are available. Experiment until you find the right shade.

REPAIRING RENDERING

Use a club hammer and cold chisel to remove all the loose rendering. Rake out some of the mortar between the bricks and brush away all dust and chippings. Make up mortar (see page 78) and thoroughly wet the damaged area with a PVA bonding agent. Push mortar on to the area with a steel float (rectangular trowel).

Level the surface by drawing a batten across the wet mortar — use a sawing motion. Before the patch is dry smooth with a float for a stucco effect, cut in the required texture with a trowel, comb, roller or brush, or throw on stones and press in to match a pebbledash effect. Before painting a smooth or textured rendered wall it is necessary to repair all the damaged spots as described above. If in doubt, tap the surface with a trowel handle. A hollow sound means that the rendering has come away and so requires repair.

GUTTERS & DOWNPIPES

Gutters collect the rainwater and melted snow from the roof. There is a slight slope (at least 1 in 120) to the downpipes — vertical pipes which carry the water to the drains. Do not confuse with the drainage system which removes house waste — see page 20.

Before the war the standard material for gutters and downpipes was cast iron. Firm and solid, but also heavy and sure to rust if not regularly painted. The introduction of plastic uPVC has made a world of difference — lightweight, rustproof, easy to erect and maintain and so on. If you have a cast iron rainwater disposal system which is faulty, replace with uPVC. There are other materials — copper, asbestos cement (no longer available), aluminium, zinc, steel and so on, but plastic is the answer. Gutters are half round (held by brackets attached to the fascia board) or ogee-shaped (screwed directly on to the fascia board).

A breakdown in the system will lead to water pouring on the fabric of the house. Carry out an inspection once a year. Look for breaks and blockages — check that the gutters are not sagging. Remove debris from the gutters by means of a trowel — always work away from the downpipe union. When the gutters are clear use a hosepipe to flush the system.

HOW TO DEAL WITH GUTTER & DOWNPIPE PROBLEMS

- **REPAIRING A SAGGING GUTTER**

The usual symptom of a sagging gutter is an overflow of water from the gutter when it is raining. Of course, the displacement may be large enough to be visible from the ground. The problem is due to a broken bracket or loosened screws. The simple answer is to attach a new bracket using new screws close to the faulty bracket. With ogee guttering you will have to remove the screws and then attach at a slightly higher level so that the sag is removed.

It is sometimes possible to repair a sagging gutter by inserting a small wooden wedge between the gutter and the bracket. Easy — but such a repair is best regarded as temporary.

- **REFIXING A LOOSE DOWNPIPE**

You must secure a loose downpipe bracket — the pipe can easily work loose in high wind and come crashing down. Remove the pipe nails from the bracket, using a claw hammer with a piece of wood against the wall to improve leverage. Remove the lower section of pipe — if made of iron and a sealant is present you will have to use a blowlamp. The next step is to remove the old plugs in the wall — replace with new plugs made out of dowels. Extend the holes by drilling if necessary — hammer home the new plugs. Now refit the pipe and bracket — drive in new nails and reseal the joints of iron pipes.

- **REPAIRING A LEAKING DOWNPIPE**

Look for the tell-tale signs of damp patches or green slime behind the pipe. Repair the leak with glass fibre bandage or self-adhesive flashing strip if you don't want to replace the section. With cast iron pipes the problem may be a break in the joint — remake the seal with a recommended mastic.

- **REPAIRING A LEAKING GUTTER**

The first task is to find whether the leak is at a joint or in the body of the gutter. Most leaks are due to faulty joints — with a cast iron pipe you should ideally remove the section, scrape off the putty, apply fresh sealing compound and then rebolt the section back in place. But iron gutters are heavy, and the usual method of tackling the problem is to paint the leaking joint with a sealing compound or seal it with self-adhesive flashing strip. With plastic guttering it is a simple job to unclip the section and replace the defective seal.

The problem may be a hole in the body of the gutter — a common problem in old cast iron gutters where rust is an ever-present problem. If the hole is a small one it can be repaired with self-adhesive flashing strip — a general decay of the iron calls for a new section rather than simple patching. Prevention is so much better than cure when dealing with cast iron gutters and pipes. Whilst they are still sound treat with a rust-neutralising product. Apply a topcoat of gloss paint.

- **CLEARING A BLOCKED GUTTER**

An overflowing gutter may mean that either the guttering or downpipe is blocked. Inspect the gutters — a thick cake of silt, leaves etc indicates a gutter blockage. Put a rag into the downpipe opening and remove the rubbish into a bucket suspended on the ladder. Brush away remaining silt and then remove rag from the downpipe. Pour water into the gutter — if it does not run away quickly you will have to now deal with a blocked downpipe.

- **CLEARING A BLOCKED DOWNPIPE**

Put a bowl at the base of the pipe to stop debris getting into the drains. Poke a stiff wire up through the shoe to remove any lower blockage. Now work from the roof — remove any rubbish from the downpipe opening and then use a piece of stout hooked wire to lift up any debris from the upper part of the pipe. Push a long bamboo cane down the pipe if there is a straight run — if all else fails the pipe will have to be dismantled.

CHAPTER 6

MATERIALS

METALS

METAL	DESCRIPTION	HOUSEHOLD USES
CAST IRON	Iron with 2 - 5% carbon. Cheap and tough but also brittle — a sharp blow can fracture it. Objects are moulded (cast) — metal cannot be drawn or twisted	Gutters, grates, boilers
WROUGHT IRON	Iron with carbon and slag. Can be worked in many ways — twisted, bent, shaped, cut etc. Suitable for welding and soldering — rusts relatively slowly	Gates, chains, screens
MILD STEEL	Despite the name, almost pure iron — carbon content is less than 0.1%. Easily worked, suitable for soldering and welding but it rusts quickly	Hinges, screws, brackets
ALLOY STEEL	Iron with other metals added, such as manganese, tungsten, molybdenum etc. Harder than mild steel, but again it rusts quickly	Chisels, saws, springs
STAINLESS STEEL	An alloy steel containing nickel and chromium. It is difficult to work but easily soldered. Widely used for kitchenware as it neither tarnishes nor rusts	Knives, sinks, pans
ALUMINIUM	Used where lightness is essential — easily worked and resistant to corrosion. It can be highly polished — major drawback is lack of strength	Foils, pans, beer cans
ALUMINIUM ALLOY	Aluminium rendered almost as hard as steel by adding small amounts of copper, manganese and magnesium. Lightweight and easily worked, but corrodes more easily than aluminium	Window frames, cladding, kettles
COPPER	An excellent conductor of heat and electricity. A soft metal, easily bent and shaped with many practical uses. Very decorative when polished, but darkens with age	Pipes, pans, cylinders
BRASS	An alloy of copper and zinc — a small amount of lead may be incorporated. A decorative metal, much used for ornaments and trimmings. Strong, bright, but darkens with age	Taps, screws, ornaments
PINCHBECK	A copper-rich brass with the appearance of gold. It was once widely used for making inexpensive jewellery, but is no longer used. Guinea Gold is similar	Antique jewellery, watches
BRONZE	Alloy of copper and tin and resistant to corrosion. Easily worked and attractive but little used around the home. Much Victorian 'bronze' is really copper plate	Door knockers, buttons, ornaments
ORMOLU	An alloy of copper, zinc and tin used to make decorative items — often gold-like. Originally, ormolu was brass gilded with gold leaf	Antique furniture, statuettes
PEWTER	An alloy of tin and lead. Dull, but can be highly polished. Once popular for kitchen and drinking utensils, but now ruled out because of lead content	Tankards, decorative plates, statuettes
LEAD	Heavy, soft, easily worked and highly resistant to corrosion. Once widely used for plumbing, but now replaced by copper and plastic because of poisoning risk	Waterproof flashing
ZINC	Somewhat similar to lead — soft, easily worked and resistant to corrosion. But it is lighter and less easily bent — not much used in the pure state	Substitute for lead flashing
SHEFFIELD PLATE	Silver sheet rolled on to one or both sides of copper sheet. Not the same as silver plate, which is done by electrolysis. No longer made	Trays, dishes, hollow-ware
NICKEL SILVER	Contains no silver at all — an alloy of copper, nickel and zinc. Nickel silver blanks are plated with silver to produce EPNS	Knives, trays, fittings
MAZAK	An alloy of zinc and aluminium, much used to produce die-cast blanks which are then brass plated to produce 'brass' objects. Check — real brass is heavy	Door knobs, ornaments, handles
BRITANNIA METAL	An alloy of tin, antimony and copper. Grey-coloured — much used by Victorians for teapots, tankards etc. Nowadays used as blanks for silver plating	Cutlery, trays, fittings
SILVER	A luxury metal — soft, easily worked but also easily scratched. Tarnishes with age — needs regular polishing. Sterling silver contains 92.5% pure silver	Cutlery, jewellery, containers
GOLD	The most prized of all household metals — reserved for rings and jewellery. Purity is measured in carats — 24 carats is pure gold, 22 carats is wedding ring gold	Rings, watches, jewellery
TIN PLATE	A coating of tin over mild steel sheet produces a metal which is easily cut, folded and soldered. The surface remains rust-free as long as the coating is not scratched	Tins, bakeware
ZINC PLATE	A coating of zinc over steel produces a rust-resistant metal known as galvanized steel or iron. It is used in sheet, rod or wire form	Wheelbarrows, wire netting, nails
COPPER PLATE	A coating of copper is frequently applied in electroplating, but it is used to serve as an undercoating for another metal such as chromium	Coating under chromium plate
CHROMIUM PLATE	Chromium has the advantage of producing a mirror-bright surface, and so is used where a gleaming finish is required — modern furniture, car trimmings, handles etc	Cheap cutlery, knobs, picture frames
EPNS	Electroplated nickel silver — the most popular type of silver plate produced in Britain. For domestic cutlery the silver thickness should be 20 microns	Cutlery, trays, fittings
SILVER PLATE	Silver coated on to any material — steel, copper, pewter, mazak, Britannia metal, plastic and even flowers and leaves. Most quality material is EPNS	Cutlery, trays, fittings
BRASS PLATE	A coating of brass on steel, mazak or plastic. Most 'brass' items are really brass plate — magnetism denotes that it is brass-plated steel	Door knockers, fire tongs, ornaments
GOLD PLATE	Tarnish-free and gleaming, such items are a sign of extravagance (e.g gold-plated bathroom fittings) or economy (gold-plated jewellery)	Jewellery, watches, taps
ROLLED GOLD	Gold sheet rolled on to one or both sides of a sheet of base metal — compare Sheffield plate. Once widely used for cases of pocket watches	Watches, jewellery, containers

WOOD

Everyone who is interested in the home needs to have some knowledge of wood and its properties. For the keen DIY enthusiast this is, of course, a fundamental requirement. He or she must buy the right type of timber at the keenest price, and it must be properly worked to produce that new cupboard, wall or bookcase. The casual handyperson may never pay a trip to the timber merchant, but driving in screws and repairing items of furniture are occasionally unavoidable. And for everyone there is the task of buying wooden fixtures and fittings — chairs, kitchen units, tables, desks and so on. This chapter tells you about the range available, together with details of fixing methods and the basic principles of working with this material.

Softwoods are used for general joinery — such as joists, floorboards, cupboard carcasses etc. Where large sheets are required we turn to one of the manufactured boards, and for a decorative effect which will not need painting we buy boards which have a veneer of an attractive hardwood on the surface. For outdoors a naturally protected wood such as teak or cedar is used, or we use preservative-treated timber.

If you are new to wood make sure you read this section before going along to buy your boards or sheets of wood. It may come as a surprise that the various woods nearly all have one drawback or other — it might be price, poor painting or staining quality, inability to soak up preservatives, resistance to standard tools ('hard to work') or softness. There are danger points to watch for when buying and a confusing set of terms to understand. Still, your DIY store or timber merchant will have someone to give advice, but don't expect to find every type of wood mentioned on page 84.

MANUFACTURED BOARDS

Manufactured board is made from wood in sheet, strip, shredded or pulped form with resins or glues bonding the pieces or pulp together. There are various types — plywood and blockboard are the most expensive; chipboard and ordinary hardboard are the cheapest. Make sure you always buy the right one for the job you have to do, and pay special care if the board will have to withstand outdoor conditions. Where water will be present you must specify an exterior or waterproof grade.

Manufactured board is sometimes regarded as an inferior material designed for people who can't afford 'real' wood. There is indeed a saving in price, but there are also other advantages. The main one is the availability in larger sheets — making up wide boards by gluing planks of timber together is not an easy task. Another point in favour of manufactured boards is the freedom from the standard defects you have to look for when buying natural timber.

For the production of finished furniture you can buy coated boards. Melamine coating is the most economical — laminate is very popular and at the top end of the range is board veneered with a decorative hardwood.

SOFTWOODS

Softwood is cut from a conifer such as pine, larch, fir or spruce. The wood is usually lighter and softer than hardwood, but not always — yew is heavier and denser than some hardwoods.

A typical softwood comes from a cool or cold climate. It is pale in colour and there are resin-bearing streaks and a number of knots. It is cheaper than hardwood and is easier to saw, plane, nail etc. This is the wood which is used for nearly all general joinery and house construction work. When the home handyman wants to buy natural (not manufactured) boards or planks for a DIY job the usual choice is between redwood and whitewood — both commonly called 'deal'.

These two woods are widely available in both rough or planed form and in a series of standard widths and thicknesses. For outdoor use you will need wood which has been pre-treated with a preservative — for indoors you will usually require a hardwood-veneered surface if you plan to stain and polish rather than paint. Not always — Scandinavian redwood is now treated with clear polyurethane varnish to produce fashionable 'pine' furniture.

HARDWOODS

Hardwood is cut from a deciduous broad-leaved tree, such as oak, mahogany or teak. The wood is usually denser and harder than softwood, but not always — balsa is much lighter than any commercial softwood.

A typical hardwood is heavy and close-grained, which means that it will take a fine polish but is harder to work with than a softwood. It is also more expensive — sometimes much more expensive, and so hardwood is generally bought either in the form of mouldings or as veneers which are applied to softwood or manufactured boards. The exception is ramin, which is available in board form from DIY shops.

There are basically two types — temperate hardwoods and tropical hardwoods. The temperate types grow in Europe and other places with cool or cold winters — the result is generally a clearly distinct patterning due to the difference between winter and summer growth. The colour is usually pale and these woods are notoriously difficult to work. The tropical hardwoods are nearly always darker and the patterning tends to be less distinct. Working is generally easier but there may still be a need to drill pilot holes before nailing.

MANUFACTURED BOARDS

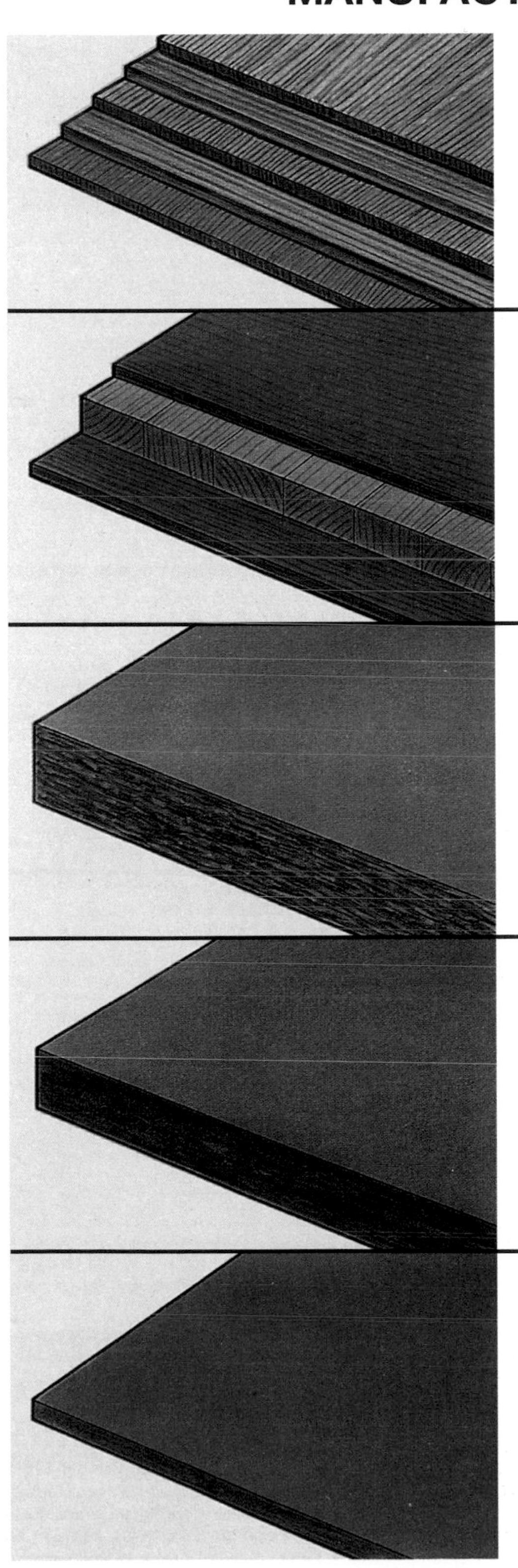

PLYWOOD

Thin layers ('plys') of wood are glued together to form a board which has neither the warping nor splitting tendency of natural wood. This property is due to each layer being laid at right angles to its partner and an odd number of layers being used to make up the finished board. The number of plys varies from 3 to 15 — the board thickness ranges from 3 - 18 mm.

There are many grades: *INT* for indoor use, *WBP* (weather- and boil-proof) or *EXT* for outdoors, *aviation* for beading, *hardwood veneered* for high-quality appearance, *structural* for maximum strength and *plank-faced* for panelling.

BLOCKBOARD

The inner core consists of strips of softwood glued together. The annual rings of the strips are at right angles to each other and this core is sandwiched between two thin layers of wood — usually birch. In top-quality blockboard these sheets are faced with decorative hardwood veneers. Board thickness is 12 - 25 mm and is worked in the same way as ordinary timber. A few words of caution: do not nail or screw too close to the end of the core strips and never paint just one face — treat both faces in the same way. Do not use blockboard outdoors.

Laminboard is a version of blockboard in which narrower strips of wood are used for the core.

CHIPBOARD

Small chips of softwood are bound together with a resin adhesive and the sheet is squeezed between rollers to the required thickness (usually 12 or 18 mm). It is cheaper than plywood and blockboard and is widely used as a base for furniture because of its even texture and resistance to warping. For maximum strength buy the *multi-layer* grade, for painting buy *painting* quality which has densely-packed small fibres on the face and for underflooring look for the *flooring* grade. A multitude of *faced* varieties are available for making furniture and worktops.

There are problems. It will bow if the support is inadequate, the cut edge may be ragged, special screws or inserts must be used for fixing and it is not suitable for use outdoors.

MDF (MEDIUM DENSITY FIBREBOARD)

The base material for fibreboard is made from the fibres produced when timber is subjected to a vacuum in a pressure chamber. These fibres are bonded with resin and then rolled — the pressure used has a profound effect on the quality of the fibreboard. Low pressures produce pinboard which is used for notice boards — high pressure produces panelboard for wall lining.

Medium density fibreboard is an exciting modern material which is very widely employed in the furniture industry but is less commonly used by the home handyman. Rather similar to chipboard, but with the great advantages that it can be cut cleanly, nailed or screwed without problems and has a surface which can be stained, polished or painted.

HARDBOARD

Pulped wood is mixed with adhesives and rolled into sheets which are 3 - 6 mm thick. This Cinderella of the manufactured boards is cheap and has little inherent strength, but has many uses around the home. *Standard* grade (smooth front face, roughened-mesh back face) is bought for covering doors, floors, drawer bottoms etc. There are *perforated* boards pierced with round holes (pegboard) or decorative shapes, and there is the *tempered* grade which has been impregnated with oil to make it water resistant.

Enamel- and *plastic-finished* boards are used where a decorative effect such as a tile or wood-panelling look is required.

SOFTWOODS

WOOD	DETAILS
CEDAR, WESTERN RED	Reddish-brown with a silky surface. Resists both rot and insects and so is popular outdoors for cladding, fences and sheds. It has its problems — colour fades with time, nails work loose and the surface is easily dented
FIR, DOUGLAS	Popular with furniture makers and house builders — very strong and quite cheap, and also knot-free. Sometimes sold as British Columbian pine — pinkish-brown and even-textured but paints badly and cracks outdoors
HEMLOCK	A general-purpose softwood from Canada and the U.S, used for doors, floors, joists etc. Strong and easily worked but not good for painting or outdoor use
LARCH	A British wood, tough and difficult to work. There are two important characteristics — it has good rot resistance and holds nails well. As a result it is used for construction work indoors and fences etc outdoors
PINE, PARANA	A fine-textured wood, attractively coloured in cream, brown or lilac and often knot-free. Very strong (used for staircases) but also temperamental — warps easily, splits outdoors and provides a poor surface for painting
REDWOOD	The most popular of all woods for the home carpenter — inexpensive, reliable, easy to work, good for painting etc. Colours range from cream to reddish-brown — commercial names include Scots pine, Baltic pine, red deal and 'pine' furniture
WHITEWOOD	Popular and inexpensive like redwood, but there are differences. It is softer with a finer texture, and the cream colour does not darken with age. Whitewood (other names — spruce, white deal) does not absorb preservatives — not for use outdoors
YEW	The softwood that thinks it is a hardwood. Yew is very heavy and close-grained — the colour is orange or brown. It is a wood used by cabinet makers and craftsmen to produce high quality articles

HARDWOODS

WOOD	DETAILS
AFRORMOSIA	A wood from tropical Africa. Close-grained and golden-brown like teak — used as a less expensive substitute in furniture manufacture. Available for the home carpenter in both solid and veneer form
ASH	A pale-coloured timber with many uses — panelling, flooring etc. The two traditional applications are bentwood chairs and tool handles. The experts will tell you to avoid boards with brown streaks
BEECH	A European wood which is often used in the furniture industry for making a stout and durable frame for veneering. The colour is ivory to pale brown and the grain is straight. Not recommended for outdoor use
CHERRY	A wood with a wavy grain and a distinctive orange sheen — more often seen as a veneer than as solid wood. A material for the cabinet maker and craftsman, but American cherry is sometimes used for joinery work
CHESTNUT, SWEET	Similar to ash but less expensive — used as a substitute for making office furniture. It is also used as a substitute for oak, which it quite closely resembles. No real drawbacks, but dark streaks can be disfiguring
ELM	Coffins, wheelbarrows and Windsor chairs are traditionally made from this brownish rough-grained timber. European elm is very durable, but now scarce because of the ravages of Dutch elm disease. Japanese elm is less robust
IROKO	A popular teak substitute — hard-wearing for both indoor and outdoor use at a significantly lower price. You will find its rich brown colour in parquet floors, furniture, garden seats etc. The texture is rather coarse
JELUTONG	A wood to buy if you wish to try your hand at carving. Very pale, soft, straight-grained and even-textured. It is also useful for home carpentry — the surface is smooth and it is easily worked
MAHOGANY	One of the great woods, now more often used as a veneer than as solid timber. Not all mahoganies are the same. African has a rich orange-brown colour and a distinctive figuring — American is more even in appearance, more expensive and more lustrous
MERANTI	A mahogany substitute from Malaysia — cheaper, redder and easier to work than real mahogany. It is quite widely available in sheet and veneer form and as mouldings — so is the closely-related lauan from the Philippines
OAK	It is not just patriotism — British oak is the strongest, straightest and most durable of all oaks. Its toughness is legendary, but it is expensive, difficult to work and glue, and splits easily when nailed. European oak is a little softer — Japanese is even lighter and not suitable for outdoors
OBECHE	Not a quality hardwood — it is a light, easily-worked timber used in the manufacture of whitewood furniture. The grain is open and the colour pale — obeche can be stained and polished
RAMIN	A very popular hardwood which you will certainly find around the house in mouldings, picture frames, furniture etc. It is a straw-coloured wood, close-textured and easy to nail. A favourite material for the home carpenter
ROSEWOOD	An expensive wood for the luxury look. The rosewood furniture you see is almost certainly veneered over a cheaper carcass. Purples and browns swirl under the high lustre finish — you can buy boards as well as veneer but you will find it a difficult wood to work
SAPELE	A mahogany look-alike — strength and colour are similar but it is less expensive. One drawback — it has a tendency to warp. Sapele is usually bought as a veneer — it polishes well but staining can produce a patchy finish
TEAK	Teak is widely used in furniture manufacture these days both in solid form and veneer, its rich brown colour marbled with darker streaks. Apart from its visual appeal it resists rot, water and fire — teak is therefore used for outdoor furniture, ships' decks etc
UTILE	Like sapele, one of the mahogany look-alikes. It has a pink-brown colour and an irregular grain — this wood is easily worked and is less inclined than sapele to warp. Widely used in the furniture industry
WALNUT	Best of all is European (especially English) walnut — mid brown with dark streaks and swirling patterns beneath a lustrous finish. Long associated with antique furniture — today's walnut table will only be veneered on a cheaper frame. African walnut is easier to obtain but is less attractive

WOOD TYPES

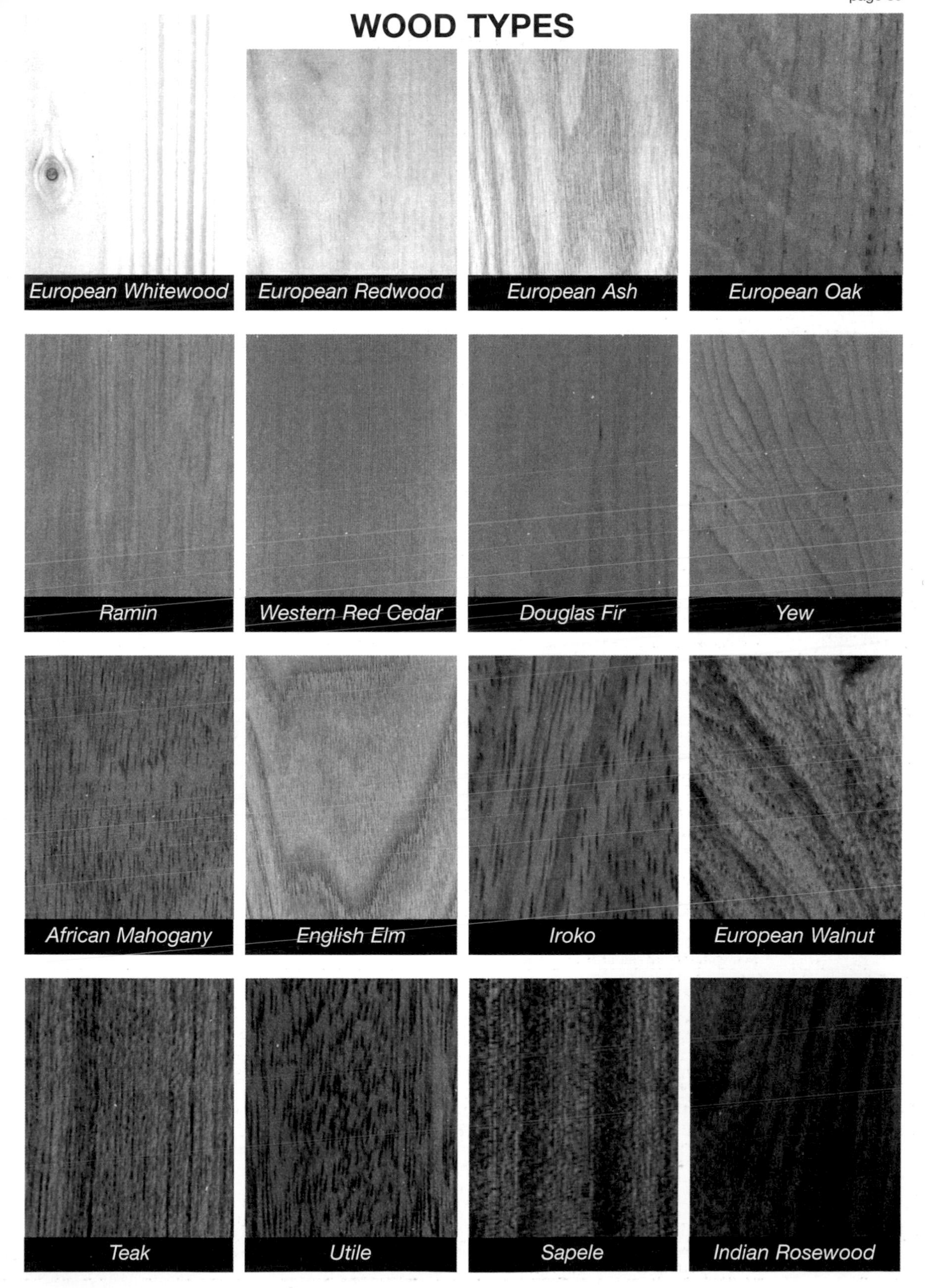
European Whitewood
European Redwood
European Ash
European Oak
Ramin
Western Red Cedar
Douglas Fir
Yew
African Mahogany
English Elm
Iroko
European Walnut
Teak
Utile
Sapele
Indian Rosewood

BUYING TIMBER

Wood can be bought from a DIY store, a builders' merchant or a specialist timber merchant. Each source has a different role to play — your local DIY store is the place to go for the popular sizes of whitewood and manufactured boards, but you will have to go to a timber merchant for sheets of decorative hardwood. When buying timber there are a number of considerations — the three basic ones are size, quality and dryness.

SIZE

Boards of softwood are sold in lengths ranging from 1.6 to 6.3 m. You can buy widths from 25 to 225 mm and thicknesses from 12 to 75 mm. If the wood is to be concealed it is usual to buy the 'rough sawn' grade — this means that the surfaces are in the state left by the power saw. Shrinkage may have taken place, so that the *actual* width and thickness may be very slightly less than the stated size — the *nominal* width and thickness. If the surface of the wood is to be seen it will be necessary to buy planed timber. Remember that planing removes about 5 mm from the nominal size. This means that the boards can be less wide and thick than stated on the label or invoice, though some suppliers include the 'actual' as well as the 'nominal' size.

Hardwoods are not sold in standard widths and thicknesses — the timber is stored as rough sawn boards and is cut and planed to your specification. Do tell the merchant whether the sizes are nominal (see above) or actual.

Buying manufactured board is more straightforward. The standard size is 2440 mm x 1220 mm, but a variety of smaller sizes is available at DIY stores.

QUALITY

Softwood is available in various quality grades but there is no single grading system for all types. As a general rule you will find that the wood stored by a builders' or wood merchant is offered in three grades. The cheapest is **carcassing** for joists, rafters etc — you must expect some knots and a moisture content of about 20 per cent. This means that some warping may occur as the wood dries out. **Standard joinery** is drier (15 per cent moisture content) and better quality — the wood to use for most DIY jobs. The top grade (**best joinery**) is expensive and should be purchased only if you intend to polish the wood (e.g a table top). There are no standard hardwood grades — it is up to you to inspect the wood and judge quality for yourself.

Make sure that wood for outdoor use is either naturally able or has been specially prepared to stand up to the elements. If it is not cedar or teak make sure that it has been treated with a preservative. Plywood should be marked EXT or WBP.

DRYNESS

Timber has to be dried before use — this increases strength, rot resistance, workability and cuts down the tendency to warp. Wood can be dried naturally by stacking it under cover in the open air (a hardwood board will take 3 - 4 years to dry after felling) or it may be kiln-dried. Furniture is made from kiln-dried wood with a moisture content of less than 13 per cent.

If the wood store has the same conditions as the place where you intend to use the wood, there is no difficulty. But if it is markedly warmer or colder, moister or drier, then you must leave the wood in its new surroundings for about a week before working with it.

LOOKING FOR FAULTS

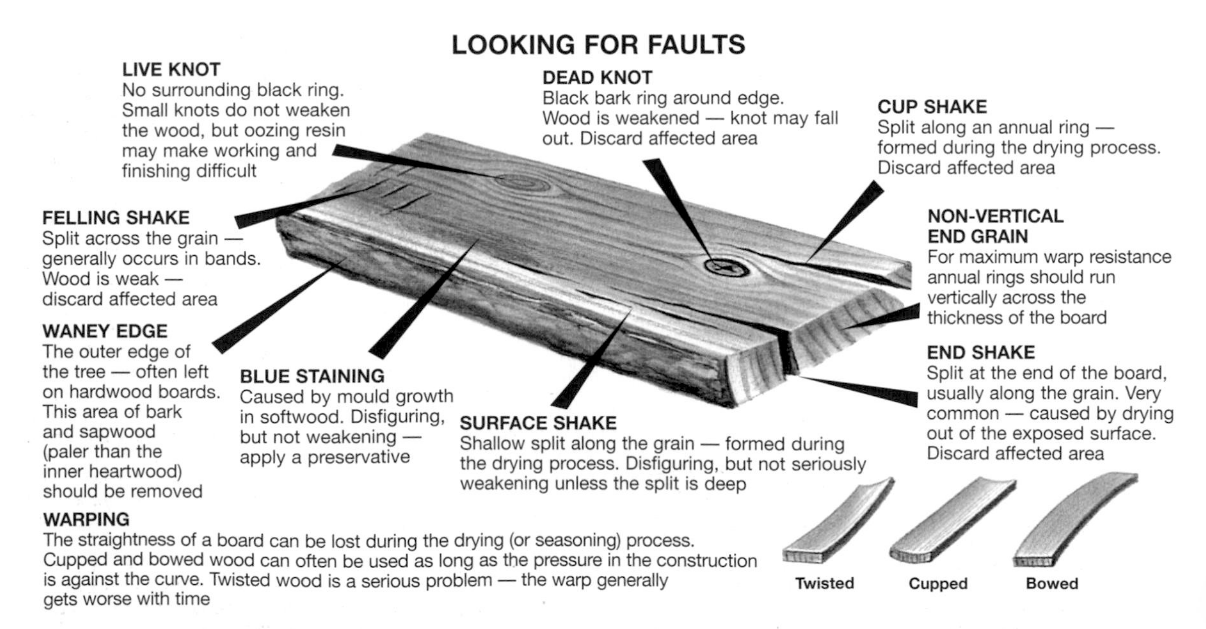

VENEERS

Faced veneers are thin sheets of decorative wood which are glued on to cheaper wood or manufactured boards. Laying a veneer on to a board is a skilled job — it is usually more satisfactory to buy veneer-faced plywood or chipboard. Edging with veneer is straightforward — veneer strips can be cut and stuck without difficulty.

MOULDINGS

Boards, sidings, posts etc are cut with a square or rectangular cross section. Wood cut with any other cross section is known as a moulding. An enormous variety is available, ranging from narrow strips for edging or picture framing to tongue-and-grooved planks for panelling or flooring. Other mouldings are used for cladding, cornices, window sashes etc.

WORKING WITH WOOD

USING A SAW

It will be necessary to have more than one saw. There are two basic types which are readily distinguished — there is the 50 - 70 cm handsaw which is used for cutting planks, boards etc and the smaller backsaw with a brass, steel or plastic strip along the back of the blade to keep it rigid. A backsaw is used for cutting joints, small pieces of board etc.

There are a few general rules to follow. Measure carefully, using a try square or a steel rule. Use a knife or sharp steel point rather than a pencil for marking — the cut fibres and very fine line will make sawing more accurate. If the cut line is hard to see, simply run a pencil point along it before you begin to saw. Widths are marked off with a marking gauge — the stock of the gauge is moved up or down to set the point at the desired width. Always saw on the waste side of the line. Take care not to wander to the other side — excess wood can be easily removed with sandpaper or a plane, but wood which has been sawn off cannot be replaced.

Use the right saw for the job in hand. Obviously you will need a handsaw and not a backsaw if the whole blade is to travel through the wood, and the number of points (teeth) per 25 mm determines the type of cut — the smaller the number, the quicker but rougher the cut.

A carpenter has a range of handsaws. A ripsaw (65 - 70 cm long) for ripping (cutting along the grain), a cross-cut saw (60 - 65 cm long) for cutting across the grain, and a panel saw (50 - 60 cm long) for cutting small planks and manufactured boards. The householder needs only one — a panel saw. The piece of wood must be firmly secured on trestles or in a vice. If the board is allowed to bow when sawing the blade will jam.

Make the initial cut by drawing the saw back gently several times, using your thumb as a guide and keeping your eye on the line and not on the saw. Now start to saw. Keep your index finger pointing downwards along the blade and apply pressure on the forward (not backward) stroke. The blade should be held at about 50° - 60° and the cut should be wedged open with a small piece of wood if the blade begins to jam. Make sure you use the whole length of the blade and let the teeth rather than brute force do the work. Take care at the end of the cut to prevent splintering — with a wide plank it is a good idea to remove the saw and cut the last few centimetres by starting again from the opposite side.

A carpenter or cabinet maker has a range of backsaws. The householder needs only one — a tenon saw.

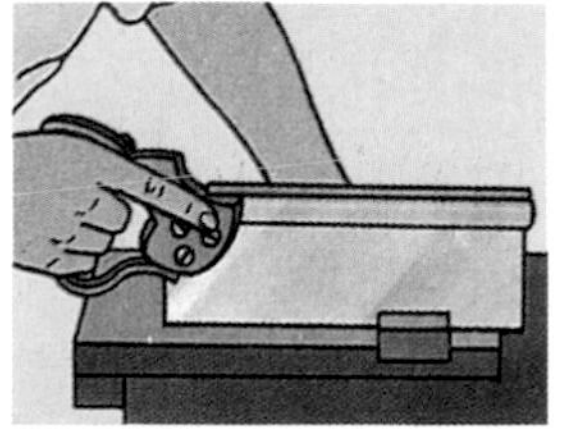

The standard tenon saw is about 25 - 30 cm long. The piece of wood must be firmly secured in a vice or a bench hook — a mitre box is used if an angled cut (mitre) is required.

Use your index finger as a guide — hold the blade horizontally and use the full length when sawing. For finer and more intricate work a dovetail saw (20 cm long) is used. This looks like a small tenon saw — for model making there is the knob-handled gents saw (10 cm long).

Choose your saw carefully if you plan to do a lot of woodwork — don't look for unbranded bargains. A hardpoint saw will stay sharp much longer than an ordinary blade, but they are more easily damaged. A PTFE-coated saw will not go rusty, and wooden handles are generally more comfortable than plastic ones. Take care of your saws. When not in use hang them up rather than leaving them on a bench or in a drawer, and rub the blade with a little light oil to prevent rust. Most saws can be sharpened at home, but it is a job best left to the experts.

USING A CHISEL

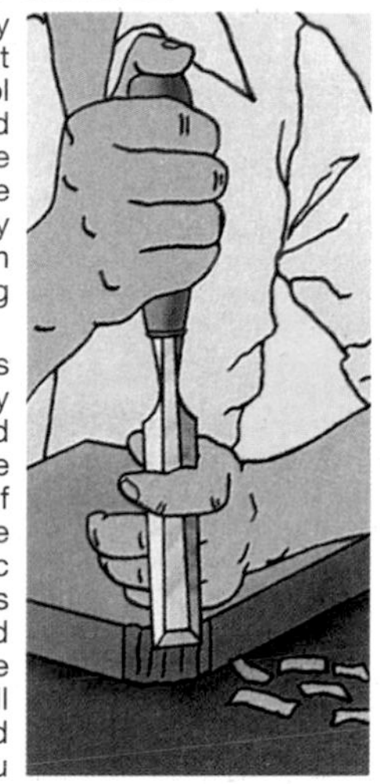

Chisels are used for many jobs around the house, but do take care. Hold the tool properly, as described below, and never use the blade as a lever where the resistance is great. Many accidents are caused each year by people ignoring these simple principles.

The best all-purpose type is the bevel-edge chisel. Buy one which is already honed and fitted with a protective guard. Paring (removal of thin strips of wood from the edge of a board) is a basic job for a chisel. The bevel is placed away from the board edge and both hands are kept behind the blade at all times. Pressure is applied with the right hand (if you are right-handed) and the left hand is used merely to guide the direction of the cut. Work slowly inward until the line marked on the board is reached. This paring technique is used for removing small areas of rotten wood from frames, cutting out housings for hinges etc.

A chisel is also used to make a mortise — a rectangular hole cut in the body of a piece of wood. Here hand pressure is not sufficient — you will need a mallet. Start work at the centre of the waste area, cutting out narrow 5 mm deep wedges. Move gradually to the edges of the mortise — finish with the bevel of the chisel facing the cut-out area.

USING A DRILL

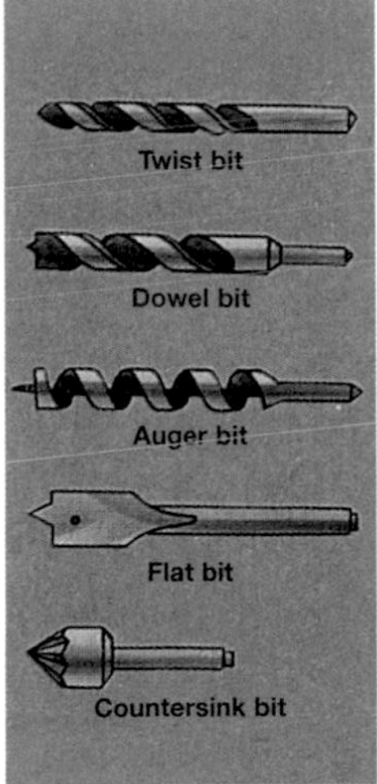

By far the most popular power tool is the electric drill, used for drilling, sanding and sawing. All sorts of improvements have been added in recent years, so deciding on the best buy is not as simple as it used to be. First of all, make sure there is a two-speed switch or a variable speed switch or dial — you need a slower speed (approx 1000 rpm) for glass, tile, metal etc than for wood (approx 3000 rpm). A hammer-action drill sounds like a good idea, but you would only need it for drilling through concrete. Finally, make sure that any attachments you require are suitable for the model you plan to buy.

There are a number of commonsense rules. You must drill at right angles to the work surface and make sure that the object you are drilling is held firmly. Do not exert too much pressure. Withdraw the bit occasionally to remove waste material during the drilling process. A drop in motor noise and a reduction in drill speed indicates that the motor is overloaded — withdraw the bit immediately and allow the drill to run at normal speed for a minute before recommencing work. Always keep the flex out of the way. Look after your drill. Have it serviced at regular intervals if used frequently, and have it repaired immediately if sparking occurs during use.

WOOD FIXINGS

NAILS

ROUND WIRE NAIL (25 - 150 mm)
The standard general carpentry nail where appearance does not matter — head is unsightly. Liable to split wood

OVAL WIRE NAIL (25 - 150 mm)
The standard general carpentry nail where appearance does matter — head can be punched below the surface

LOST HEAD NAIL (12 - 150 mm)
Round or oval. Used in general carpentry and flooring — the small head is easily punched below the surface

PANEL PIN (12 - 50 mm)
A slender version of the lost head nail — widely used for fixing mouldings, attaching plywood and cabinet making

FLOOR BRAD (20 - 150 mm)
Flat-tipped rectangular nail made for fixing floorboards to joists. Strong, unlikely to split wood but now hard to find

HARDBOARD PIN (12 - 38 mm)
Square-sectioned nail used for hardboard, thin plywood etc. Diamond-shaped head easily tapped below the surface

CLOUT NAIL (12 - 50 mm)
Short nail with an extra large head. Used outdoors for fixing fencing etc

TACK (6.5 - 25 mm)
Small, sharply-pointed nail used to attach fabric to wood frames and carpets to floors. 'Improved' tacks are stronger

SPRIG (12 mm)
A headless tack for fixing glass in wooden frames

Nailing is the most popular way of attaching one piece of wood to another — it is quick, inexpensive and all you need is a hammer and some nails. Simple — but not as simple as the novice may believe. There is a technique to learn and there are many types of nail from which you have to choose.

Most nails are made from mild steel wire — round or oval in cross-section. A blunt-pointed nail gives a more secure bond than a sharp one and oval nails should have the wide side running along the grain. Brad nails are rectangular in cross-section — the risk of wood splitting is reduced.

Not all nails are made of mild steel. There are galvanised and non-ferrous ones for use outdoors or in some hardwoods which are stained by mild steel. There are also steel ones for driving into masonry (see page 53).

(1) Nail thinner piece to thicker one. Nail length should be three times the thickness of thinner board

(2) Hold the nail near tip — slope it slightly away from you. Secure it in the wood with rapid light taps. If nail is too small to hold, use cardboard strip. Pull away strip before nailing home

(3) Hold hammer close to end of handle. Swing the hammer from the elbow — keep hammer head in a straight line with the length of the nail. Nailing at an angle increases strength of the bond

(4) Use a nail punch to drive head below surface

SCREWS

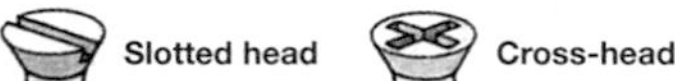

The slotted-head screw is the traditional type, but the blade can easily slip. Cross-head screws need a smaller range of screwdrivers and a more positive grip is obtained

COUNTERSUNK HEAD SCREW (6.5 - 150 mm)
The most popular type — the standard screw when you wish to attach wood to wood. The head can be driven below the surface

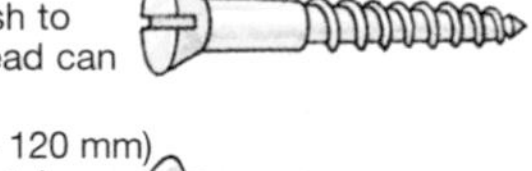

ROUND HEAD SCREW (6.5 - 120 mm)
Mainly used to attach thin metal or plastic to wood — the standard screw for brackets and other items without countersunk holes

RAISED HEAD SCREW (6.5 - 60 mm)
A hybrid of the countersunk and round screw — usually plated and used with decorative fittings which bear countersunk holes

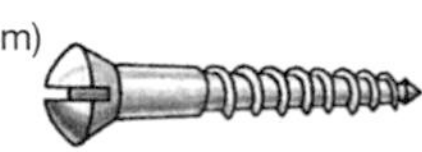

MIRROR SCREW (20 - 60 mm)
A decorative chromium-plated domed cover hides the countersunk slotted head

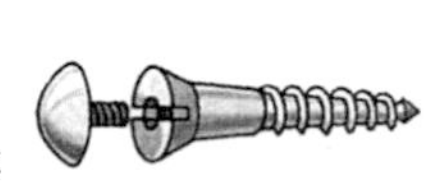

CHIPBOARD SCREW (12 - 60 mm)
A cross-head screw which has a very short shank — designed for chipboard

COACH SCREW (25 - 300 mm)
A heavy-duty screw. The head is turned with a spanner and not a screwdriver

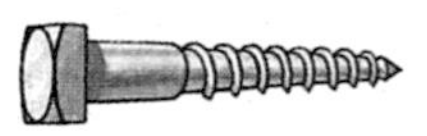

Screwed joints are stronger than nailed ones, and the parts can be readily dismantled by unscrewing. But there is more involved than brute strength — guide holes must be made before you try to screw two pieces of wood together. A bradawl will do for softwood and small screws, but a drill is usually required.

A screw is made up of three parts — the head, the smooth shank and the corkscrew-like thread. The size is the gauge number of the shank — for domestic use the range is from 4 (smallest) to 12 (largest). The length of a screw is the distance from the top of the head to the tip of the thread.

Most screws are made of mild steel, but you will often have to use other types. There are brass, aluminium and stainless steel ones for outdoors — plated finishes are for internal use only.

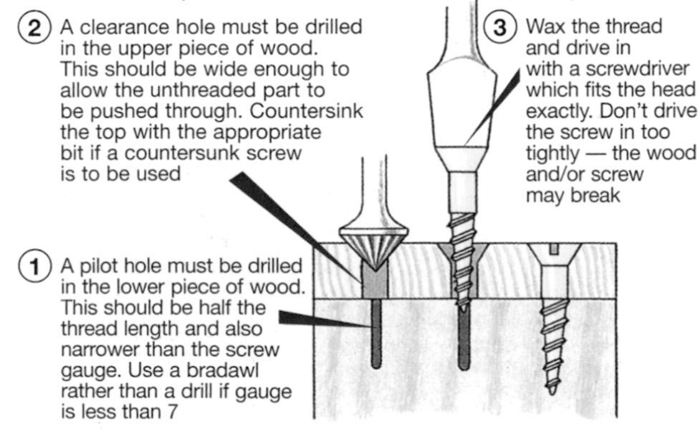

OTHER FIXINGS

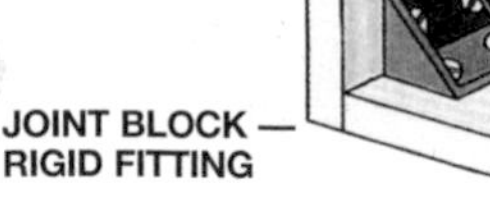

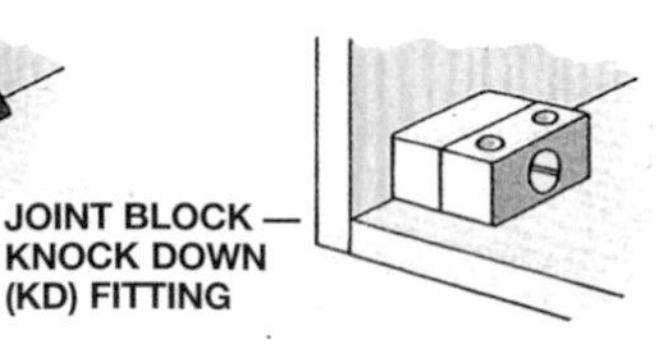

PAINT, STAIN & VARNISH

Paint is cheaper than wallpaper, and painting is by far the most popular DIY job. The task is easier than it used to be — there are now non-drip paints, peel-off strippers and solid emulsions for simple roll-on application. Still, the age-old warnings remain — you must spend time and take care over preparation and you must choose the right paint system. Don't guess which system to use — read this section and check the manufacturer's leaflet. Bare wood may require a knotting-primer-undercoat-topcoat system — a sound wall which is to be painted in a similar shade may require just one coat of vinyl emulsion.

Painting outside woodwork is less popular, but it is more vital than indoor decoration. Exterior paint has an important protective job to do as well as a beautifying one. It is certainly harder than painting indoors — some paint stripping is nearly always necessary and working near the top of a ladder is not for everyone. Repainting the outside woodwork is necessary every 2 - 5 years. Paint is made up of three basic parts. There is the *pigment* which provides colour and covering power. Next, the *binder* holds the pigment together and bonds it to the painted surface. Finally there is the *liquid carrier* which holds the other ingredients — it is nearly always oil or water, but occasionally a volatile solvent is used. The two basic paint surfaces are *matt* (dull) and *gloss* (shiny), but you can buy *semi-gloss* paints with a range of sheens.

THE PAINT TO USE

There is a wide array of types, but for most purposes the choice is quite simple. For wood and metal a gloss oil-based paint is the one to use — it will give the toughest and longest-lasting surface but it will also show up surface imperfections much more than a matt or semi-gloss type. If you are decorating stripped or new wood or an outdoor iron object you must use a primer. Painted surfaces do not need a primer — go straight on to the next step of putting on an undercoat. Finally, apply a topcoat of gloss paint — a non-drip gloss does not need an undercoat. The number of topcoat layers required will depend on see-through — one may do but you might need two.

Indoor walls and ceilings are generally painted with a water-based emulsion paint — a roller is quicker than a brush. No undercoat is used — apply two or three coats of emulsion.

Besides these standard paints there are a much larger number for special situations — see page 91 for details.

EQUIPMENT

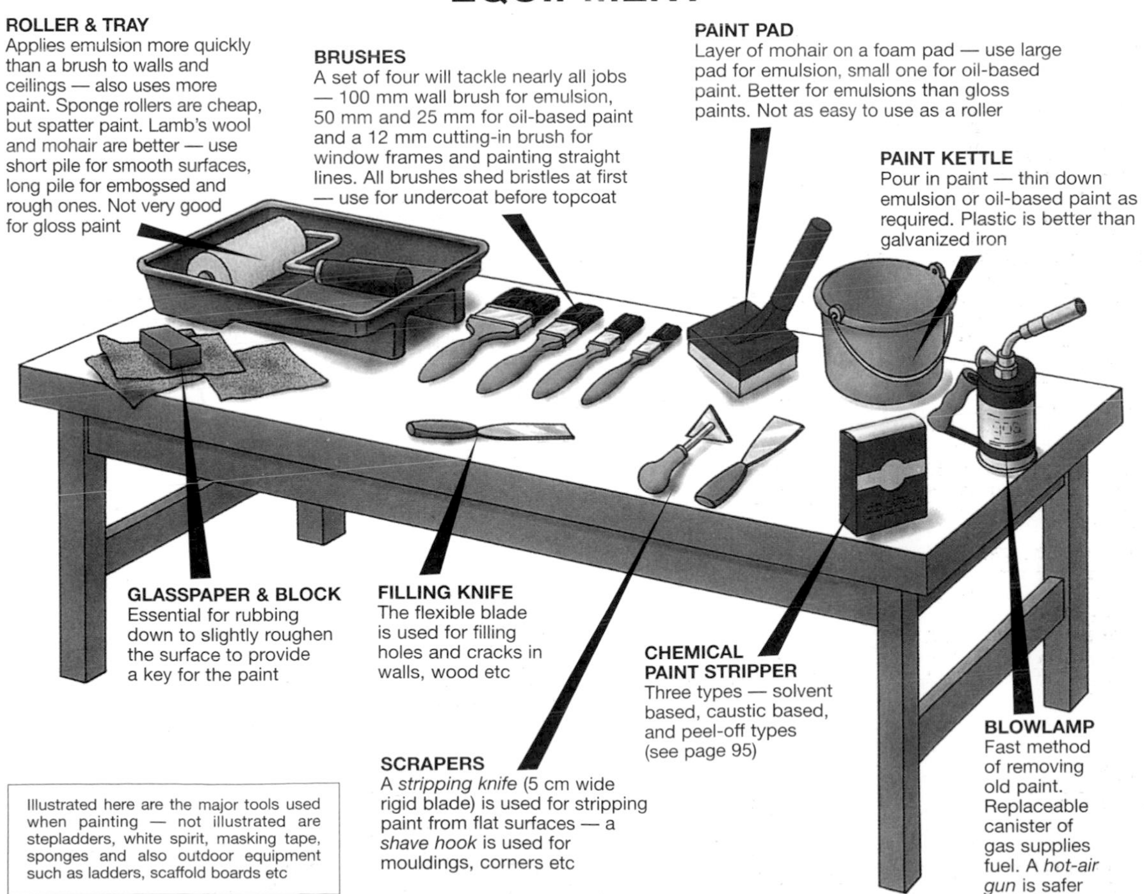

ROLLER & TRAY
Applies emulsion more quickly than a brush to walls and ceilings — also uses more paint. Sponge rollers are cheap, but spatter paint. Lamb's wool and mohair are better — use short pile for smooth surfaces, long pile for embossed and rough ones. Not very good for gloss paint

BRUSHES
A set of four will tackle nearly all jobs — 100 mm wall brush for emulsion, 50 mm and 25 mm for oil-based paint and a 12 mm cutting-in brush for window frames and painting straight lines. All brushes shed bristles at first — use for undercoat before topcoat

PAINT PAD
Layer of mohair on a foam pad — use large pad for emulsion, small one for oil-based paint. Better for emulsions than gloss paints. Not as easy to use as a roller

PAINT KETTLE
Pour in paint — thin down emulsion or oil-based paint as required. Plastic is better than galvanized iron

GLASSPAPER & BLOCK
Essential for rubbing down to slightly roughen the surface to provide a key for the paint

FILLING KNIFE
The flexible blade is used for filling holes and cracks in walls, wood etc

CHEMICAL PAINT STRIPPER
Three types — solvent based, caustic based, and peel-off types (see page 95)

BLOWLAMP
Fast method of removing old paint. Replaceable canister of gas supplies fuel. A *hot-air gun* is safer

SCRAPERS
A *stripping knife* (5 cm wide rigid blade) is used for stripping paint from flat surfaces — a *shave hook* is used for mouldings, corners etc

Illustrated here are the major tools used when painting — not illustrated are stepladders, white spirit, masking tape, sponges and also outdoor equipment such as ladders, scaffold boards etc

TYPES OF PAINT

PRIMER/SEALER

A sealer prevents stains and other undesirable materials bleeding into the paint — a primer bonds tightly on to the surface and prevents the paint soaking into the surface. Most priming products serve both functions, adhering to metal, wood, brick etc and providing a smooth and satisfactory base for the undercoat or topcoat.

A primer is not always necessary. The main use is on bare wood and on metal surfaces, and also on concrete and stone.

UNDERCOAT

The second stage in a full paint system — it is applied immediately after priming to provide a smooth surface for rubbing down to give a key for the topcoat. Colour should be close to but not the same as the topcoat.

An undercoat is not always necessary. If the old paintwork is sound and is quite similar in colour to the new paint, you can rub down and apply topcoat. Non-drip gloss and emulsion paints do not need an undercoat.

TOPCOAT

The final part of the paint system — the layer which shows. It must be decorative but it must also be protective — strong enough to withstand knocks in the hall and condensation in the kitchen and bathroom. Outdoors it must keep out water and frost.

A range of textures can be produced by sponging with a second colour, dabbing with a rag or patterning with an embossed roller. Such techniques are best left in expert hands.

STANDARD PAINTS

TYPE	NOTES
OIL-BASED	
Alkyd resin paint	Matt oil-based paints contain alkyd resins — gloss and semi-gloss ones may be made with alkyd or polyurethane resins. There are differences — alkyd resin paints are glossier and last a little longer outdoors than polyurethane ones. A basic paint for woodwork and metal indoors or out — make sure the undercoat is recommended for use with the chosen topcoat. Coverage is approx 15 sq.m per litre
Polyurethane resin paint	A basic paint for woodwork and metal indoors and out. Gloss is the usual form, drying more quickly than alkyds and providing maximum durability and water resistance. Coverage is approx 15 sq.m per litre
Polyurethane resin paint (non-drip)	Non-drip (also known as thixotropic or jelly) gloss paint is a boon for the inexperienced — it only turns into liquid when brushed out, so there are no irritating drips and runs. No undercoat is needed, but there are a few drawbacks. Coverage is less than with a liquid paint (approx 11 sq.m per litre), brush marks are more noticeable and it is more difficult to use in fine mouldings and around windows
Enamel	The proper meaning is a coloured glaze produced by heat treatment. Nowadays the word is used to describe a high-quality gloss paint in which the pigments are very finely ground. It is used without a primer or undercoat to produce a glass-smooth effect
WATER-BASED	
Vinyl emulsion or Acrylic emulsion	The basic paint for walls and ceilings indoors — often thinned with water before use. Easy to apply, but a gloss surface must be thoroughly rubbed down before applying emulsion. Matt dries quickly and is the preferred type where the surface is imperfect. Semi-gloss (silk or sheen) is recommended for kitchens, bathrooms, and on embossed papers. Gloss types are available, but the lustre is inferior to an oil-based paint. Coverage is approx 11 sq.m per litre
Solid emulsion	Matt and semi-gloss finishes are available in non-drip form, the rectangular tray containing a jelly-like formulation for roller use. Very useful for the beginner — the easiest of all paints to use
Distemper	The forerunner of all water-based paints — pigment, natural oil binder and water. Not very durable — still found on old walls but now replaced by modern emulsion paints
SOLVENT-BASED	
Lacquer	Paint dries as the inflammable solvent evaporates — finish is similar to enamel treatment. Commonest type is touch-up cellulose lacquer in aerosol form for car bodywork repairs

SPECIALIST PAINTS

TYPE	NOTES
Microporous paint	Microporous (or breathing) paint is a water-based product containing acrylic resin — it is applied to bare wood. This type of cover cannot be applied over a surface which is already painted — strip down to bare wood. The great advantage is the ability of moisture trapped in the wood to escape, and the film is flexible. This means that the cracking and bubbling associated with traditional gloss paint when used outdoors can be avoided. Not all experts are convinced that microporous paints are the complete answer, but they are widely used in the U.S and Scandinavia
Masonry paint	Ordinary emulsion paint should never be used outdoors — masonry paint is a special grade which can resist the effect of rain, frost, sunlight, ultra-violet rays etc. It usually contains sand, crushed stone or other aggregate to provide a surface texture and to fill small cracks. It provides a waterproof coating over brick, stone or rendering
Cement paint	A Cinderella product but it can be used on new brick, concrete and cement under damp conditions. It is bought as a powder and mixed with water
Anti-condensation paint	There are several brands which can deal with mild condensation and are recommended for kitchens and bathrooms. They work by insulating the surface — some also contain absorbent particles such as clay or vermiculite
Fire-retardant paint	Old oil-based paint is highly inflammable, thus posing a problem in high fire-risk areas. A number of paints are available which can slow down the combustion rate of the material on which they are painted. Emulsion type is useful for covering expanded polystyrene tiles
Bituminous paint	A black or brown paint which produces a waterproof layer — used for painting gutters, tanks, exposed walls etc
Textured paint	An indoor paint which forms a raised pattern surface after application, either automatically or by means of a roller or scraper
Floor paint	Brick, concrete, tile and stone floors can be painted with a special epoxy resin material. Do not use ordinary paint — it is not sufficiently durable
Rust-resisting paint	Enamel paint which prevents but does not neutralise rust. No primer is necessary — available as a smooth or hammered finish
Heat-resisting paint	A boiler flue pipe is the only area where you are likely to need a paint which will withstand very high temperatures. Black and aluminium finishes are the only types available
Other paints	Anti-mould, blackboard, metallic (including gold, silver and hammered aluminium), anti-burglar for drainpipes and harmless phosphorescent paint for doorbells are manufactured, but some are hard to find in the shops

PRIMERS/ SEALERS

TYPE	NOTES
Knotting	A shellac-based varnish which prevents resin from oozing out of the knots in softwood. If left untreated the resin would bleed into the paint
Multi-purpose primer	Other names include all-purpose and universal primer. This is the product to use on wood, metal and plasters unless there is a special problem. It blocks absorbency and forms a smooth layer which then requires an undercoat or topcoat. Coverage on wood is approx 7.5 sq.m per litre — more on metal, less on plaster
Wood primer	A white paint used as a single coat to prime bare wood and manufactured boards. Use neither the pink grade which contains lead nor red lead primer
Primer/sealer undercoat	A water-based acrylic material which seals, primes and undercoats wood or plaster in one operation. Unfortunately water tends to raise the grain of softwood, so rubbing down before and after priming is necessary
Aluminium wood primer	Use on hardwoods, highly resinous softwoods, badly stained surfaces, creosoted wood or wood stripped with a blowlamp
Zinc chromate primer	Use on metal before painting
Rust-neutralising primer	Use on metal before painting. Added advantage is conversion of any rust which is present into harmless magnetite
Alkali-resisting primer	Use on new cement, concrete, brick or plaster before using an oil-based paint
Stabilising primer	Use on walls with a flaking or powdery surface — remove as much loose material as possible before treatment

PAINTING INDOORS

PREPARATION

Remove small pieces of furniture to another room — move larger items to the centre of the room and cover with a dust sheet. Curtains, pictures etc should be taken away and floor coverings should be covered. Remove handles from the doors.

Now prepare the surfaces in the correct sequence: ceiling → walls → woodwork/metal. Do not skimp this work — beginners are amazed how long a professional takes to prepare a room for painting and how short a time it takes to do the actual painting!

CEILING

The job is simple if the existing emulsion paint is sound — merely wash down with dilute detergent or sugar soap, remove with plenty of clean water and let the surface dry thoroughly. Look for cracks — these must be filled flush with the surface (see page 52). Look for stains — these must be spot-treated with the appropriate primer/sealer (see page 91). Plaster and plasterboard do not present any problems — merely dust down thoroughly before painting and make sure that new plasterwork is left for at least four weeks before painting. Equally easy to prepare is wallpaper which is firmly attached to the ceiling. Never remove sound paper.

Unfortunately ceiling preparation is often more difficult than described above. Loose paper will have to be stripped and all adhesive washed off. Wallpaper which has been painted with distemper will have to be removed and so will flaking emulsion paint.

WALLS

Walls covered with wallpaper, emulsion paint, plasterboard or plaster are quite simple provided that the surface is sound. Follow the rules for ceilings described opposite — wash the walls with a sponge, moving upwards from skirting board to ceiling. Avoid wetting light switches, wall lights etc.

All holes and cracks must be filled, and all loose paint must be removed. The surface should be thoroughly rubbed down with glasspaper after such work. Spot prime all repaired or scraped parts of the wall. Gloss or semi-gloss paint must be rubbed down with glasspaper. Preparation can be a lengthy job. Dampness or mould growth must be dealt with at this stage — see Chapter 7. The walls may have a large number of cracks or holes — hang lining or textured paper after repairing the faults and before painting.

WOODWORK

Never strip away paint unless it is defective or if the layer is preventing doors or windows closing properly. If stripping is necessary, see page 95. If not, wash down thoroughly, rub down with glasspaper and finally remove all dust before painting. Holes and cracks should be repaired with wood filler and the surface spot-treated with primer after rubbing down.

IRON & STEEL

Rub with white spirit. Wash thoroughly and allow to dry. If rust is present remove with a wire brush, rub down and apply a rust-neutralising primer.

TECHNIQUE

Dip the brush into the paint to cover half the bristle length. Wipe off excess paint on the side of the tin — not necessary with non-drip paint. A paint roller is loaded with paint by pushing it back and forth in the front of the tray and then again pushing it back and forth on the sloping back of the tray to spread the paint evenly over the roller. Paint the edges with a brush before you start — then roll slowly and evenly in criss-cross fashion until the whole area is covered. Remember to remove the roller gently from the surface to avoid splashing

Matt emulsion

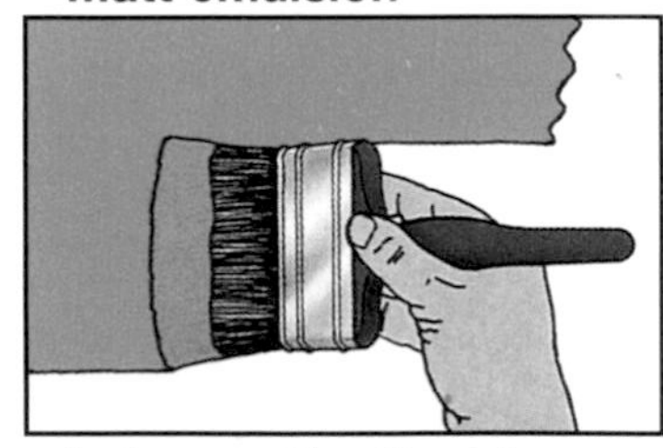

Laying on and brushing out
Apply a horizontal band of paint about 20 cm wide — brush out sideways

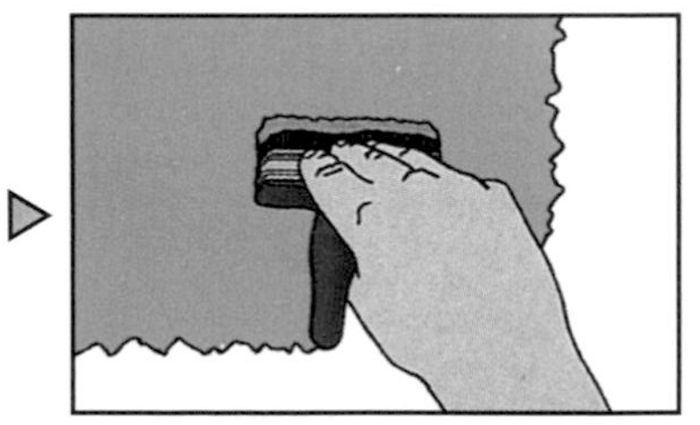

Laying off
Finish off with light upward strokes in a criss-cross pattern

Gloss paint

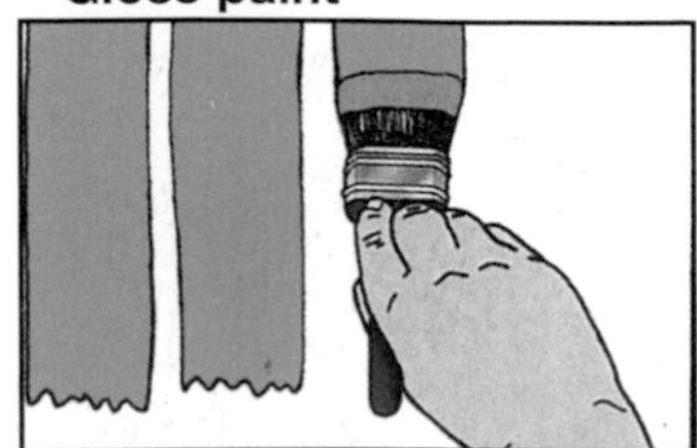

Laying on
Apply the paint from the brush in two or three vertical strokes

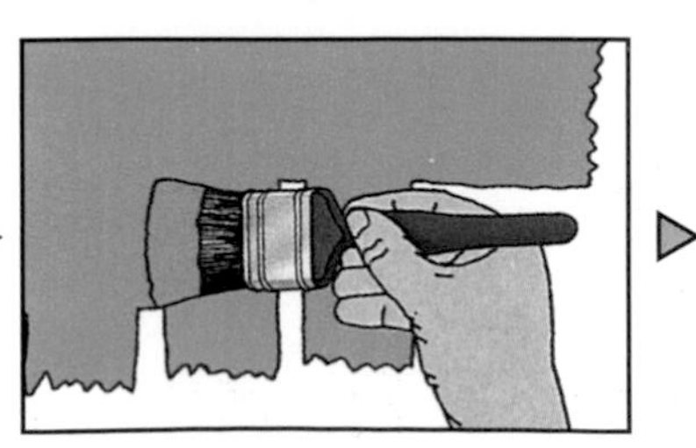

Brushing out
Spread out these vertical strips of paint by brushing sideways. Brush out sparingly with non-drip paint

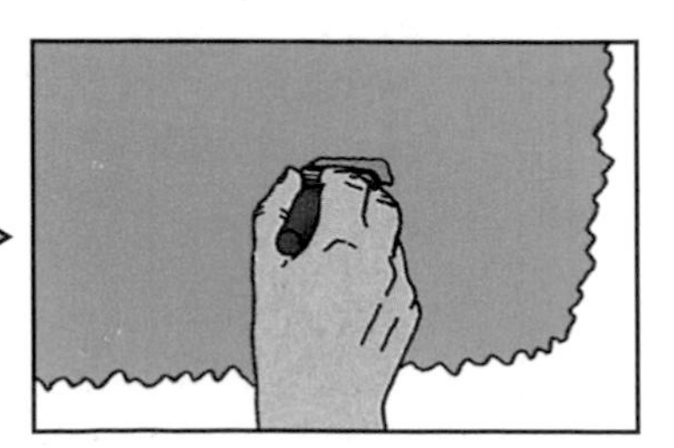

Laying off
Finish off with light upward strokes. Lay off sparingly with non-drip paint

TACKLING THE JOB

The painting sequence

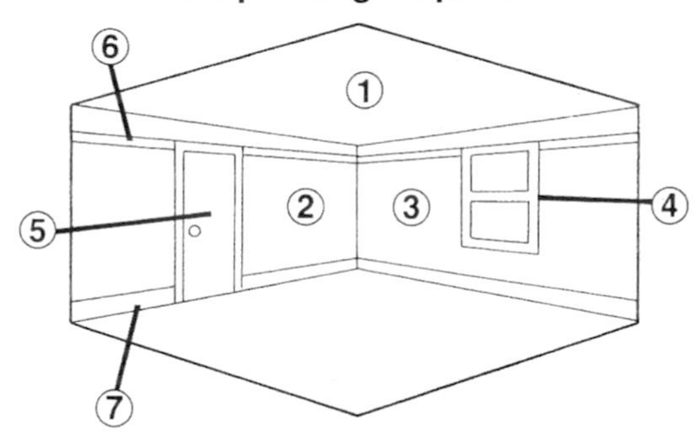

Holding the brush

Hold a small brush like a pencil

Hold a large brush like a table-tennis bat

CEILING

Work in 60 cm bands away from the window wall, these bands stretching from one wall to the opposite one. Work quickly so that the edge of each band is still wet when you start the next one. Start early in the day to ensure that the whole ceiling can be painted in one session.

WALLS

Work in 60 cm bands away from the window — start painting a wall in the top right hand corner (if you are right-handed) and end at the left hand corner above the skirting board. Start early in the day to ensure that the whole wall can be painted in one session. Paint ('cut in') the narrow strip around the door and window frames after the main body of the wall has been painted. Close the windows when working.

WINDOWS

Start early in the day so that the edges will be dry before nightfall, thereby allowing the window to be closed. There is a clear-cut painting sequence. With a sash window the top sash is painted first, then the bottom sash and finally the frame and rebates. See page 95 for the casement window sequence. Scraping paint off the glass with a razor blade is a tedious job — for a neat finish either stick masking tape around the outer edge of the panes before painting, or use a paint shield when painting. Remove masking tape when the paint is dry.

BARE WOOD

New or stripped wood will need priming — softwood knots should be painted with knotting before applying a primer. Universal primer is quite satisfactory indoors, but blowlamp-stripped wood, hardwood, stained wood and preservative-treated wood should be painted with an aluminium primer. Fill in cracks and holes and then rub down. Spot prime the filled areas and then apply an undercoat, where necessary, or one or two applications of topcoat.

DOORS
Flush door

Open the door and insert a small wedge at the base. Make sure the top edge, keyhole etc are clean before you begin. With gloss paint rub down each coat with fine glasspaper until the final topcoat is applied. Do not have too much paint on the brush when painting mouldings — avoid a build-up at the edges. Work quickly so that the painted sections are joined together whilst the paint is still wet. Complete the door in one session.

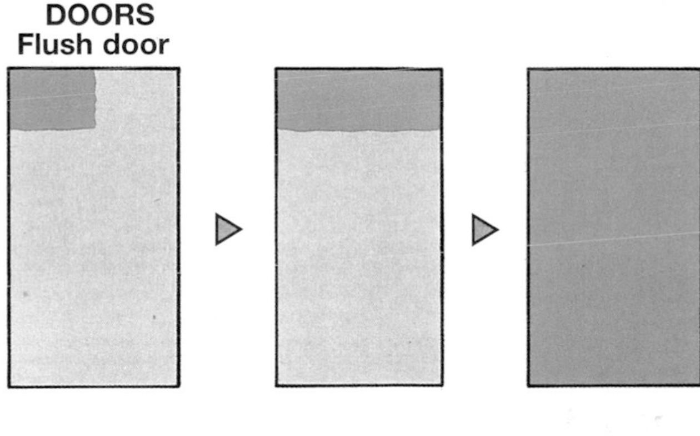

Panel door

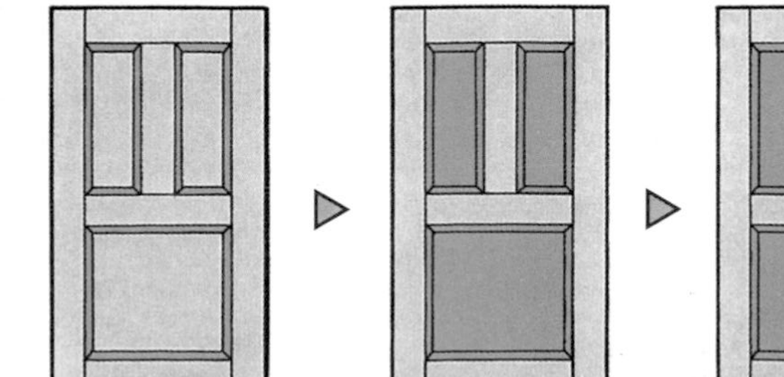

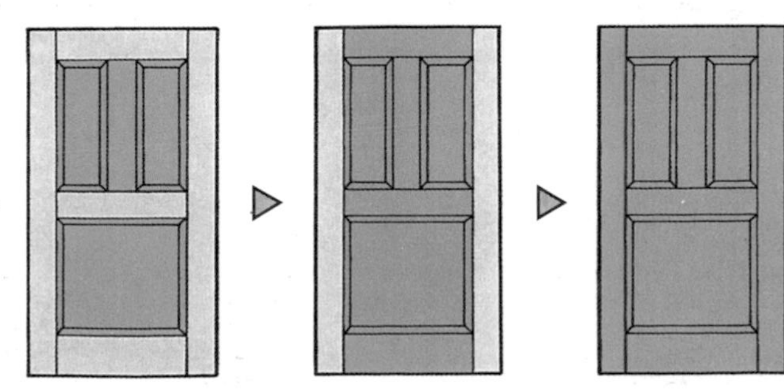

PAINTING OUTDOORS

PREPARATION

The best time to paint the outside of the house is in early autumn — try to choose a settled spell in September or October and make sure that the work is finished before the onset of winter. If autumn is not possible, choose early summer. Successful house painting is threatened by rain (paint will peel and later blister), hot sun (paint will quickly blister if the wood is damp) and frost (gloss paint will dry with a dull finish and masonry paint will be damaged).

Before you can begin to prepare for painting it is essential to carry out any necessary repairs. Broken windows must be reglazed, rotten wood replaced or treated, brickwork repointed where necessary, cracked putty renewed, dampness eradicated and faulty gutters and downpipes repaired or replaced. Ladders will be needed, but a scaffolding tower is a much better way of reaching the upper part of the house. Do take care — read pages 74 and 77 and make sure that children and pets are kept away from under the ladder. Tie a long board to the lower rungs if the ladder has to be kept in position overnight.

The basic principle is to prepare and then to paint from the top of the house down to ground level so that neither dislodged dirt nor paint will fall on to newly-painted work. There are two basic ways of tackling exterior painting — some experts recommend that you prepare and then paint each section in turn, but it is generally felt that it is better to do all the preparation first and then get on with the painting. The choice is up to you, but whichever way you decide the preparation and painting sequence shown below should be followed. Before you begin, cover plants, paths etc with polythene sheeting.

The preparation and painting sequence

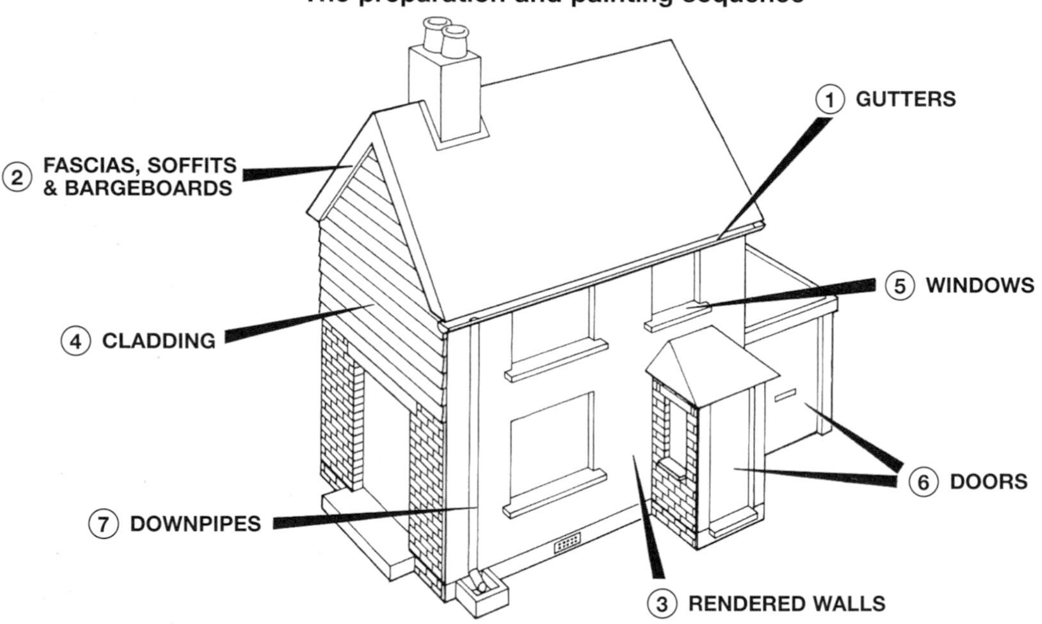

① **GUTTERS**	Clear away all rubbish. Wire brush metal guttering to remove loose rust — paint with a rust-neutralising primer.
② **FASCIAS, SOFFITS & BARGEBOARDS**	Rub down with glasspaper if the paint is sound. All flaking paint must be removed and the bare patches thoroughly rubbed down. Apply a primer after dusting. Work along the grain — double-coat the end grain. If flaking is severe, you will have to strip off all the paint — see page 95.
③ **RENDERED WALLS**	Brush down the surface, working from the eaves to ground level. Repair cracks and replace loose rendering — see page 79.
④ **CLADDING**	Rub down with glasspaper after filling cracks and holes. Replace or treat rotten wood — see page 107.
⑤ **WINDOWS**	Wire brush metal windows — rub down wooden window frames with glasspaper. You must deal with flaking paint — see step ② above.
⑥ **DOORS**	Treat as step ②. Hardwood doors are better stained and varnished than painted — see page 97.
⑦ **DOWNPIPES**	Treat as step ①.

TACKLING THE JOB

Stripping paint

The quick and cheap way is to use a **blowlamp**. Have a bucket of water handy and place a tray below the area to be treated. Hold the nozzle about 15 cm away from the surface and keep the flame moving by swinging the nozzle back and forth. When the paint has started to melt, scrape off with a stripping knife and shave hook. Always work from behind the blowlamp and scrape in the direction of the grain. There can be problems — lead paint should not be stripped in this way, wood can be charred if the flame is not kept moving and glass can crack when window frames are treated. A blowlamp should be reserved for flat areas without mouldings and where there is no danger of fire.

A **hot-air gun** is safer — it works like a hair dryer. It is just as speedy as a blowlamp and by using directional nozzles you can remove paint from window frames. It is heavy to hold and you do need an electric cable, but it is still the best choice if you have to strip a large area.

A **chemical stripper** is expensive compared to the other methods, but is the one to choose for a small area or for intricate mouldings. There are three types — solvent strippers and caustic ones, and there is also the peel-off type which allows you to remove all the paint by just peeling off the strip about an hour after treatment. Chemical strippers call for precautions — read the label carefully.

Painting

Make sure that the paint is recommended for exterior use. When working from a ladder use a paint kettle -— it should be less than half full and suspended from a rung by means of a butcher's hook. Wait until the dew has gone before you start painting.

① GUTTERS

Treat the inside with two coats of bituminous paint or with gloss paint. The outside of the gutter should be painted with undercoat and a gloss topcoat. Plastic gutters can be painted if first thoroughly cleaned with a detergent solution.

② FASCIAS, SOFFITS & BARGEBOARDS

Start at the ridge and work downwards to the fascia boards (see page 75 for the meaning of the words). After priming all bare patches and replacing or treating rotten wood all of this exposed roof timber should be painted with undercoat and then one or two topcoats of gloss paint.

③ RENDERED WALLS

Start from the top right hand corner — use cement paint, exterior-grade emulsion or masonry paint. A 100 mm brush is the one to use, although you will find it quicker to use a roller than a brush. A roller with an extension pole will allow you to get to the higher reaches without having to take your ladder or scaffold there. Speed is important — you should paint the whole wall in a single session.

④ CLADDING

If previously painted, use undercoat and one or two coats of gloss paint. If stained use a reliable preservative.

⑤ WINDOWS

See step ⑥ for general details. Windows should be painted in a set sequence, as shown below for casement windows and as described on page 93 for sash windows.

As with window interiors you should either stick masking tape around the outer edge of each pane before painting or use a paint shield when painting. The paint should go a few millimetres over the putty to prevent rainwater seeping in between the glass and putty.

⑥ DOORS

The standard system for all wooden surfaces in exposed situations is undercoat plus two coats of gloss paint. Rub down between each coat. Bare wood will need priming and perhaps knotting before using the standard system. For new doors you can use one of the new one-coat microporous paints which require neither primer nor undercoat. As an alternative you should always consider staining and varnishing for hardwood doors.

⑦ DOWNPIPES

Make sure that the surface is properly primed. Apply undercoat and gloss topcoats — hold a piece of cardboard behind the pipe to keep paint off the bricks. If you are changing from a bituminous paint to a standard oil-based one you will need to use an aluminium primer. Start at the top and work to ground level, applying the same undercoat and topcoat as in step ①.

HOW TO AVOID & DEAL WITH PAINT PROBLEMS

BEFORE YOU START PAINTING

If you are new to painting read this chapter and the instructions which come with the paint. Stir paint with a broad piece of board or plastic — do not use a narrow cane or stick. Use a circular motion, moving the stirrer up and down. Do not stir non-drip.

Paint which has been stored for some time may pose a problem. A layer of water on top of emulsion paint should be poured away — a skin-like layer on top of an oil-based paint should be cut away and the contents strained through the fabric from a pair of old nylon tights.

Many paints can be thinned before use, but you must carefully follow the instructions on the can.

BITTINESS

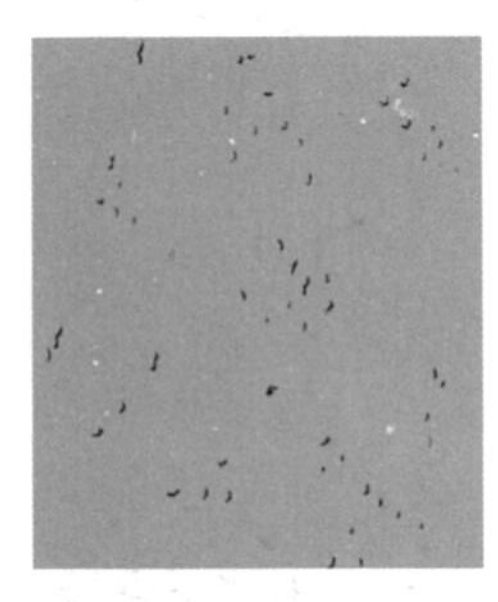

The cause of small pimples on the surface is dust. This dust may have come from the brush if not all of the surface was cleaned before you started or from the air when painting outdoors in an urban area. Another possibility is inadequate wiping after rubbing down the surface with glasspaper.

If bittiness is present, rub down with fine grade wet-and-dry glasspaper when the paint is dry. Wipe away all traces of dust and apply a fresh coat of paint.

SAGS & RUNS

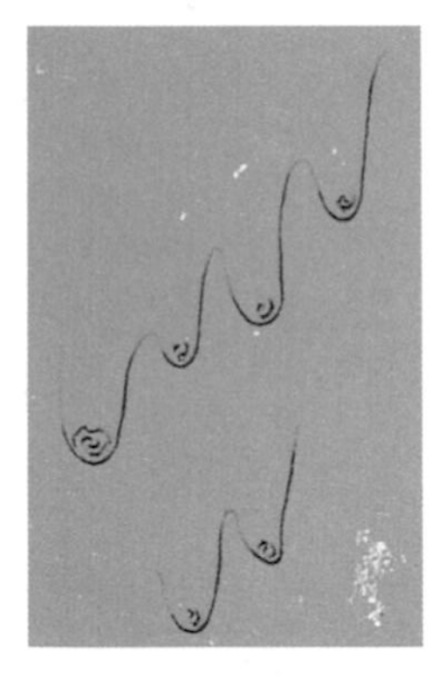

The tell-tale sign of a beginner. These tear-like streaks can be caused in several ways, but the usual reasons are loading the brush with too much paint and/or not spreading it out sufficiently. Sags and runs occur most frequently with gloss paint — with this type of covering you must lay on, brush out and lay off properly as described on page 92.

If the paint is still wet you may be able to brush out and lay off to remove the trouble. This is not usually practical — let the paint dry for several days and then carry out the treatment described for bittiness.

BRUSHMARKS

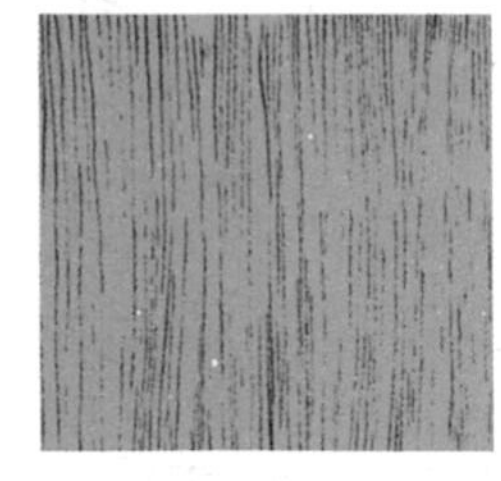

Another common problem with several possible causes. The paint should form a smooth and even layer after laying off — the presence of clearly defined streaks when the paint is dry usually indicates that the bristles were sub-standard or the paint was too thick. Other possible causes are insufficient rubbing down of a gloss surface before painting and overloading the brush.

SLOW DRYING

It is quite normal for paint to take a long time to dry in cold weather — have patience. Paint failing to dry at normal temperature is a serious problem — it usually indicates that the surface was either wet or greasy at the time of painting. You will have to strip off the paint, prepare the surface properly and then repaint.

BLISTERS

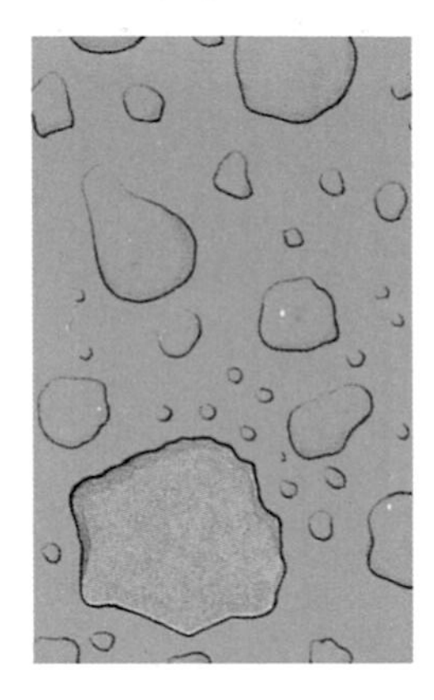

The cause of bubbles is a build-up of water vapour under the airtight and watertight skin formed by the paint. The water vapour arises from damp which was already present before painting or was able to creep into the wood after painting. In cold weather the dampness does not deform the paint — in hot, sunny weather the dampness vapourises and the blisters appear.

Isolated blisters can be cut out and the space filled with a fine surface filler. The surface should be rubbed down and repainted. If there are a large number of blisters, the only answer is to strip off the paint and begin again.

LACK OF GLOSS

It is often difficult to pin-point the cause. It will occur if the work was done in frosty weather or if the film was affected by water — it also happens when too much thinner is added to the paint. A common cause is poor priming or leaving insufficient time between coats.

GRINNING

A technical term for see-through and the cause is usually obvious — too much thinning, too little stirring, overbrushing or the wrong undercoat. Rub down and apply another topcoat.

WRINKLES

This crinkled effect is associated with gloss paint applied too thickly or to a badly prepared surface. Dampness or soft paint below the topcoat can also cause wrinkling. Strip off and repaint.

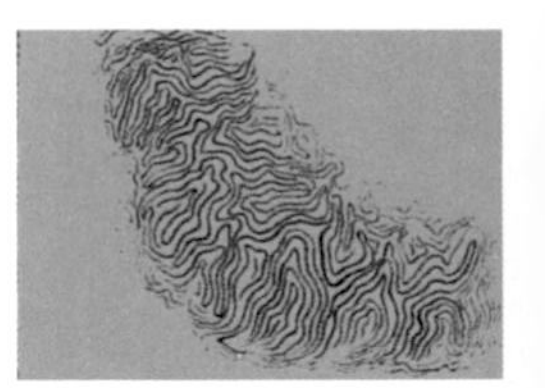

FLAKING

The peeling or lifting of new paint shows that the surface was badly prepared. Dust is the usual cause with a water-based paint — dampness or a wet undercoat is the usual culprit with an oil-based paint.

Flaking of old paint has a different cause. It may indicate rot or simply a break down of the film due to damp, frost, hot sun etc. Strip off, prepare thoroughly and repaint as soon as possible.

AFTER YOU FINISH PAINTING

If you have to stop painting for a short time, merely wrap the brush in aluminium foil. Overnight the brush should be immersed in water or brush cleaner as appropriate. Never stand it in a jam-jar. Drill a hole in the handle of the brush, insert a piece of wire and suspend in the liquid so that the bristles do not touch the bottom of the container.

When the painting job is finished, scrape off excess paint from the brush by pulling a knife away from the handle to the tips of the bristles. Wipe off paint on newspaper, wash out paint with cleaner recommended on the tin and then wash in warm water before hanging up to dry.

WOOD FINISHING

The purpose of **painting** is to provide an attractive and protective surface which obliterates the texture of the wood. The purpose of **wood finishing** is to provide an attractive and protective surface which enhances the natural beauty of wood.

All cracks and holes must be filled with a proprietary stopper. Keep this work to a minimum — stopping can be obtained in various wood shades but staining can result in the highlighting of these repaired areas. If the wood has an open grain the pores should be filled with a grain filler if you are aiming for a luxury finish. The final step is to sand the wood until it is perfectly smooth. Wipe it down until it is completely free from dust.

BLEACHES

Bleaches make the wood lighter. They are often used when the bare wood has been discoloured over part or all the surface. Buy a two-part bleach system and follow the instructions exactly.

STAINS

Wood stains (wood dyes) colour the surface and often enhance the grain. They usually approximate the shades of hardwoods, and a wide range of wood types is available. Purists claim that new wood should not be stained prior to polishing or varnishing, but for most people the somewhat insipid appearance of whitewood needs to be improved by the richness of a stain. For the adventurous there are stains in bright colours rather than hardwood shades — red, blue, green, yellow etc. They may look horrible or stunning, depending on the object which has been stained and the surroundings.

There are oil-, spirit- and water-based stains. Both the oil- and spirit-based ones can raise the grain — oil-based stains are the most popular. Buy the shade which is closest to the colour you want and buy the varnish at the same time — it should be produced by the stain manufacturer to ensure that the two will be compatible. Once the wood has been properly prepared you are ready to start work. Apply a dab of stain to an inconspicuous part or an unwanted piece of the wood to see if the colour is right.

Pour some stain into a saucer. Apply with a piece of soft, clean and lint-free cloth. Try not to put on too much liquid. If the wood is too pale when dry, apply a second coat. If it is too dark, rub down with fine glasspaper.

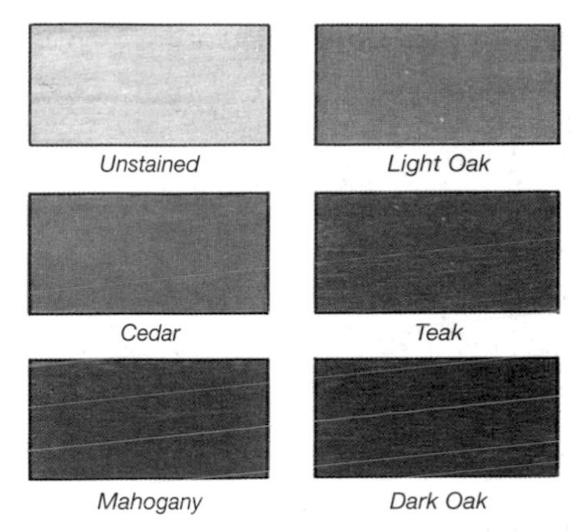

Unstained *Light Oak*
Cedar *Teak*
Mahogany *Dark Oak*

OIL FINISH

The traditional finish for hardwood doors, window frames etc is a mixture of raw and boiled linseed oil with a little turpentine. There are several problems — the surface remains slightly gummy, attracts dust and darkens with age. It is much better these days to use teak oil or Danish oil which gives a longer-lasting finish and a satiny sheen.

WAX FINISH

A mixture of beeswax and turpentine. Many coats are needed and wax finishing is not often recommended. The surface attracts dust and is neither heat-resistant nor durable.

SHELLAC VARNISH

The traditional varnish which has been used on furniture for ages. It is thinned with methylated spirits and applied quickly over the surface. Each coat is lightly rubbed down with fine steel wool before the next one is applied, and the process is repeated until a smooth, glassy surface is obtained. French polishing is a skilled refinement of this simple technique and several brands of French polish are available. All shellac varnishes suffer from the drawback that the attractive surface does not stand up to heat, water stains, spilt alcoholic drinks nor hard wear.

POLYURETHANE VARNISH

This is the type of finish you are most likely to find in your DIY shop. There are interior and exterior grades and gloss, semi-gloss and matt types. The finish is ideal indoors — hard-wearing, heat-resistant, water-repellent and so on. It is also recommended for outdoor use, but it is not particularly hard-wearing when subjected to bright sunlight.

Apply with a soft brush — it is vital that the first coat should be diluted with 10 per cent white spirit for softwoods (25 per cent for hardwoods). This coat sinks into the wood and should be left to dry for at least 12 hours in a dust-free atmosphere. Rub down with fine steel wool, remove the dust with a rag damped with white spirit and apply a second coat. About four coats are required to produce a satisfactory finish. Indoors the effect may seem rather artificial. A more natural appearance can be obtained by using a matt grade which is then wax polished.

TWO PART PLASTIC RESIN

Plastic resin (also called cold cure lacquer) is produced by mixing a resin with a hardener. The clear varnish forms an extremely hard and chip-resistant surface for table tops.

COLOURED VARNISH

The wood is stained and finished in one operation which saves time. There are gloss, semi-gloss and matt types. But you can't apply many coats — the surface gets darker with each additional coat. If the surface is chipped unstained bare wood is revealed.

MICROPOROUS STAIN

A stain for outdoor use with the same advantages as microporous paint (see page 91).

FABRICS

ACETATE Silky fibre made from cellulose. Neither creases nor shrinks, but is not hard-wearing. Usually used in blends. Typical trade names: Dicel, Lansil.

ACRYLIC Woolly fibre made from an oil by-product. Crease-resistant and hard-wearing — used alone or in blends to add toughness to natural fibres. Typical trade names: Dralon, Acrilan, Orlon.

ALPACA Fine hair from S. American animal — Llama is shorter and coarser. Blended with wool or cotton.

ANGORA Soft and silky hair from Angora rabbit. Blended with wool or artificial fibre for knitwear.

ASTRAKHAN Fabric imitation of the curly fur of Astrakhan lamb.

BATIK Fabric bearing a pattern produced by dyeing, the areas not to be coloured being protected by a wax coating.

BATISTE Fine and smooth fabric made occasionally from wool but more usually cotton. Similar in texture to cambric.

BOUCLE Fabric made from 3-stranded looped wool or artificial fibre — used for ladies' suiting.

BROCADE Fabric with a raised pattern which is woven into the cloth.

BRODERIE ANGLAISE Fabric, usually cotton, with a cut-out embroidered design which is nowadays machine-made.

BRUSHED NYLON Nylon fabric brushed to raise a fine nap of fibres — cloth has a warmer and softer feel than ordinary nylon.

BUCKRAM Stiffening fabric made of cotton or jute treated with gum.

CALICO Cotton fabric with a firm, close weave and a dull finish. It may be bleached or unbleached.

CAMBRIC Fine and smooth fabric made from linen or cotton. Similar in texture to batiste but the surface is shiny.

CAMELHAIR Woven wool imitation of fabric made from camel hair.

CANDLEWICK Cotton or artificial fibre fabric patterned with tufts of yarn. Used for bath mats and bedspreads.

CANVAS Strong fabric woven from coarse yarn — hemp, linen, cotton or artificial fibre. Unblended with a tight weave — more open weave used for embroidery canvas.

CASHMERE Soft and silky hair from Cashmere goat. Blended with wool for suiting and knitwear.

CELLULAR Cotton, wool or blended fabric with a honeycomb weave.

CHEESECLOTH Cotton or blended fabric with an open gauze-like weave.

CHENILLE Velvet-like fabric made of silk, cotton, wool or artificial fibre.

CHIFFON Semi-transparent fabric with a slightly crinkled surface. Very fine — made from silk, viscose or cotton.

CHINTZ Cotton woven fabric, always glazed on the surface and nearly always with a design of flowers and/or birds.

CLYDELLA Trade name for a popular blend of wool and cotton.

CORDUROY Ribbed woven fabric made from cotton or cotton blends. Hard-wearing — used for suiting.

COTTON Natural fibre from the seed pod of the cotton plant. Cotton fabric is absorbent, strong and dyes well, but creases easily if it is not resin-treated.

CREPE Crinkled fabric — various processes used on cotton, wool, silk, polyester etc.

CREPE DE CHINE Highly crinkled, glossy fabric made from silk originally but nowadays from artificial fibre.

DAMASK Jacquard-woven fabric with intricate designs and plain colours. Glossy — used for table linen and soft furnishings.

DENIM Twill-woven cotton fabric with a coloured warp and grey weft. Hard-wearing.

DRILL Coarse cotton fabric with a twill weave — used for uniforms, sails etc.

DUCK Heavy type of canvas.

FELT Fabric made of fibres (usually wool) bonded together by shrinking and rolling so that they interlock.

FLANNEL Woven woollen or woollen blend fabric which is both lightweight and soft.

FLANNELETTE Imitation flannel made from cotton or artificial fibre. Surface is brushed to produce downy finish.

FUR FABRIC Fabric made from cotton or artificial fibre to look like animal fur.

GABARDINE Hard-wearing, twill-woven wool, cotton or artificial fibre — recognised by its fine diagonal ribbing.

GEORGETTE Semi-transparent crepe woven from fine yarn — silk or artificial fibre.

GINGHAM Cotton or cotton blend fabric with a distinct checked or striped pattern.

GROSGRAIN Silk (nowadays artificial fibre) fabric with a distinctly ribbed surface.

HESSIAN Strong and coarse fabric woven from hemp and jute. Used for upholstery, linings etc.

HOPSACK Loosely-woven fabric made from cotton, linen or artificial fibre. Used for suiting.

JACQUARD WEAVE Weaving process which produces intricate patterns on looms controlled by cards bearing a series of holes — an example of early automation.

JERSEY Knitted fabric made from cotton, wool, silk or artificial fibre.

LACE An intricately patterned fabric with an open weave. Once hand-made from cotton — now produced by machine from cotton or artificial fibre.

LAWN Fine and lightweight woven fabric made from cotton or cotton blend.

LINEN Natural fibre from the stems of the flax plant. Linen fabric is absorbent, very strong and lustrous but creases and shrinks unless treated. Nowadays used in blends.

LYCRA Synthetic rubber material — usually blended with other fabrics.

MERCERISED COTTON Cotton fabric given added strength and lustrous finish by treatment of the yarn.

METALLIC FABRIC Shiny fabric produced from plastic-coated aluminium 'yarn'. Typical trade names: Lame, Lurex.

MODACRYLIC Type of acrylic which is flame-resistant. Typical trade names: Teklan, Dynel.

MODAL Viscose fabric which resembles cotton — absorbent and strong. Trade name: Vincel.

MOHAIR Fabric made from angora — often used as a blend with wool for knitwear and suiting.

MOIRE Fabric with watermarked swirling pattern and a ribbed weave — sometimes called watered silk.

MOQUETTE Carpet-like upholstery material with cut or uncut pile, made from wool, cotton or artificial fibre.

MUSLIN Plainwoven cotton with a somewhat loose weave.

NEEDLECORD Finely-ribbed corduroy.

NET A collective term for fabric loosely woven as a mesh.

NYLON Artificial fibre made from an oil by-product, famed for its strength, hard-wearing qualities and crease-resistance, but notorious for its non-absorbency. Typical trade names: Bri-nylon, Enkalon, Antron.

OILSKIN Fabric of natural or artificial fibre coated to make it waterproof.

ORGANDIE Delicate, semi-transparent fabric made from cotton or artificial fibre — silk version known as organza.

PERCALE Combed cotton or cotton-blend fabric — closely woven like cambric.

PIQUE Stiff fabric, usually made from cotton, embossed with a ribbed or other patterned finish.

PLAIN WEAVE Weaving process without any frills. Warp and weft cross over each other in an over-under-over-under pattern.

PLISSE Puckered cotton fabric.

PLUSH Velvet-like material with a rather open weave.

POLYESTER Artificial fibre made from an oil by-product, widely used in cotton blends to improve crease-resistance and wear-resistance. Strong like nylon, but it does not stretch. Shrink-proof and moth-proof but it is non-absorbent. Typical trade names: Crimplene, Terylene, Dacron.

POLYVINYL CHLORIDE Plastic coating (PVC) applied to fabric to make it waterproof.

POPLIN Closely-woven cotton or cotton blend fabric. Strong with fine ribbing.

RAYON Artificial fibre made from cellulose. Two types — acetate and viscose.

SAILCLOTH Stiff cotton canvas, strong and ribbed.

SATEEN Type of satin made from cotton.

SATIN Lustrous fabric with a smooth surface made from silk or artificial fibre blends.

SATIN WEAVE Weaving process where warp thread goes over-over-over-over-under the weft threads (compare plain weave).

SEERSUCKER Cotton fabric with crinkled stripes or checks.

SERGE Heavyweight wool or wool blend fabric, twill-woven and a popular material for uniforms.

SHANTUNG Silk or silk-like fabric with an uneven surface.

SHEER A collective term for thin, semi-transparent fabrics.

SILK Natural fibre from the cocoon of the silkworm. Strong, luxurious, warm, elastic but damaged by several things including sunlight and perspiration.

TAFFETA Shiny, closely-woven fabric — once made from silk but nowadays from artificial fibre.

TRIACETATE Artificial fibre made from cellulose and cotton. Somewhat similar to acetate but it is more resistant to wear, dirt and heat. Used in blends for weaving and knitting. Typical trade names: Tricel, Tricelon.

TULLE Net made from silk or artificial fibre — used for trimmings.

TWEED Coarsely-woven woollen fabric, often patterned with some form of check.

TWILL WEAVE Weaving process designed to produce diagonal ribbing. Herringbone is a variety of twill weave.

VELOUR Woven wool or cotton fabric with a velvety pile.

VELVET Fabric with a dense, smooth pile on one side. Made from many yarns — cotton, silk and a variety of artificial fibres.

VELVETEEN Velvet-like fabric made from cotton or cotton blend. The pile is short.

VISCOSE Silky fibre made from cellulose — sometimes called viscose rayon or rayon. Soft and absorbent but not hard-wearing and can be marked by water. Usually used in blends. Typical trade names: Darelle, Evlan.

VIYELLA Trade name for a popular twill-woven wool and cotton blend.

VOILE Soft, semi-transparent, plain-woven fabric.

WHIPCORD Cotton or woollen twill-woven fabric with distinct ribbing.

WINCEYETTE Soft, twill-woven fabric made from brushed cotton or cotton blend.

WOOL Natural fibre from the fleece of sheep. Warm, elastic, crease-resistant, absorbent etc but shrinkage and matting after washing can be a problem. Nowadays often used in blends.

WORSTED Fabric woven from wool yarn which has been combed to produce a fine and smooth surface.

PLASTIC SHEETING

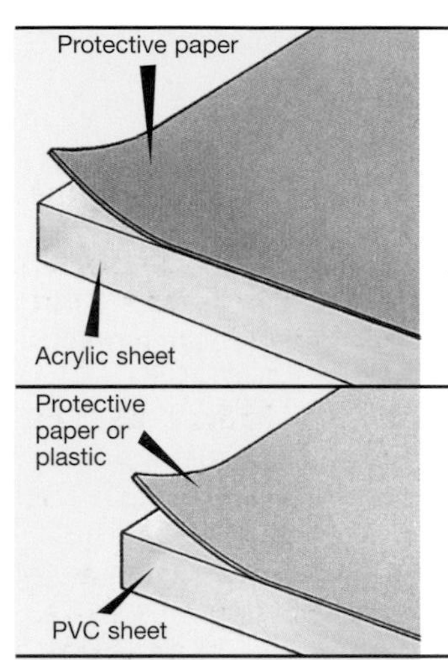

RIGID ACRYLIC

Rigid and almost unbreakable, clear or milky, flat or corrugated, acrylic sheet is the most popular glass substitute. When coloured it is also a decorative material, as illuminated shop signs clearly demonstrate. Mark cutting lines and drilling holes on the protective paper cover before you begin to shape acrylic sheet — use a tenon saw for cutting and a hand drill (not a power one) for making holes. Smooth sawn edges by rubbing with glasspaper and then remove paper cover.

Acrylic sheet can be bent or shaped by covering in metal foil and leaving exposed the area to be softened. The sheet is then held near a radiant heater until the area to be worked is rubbery — shape as desired and keep rigid until cool.

RIGID PVC & OTHER PLASTICS

Rigid PVC (vinyl) sheet is a glass substitute which is designed for industrial and amateur use. It is employed as an alternative for the more popular acrylic sheet where very high heat resistance is required — for example light diffusers on fluorescent tubes. Corrugated PVC is used for roof lights where its fire resistance and high impact strength are important advantages. Polycarbonate is a lightweight, tough and transparent sheet.

Decorative layer of coloured or printed paper impregnated with melamine resin

Backing layer of 5-6 sheets of kraft paper impregnated with phenolic resin

PLASTIC LAMINATE

The introduction of plastic laminates has proved a great boon to both the furniture maker and the DIY enthusiast. Carcasses of chipboard, MDF or plywood are covered with it to provide most of the worktops and some of our kitchen and bathroom furniture. Each sheet is made up of several layers of resin-impregnated paper which are bonded together under heat and pressure to form a laminate 0.8 - 1.5 mm thick. Sheet width is generally 120 cm and it is cheaper to buy off-cuts than whole boards. The range of grades, colours and textures is enormous.

There are two ways to cut the sheet. You can either use a fine-toothed saw or you can cut it in the same way as glass — see page 65. Cut the sheet slightly larger than the space to be covered. Use a contact adhesive which allows some adjustment after the two surfaces are brought together. Spread the adhesive on the back of the laminate and on top of the surface to be covered, and leave for about 15 minutes. Now bring them together, press firmly everywhere and leave to dry. Finally, remove the excess laminate from the edges with a plane or file.

Decorative layer of coloured or printed paper impregnated with melamine resin

Chipboard

MELAMINE-FACED CHIPBOARD

Melamine-faced chipboard is widely used to produce inexpensive furniture — it is cheaper than either wood covered with plastic laminate or veneer. The decorative layer is bonded under heat and pressure to chipboard — the popular finishes are white and woodgrain.

Shelves and simple pieces of furniture can be constructed using this material. Melamine-faced chipboard is easily cut with a fine-toothed tenon saw and pieces are put together with KD fittings and chipboard screws (page 88). There is a range of board sizes — 90 - 240 cm long, 15 - 90 cm wide and 15 mm thick. The boards are finished on both sides and edging strip is available which merely requires smoothing down with a warm iron. Melamine-faced chipboard is not as hard-wearing as plastic laminate.

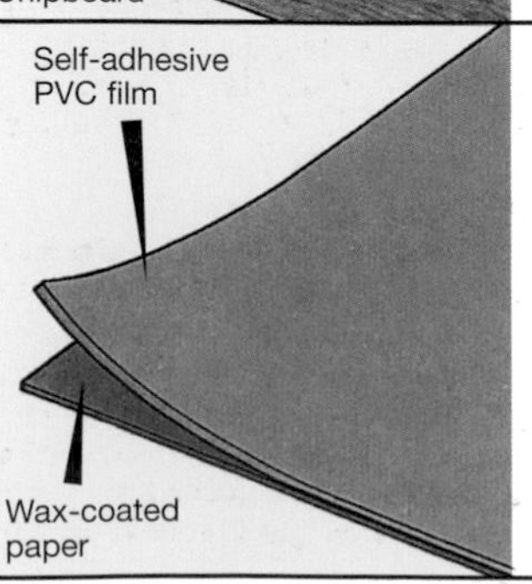

FLEXIBLE PLASTIC

The reasons for the popularity of stick-on plastic sheeting are the simplicity of application and the enormous range of colours, patterns, surface textures etc. The flexible sheeting is bought in 45 cm wide rolls and the decorative self-adhesive film is peeled away from the waxed paper backing after it has been cut to size. Almost any surface can be covered, but you must be careful to avoid creases and bubbles when pressing down the film. The surface is washable and stain-resistant, but it will not stand very high temperatures nor resist scratching by sharp objects. When covering a shelf, cupboard door etc make sure that there is at least a 3 cm overlap on the reverse side.

Plain colours, simple patterns and wood look-alikes are the favourite flexible plastics, and either a matt or shiny smooth surface is generally chosen.

CHAPTER 7

PROBLEMS

No matter how small your house may be or how recently it was built, there will be problems from time to time. It is not just a matter of the structure developing faults with age. Tower blocks are demolished with dwellings built centuries ago standing nearby — in the old days wood was thoroughly seasoned and basic techniques have stood the test of time. However, many materials have improved dramatically and the owner of a new house has the safeguard of the National House Building Council's 10 year guarantee against major defects. Don't expect the builder to repair every fault which may develop during that period — your Agreement will show that his responsibilities are quite specific.

Problems are not always a matter of structural failure — they are more likely to be due to one of the services or a piece of equipment going wrong. Then there are all the living problems, ranging in size from tiny mites and fleas to noisy neighbours. So there will be problems, both large and small, and there are two golden rules to follow —

Prevent as many problems as you can before they start.

Tackle problems which occur as quickly as you can.

So many troubles can be prevented with a little forethought and attention — frozen pipes, excess heat loss, foundations damaged by tree roots, house fires due to faulty electrical wiring etc. Some problems can't be prevented, but tackling the trouble promptly can stop it from becoming a major one. Rot in a door or window frame should be tackled immediately — so should unsteady furniture, loose roof tiles, pest infestations and so on. Clearly the two golden rules given above are vital, and to follow them there are several steps you must take. A checklist is set out below.

HOW TO AVOID & DEAL WITH PROBLEMS

- **LEARN TO KNOW WHAT TO LOOK FOR**
  The way to spot problems is dealt with in several sections of this book. Service troubles — gas, electricity, plumbing, drains etc are dealt with in Chapter 2. Study Chapter 4 for the way to deal with general difficulties inside the house and Chapter 5 for exterior problems. This chapter brings together the remaining problems which can occur — a frightening array of minor and major headaches. Take heart — you will never experience most of them, but it is still necessary to know what to do in an emergency.

- **DON'T TACKLE THE JOB YOURSELF UNLESS YOU KNOW WHAT TO DO**
  This book tells you how to tackle many simple repair jobs for yourself but advises you to seek professional help when there is a serious and complex problem. DIY is a splendid hobby and can save you a great deal of money in maintenance and construction work, but most repair jobs call for experience, and that cannot be gained by reading a book. In particular avoid tasks involving tall ladders unless you have a head for heights.

- **LOCATE THE MAIN TAPS AND SWITCHES**
  Find out how to turn off the main stopcock and gas tap before an emergency arises — instruct the other adult members of the family. Keep spare fuse wire or fuses and a torch in a handy place.

- **MAKE SURE THAT YOU USE A QUALIFIED PROFESSIONAL**
  Never employ people who just knock on the door and offer to build a wall, resurface a drive or repair a roof because they have "material left over from the last job". Try to use someone who has done satisfactory work on a previous occasion for you or a friend, and who is a member of the appropriate professional body.

- **HAVE A HOUSE-SAVING KIT**
  In addition to a basic tool kit (see Chapter 9) and first aid box there should be waterproof tape for tackling leaking pipes, a selection of fuses, a fire blanket and fire extinguisher, and some form of emergency lighting and heating in case of a power failure. These are the basics — there are many more items for the keen and the cautious.

- **HAVE A LIST OF EMERGENCY PHONE NUMBERS**
  This should include the electrician, police station, doctor, 24 hour plumbing service and the emergency gas service.

- **HAVE YOUR EQUIPMENT SERVICED REGULARLY**
  Major electrical and gas items need regular servicing — for some equipment such as central heating it is essential. If you have moved into an old house or if you have not had your wiring inspected for many years, ask your electricity supplier to check the system.

CONDENSATION

Everyone has seen the effect of **superficial condensation** during periods of cold weather. The warm air in the kitchen or bathroom contains a large amount of water vapour. On contact with a cold surface water droplets appear. Mirrors and tiles are easily wiped and so the problem is sometimes ignored, but if condensation is excessive you must take remedial action or the structure and its contents may be damaged. Water trickling on to woodwork can lead to rot — it will result in rust if left on steel window frames. Condensation can lead to mould growth on walls. Less easily detected but much less common is **interstitial condensation** which occurs within the bricks of external walls.

An average family produces about 20 litres of moisture in the air of the home each day, and this has to go somewhere. Cooking, washing and bathing are, of course, the main sources, but you produce 1 litre of water vapour per day simply by breathing and perspiring! The trouble is that in recent years we have done everything we can to stop heat from escaping — there is draughtproofing around doors, modern sealed windows, loft insulation, blocked-up chimneys and so on. The heat is kept in, but so is the water vapour.

Tackling the problem There is quite a lot you can do without having to spend any money. In a well-heated and insulated home the trouble is due to inadequate ventilation coupled with too much moisture in the air. In the kitchen do not let kettles and pans boil unnecessarily — close both the bathroom and kitchen doors when the rooms are steamy and open the windows slightly when they steam up. Open living room and bedroom windows for at least a few minutes each day to allow a change of air. Consider anti-condensation paint instead of gloss paint when you next decorate, and try cork tiles or carpet on the floor instead of cold ceramic tiles. Leave some space in wardrobes to allow air movement.

In an older house with little insulation the condensation problem is probably due to inadequate heat. Some background heat is necessary during the day — rooms which receive heat for just a few hours each day can be badly affected by condensation. Never use paraffin heaters if there is a dampness problem — a litre of paraffin or bottled gas produces a litre of water vapour.

Unfortunately, the most effective measures do cost money. A kitchen should be fitted with an extractor fan, a tumble drier should be vented to the outside and windows should be double glazed. There are ways to remove water vapour from the air. Containers of moisture-absorbing crystals can have only a small benefit — where the problem is serious an electric dehumidifier may be necessary.

Trouble in the roof Loft insulation keeps the house warmer in winter but it also keeps the loft and its timbers much cooler. If water vapour is allowed to rise up into the loft and then not allowed to escape, condensation can occur on the structural timber and this may lead to rot. The answer is to place polythene sheeting on the loft floor before laying down the insulating material and then ensure that there is some ventilation through air bricks or tile vents.

STORM DAMAGE

Winds below 50 mph rarely cause damage to a well-built house, but even moderate winds can blow over garden umbrellas, dustbin lids etc. It is not practical to take too many precautions against the risk of gale damage, but if your home is particularly exposed it would be wise to take some safety measures. Have the roof tiles, chimney and TV aerial inspected regularly — cut back tree branches which could break windows in a gale and keep a supply of sheet polythene handy.

During a gale-force storm close windows securely and unplug the TV if it has an outside aerial. If a window is broken, block it immediately with hardboard, tarpaulin or polythene sheet. If a roof tile is heard to fall, don't go out to inspect the damage until the storm has passed. At the end of the storm call a builder immediately if there has been damage — otherwise check the roof for slipped tiles and the gutters for blockages. A temporary repair of a lost roof tile may be possible by pushing a large sheet of polythene between the battens and the tiles surrounding the hole. After a snowstorm clear away any snow which may have collected in the loft.

SMELLS

There are two types of unpleasant odour which afflict the householder — temporary smells and persistent ones. Temporary smells include fresh paint and tobacco smoke (a bowl of vinegar is claimed to remove the odour), bonfire smoke (have a word with your neighbour — see page 106) and burnt food. For all temporary smells an air freshener block or aerosol is useful — but make sure that the aroma of the aerosol is not more unpleasant than the smell you are trying to mask. Rubbish in kitchen bins and outdoor dustbins should always be contained in plastic bags — use mothballs or a proprietary dustbin product if there is an odour problem with the bin in summer. Remove fish smells from pans by pouring in cold tea — leave for 30 minutes before washing. Smells are generally not a problem in the average home. Air fresheners are fine, but the prime way of achieving freshness is to air each lived-in room by opening the window for at least a few minutes every day.

Persistent odours are much more worrying. A foul lavatory smell usually indicates a blocked drain — seek expert help. A musty smell is caused by mould growth or rotting wood — locate and tackle the problem at once.

EFFLORESCENCE

A white deposit frequently appears on the surface of new brickwork. This is due to the water-soluble salts within the bricks being drawn to the outside as the walling materials dry out. Once at the outer face of the brickwork these salts crystallise and appear as a white fluffy film.

On outside brickwork there is no problem — efflorescence is quite normal and all you have to do is to remove the deposit with a wire brush until it ceases to appear. Never try to scrub it away with water — you will only make matters worse by bringing fresh salts to the surface. On inside walls it can be a problem by disfiguring or even dislodging the paper. To prevent efflorescence reappearing it is necessary to strip off damaged paper, leave the surface to dry, brush off the deposit and then treat the surface with a proprietary sealer before redecorating.

Efflorescence should not persist after two years. If it continues to appear you should consult a builder. It could mean that dampness is entering the wall from a leaking pipe, faulty damp-proof course etc and there could be serious trouble if the fault is left unattended.

MOULD

Patches of mould, usually greenish-black but occasionally brown or red, can occur on many surfaces in the home — furnishings, leather, clothes in a drawer, wallpaper and so on. The most likely areas to be affected are painted wood and surfaces in the kitchen or bathroom.

Mould (referred to as 'mildew' on fabrics) receives scant attention in most homecare books — it is dismissed as harmless. This is regrettable. First, it is not harmless. It is true that mould does not damage timber like the wood-rotting fungi but the air-borne spores of some types of mould can pose a health hazard by causing breathing problems. Secondly, the presence of mould indicates that the environment is not right — either damp is creeping through the walls or there is too little ventilation.

Remove mould when it appears. Wipe down the area with a solution of 1 part bleach/6 parts water and leave for a day before scraping away the surface growth. Remove and burn mouldy wallpaper. When redecorating use a fungicidal sealer and a fungicidal wallpaper paste. The long-term answer is to find and remove the cause — read the sections on condensation and damp.

NOISE

Little can be done about road traffic, trains, low-flying aircraft etc to stop the noise at source. It is up to you to lessen the problem by installing improvements in your home — sealing strips around windows and doors, wide-gap double glazing, heavy curtains which are drawn at night, thick loft insulation and so on. If you live in a high-noise area you may qualify for a grant.

We accept the noise of our own equipment much more than that of our neighbours — the main offenders are TV/radios, lawn mowers, power tools and washing machines. By far the worst problem is the blaring stereo late at night — the only satisfactory answer is to persuade your neighbour to turn down the equipment, move it away from the party wall and/or close the windows. If the noise persists and is both regular and unreasonable, complain to your local council.

STAINS

- The correct method of stain removal depends on the fabric, the substance which has been spilt and the age of the stain. Never guess what to do — some treatments can do more harm than good. For example, soaking in hot water instead of cold may fix a stain in the cloth.
- Treat all stains as soon as possible — once they have dried removal may be very difficult. Dab or scrape off as much as you can and then take appropriate action. Pour salt on wine which has been spilt on a carpet and brush off after an hour — for spilt grease cover the area with talcum powder and leave for 30 minutes before brushing off. With non-greasy stains on washable fabrics (except silk, wool and non-colourfast materials) rinse thoroughly in cold water. If the stain remains, soak overnight in a heavy-duty washing powder containing enzymes — make sure the fabric is suitable for soaking. Rinse and wash normally.
- A simple technique may be inappropriate or may not work. You have two choices. Firstly, you can take the item to a dry cleaner or call in a specialist company for a carpet or upholstery. This is the preferred course of action for delicate fabrics such as silk and for materials you can't identify. Mark the stained area by tacking with cotton and tell the assistant the cause of the stain. The second alternative is to try to remove the stain yourself. There are numerous proprietary dry-cleaning products at your supermarket — in addition there are many common household products such as ammonia, methylated spirits, bleach etc which can be used to remove one or more types of stain. Consult the chart below. Use dry-cleaning fluids with care. Make sure the room is well-ventilated and don't smoke. Read both the instructions and precautions before use. Test the product first on a small and inconspicuous part of the fabric. Place the wrong side uppermost on an absorbent pad and dab (don't rub) with the cleaner. Work from outside the stain inwards.

STAIN	WASHABLE MATERIAL	NON-WASHABLE MATERIAL
ADHESIVES	**Contact, Clear** Dab with nail polish remover. Not suitable for acetates — use lighter fuel instead **Epoxy** Removal extremely difficult when dry. Dab with methylated spirits. Not suitable for acetates — use lighter fuel instead **Latex** If wet, wash off with cold water. If dry, peel off — remove residue with dry-cleaning fluid **PVA** Dab with methylated spirits — not suitable for acetates	Dab with nail polish remover. Not suitable for acetates — use lighter fuel instead Removal extremely difficult when dry. Dab with methylated spirits. Not suitable for acetates — use lighter fuel instead If wet, sponge off with cold water. If dry, peel off — remove residue with dry-cleaning fluid Dab with methylated spirits — not suitable for acetates
BEER	Cold rinse. Soak overnight in biological washing powder. Wash	Sponge with solution of 1 part vinegar/5 parts water. Sponge with clean water. Dab dry with kitchen paper
BIRD DROPPINGS	Scrape off as much as possible. Cold rinse. Soak overnight in biological washing powder. Wash. Bleaching of white fabric may be necessary	Scrape off as much as possible. Take to the cleaners
BLOOD	If wet — soak in a strong salt solution. If dry — cold rinse. Soak overnight in biological washing powder. Wash	Sponge with solution of 3 drops ammonia/1 litre water. Sponge with clean water. Dab dry with kitchen paper
BUTTER	See GREASE	See GREASE
CANDLE WAX	Place cloth in the refrigerator — when cold scrape off as much as possible. Place blotting paper over and under wax — rub with warm iron. Repeat with fresh paper until clear	Cool area with ice cubes in a plastic bag. When cool scrape off as much as possible. Place blotting paper over wax — rub with warm iron. Repeat as necessary
CHEWING GUM	Place cloth in the refrigerator — peel off hardened gum. Remove residue with dry-cleaning fluid. Wash	Cool area with ice cubes in a plastic bag — peel off hardened gum. Remove residue with dry-cleaning fluid
CHOCOLATE	Scrape off as much as possible. Cold rinse. Soak overnight in biological washing powder. Wash	Scrape off as much as possible. Use dry-cleaning fluid
COFFEE	Cold rinse. Soak overnight in biological washing powder. Wash. If not removed, sponge with solution of 1 tablespoon borax/500 ml water. Wash	Sponge with solution of 1 tablespoon borax/500 ml water. Sponge with clean water. Dab dry with kitchen paper
CRAYON	Sponge with methylated spirits — not suitable for acetates. Dab dry with kitchen paper. Wash	Sponge with methylated spirits — not suitable for acetates. Sponge with clean water. Dab dry with kitchen paper
CREAM	Cold rinse. Soak overnight in biological washing powder. Wash. If not removed, dab with nail polish remover — not suitable for acetates	Use dry-cleaning fluid or a stain-removal bar
EGG	Cold rinse. Soak overnight in biological washing powder. Wash	Use a stain-removal bar

STAIN	WASHABLE MATERIAL	NON-WASHABLE MATERIAL
FRUIT JUICE	If dry, rub with glycerine and leave for 1 hour. Cold rinse. Soak overnight in biological washing powder. Wash. If not removed, soak whites in solution of 150 ml hydrogen peroxide/500 ml water/5 drops ammonia	Sponge with cold water. Rub with glycerine and leave for 1 hour. Dab dry with kitchen paper. Use dry-cleaning fluid
GRASS	Cold rinse. Soak overnight in biological washing powder. Wash. If not removed, sponge with methylated spirits or use a stain-removal bar	Use a stain-removal bar
GRAVY	Cold rinse. Soak overnight in biological washing powder. Wash	Use dry-cleaning fluid or a stain-removal bar
GREASE	Dab with dry-cleaning fluid. If stain persists, try a stain-removal bar. Wash	Use dry-cleaning fluid or a stain-removal bar
INK	**Washable ink** Cold rinse. Soak overnight in heavy-duty washing powder. Wash. If not removed, sponge whites with lemon juice and salt **Ball point, Felt tip** Sponge with methylated spirits — not suitable for acetates. Dab dry with kitchen paper. Wash	Sponge with dilute detergent. Sponge with clean water. Dab dry with kitchen paper Take to the cleaners
IRON MOULD	Sponge with lemon juice — leave for 30 minutes. Wash	Sponge with a proprietary rust remover
LIPSTICK	Scrape off as much as possible. Sponge with methylated spirits — not suitable for acetates. Dab dry with kitchen paper. Wash	Scrape off as much as possible. Take to the cleaners
MARGARINE	See GREASE	See GREASE
MILDEW	Cold rinse. Soak overnight in biological washing powder. Wash	Take to the cleaners
MILK	Cold rinse. Soak overnight in biological washing powder. Wash. If not removed, sponge with solution of 1 tablespoon borax/500 ml water. Wash	Sponge with solution of 1 tablespoon borax/500 ml water. Sponge with clean water. Dab dry with kitchen paper
OIL	See GREASE	See GREASE
PAINT	**Oil-based** Scrape off as much as possible. Sponge with white spirit then soapy water. Wash **Water-based** Cold rinse. Soak overnight in heavy-duty washing powder. Wash	Scrape off as much as possible. Sponge with white spirit. Sponge with clean water. Dab dry with kitchen paper Take to the cleaners
PERSPIRATION	Sponge with solution of 2 tablespoons vinegar/500 ml water. Wash. If not removed, use a stain-removal bar	Sponge with solution of 2 tablespoons vinegar/500 ml water. Sponge with clean water. Dab dry with kitchen paper
RUST	See IRON MOULD	See IRON MOULD
SCORCH MARKS	Soak in solution of 1 tablespoon borax/500 ml water. Wash	Sponge with solution of 1 tablespoon borax/500 ml water. Sponge with clean water. Dab dry with kitchen paper
SHOE POLISH	See CRAYON	See CRAYON
SPIRITS	Cold rinse. Soak overnight in biological washing powder. Wash	Sponge with methylated spirits — not suitable for acetates. Sponge with clean water. Dab dry with kitchen paper
TAR	Scrape off as much as possible. Sponge with eucalyptus oil. Wash	Scrape off as much as possible. Use dry-cleaning fluid
TEA	See COFFEE	See COFFEE
URINE	Cold rinse. Soak overnight in biological washing powder. Wash. If dried, soak first in dilute vinegar	Sponge with dilute vinegar. Sponge with clean water. Dab dry with kitchen paper
VOMIT	Scrape off as much as possible. Rinse under tap. Soak overnight in biological washing powder. Wash	Scrape off as much as possible. Sponge with water containing a few drops of ammonia. Sponge with clean water. Dab dry with kitchen paper. If smell persists, use a stain-removal bar
WATER	Spots on silk, velvet etc — hold in front of steaming kettle	Hard water spots on sinks, basins etc — wipe off with solution of 2 teaspoons vinegar/500 ml water
WINE	Rub with lemon juice and salt. Leave for 1 hour. Wash	Sponge with warm water. Sprinkle with salt. Leave for 1 hour. Brush off

Most of the above remedies have been used for many years, but neither success nor safety to fabric can be guaranteed. Much depends on the age of the material, ingredients in the stain, etc. If in doubt, seek professional help

SUBSIDENCE

Subsidence occurs when the foundations of a house move downwards so as to cause structural damage. Upward movement is called *heave*. The possible causes are many and varied. First of all, the subsoil may move. Clays shrink and swell according to the water content, so that a very dry summer or a very wet winter may put a great strain on the foundations. A number of factors can attack the stability of the subsoil irrespective of its type — flooding, old mine-workings, underground streams, uptake of water by tree roots, the presence of rotting wood or rubbish, insufficient settlement time prior to building and so on. Finally (and rarely), the foundations themselves may have been improperly laid.

After the causes, the symptoms. Doors may stick and windows fail to open but the characteristic feature is the appearance of cracks in the wall. If there is subsidence then you may face a serious problem. You will need to call in a surveyor immediately and the work involved will be expensive and disruptive.

Fortunately, not all wall cracks are caused by subsidence. In fact, only rarely do cracks indicate this frightening problem. In a new house you will find that fine cracks start to appear on some ceilings and internal walls — the main cause is shrinkage as the wood, plaster, mortar etc dry out. These shrinkage cracks are nothing to worry about — they are easily covered by decorating. Keep them to a minimum by maintaining the house on the cool side with good ventilation during the first few months after construction. In addition to shrinkage cracks there may also be settlement ones — fine cracks caused by the building settling down on its foundations.

In older houses delayed settlement cracks sometimes occur. The problem is to determine whether you are dealing with a settlement crack, which can usually be dealt with quite simply, or with a subsidence crack, which calls for immediate attention by a surveyor. Look at the width of the crack — openings which measure less than 3 mm across are rarely worrying, but they may be the first sign of subsidence. Next, look at the location — cracks near a corner of the house or running diagonally from doors or windows can mean subsidence, especially if the crack occurs both inside and outside the house. Long cracks are much more worrying than short ones, and cracks along the join between an extension or garage and the house may indicate that the added-on building has subsided. Finally, carry out the glass slide test described on page 79.

If the signs point to subsidence or if you are in any doubt, call in a qualified surveyor. Leave any recommended works to a qualified builder. The work may consist of underpinning the foundations and some shoring up of the wall or walls. Steel tie rods may be sufficient to hold the affected wall, but with a badly affected house the only course of action may be to rebuild the damaged area. Insurance cover depends on the wording of the policy — check it. The cost will be high. With a new building there is the 10 year guarantee.

Obviously it is better to prevent subsidence than to try to remedy it. There is nothing you can do about the subsoil, foundation geometry etc but you can avoid the tree root trouble which can cause subsidence in clay soil. Do not plant a tree within 15 m of the house if you expect it to grow to a considerable height. Even small trees should be at least 5 m away. Instant removal may not be the answer — some trees are protected by law and the sudden change in the water content of a clay subsoil following felling may actually cause heave.

FLOOD

If you live in an area which is prone to flooding you should have the necessary precautionary materials on hand — sacks and sand for making sandbags and some form of emergency lighting and heating.

When a flood alert is issued the local police helped by the fire brigade will take charge — follow their instructions. If they cannot get to you in time, follow the standard drill. Put sandbags (or soil in plastic carrier bags as a substitute) along the threshold of all outside doors and air bricks to impede the entry of water. Take as much as you can upstairs — drinking water, food, coats, torch, reading material, battery radio, mobile phone and valuables. Take up ground-floor carpets if possible. Finally, switch off the electricity at the mains and go upstairs.

The real headache begins once the flood water has receded. Do not switch on the electricity or drink the water until you are told to do so. Open windows and doors — wash down walls and remove carpets. Keep rooms heated. Drying out will take about 4 - 6 months — do not be in a hurry to redecorate.

NEIGHBOURS

Sometimes your neighbours can cause annoyance or difficulty without meaning to do so. Point out that planting a tree too close to your house may cause trouble for which they will be legally responsible. If branches overhang your property you have a right to lop them off, but be polite and inform your neighbours first. Let your deeds resolve any boundary disputes — if the boundary is not clear then explain that a fence is considered to be yours if its posts are on your side. It may not have occurred to your neighbour that the proposed high wall or extension will cast a shadow on part of your house — simply explain that you have a legal 'right to light' if that part of your house has been unshaded for at least 20 years.

Unfortunately there are many neighbour problems which are due to pure selfishness. Bonfires, excessive noise, parking on your property, dangerous pets — the list is almost endless. If the problem is isolated (a noisy birthday party etc), grin and bear it. If it is persistent, do something about it. In the first instance, talk it over — be as friendly as you can. If that fails discuss the matter with your local council.

WOOD DECAY

There are many fungi which can infect timber, but the only two you have to worry about are dry rot and wet rot. In both cases air-borne spores infect the wood and wood-rotting strands (hyphae) spread outwards. This initial attack only takes place if the wood is damp or wet and has been so for some time. There are no cures, so prevention is extremely important. Protect your home against damp and use preservative-treated wood in high-risk areas.

The only insect likely to trouble you is woodworm — the grub (larval) stage of a number of beetle species. Once again prevention is much better than cure.

Most softwoods have little or no natural resistance to attack by rots or woodworm, so a preservative is needed to bestow chemical protection. New softwood timber which is to be placed in an exposed or damp situation should be pressure-treated with a proven preservative. The purpose of a paint-on stain/preservative is to provide colour and top-up protection.

DRY ROT

Dry rot begins in a damp, poorly ventilated place — the favourite sites are suspended wooden floors, cellar timbers, leak-affected structural timber and the back of skirting boards. Unlike wet rot it prefers damp (20 per cent moisture) and not wet timber, and it does not affect wood outdoors. It is less common than wet rot but the effect is usually more serious because of the way it spreads. Once the fungus has taken hold a mass of cottony threads develop and from them long root-like strands appear which seek out fresh wood to attack. These strands can pass through plaster, mortar and even brick. In this way dry rot can move from basement to roof timber and from one semi-detached house to another.

Detecting dry rot is often not easy because it usually attacks timber which is hidden from view. There is a musty, mushroom-like odour and the wood is soft when prodded with a screwdriver. Woolly growths may be seen above a skirting board, and dried-out rotten wood has cracks both along and across the grain to form cube-shaped blocks which crumble when touched. After many months pancake-shaped fruiting bodies are formed on timber or plaster. Spores look like red dust — its presence is a sure sign that there is dry rot.

Don't try to tackle dry rot unless you have the necessary experience. All infected wood will have to be cut back 1 metre beyond the diseased area and all strands removed from plaster, brickwork etc. Dry rot fungicide is applied to the rest of the wood and the source of dampness discovered and eradicated.

WET ROT

Wet rot attacks wet (at least 30 per cent moisture) and not moist timber. Unlike dry rot it will not spread to moist timber, and it is active outdoors as well as inside. The effect is often localised, but windowsills, window and door frames, doors and fenceposts can be destroyed. Rafters and joists in leaking roofs are sometimes attacked. Detection of wet rot on visible timber is usually quite straightforward. Paintwork bubbles up and the timber below is soft. Rotten wood is dark brown with cracks along the grain.

Keep dampness out of the house in order to prevent the problem — make sure wood is allowed to dry out properly after a leak. Outdoor rot-susceptible timber should be properly maintained with paint or with a stain/preservative.

To get rid of wet rot you will have to cut out the rotten timber and replace it with preservative-treated wood. For small areas of rot you can use a wood repair system. This saves you having to insert a new piece of wood — all you have to do is cut away the rotten area and paint with hardener. The original level is restored with filler — preservative tablets are inserted into the surrounding sound wood.

WOODWORM

The presence of woodworm is all too obvious — a peppering of small round holes on the surface. These are the exit holes through which the adult beetles departed after spending several years as grubs tunnelling through the wood. Below the surface there will be a network of tunnels — on the surface there will be tiny piles of dust (frass) if the pest is still active. The most usual type of woodworm is the furniture beetle — 6 mm long with exit holes 1 - 2 mm in diameter. Other woodworms include the death-watch beetle on old hardwoods. The grubs of the furniture beetle prefer damp rather than dry wood, softwood rather than hardwood and are especially fond of plywood and glue.

The problem may start with a female beetle flying into your home and laying its eggs — unfinished wood is preferred and painted or polished wood is avoided. It is much more likely to have begun with the introduction of infested wood.

You can treat an infestation in furniture with an aerosol containing woodworm insecticide. After injecting the liquid into the holes, spray the surface thoroughly and apply a repeat spray a few months later. Call in a specialist company if structural timber has been affected.

DAMP

At least 15 per cent of British homes show decoration damage due to dampness — it is a serious problem. The visible symptoms (damaged decoration, peeling wallpaper etc) are bad enough, but the hidden results can be even more worrying. Structural woodwork may be weakened by wet rot and the health of the family can be harmed by the mouldy, moist atmosphere when the temperature is low.

Take damp seriously. Inspect the outside of the house regularly to make sure the defences are sound. If you spot damp patches indoors, take remedial action. If in doubt, seek reputable and impartial advice — in some cases it will be necessary to seek professional help to cure the problem, but don't accept the usual 'rising damp' diagnosis without a second opinion.

TYPES OF DAMP

TRAUMATIC DAMP
Water from an **inside source** reaching the wall/ceiling.
Recognition: Caused by leaking pipe, drain, tank or radiator. Size of patch steadily increases — not related to rainfall, temperature, season etc

PENETRATING DAMP
Water from **rain** or **snow** reaching the wall/ceiling
Recognition: Patches may be some distance away from the point of entry, but patches around windows usually indicate poor sealing or faulty windowsill, and long vertical stain on upper floor indicates a faulty gutter downpipe. Patches expand after heavy rain. Associated with exposed N and W facing walls and with old houses

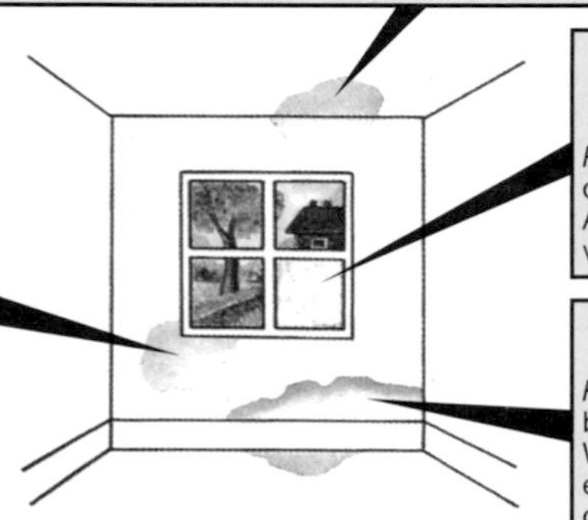

CONDENSATION
Water from the **air** condensing on the wall/ceiling/room surfaces/furnishings/clothing
Recognition: Water drops on windows, mirrors etc — damp and sometimes mouldy patches on walls. Associated with steamy rooms, cold weather and poor ventilation

RISING DAMP
Water from the **ground** reaching the floor/wall
Recognition: Wallpaper peeling away from skirting board, lifting floor tiles, discoloured patch on wall. Wall patch can rise to 1 m — tidemark present. Patch expands in winter. Associated with old houses. Not as common as some companies would have you believe

FINDING THE CAUSE OF THE TROUBLE

Go outside just after a heavy rainstorm. Water will still be flowing through the gutters and downpipes but looking upwards will not be a problem once the rain has stopped. Take a notebook and pencil.

TESTING FOR DAMP

Ideally you should detect damp before any visible signs are present. You can buy a battery-operated damp meter — two prongs are inserted into the mortar, plaster etc and a light indicates dampness. Once a patch appears it may be easy to find the cause. However, it is often difficult — a wet patch at the bottom of the wall may be rising or penetrating damp, and in a cellar it is sometimes a combination of the two. Use the **aluminium foil test**. Dry the damp patch with a heater and then attach a piece of foil with adhesive tape. Inspect it some time later. Water on the surface indicates condensation — water on the back of the foil after removal from the wall indicates penetrating, traumatic or rising damp. If the problem is serious you should call in a surveyor. Call in a damp-proofing company if you wish, but remember that some of these companies tend to be unduly pessimistic.

CRACKED FLAUNCHING
Repair needed

UNCAPPED CHIMNEY POT LEADING TO CLOSED-OFF FIREPLACE
Chimney breast may be stained. Fit half round tile — see page 77

DEFECTIVE FLASHING
Repair needed — see page 77 or call in a builder

DEFECTIVE TILES OR SLATES
Slipped, broken or missing tiles or slates will let in water — see page 77. Inspect from outside — also look for dripping by standing in loft on a rainy day

DEFECTIVE GUTTERING
See page 80

DAMAGED FELT
Look for bubbles and cracks. Carry out temporary or permanent repair — see page 77

DEFECTIVE WINDOWS
Gaps between frame and wall will let in penetrating damp — so will rotten woodwork or blocked groove under sill

DEFECTIVE DOOR
Gaps between frame and wall will let in penetrating damp — so will rotten woodwork or a defective weather bar at base

BRIDGED DAMP-PROOF COURSE
Dpc may be bridged by earth or covered by a path. Gap between dpc and ground level should be at least 15 cm

POOR BRICKWORK
Cracked bricks and missing mortar can lead to water entry — see page 79

BLOCKED AIR BRICK
Remove leaves, soil etc

LEAKING DOWNPIPE
Can cause serious penetrating damp — see page 80

DAMAGED RENDERING
Cracked or broken rendering will let in water. Repair needed — see page 79

CAUSES AND CURES

RISING DAMP

- **NO DAMP-PROOF COURSE** Rising damp is caused by water in the ground being sucked up through the brickwork and mortar. If no damp-proof course (dpc) is present it will be necessary to insert one, but make sure that rising damp is really the cause of your problem.
- **DEFECTIVE DAMP-PROOF COURSE** Builders have had to include a dpc since 1875, but some of the earlier ones were brittle and in some older houses a broken dpc can be found. If rising damp has resulted from a break in the dpc, use one of the four methods of replacement shown below. The problem area may be limited — don't repair more than you have to.

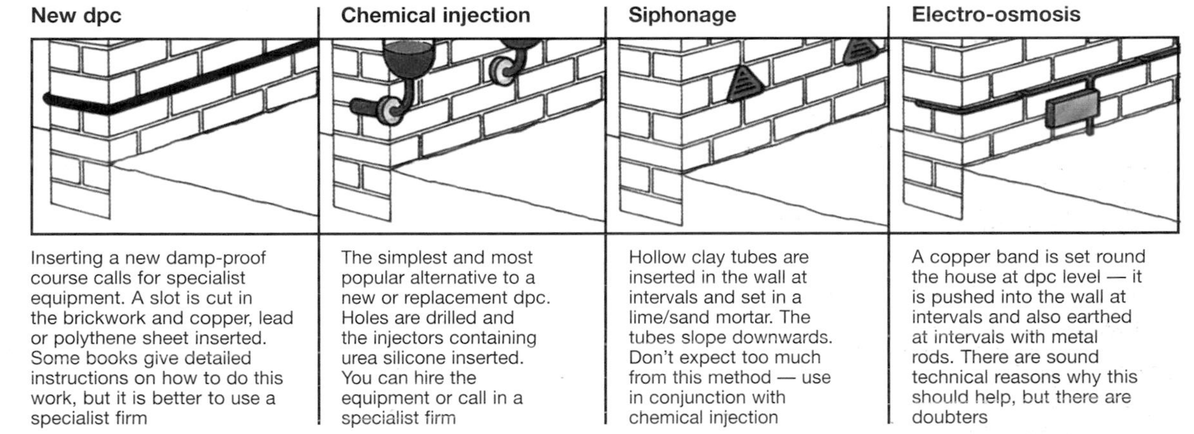

New dpc
Inserting a new damp-proof course calls for specialist equipment. A slot is cut in the brickwork and copper, lead or polythene sheet inserted. Some books give detailed instructions on how to do this work, but it is better to use a specialist firm

Chemical injection
The simplest and most popular alternative to a new or replacement dpc. Holes are drilled and the injectors containing urea silicone inserted. You can hire the equipment or call in a specialist firm

Siphonage
Hollow clay tubes are inserted in the wall at intervals and set in a lime/sand mortar. The tubes slope downwards. Don't expect too much from this method — use in conjunction with chemical injection

Electro-osmosis
A copper band is set round the house at dpc level — it is pushed into the wall at intervals and also earthed at intervals with metal rods. There are sound technical reasons why this should help, but there are doubters

- **BRIDGED DAMP-PROOF COURSE** Earth may be piled against the bricks above the dpc to raise a bed or rockery. Remove the earth to create the statutory gap of 15 cm between ground level and the dpc. A raised path is a more difficult problem — relaying may be the only answer. A less common way of bridging the dpc is by rendering or plastering over it, thereby linking the moist earth with the upper bricks.

TRAUMATIC DAMP

Trace leak — it may be necessary to lift some floorboards to find it.

PENETRATING DAMP

- **DRIVING RAIN AGAINST A SOUND WALL** Rain should not penetrate through a sound cavity wall, but penetrating damp can seep through a solid wall if the mortar is a lime/sand mix. Large patches of damp on the inside face are the result, and waterproofing the exterior is the answer. The cheapest method is to paint on a silicone water-repellent. Rendering is the traditional way of waterproofing exposed walls — very useful but it will do more harm than good if not properly applied.
- **DRIVING RAIN AGAINST AN UNSOUND WALL** Cracks in brickwork and missing mortar can let in water. Cracked and blistered areas on a rendered wall are even more serious. The cure is obvious — have the faults repaired.
- **DRIVING RAIN AGAINST A DEFECTIVE WINDOW** Damp patches on an internal wall around a window show that something is wrong outside. Dampness at the base usually indicates a sill problem — clean the groove under the sill and check the sealing. Dampness at the sides or at the top may indicate a damp-proof course problem — consult a builder.
- **ROOF & GUTTER PROBLEMS** See Chapter 5.
- **CAVITY WALL TIE PROBLEMS** The tell-tale sign is a line of regularly-spaced round spots on the wall which may be damp or mouldy. The ties may have been fixed wrongly or may have been covered by mortar carelessly dropped during the building operation. Call in a builder.

CONDENSATION

See page 102

COVERING DAMP

There are many brush-on solutions and stick-on sheetings for covering damp inside walls, but they are not cures. The problem of dampness in the wall remains and may be driven to other parts. Despite this limitation these masking agents do have an important role. They are useful when you wish to redecorate soon after curing a damp problem and are also useful when decorating a below-ground room where there is just no way of curing the inherent dampness. However, masking agents should not be used as a substitute for curing damp.

The simplest systems involve brush-on solutions. Bituminous emulsion is the cheapest but the synthetic rubber products are more effective. Other types are available — check whether priming is necessary and what precautions are required. It is also wise to check if there is hydrostatic pressure against the wall. Water will seep through a hole drilled through a brick — if it does then use an epoxy damp-proofing system.

Some people prefer to use a lining material rather than a brush-on liquid. The popular one is aluminium foil — walls are washed down, cracks are filled and the lining foil laid using the recommended special adhesive. A popular alternative for cellars and basements is corrugated waterproof lathing which is bought in a roll. The old wet plaster is removed and the corrugated sheeting nailed to the wall. Plasterboard can be attached to the new surface.

The traditional way to cover a damp wall is by tanking — preservative-treated battens are nailed to the wall which is painted with an anti-mould solution. A vapour barrier and then plasterboard are attached to the battens.

PESTS

You share your home perhaps with a family, perhaps with a pet or two, but quite certainly with thousands of unwelcome living things. Not all are harmful — spiders and silverfish do no harm, but many people find them distasteful and so they get linked with the others as 'pests'. By far the largest group in number are the microscopic mites and by far the most frightening are the mammalian pests — rats, mice and bats. You will never have a pest-free home but by carrying out proper precautions and having the right remedies on hand you will not be troubled by their presence.

Precautions include good hygiene — old food scraps, crumbs left in drawers etc attract flies, mice, cockroaches and ants. Move compost heaps away from the house and fill gaps along skirting boards and around outside pipe entry points.

Cures come in many forms. As a standby have a general-purpose and safe aerosol on hand. Always read the label before you buy or use an insecticide or other pest killer. Do not spray food and store away from pets and children. A serious infestation of wasps, rats etc may be beyond you — get in touch with your local Environmental Health Department.

ANTS

Small insects less than 8 mm long with a distinct waist — usually black but sometimes red. Spray with an Ant aerosol — trace back to the nest if you can and pour in boiling water. Puff an Anti-ant powder into the entrance

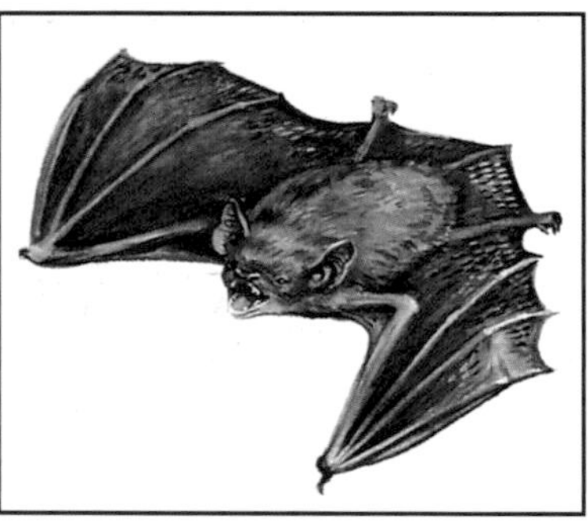

BATS

The bats in your room or behind the cladding are harmless and will not fly into your hair, but many people are still afraid of them. The commonest type is the pipistrelle. Don't try to get rid of them or even block their access into your home — it's illegal. Contact the Nature Conservancy Council who will move them for you

BED BUGS

Fortunately rare these days, but they may be there when you move house or buy second-hand bedroom furniture. The flat 3 mm round insects feed on human blood — irritating bites in the morning and a strange smell indicate their presence. Killed by insecticidal aerosols, but leave eradication to the Environmental Health Department

CARPET BEETLES

The 3 mm long grubs of the carpet beetle and fur beetle attack carpets, woollens, fur etc — now more serious pests than clothes moths. Tell-tale sign is the presence of cast-off furry skins. Destroy birds' nests in roof (the favourite hiding place) and get rid of fluff in drawers, wardrobes etc. Spray with Carpet Beetle Killer

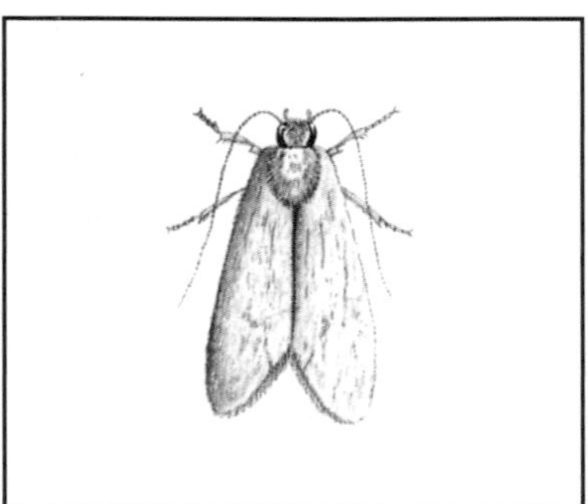

CLOTHES MOTHS

A plain-looking moth, pale brown and 8 mm long. They do no harm — it is the 20 mm white grub which eats wool and wool-mix blankets, carpets, clothes etc as well as fur. Perspiration and food residues act as an attractant. Store items in plastic bags with a moth repellent. Spray with an aerosol Moth Killer

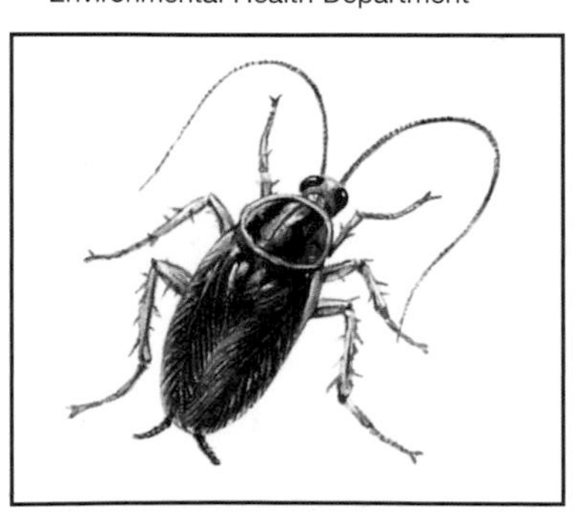

COCKROACHES

Brown beetles, 10 - 25 mm long, which come out of crevices at night to feed. They leave behind an unpleasant smell and perhaps food poisoning. Do not confuse with the harmless black beetle, which does not have the rapid scuttling movement of the cockroach. Spray kitchen nooks and crannies with a suitable aerosol. Repeat treatment

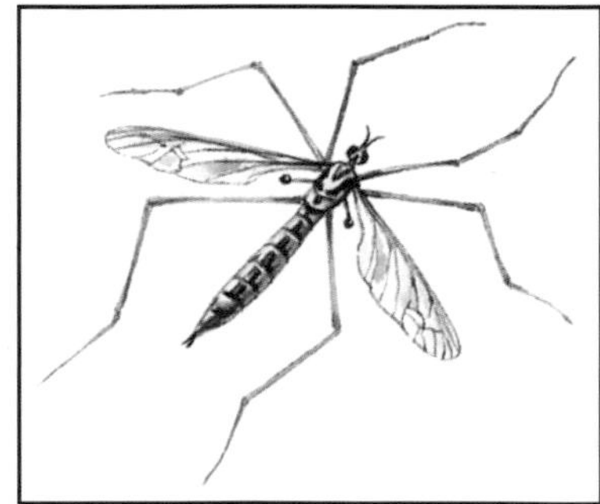

CRANE FLIES

Better known as daddy-long legs — large spindly insects with gossamer-like wings. Harmless, but its grubs are the plant-destroying leatherjackets hated by gardeners. The flies appear in late summer — they can be annoying and should not be left to lay eggs on someone's lawn. Kill with a fly swatter or a suitable aerosol

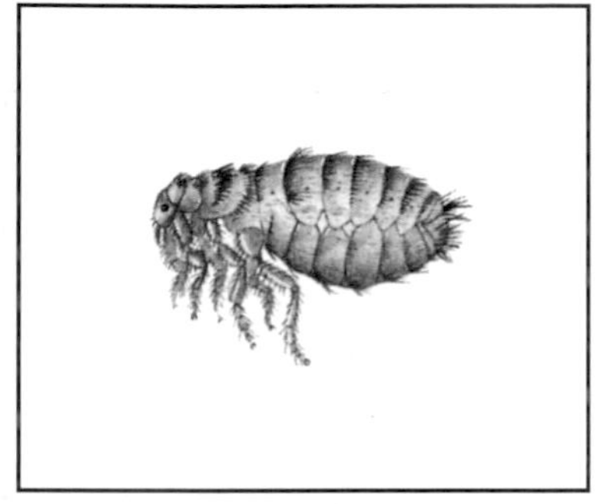

FLEAS

Small red bites which are extremely itchy usually indicate a flea problem — your dog or cat will generally have been the carrier. Fit it with a Flea collar or ask your vet for one of the modern flea treatments. Burn infested bedding and vacuum carpets etc thoroughly. Spray cracks and crevices with a suitable aerosol

FLIES

The one you are most likely to see is the common housefly, but it can be a bluebottle (large, noisy, shiny blue), stable fly (housefly-like, but bites humans) or a cluster fly (housefly-size, but hairy and joins with others to form autumn swarms in upper rooms). Keep food covered and kitchen surfaces clean. Spray with a suitable aerosol

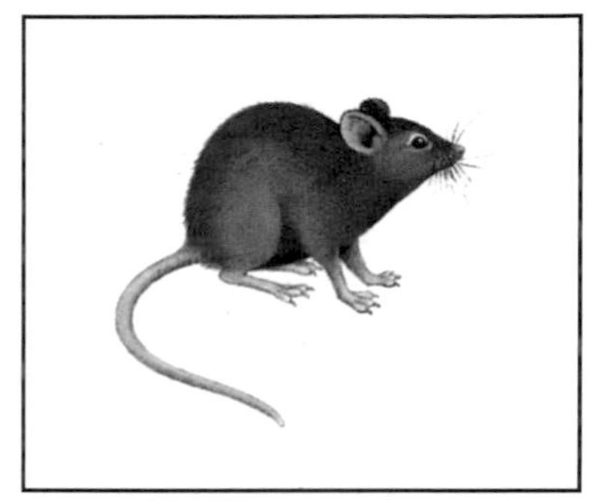

MICE

The tell-tale signs are nibbled food and packages plus the presence of small droppings. Both the house and field mouse come indoors — tackle the problem quickly as both contaminate food, can carry food poisoning and may gnaw through electric cables. Use a Mouse bait and block entry points — use a trap if all else fails

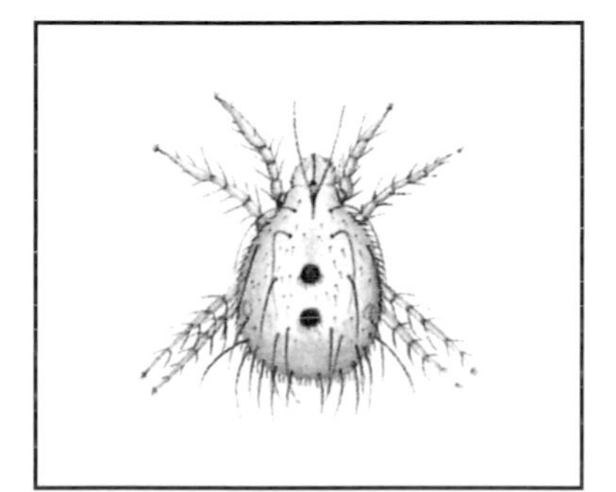

MITES

Tiny creatures just visible to the human eye — look like particles of dust on the move. The house dust mite lives on particles of dead skin — the furniture mite is found in upholstery. If you are allergic to the house dust mite you will start to wheeze — asthmatic people should use plastic filled pillows and vacuum bedrooms daily

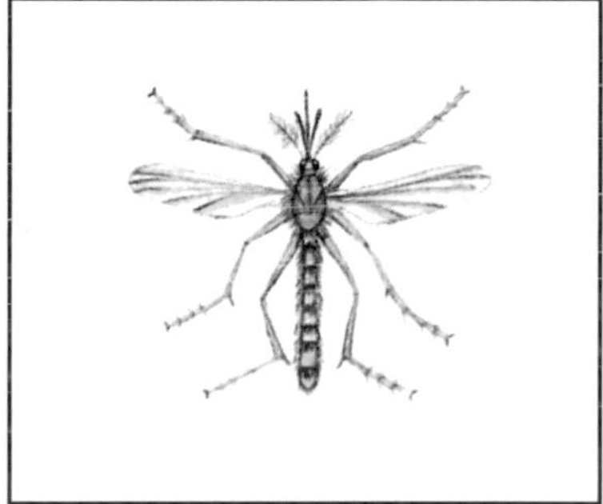

MOSQUITOES

A term loosely applied to tiny buzzing insects — midges are really flies, gnats are true mosquitoes which don't bite and there is the gnat look-alike which does. Biting mosquitoes are occasionally a problem — cover the surface of water-butts, guttering etc with a thin layer of paraffin. Spray insects with a suitable aerosol

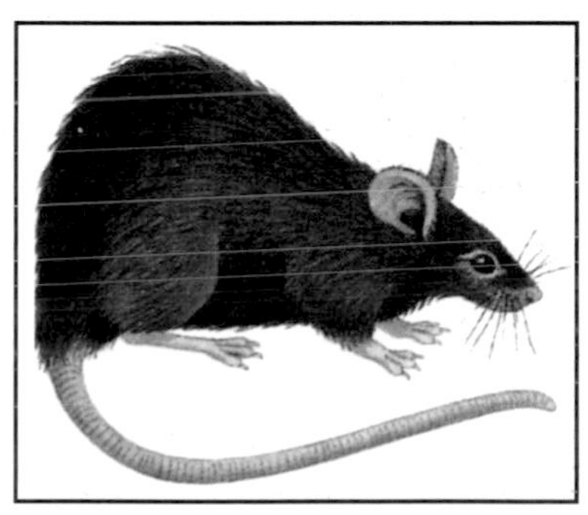

RATS

The most frightening household pest. The scurrying brown rat is about 20 cm long which makes it our largest trespasser, and it can be a carrier of a number of diseases. Cables and pipes can be damaged. Get in touch with your Environmental Health Department straight away. DIY control involves using Rat bait

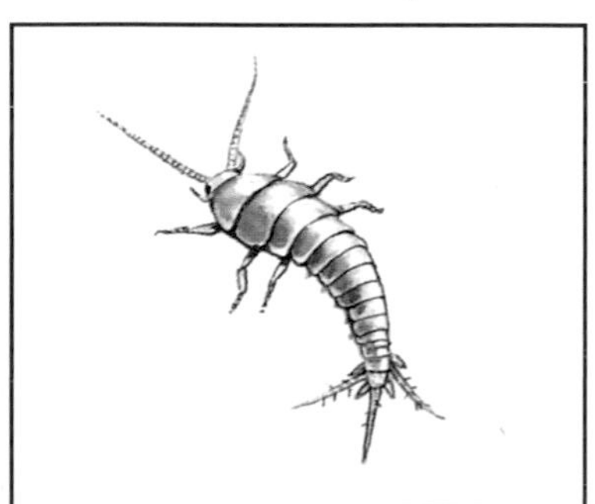

SILVERFISH

A pest of damp areas — silvery-grey, cigar-shaped, 10 mm long. Not often seen as it feeds at night, but sometimes trapped in baths and basins. Rarely causes any damage, but sometimes eats wallpaper paste. Not a problem but the dampness they indicate could well be. Kill with a suitable aerosol if they are a nuisance

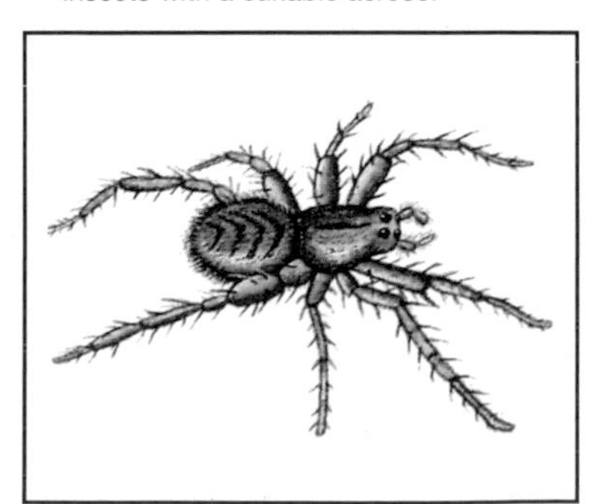

SPIDERS

All are harmless, but this is no comfort to people who are terrified of them. Cobwebs on wooden cladding often indicate dampness below — their presence indoors indicates nothing except the absence of regular dusting. Lift and move outdoors if you are not squeamish — use a plastic spider transporter if you are

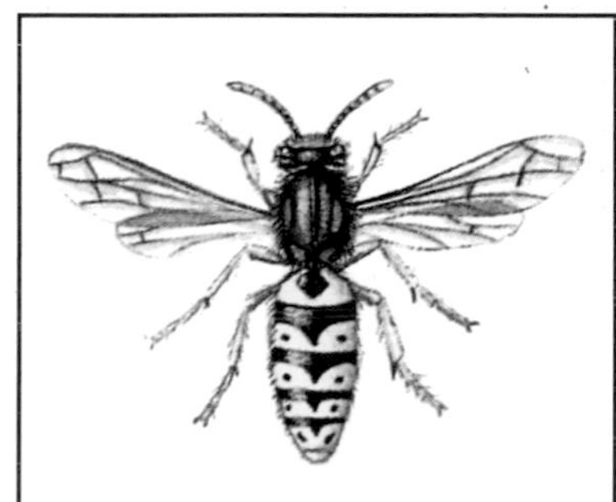

WASPS & BEES

A nuisance in early autumn. Hornets (twice the size of ordinary wasps) are fortunately uncommon. Bumble bees may be more frightening than wasps but will rarely sting if not disturbed. Let bees escape through an open window — spray wasps with a suitable aerosol. For nest removal consult the Environmental Health Department

HEAT LOSS

Of course, all the heat produced by fuel is eventually 'lost' — the house cannot hold its warmth for ever. The purpose of insulation is to slow down the rate of loss so that you can gain as much benefit as practical before the warmth produced by gas, oil, electricity etc is dissipated to the air outside.

In an uninsulated house about three-quarters of the heat you pay for is lost to the environment before you have derived the proper benefit from it. With good insulation and the efficient use of fuel this loss can be halved (see page 28). This sounds most attractive, but do be clear on two points: You cannot cut down heat loss altogether by turning your house into an airtight box, nor would it be desirable to do so. There must be enough ventilation to keep condensation in check (page 102) and to allow gas and coal fires to burn efficiently.

Not all forms of insulation are worthwhile unless you are seeking maximum heat conservation. It certainly pays to seal gaps and to draught-proof doors and windows, and you should always ensure that there is some loft insulation. With double glazing, however, it will take some years before you will recover the cost in saved fuel.

The actual heat loss which takes place in a particular home depends on the situation. The prime controlling factor is the amount of insulation present — new homes are built to a much higher standard than old ones. A flat-roofed bungalow will lose considerably more heat through the roof than a 3-storeyed house with a pitched roof. Any apartment or terraced house will lose less heat through the walls than a detached house. But no matter what style of home you occupy there can be no doubt that some thought and a little money spent on insulation can cut your fuel bills.

It is not just a matter of cutting fuel bills. Draughts and cold corners in an uninsulated house can make life distinctly unpleasant in the depths of winter. Insulation can be expensive — if money is short begin with draught-proofing and then go on to lagging the hot water cylinder and insulating the loft.

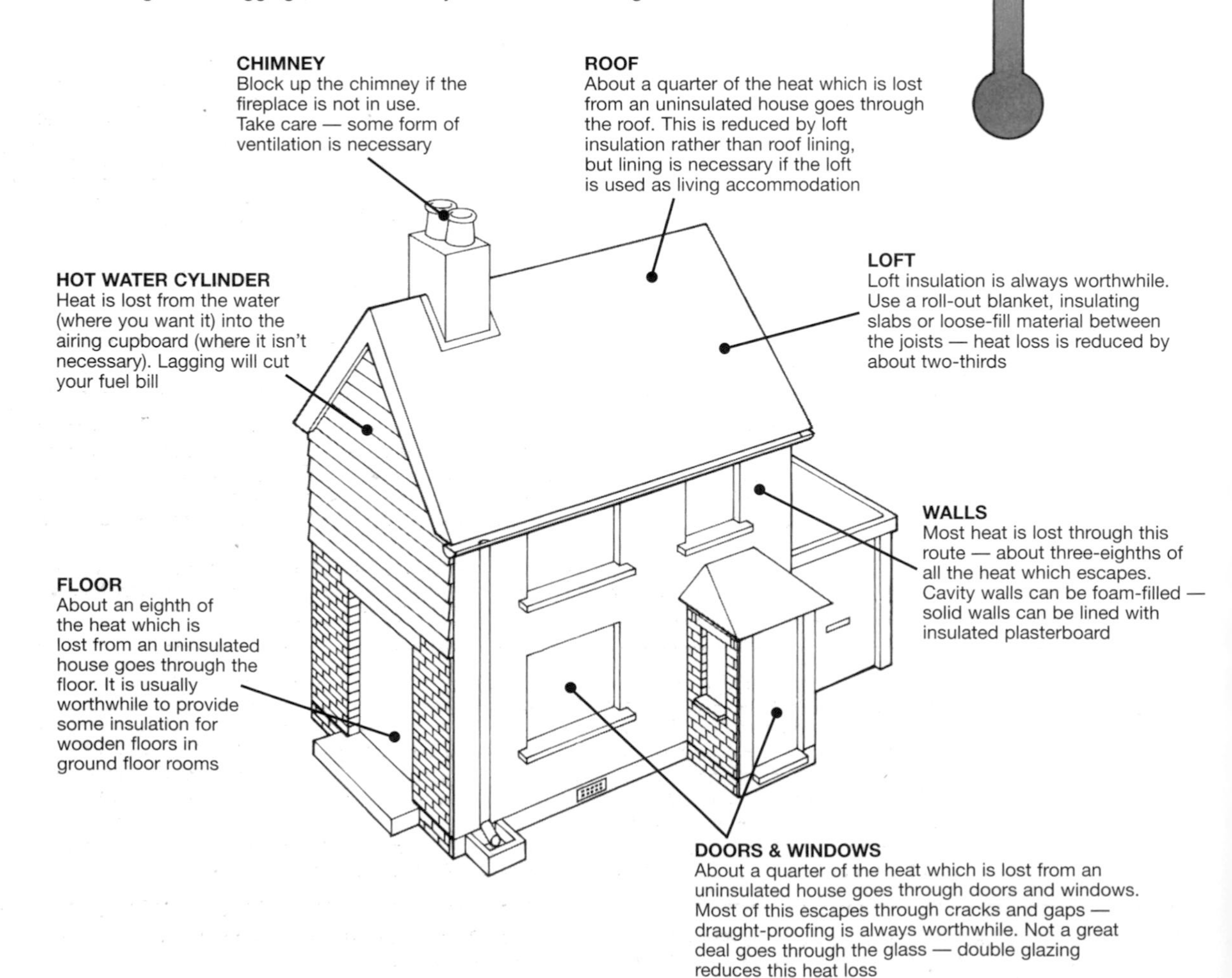

CHIMNEY

An unused fireplace is a significant escape route for warm air in winter. Unlike a badly fitting window you do not feel a direct draught, but an appreciable amount of heat is escaping. Blocking off the fireplace is the obvious solution, but to do so without blocking off the chimney is asking for trouble. The chimney pot must be capped, either with a half round tile (see page 77) or a special ventilator. Note that the chimney must not be blocked completely — some ventilation is essential to prevent condensation.

ROOF

Heat loss from the top of the house is reduced by insulating the floor of the loft rather than the surface under the tiles. There is an exception — if the loft is to be used as a room it is necessary to insulate the roof itself as well as the area between the joists.

There are several methods of roof lining. If there is already a sloping ceiling covering the roof battens you can cover it with expanded polystyrene sheeting, or insulation slabs can be slid into the space between the ceiling and the tiles — there should be at least 5 cm air space for ventilation. If the roof is unlined you will need to cover the space between the battens with strips of roofing felt or polythene and then polystyrene slabs. The final step is to nail thermal plasterboard on the battens to form a ceiling.

HOT WATER CYLINDER

The easiest method of insulation is to fit a padded jacket — see page 18. This should be at least 8 cm thick and the cap and all cables should be left uncovered.

LOFT

Vacuum the area between the joists before you begin, and replace rotten timber. Never stand or kneel on the floor — walk on the joists or on a stout board placed across them. Insulation will create a number of potential problems. Freezing-up will be more likely, so insulate pipes and the cold water cistern (see page 18) — do not lag the floor below the cistern. There will also be an increased risk of condensation — it is a good idea to place polythene sheeting under the insulation to prevent the upward movement of water vapour. The vital step is to ensure that there is adequate ventilation despite insulation. If there are air gaps at the eaves or between the tiles then nothing more need be done. If the roof has been lined and the gap at the eaves blocked then you should drill a series of air-holes in the soffits — cover with fine wire netting.

METHOD 1
Roll-out blanket of 10 cm thick glass fibre or mineral wool — wear gloves, long sleeves and a face mask. Start at the eaves and unroll steadily to the centre of the roof. Push blanket under electric cables

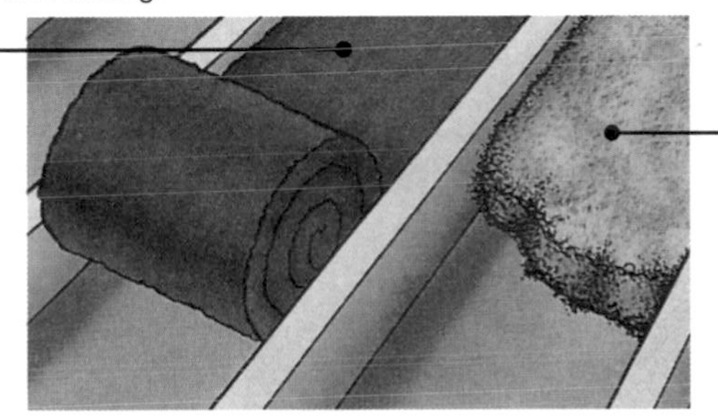

METHOD 2
Loose-fill granules of cork, vermiculite, expanded polystyrene or mineral wool. Easier than method 1, but more expensive and more difficult to keep in place. Use a piece of board to form a smooth layer 5 cm below top of joists

Flat roofs are difficult to insulate. The only practical method is to cut down heat loss by covering the ceiling below. Use expanded polystyrene tiles or thermal plasterboard.

WALLS

Filling the space in cavity walls will reduce heat loss — the cost is recovered in 4 - 5 years. This is not a DIY job and you must seek professional advice before you go ahead. Ask a surveyor or architect whether it is practical for your house — it may not be (timber framing, exposed location etc). If suitable, choose a firm which is registered with the appropriate body, and let them obtain the necessary local authority permission. There are several methods — mineral fibre threads, expanded polystyrene beads and urea-formaldehyde foam.

Solid walls call for different measures. Place aluminium foil behind the radiators to reflect heat back into the room. The easiest structural way to cut down heat loss is to dry-line the room with thermal plasterboard. It must be 5 cm thick to be worthwhile and that will reduce the size of the room.

DOORS & WINDOWS

Test for draughts with a candle — deflection of the flame indicates a draught. For hinged windows the cheapest way is to fit self-adhesive foam strips to the frames. When the window is closed the strip should be slightly compressed. Unfortunately these strips stay permanently squashed after a short time — metal strips and plastic compression seals are more satisfactory but they are more expensive.

Sash windows should be fitted with nylon pile draught excluders. The sides of doors can be fitted with inexpensive foam strip or with dearer but more efficient aluminium strips fitted with plastic seals. You will need a threshold strip at the bottom of the front door.

Look out for other problem areas. Fit a letter-box flap which fits tightly, seal gaps between door or window frames and walls, and block holes at the entry points of pipes into the kitchen.

FLOOR

Tackle the floor insulation problem by filling holes in the floorboards, sealing gaps between the floor and skirting boards, and by using a thick underlay beneath the carpet.

FIRE

Domestic fires are the most serious of all home problems. At best the result is upsetting with some damage — at worst there is loss of life and property. The advice is to stay calm and remember what to do, but the problem is that it is so often a time of panic which leads people to do the wrong thing.

There are about 50,000 domestic fires each year attended by the fire brigade. Small fires which could have got out of hand exceed that number, so it is sensible to take wise precautions (see Chapter 8). The golden rule is to **tackle a small fire promptly and calmly if you have the equipment to do so, but to leave a large fire or a furniture fire with billowing smoke and call the fire brigade immediately**.

Dealing with small fires

The way to put out the flames will depend on the type of fire — water in some cases will do more harm than good. There are a few general rules:

- Get everybody out of the house
- Make sure you have a clear escape route
- Tackle the blaze, but if possible get someone to ring the fire brigade in case it gets out of hand
- If it does get out of hand or choking smoke is driving you back, close all the doors as you quickly leave and wait for the fire brigade outside the house

FRYING PAN FIRES are very common but fortunately are usually easy to extinguish. Switch off the burner if you can and then use either a fire blanket or a damp towel. Hold the blanket or cloth in front of you and drop it over the top of the pan to cover it completely. Turn off the stove if you haven't already done so and leave the pan undisturbed until it is cool. Two don'ts — don't ever use water and don't ever try to lift a burning pan.

ELECTRICAL FIRES are another common type of domestic fire. Switch off the supply and pull out the plug if you can. If you have been able to do this, then the flames can be dealt with by using water or a foam extinguisher. Water must never be used if the electrical supply is still on — use a dry powder extinguisher instead.

PORTABLE HEATER FIRES can be extremely dangerous. If the fuel is paraffin you should stand well away and extinguish with water. Never try to move a burning appliance. Tackling a bottled gas heater should be left to the fire brigade if you can't switch off the gas supply.

FURNITURE FIRES Water or foam can be used, but watch out for smoke. Modern cushions and upholstery often give off a highly toxic gas when burning — such fires should be dealt with by the fire brigade.

OTHER FIRES can be extinguished with water, earth, blankets, sand etc. The general principle when using an extinguisher is to direct around the edge of the fire rather than into its heart.

Dealing with large fires

If you are in the room, back quickly to the exit and close windows and doors if you can. The first priority is to get everyone out and having a pre-arranged drill can be a life-saver. Pull doors closed as you leave and call the fire brigade at once by dialling 999 — speak slowly and give them clear details. Keep everyone together outside the house — don't let anyone go back in to collect valuables, pets etc.

You may be unlucky enough to be trapped. If possible move to a room with a window facing the street and then close the door, blocking the air space at the bottom with a rug or other material. Shout for help from the window, but stay close to the floor at other times. Do not jump unless it is absolutely necessary. If there is no other choice, throw down as much soft material as you can, turn inwards and lower yourself down by your arms. Let go.

CORROSION

The surface of bare metal in contact with air forms a metallic salt which is different from the metal itself. Some of the metal is lost in the process — the metal has corroded. This corrosion layer may be very thin as with the tarnish of silver and the patina of bronze, or thick enough to weaken the metal as in the case of rust on iron and steel.

Most corrosive films are not harmful — this applies to aluminium, zinc, silver, copper, brass and bronze. It may, however, be unsightly — it can be prevented on decorative brass and copper ornaments by spraying with a transparent resin film or it is removed from tarnished objects by polishing. Aluminium is rubbed down before priming and painting — zinc should be painted without rubbing down.

The trouble with rust is that it develops on ferrous metals very quickly and the process continues as long as moisture and air are present. To prevent rust on new metal apply a rust-preventing primer and then an undercoat and topcoat. If rust is present you need a tannate-based primer. Brush away loose rust and rub down the surface until smooth. Paint on the tannate primer — this converts the remaining rust into harmless magnetite and forms a rust-preventing undercoat. Apply two coats and then a topcoat.

CHAPTER 8

SAFETY & SECURITY

Unlike some of life's problems neither accidents nor robberies at home are inevitable — most domestic injuries can be avoided without having to spend any money on safety measures, and many burglaries and break-ins can be prevented by care and commonsense without the need of a sophisticated alarm system. There are many myths and misconceptions — it is helpful to get rid of these mistaken ideas. Electrocution and fires are often thought of as the great killers. Take great care by all means, but only 1 per cent of fatalities are due to electricity, and fires account for 10 per cent of the home accident deaths in the U.K. Most deaths are due to falls by the elderly, suffocation and scalding of the very young, and accidental poisoning. Most burglaries take place in the daytime and most of them involve entry through an open door or by gently forcing a defectively secured window or door. Few burglars like a challenge unless the house is known to contain valuables — they go elsewhere if the property is properly secured.

SAFETY

SAFETY MEASURES AROUND THE HOUSE

- Follow the **GLASS** safety code on page 65. Do not have loose rugs near windows.

- **FLOORS** cause many accidents. Lino, tiles and vinyl can be slippery — carpeting, cork and cushioned vinyl are safer. If there are children or old people in the house make sure that there are no loose rugs, heavy coatings of wax polish, frayed carpets or wet patches.

- **FIRE** can break out in any room in the house. The kitchen is the prime danger area, but read all of page 116 for the specific problems that may arise in each room. There are some general points. Never drape clothes over a heater or in front of an open fire to dry, and have electrical and gas equipment serviced regularly. Cigarettes cause many fires — use a deep ashtray and keep matches and lighters well away from children. Don't hang mirrors in front of fires and store all inflammable liquids away from sources of heat or bright sunlight.

  Each fuel presents its own problems. Read the safety measures for **electricity** (page 9), **gas** (page 12), **coal** and **wood** (page 13) and **liquid fuels** (page 14).

  There is a wide range of fire detection and fire fighting equipment available. A fire blanket stored in the kitchen is recommended — so are smoke detectors. There are mixed views about domestic fire extinguishers — you should certainly have one in the car and a dry powder type in the garage. A multi-purpose extinguisher in the hall is a useful precaution, but you ought to get out of a burning house rather than trying to deal with it yourself.

  Despite all your precautions there may still be a fire. Read what to do (page 114) before an emergency occurs.

- **TOXIC LIQUIDS** and **POWDERS** must be stored safely. Throw away all unlabelled packages and take old prescriptions back to the chemist. Medicines should be kept in a locked cupboard away from children. Keep pesticides and DIY products in the shed or garage — never throw empty aerosols on the fire. If there are precautions on the label you must read them before use.

- It is a sad fact that the growing interest in **DIY** has led to a disturbing increase in accidents. Half the injuries are due to either cuts from sharp tools or falls. Learn to use saws, chisels etc in the proper manner (page 87) and don't climb a ladder unless it is secure (page 74). A circuit breaker should be present when using electrical equipment outdoors (page 9) and buy a simple metal detector to test for cables and pipes before drilling into walls. The golden rule is to avoid all jobs with a potential hazard unless you know what you are doing and have the proper equipment and safety clothing to do it.

- Look for **SAFETY LABELS** when buying equipment and furniture.

- Learn the way to lift **HEAVY OBJECTS**. Bend your knees and not your back. Let your leg muscles do the work — not your shoulder muscles. Know your limitations — use a trolley when the object is too heavy for you.

- Have a properly equipped **FIRST-AID CABINET**. Learn the rudiments of first aid in case of an emergency but this does not mean that you have to be a skilled first aider. In case of a serious accident seek medical help immediately — this is no place for DIY.

SAFETY IN THE KITCHEN

The oven and hob are the danger areas. The hob should be away from doors and curtains — and draughts if gas-fuelled. Don't fill a pan more than half way with oil, and dry food before placing in hot fat. Always turn handles so that they do not project beyond the hob or over a lighted burner. Do keep small children well away — fit a guard rail to the hob. Don't leave pans on the stove if you leave the room, and never let flex trail close to the hot plates or rings. Open oven doors slowly and use gloves to remove hot containers.

Do not use either gloss paint or expanded polystyrene tiles on the ceiling. Lift up spilt food and mop up spilt liquid from the floor immediately.

Never connect electrical equipment to a light socket.

Take care with kitchen knives. They should not be kept loose — store in a wall rack placed well above little fingers or keep in a knife block. Always cut on a level and firm surface — keep your fingers well away. Take care when opening cans.

SAFETY IN THE BEDROOM

Do not smoke in bed. Take care with hot water bottles — do not use boiling water and remove from children's beds before they go to bed.

Nightgowns should be made of flame-resistant material — keep all fabrics away from radiant fires.

Electric blankets can cause problems — they should not be damp, creased or worn.

A bedside lamp will avoid you stubbing your toe or tripping over things in the dark — never try to dim the lamp by putting cloth over the shade. Have a night-light in a child's room.

If the windows are double glazed, make sure bedroom ones can be opened in case of an emergency.

SAFETY IN THE BATHROOM

Don't take any electric equipment into the bathroom, apart from an electric razor or toothbrush. Switches should be the pull-cord type and both light fixtures and heaters must be well away from wet hands.

Baths should have an anti-slip base — so should the shower. Turn on the cold tap in the bath before adding the hot water. Read about showers on page 38.

Never put bleach and cleaner into the toilet at the same time — chlorine gas can be produced and the effect is most unpleasant and can be dangerous.

Safety for the elderly

Seven out of every 10 home fatalities involve people who are over 65 years old. Falls are the main problem. Use the following check list — no loose tiles or other floor coverings, good lighting near stairs, firm hand-rail on stairs, no climbing on chairs or stools to reach high objects and no wax polish on floors.

The elderly must also avoid vigorous exertion in cold weather after a period of inactivity. Spring digging and spring lawn mowing take their toll each year. More widely publicised is hypothermia — the room temperature must always be above 10° C for elderly people.

For the elderly who live alone there are help-summoning systems. Pressing the button on the neck-worn unit brings assistance. They are not expensive — ask your local Council for details.

SAFETY IN THE LIVING/DINING ROOM

Be careful with hot drinks — keep them well away from babies and toddlers, and do not rest a cup on the arm of a chair.

Wear oven gloves to move oven-to-table dishes into the dining room — warn the family that the casserole or pan is hot.

Make sure that toys are safe — no tiny detachable bits or sharp points for toddlers, no loose eyes on teddies etc. Watch your own safety — there are many accidents caused each year by adults tripping over playthings.

Smouldering upholstered furniture can be lethal — look for the green match-resistant label when buying.

Pull out the TV plug when you plan to be away. This is especially important when you are going on holiday.

Don't empty ashtrays into a waste-paper bin, and don't smoke if you often fall asleep in front of the TV.

Avoid trailing flexes, multi-way plugs and flexes under carpets.

SAFETY IN THE HALL

A staggering 100,000 people are hurt each year by falling down the stairs, and nearly half the injured are small children. Follow the rules — a firm hand-rail, nothing left on the stairs, good lighting, no loose mats near the stairs, a non-slip surface on the treads and no sharp-cornered objects near the top or bottom of the staircase.

A gleaming hall floor may look nice, but it can be a menace for the young or very old.

Remember the stairs and hallway are your escape route in case of fire — keep clear of hazardous objects. Obviously you must do all you can to prevent the staircase burning in case of a fire when you are upstairs — do not store paper, rags, inflammable liquids etc under the stairs. On your way to bed at night, close all the doors along the hall. This will help to prevent flames and smoke from spreading in case of a fire.

It is essential that the hall should be well-lit. Switches at the bottom and top of the stairs are most useful.

Safety for children

One out of every 10 home fatalities involves a child who is under 5 years old. Parental carelessness is the major problem before the toddler stage, and then childhood curiosity becomes a major factor.

Never use a pillow during the baby's first year. Never leave a baby alone in the bath or alone with a feeding bottle. Keep all small objects away — so many accidents are caused each year by babies swallowing beads, buttons, peanuts, crisps, sweets etc.

The toddler stage brings extra problems. You will need a safety gate at the bottom and top of the stairs and perhaps one at the kitchen door. Fit safety catches to upstairs windows and fit corner cushions to sharp furniture edges. Keep plastic bags out of reach and store dangerous liquids in a safe place. Obviously this means medicines, disinfectants, paints, pesticides etc but for young children it also means alcoholic drinks, detergents and many other apparently safe liquids. Fit a child-resistant catch on the door of the sink cupboard and cover electric sockets.

SECURITY

There are basically two types of housebreaker — the professional burglar and the sneak thief. The professional burglar will have generally chosen his target with care — he will know or strongly suspect that valuables are present. His first job will be to inspect the property to see the easiest point of entry, the safest escape route, signs of you being away and so on. The professional usually likes to have ample time in which to work and does not leave a deliberate trail of destruction from room to room. Damage is done only if he has to break into things to get to the objects he is searching for. Once found, the burglar leaves as quickly as possible. Report to the police immediately anyone who seems to be paying undue attention to your house. You will have to make your house secure, using the Security Plan on page 118.

For most of us the professional burglar is not the problem. The majority of break-ins are carried out by sneak thieves. About three-quarters of them are children or teenagers who are looking for easy access. If they can't find it, they move on elsewhere and the result is often senseless vandalism. Insurance cannot cover the deep sense of shock suffered by the unfortunate victim. The answer is to make the sneak thief go elsewhere — he will not have made your home the object of his day's work. The house should look occupied at all times and entry must be made difficult at all times. To see if your house is secure, you can follow the excellent police advice — go out and lose your key! Of course you needn't actually lose your key, but do see how you could enter the empty house without a key and by causing little or no external damage to gain entry. You will probably find it can be done quite simply. Read the Security Plan on the next page.

WHAT A THIEF LOOKS FOR

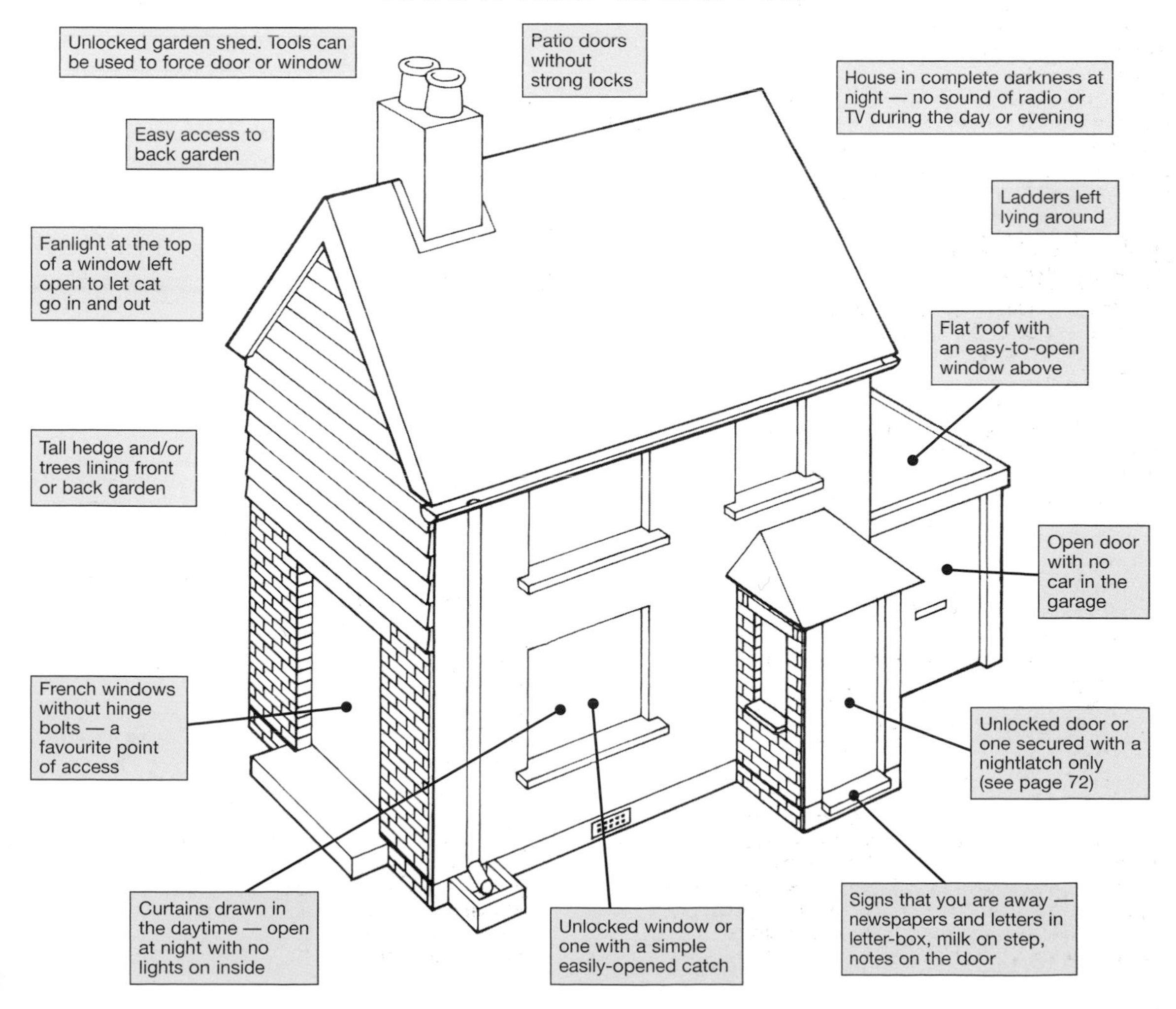

THE SECURITY PLAN
— the 6 steps to a safe home

1 **Put valuables away** Keep share certificates, house deeds, precious jewellery etc in a safe deposit box in a bank or security company. If you have to keep large amounts of money at home, consider a safe.

2 **If you can't, take security measures** Don't talk about your valuables, money or forthcoming holidays in a public place. Never place valuables in a room where they can be seen by passers-by. Mark items with special ink which becomes visible under UV light — use your postcode plus house number. Insure valuables adequately — take photographs and keep an inventory.

3 **Install the essential security items** There are hundreds of security items on the market — but only a few are essential. Nine out of every 10 entries are through open or inefficiently closed doors or windows. A simple nightlatch on the front door can be opened very easily — you need a mortise deadlock (see page 72). Downstairs windows need key-operated window locks. French windows need hinge bolts and sliding patio doors should have a key-operated security lock.

4 **Carry out the essential drill before you go out**
If leaving for a short time —

- Lock the external doors and windows — close the garage door.
- Switch the radio on. If going out at night switch on at least one light after drawing the curtains of the room. Switch on an outside light if there is one.

If going on holiday —

- Cancel the papers, milk and any other regular deliveries.
- Keep the curtains open. Lock the external doors and windows — close and lock the garage door and lock the garden shed.
- Arrange with a neighbour to keep an eye on the property. This will call for throwing away free newspapers, pushing mail through the letter-box and perhaps cutting the lawn.
- Most experts believe that you should not lock drawers nor internal doors when the house is unoccupied.

5 **Don't ask for trouble** Don't do any of the silly things which make the job of a thief easier. The list includes leaving the back door open when watching evening TV, and leaving the key under the mat. Notes to tradesmen pinned to the front door are another open invitation. Don't leave the key for a window lock on the window frame. Change the locks when you move house.

6 **If you are cautious, nervous or have valuables, consider the optional extras** Fit a door chain on the front door, plus a door viewer if you are nervous. The back door will need a deadlock like the front one. Insurance companies may advise you to have key-operated bolts at the top and bottom of doors which open to the outside. Fit key-operated locks to upper as well as the downstairs windows. Double glazing is a great deterrent.

Install a strong porch light. Fit a light sensor switch in one or two rooms which turns on the light at night and off at dawn. Leave on all the time, not just when you are away. Alternatively you can buy time switches which can be set to turn on the lights at either pre-set or random times. Install an outside light which switches on for a few minutes when you (or an intruder) approaches. Don't try to illuminate your house like a Christmas tree on the nights when you are away — a burglar will know you are out if it doesn't look normal.

Burglar alarms are useful — they will frighten off an intruder and warn neighbours of a break-in. Magnetic alarms are the most reliable type, but they are also the most complex and the most expensive. Windows and doors are fitted with magnetic contacts which when opened cause the alarm to ring, and pressure pads are fitted below carpets. Easier to install are the infra-red and ultra-sonic systems, but some of these can be triggered off by draughts. There are still more additional extras — a barking dog can be as good as a burglar alarm, sticky anti-burglar paint can be used on drainpipes and battery-operated personal alarms can be installed by the front door or bedside. An optional extra which will cost you nothing is to obtain advice from your Crime Prevention Officer — ring the police station and he will visit your home.

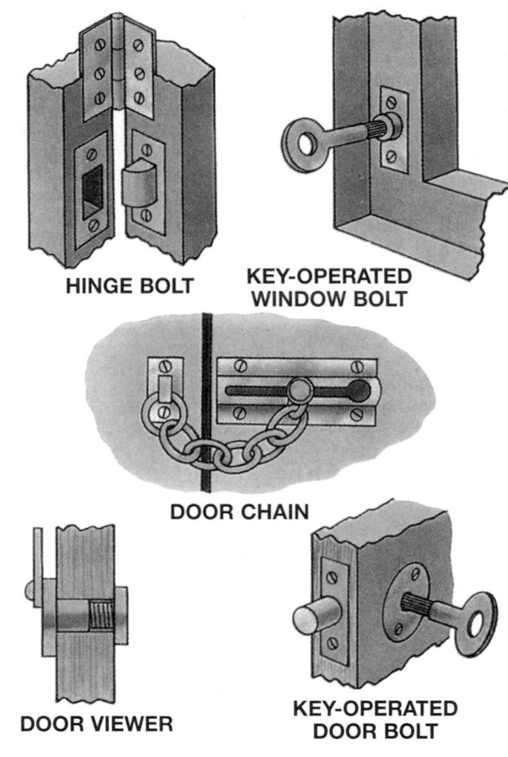

The Neighbourhood Watch Scheme

There is nothing new or very clever in the basic concept — Neighbourhood Watch is merely a development of the age-old good neighbour policy, plus some police involvement. There is no well-defined set of rules for starting up a scheme. There are many variations, but the basic principles are generally the same. A police Crime Prevention Officer calls on each house in a street or group of streets to explain the scheme and to enlist support. There are window stickers for the participants, and each member of the scheme takes on the duties of watchfulness without legal liability.

There is no have-a-go or vigilante element. Suspicious actions are reported immediately to the police station, security problems are often discussed and when a member goes on holiday he appoints a key holder. The measure of involvement is agreed by the group.

Burglary the easy way

The most surprising aspect of home security is that many thousands of burglaries do not involve break-ins. A quarter of all home robberies involve a thief who simply enters through an open door or window. Another method of unforced entry is by the person who calls "from the water board, electricity office, the Council to assess the rates" and so on. Never say yes until you have been shown some item of official identification. Read it — if in doubt call the office before allowing entry.

Don't put your name and address on keys, and if possible keep your keys separate from a purse, handbag etc which contains identification information.

The most despicable form of non-forced entry is the false telephone call supposedly from the police to say that there has been an accident. The recipient understandably rushes out without closing doors, windows etc. Ring the number back if you have the presence of mind, or ask a neighbour to keep an eye on things.

CHAPTER 9

HOME CARE

Most of this book is devoted to the way the home is made, decorated and equipped. Dangers and faults are dealt with, and the ways to tackle simple repairs are described.

This final chapter deals with everyday upkeep — the cleaning and general maintenance of the fixtures and fittings which fill your home. If you do not have someone to do this for you then these are DIY tasks. This aspect of home DIY takes up only a tiny part of the book, but absorbs a large part of the working day of the person whose job is to look after the house. The basic reason is that most home care jobs are time-consuming but are both simply described and usually already understood. It is not words but equipment plus energy which are required.

ANODISED ALUMINIUM

Trolleys, trays, saucepan lids etc. Remove marks with a damp cloth — polish with a dry one. Do not put in a dishwasher.

BASINS & BATHS

Remove tide marks with a small amount of washing-up liquid on a cloth. **Porcelain-enamelled** and **vitreous-enamelled** baths should be cleaned with a cream cleaner. Check that it is recommended for vitreous enamel — there will be a V on the label. Never use an abrasive powder cleaner as it can scratch the surface.

Acrylic plastic baths should be wiped down with a mild detergent. Fine scratches can be removed with silver polish and a soft cloth.

In hard-water areas scale and stains build up under and around taps and around plugholes. Buy a proprietary bath-stain remover and follow the instructions exactly.

BLANKETS

Check the care label before washing — if in doubt, use the wool programme on your washing machine. If the machine is too small for this job, take the blanket to a launderette or to the cleaners.

Washing is straightforward, but drying can cause problems. In a washing machine the spin should be for a very short time and when the blanket is to be hung out to dry it is essential that it is damp and not wet when put on the line.

BRASS

Utensils: Wash in hot water and detergent. Rinse and dry, then treat with brass or copper polish. If stained, rub with cut lemon sprinkled with salt.

Ornaments: If unlacquered, use brass or copper polish. If lacquered, clean with a soft duster. The lacquer coating breaks down in time, especially if the object is constantly handled. Remove remaining lacquer and the tarnish with acetone. Polish, then respray with transparent lacquer.

BRONZE

Clean with a soft duster. If dirty, wash in hot water and detergent. Rinse and dry. If stained or coated with verdigris, remove as much as you can with a wire brush or knife, then rub surface with paraffin.

CANE

Clean with a soft duster. If dirty, wash with warm salty water — rinse and dry. Do not soak cane or wicker — just wipe down with the solution and leave outdoors to dry.

CARPETS

Regular vacuuming not only makes a carpet look better, it also prolongs its life by removing grit. The usual routine is to vacuum about once a week, but spilt food should be brushed up as soon as possible. Matting should be lifted periodically so that the floor below can be cleaned.

Uneven wear can be a problem. Move furniture about occasionally if you can — place rugs at entry points from outdoors and over the foot zone in front of much-used armchairs. If an area has been crushed by furniture, dampen the patch and then vacuum.

Stains are another problem — the appropriate treatment can be found on pages 104 – 105. Act quickly — mop up spills with paper towels or rags then squirt affected area with a soda water syphon. Cover grease with talcum powder as soon as possible. The exception to speedy treatment is mud — leave it to dry before scraping or brushing off. With fitted carpets keep a few scraps at laying time — use them for testing the safety of stain removers if one is required at some later date.

At intervals of a few months or a few years (depending on the amount of wear) you will have to shampoo the carpet. There are various DIY systems — dry, wet, aerosol etc. It is a good idea to hire an electrical shampooer for this job, and if the carpet is badly stained you should consider using a professional cleaning company who will come to your home. Always obtain a quote before cleaning starts.

CHROME

Clean with a soft duster. If dirty or stained, wash in hot water and detergent. Rinse and dry, then polish with chrome cleaner.

COOKER

Don't let burnt food accumulate on or in the cooker — wipe off spills immediately and brush out the oven after use. Switch off the electricity or gas before you start to clean the cooker. Soak all movable parts (trays, shelves etc) in warm water and a biological detergent — rub stubborn stains with a nylon brush. Rinse and dry thoroughly.

Clean the vitreous enamel body of the cooker with a cream cleaner — use a proprietary oven cleaner for the inside. Never use an abrasive material on the lining of an oven. Wash the oven window with bicarbonate of soda on a damp cloth. Oven cleaning is an unpleasant job — a welcome advance has been the self-cleaning oven.

COPPER

See BRASS.

CROCKERY & CHINA

Ideally you should wash up immediately after the meal is finished. If this is not possible, rinse and then soak the dishes in cold soapy water. Use a good quality washing-up liquid and warm water — use a brush to remove food from crevices and never use abrasives or scourers on bone china or porcelain. Rinse in clean warm water and leave to dry. With delicate crockery you must avoid sudden changes in temperature which can cause cracking. Stains can be a problem. Remove tea and coffee stains in cups with a hot washing soda solution.

With a dishwasher load after every meal and switch on each evening. Check that the items are dishwasher-proof.

CURTAINS

Accumulated dust can destroy your curtains. Vacuum heavy drapes and dust down others, but all curtains need occasional washing or cleaning.

Lined and heavy curtains should be dry cleaned. At the other end of the scale net curtains are easily washed — soak for 15 minutes to loosen the dirt and then wash as recommended on page 37. Dry by hanging along a rod. Other curtains are less easy to wash — remove hooks and take down the hem before you begin.

CUTLERY

Wash cutlery immediately after use — rinse if washing is not possible. The reason is that many foods stain silver plate, and salt affects stainless steel. Keep non-metal handles out of the water if cutlery is left to soak.

Use hot water and washing-up liquid. Rinse and dry — store silver-plated cutlery in a felt-lined box.

FLOORS

Sweep or dry-mop the floor regularly — daily if possible. The correct method of cleaning depends on the type of floor, so there can be few general rules. Choose a non-slip product where wax polishing is recommended, and do not use too much water when mopping is recommended. Above all, never build up a thick layer of slippery wax.

Wood: Sweep the floor regularly — daily if possible. Wash only occasionally. If the floor is unsealed it will be necessary to oil or wax polish the surface every 2 months. It is better to apply a sealer which only requires cleaning with a moist mop.

Linoleum: Wipe over with a damp cloth — do not soak the floor with a wet mop. Polish occasionally with a water-based emulsion.

Vinyl: Wipe over with a cloth dampened with mild detergent — do not soak the floor with a wet mop. Remove scratch marks with fine steel wool.

Quarry tiles: Use a detergent solution or a proprietary floor cleaner. Mop sealed floors — scrub unsealed ones. Polish when dry with self-shine tile polish — use very sparingly.

Cork: Wipe over sealed tiles occasionally with a damp cloth — polish with a water-based emulsion. Unsealed tiles should be treated with non-slip wax polish.

FURNITURE

Antique wood: Dust regularly and store properly — keep out of direct sunlight and turn down the central heating to avoid over-dry air. A little furniture cream can be applied occasionally — but the treatment of antique furniture should be left to the experts.

Oiled wood: See page 97. Dust regularly and rub twice a year with a cloth and a little teak or Danish oil. Apply sparingly.

Waxed wood: See page 97. Dust regularly and rub occasionally with wax polish.

Varnished wood: See page 97. Dust regularly and polish occasionally with furniture cream or a silicone-based liquid polish. A range of spray polishes is available.

Painted wood: See PAINTWORK.

Minor repairs:

Removing water and heat rings and spots

Cold liquids cause dark stains on polished surfaces — white stains are usually due to alcohol or hot tea/coffee. Apply metal polish to a soft cloth and rub it over the stain, working along the grain. Polish the area after treatment. Superficial stains will be removed — deeper stains call for stripping off the old surface and applying a new one.

Removing scratches

There is no easy way to remove a deep scratch — stripping and refinishing is the only way. It is often possible, however, to disguise a scratch with a wax crayon or with coloured varnish.

Removing bruises and dents

Shallow dents can be removed by a simple steam treatment in softwood, but the chance of success with hardwood is much less. Spread a damp cloth over the damaged area and run a warm iron over the surface. The damp heat swells the grain and fills the dent.

Removing veneer blisters

Cover affected area with a cloth and run a warm iron over the area.

GLASS

Coffee tables, shelves etc. Treat in the same way as WINDOWS, using a proprietary window cleaner or a 1 part water/1 part vinegar solution. Remove fine scratches by rubbing the surface with metal polish before washing.

GLASSWARE

Deal with the glassware first when washing up. Use hot soapy water — rinse in warm water and dry immediately to avoid streaking. Never stand or store glasses on their rims — always keep them upright. Standing tumblers inside each other can save space, but they often get stuck. To free them, stand the lower one in hot water and fill the upper one with ice.

Deal with stained decanters and vases by filling with a warm solution of biological detergent — leave overnight. If scale or other film still remains, fill the container with a solution of salt and vinegar in warm water — again leave to stand overnight.

GLOVES

Washable gloves are easily cleaned — put them on and immerse your hands in warm soapy water. Squeeze your hands together, and then repeat the process in clean water to remove the soap. Dry on a towel at room temperature.

Non-washable gloves are more difficult to clean. If dirt is the problem, try an India rubber. If grease spots are the trouble, dust with Fuller's Earth and leave overnight. Brush off the powder — repeat if necessary.

GOLD

Rub with a soft duster. To restore the shine wash in warm water to which a mild detergent and some household ammonia has been added. Rinse, dry and burnish with a soft cloth.

IRON

The sole plate may become coated with starch, size or burnt fabric. Try scraping with a strip of wood and then rubbing with a nylon scourer. If this fails turn the iron on and when the sole plate is warm to the touch, switch off and rub soap over the affected area. Rub the sole plate on a piece of unwanted cloth.

IVORY

Unlike antique furniture, ivory should be kept in a sunny spot. Dust regularly — use a paintbrush to clean intricate carvings. Never put in water.

JEWELLERY

You can buy a jewellery kit to polish settings but do be careful when trying to clean stones. Diamonds, onyx, topaz, emeralds, rubies and many others are cleaned by being dipped into warm soapy water and then brushed gently with a soft brush before drying with a chamois leather. Diamonds are dipped into surgical spirit (or gin!) for their final sparkle. But some precious stones, such as turquoise and opal should not be put into water. Simply rub with a chamois leather, but as with all valuable jewellery the best plan is to take it to a professional.

KETTLE

Descaling is necessary at regular intervals in hard-water areas. Cover the element with 1 part vinegar/1 part water and bring to the boil. Leave overnight, empty and rinse. Boil water twice and empty before bringing the kettle into service again.

LAMPSHADES

Plastic and glass can be washed — all other types should be dusted. Plastic lampshades become very dusty — rub with an anti-static cloth before replacing.

LAUNDRY

There is an enormous range of washing aids these days, but there is no common labelling code to tell you which type you are buying. The best plan is to try several brands until you find the one that suits you.

Heavy duty powders are by far the most popular — the soap-based ones are suitable for soft-water regions but in a hard-water area you will require a synthetic detergent. Some contain enzymes — the so-called 'biological', 'low-temperature' and 'all-temperature' washing powders. These powders are especially useful for removing protein stains such as blood and perspiration, but it seems that some people may develop a rash from enzyme-based powders.

Low-foaming products are used in front-loading machines which would not function effectively with lots of suds. The word 'automatic' appears on the label — a few are enzyme-free but most are biological. Liquids are available.

Light duty products include the liquids, powders and flakes used in hand-hot or cool water — the products used for hand washing.

Fabric conditioners reduce static and maintain the softness of woollens, brushed fabrics and towelling.

Enzyme-based pre-washers are used to remove stains from heavily-soiled articles before washing.

Stiffeners are used to add body to fabrics before ironing. Both powder and spray starches are available.

Sort laundry before washing — if you plan to wash a mixture in one load, you must use the gentlest programme (see page 37). Empty pockets and close zips, brush off dirt and tie up loose ribbons. Treat woollens with care — never wash by machine unless the label recommends it. The standard programme for woollens is to wash by hand and rinse in warm water, and then roll the article in a towel to remove excess moisture. Finally, spread out the garment on a flat surface away from heat and sunlight.

LAVATORY

Clean daily, using a specific lavatory cleaner. Sprinkle inside the pan and after the recommended soaking time clean the inside with a lavatory brush. You can use household bleach as an alternative to a lavatory cleaner, but you should never mix the two together. Wash the seat and outside with warm water and a mild detergent.

LEATHER

Leather furniture is expensive and should be looked after. Dust regularly and occasionally treat with a hide cleaner. Use sparingly, and do not use an ordinary or general-purpose polish. If the leather has become stiff, use saddle soap — if faded, touch up the light spots with leather stain.

MIRRORS

Use a proprietary cleaner — the problem with water is that it can damage the silvering behind the glass. Cleaning with crumpled newspaper and a thin coating of glycerine will prevent the steaming up of bathroom mirrors. Hair lacquer spots are sometimes a problem on bedroom and bathroom mirrors — remove with methylated spirits before cleaning in the normal way.

PAINTWORK

The standard method of cleaning paintwork is to wash with warm water and a little washing-up liquid. Rinse and dry. A few tips — dust door tops, cupboard tops etc thoroughly before washing and work downwards from ceiling to floor. Never use washing powder.

Grimy paintwork calls for a different treatment — sugar soap solution and a pail of rinsing water. Rub one patch at a time with a sponge until the dirt is removed — rinse with clean water and dry with a cloth before going on to the next section. Most experts recommend that you should work from ground level upwards, but previously-cleaned patches can be streaked if you follow this advice.

PEWTER

Wash in warm soapy water and dry thoroughly. Burnish with a cabbage leaf.

PLASTICS

Plastic sheeting and surfaces: See page 100 for descriptions. Wash with warm water and a mild detergent. Do not rub laminates with a dry duster.

Plastic utensils and crockery: Wash by hand if not labelled as dishwasher-proof. Keep polyethylene utensils away from naked flames.

POTS & PANS

Soak immediately after use and then clean with a pan scourer and hot soapy water. Burnt-on food can be removed by soaking overnight in a biological detergent. Apart from these general rules there are specific instructions for the different materials.

Aluminium: Avoid harsh abrasives and allow pans to cool before washing. Black stains can be removed by boiling dilute vinegar or an acid food (e.g rhubarb) in the pan. Dry cookware immediately after washing.

Vitreous enamel: Avoid harsh abrasive cleaners and abrasive pan scourers — use a cream cleaner approved for enamel. Remove stains with dilute household bleach.

Cast iron: Frying pans should only be washed if they cannot be cleaned by the recommended method — a small amount of oil rubbed in with kitchen paper.

Stainless steel: Avoid harsh abrasive cleaners and abrasive pan scourers. Dry immediately after washing — polish occasionally with a stainless steel cleaner.

Non-stick surfaces: Follow the maker's instructions — avoid harsh abrasive powders and abrasive pan scourers.

Tinware: After baking wash and wipe the cake tins and place in the still-warm oven to dry thoroughly.

SHOES

Wash off surface dirt before polishing — allow to dry. Shoes must be polished regularly to feed and protect the leather as well as to improve the appearance. Once it was a matter of brushing a good quality wax polish into the leather (especially the welt) and then brushing the surface with a polishing brush before buffing with a soft cloth. Nowadays there are all sorts of products — creams, aerosols, self-shining liquids, sponge-headed applicators and so on. Be guided by the assistant — follow the instructions. Scuffed shoes will need a renovating polish — tight shoes call for a leather-expanding product. Rub patent leather shoes occasionally with a little petroleum jelly.

SILVER

Silver and silver-plated articles should be polished regularly to prevent the development of tarnish. Many silver cleaners are available — the impregnated wadding type is the most popular. Tarnish is a problem on intricately-modelled pieces — use a silver-cleaning dip and follow the instructions exactly. After polishing rub with a soft duster — silver-cleaning cloths are available which delay tarnish formation. For badly tarnished items you can try Silver Solution which silver-plates articles when rubbed on.

SINKS

Wash regularly with hot water and washing-up liquid. Never use harsh abrasives to remove stains — clean stainless steel sinks with a specific cleaner and use a cream cleaner on vitreous enamel ones.

STAINLESS STEEL

Despite the name, stainless steel can be stained or pitted by a number of agents — salt, acidic foods, bleach, some detergents etc. Always wipe stainless steel immediately after washing — even when taken from the dishwasher. Wipe with lemon juice or a cut lemon to brighten the surface. For specific instructions see CUTLERY, POTS & PANS and SINKS.

STEEL

Iron and steel pans, knives etc should be washed in hot water and detergent — remove deposits with an abrasive powder or steel wool pad. Rinse and dry immediately.

STONE

Never wash stone with soapy water — the residual scum will be hard to remove. Wipe or scrub with washing soda in hot water — rinse with plain water.

SUEDE

Despite what others do, never use a wire brush. Suede coats, jackets and shoes should be brushed with a rubber brush. Treat grubby spots with oatmeal — leave for a couple of hours and then remove with a soft brush. Treat occasionally with suede dressing (shoes) or suede cleaner (clothing).

TILES

Wipe with warm water and washing-up liquid. Alternatively use a spray or aerosol window cleaner. Clean grouting with a brush and dilute household bleach. Rinse and dry.

UPHOLSTERY

Remove cushions from sofas and armchairs before thoroughly brushing or vacuuming. Pay special attention to the edges and crevices — old crumbs can attract mice. Reverse cushions when replacing them to ensure even wear.

Stains should be dealt with promptly — see pages 104 - 105. Cleaning is necessary once or twice a year — consult the care leaflet which came with the furniture. Most fabrics can be treated with dry-foam upholstery shampoo but some cannot. These fabrics (velvet, tapestry, silk, wool) should be left to a professional cleaner. Dry clean or wash loose covers — if washed, replace on chairs whilst still damp. Vinyl and other plastic should be wiped with a soft cloth and a mild detergent. You can use a cream cleaner or spray polish recommended for plastics, but never use abrasives, solvents or wax polish.

VENETIAN BLINDS

Dust regularly — wear an old pair of cotton gloves and run your hand along the slats.

VINYL

See PLASTICS.

WALL COVERINGS

Gently dust or vacuum wallpaper to prevent griminess. If the paper has dirty patches, rub the affected areas with stale white bread.

Washable wallpapers should be cleaned with a sponge dampened with water and a little washing-up liquid. Avoid over-wetting the surface — work up and down, not side to side.

Vinyls are much more resistant to water — they can be lightly scrubbed to remove marks and grease.

Fabrics need gentle handling. Use a long-handled soft brush or a vacuum fitted with a brush attachment. Do not use liquid cleaners.

WINDOWS

The traditional method of washing windows is to use a bucket of warm water and a couple of wash leathers (chamois leather, synthetic chamois leather or lint-free cloth). Wash with one, wrung out so that it is damp and not wet, working from the edges to the middle. The other cloth should be almost dry — wipe over the washed surface.

Wash windows on dull, frost-free days. If the windows are very dirty add a little washing-up liquid to the water. Change the water frequently.

It is much quicker but more expensive to wash windows with a spray-on or aerosol window cleaner — a solution of 1 part water/1 part vinegar is a cheap substitute. Simply spray on a fine film and then wipe off with a clean cloth. For sparkling glass, finish off with crumpled newspaper.

THE BASIC TOOL KIT

Buy a basic tool kit of essential items — purchase them individually or as a boxed set. These are the tools you will use most often and you should always get the best you can afford. Add to these basic items as your needs and interest grow. Remember that many items can be hired these days, so it is foolish to buy an expensive item if it is to be used very rarely. Keep tools on racks on the wall — tool-hanging clips on a pegboard are one of the best storage methods. Apply a thin coating of oil on steel surfaces after use and keep all tools well away from children.

ELECTRICAL TOOL KIT
See page 9

HAMMERS

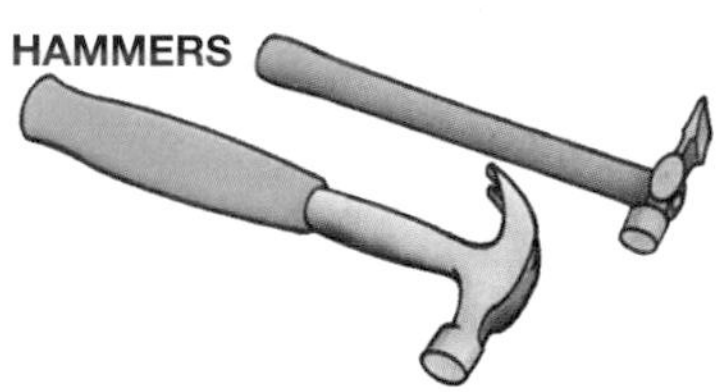

450 gm claw hammer with steel shaft for general woodworking jobs

110 gm pin hammer with wooden shaft for delicate woodworking jobs

SAWS

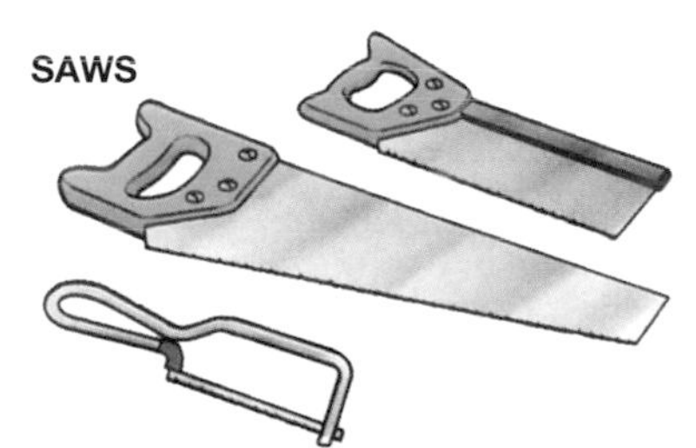

Panel saw (50 - 60 cm) for general woodworking jobs — see page 87

Tenon saw (25 - 30 cm long) for jointing and small woodworking jobs — see page 87

Junior hacksaw (15 cm blade) for cutting metal and plastic

SCREWDRIVERS

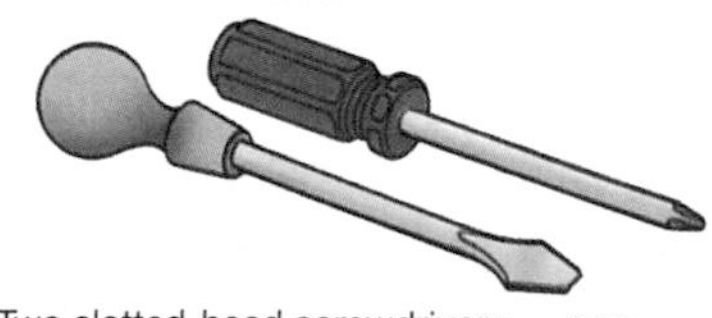

Two slotted-head screwdrivers — one for 6 - 8 gauge screws and the other for 10 - 12 gauge screws. See page 88

One cross-head screwdriver — use with Phillips or Pozidriv screws

FLEXIBLE TAPE

3 m steel tape. Look for essential features — return spring, thumb lock and both metric and imperial markings

STEEL RULE

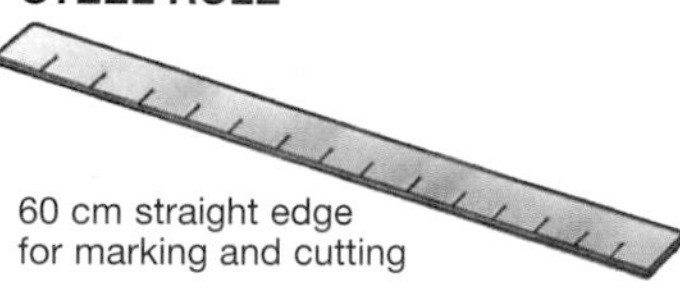

60 cm straight edge for marking and cutting

FOLDING RULE

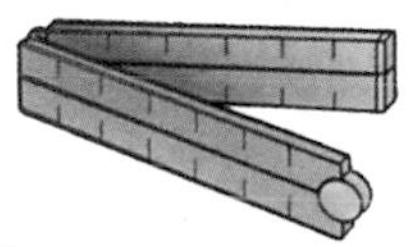

Boxwood or plastic 1 m folding ruler — useful in confined spaces

SPIRIT LEVEL

Metal or plastic body about 60 cm long. Buy one with both horizontal and vertical vials set in the body

BRADAWL

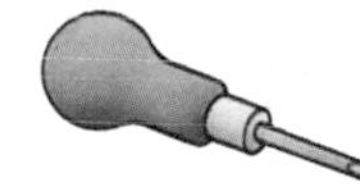

Small chisel-like point for starting drill or screw holes. A gimlet has a corkscrew-like tip

COMBINATION SQUARE

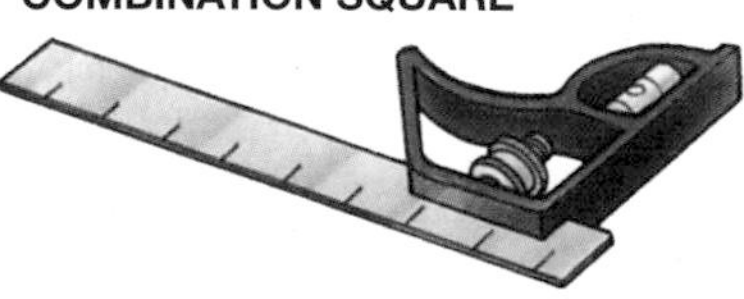

Somewhat complex for a basic kit, but extremely useful. Buy one with a 30 cm metal rule, try square and protractor for marking angles on wood, and a spirit level

SURFORM

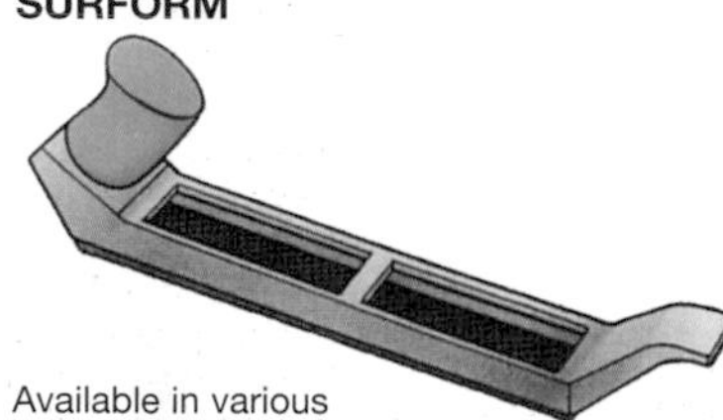

Available in various shapes and sizes — used for shaping wood, plastic and metal

CHISELS

Two chisels — blade widths 6 mm and 25 mm. Check for plastic handles and slip-on blade covers. See page 87

DRILL

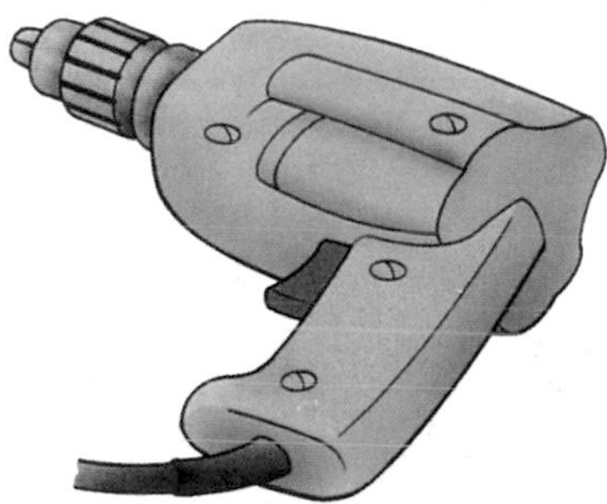

10 mm chuck, 2 speed electric drill plus a range of bits (4 - 10 mm) are the basic kit. Buy accessories (sanding disc, circular saw etc) as required

BOLSTER CHISEL

5 cm wide blade — used for lifting concrete, plaster and floorboards

ADJUSTABLE SPANNER

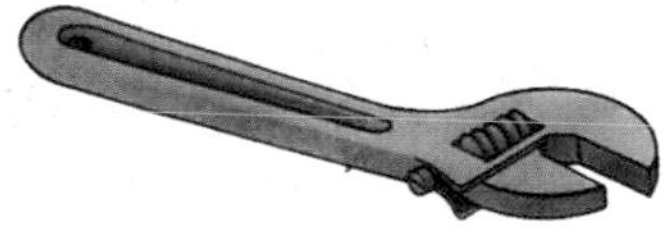

Usual type is a crescent spanner adjusted by a screw at the top of the handle

SANDING BLOCK

Block of wood with glasspaper wrapped round for smoothing or keying surfaces

MISCELLANEOUS ITEMS
Oil can, screws, nails and washers, adhesives and fillers, pencil, scissors, plumbline, goggles, rubber gloves, glasspaper, ladder, string, wall plugs, oilstone, putty knife, scraper

CHAPTER 10

INDEX

Acknowledgements

The author wishes to acknowledge the painstaking work of Gill Jackson, Angelina Gibbs and the late John Woodbridge. Grateful acknowledgement is also made for the help received from Barry Highland (Spot On Digital Imaging Ltd) and Brian O'Shea.

Many people provided information, artwork or photographs for the various sections of the book. Included here are Aga-Rayburn, Armitage Shanks Ltd, David Baylis, Dr Tim Baylis, BEAB, Berry Magicoal Ltd, Black & Decker Ltd, Bosch, Brabantia (UK) Ltd, Braintree District C
Carpet Manufacturers Association, British Flat Ro
Glass Manufacturers Association, Glen Dimplex Gr
Bluebridge Farm Studio, Hotpoint, Husqvana Ltd,
Miele Company Ltd, Morphy Richards, Moulinex L
Chartered Surveyors, Shires Bathrooms Ltd, Solid
Research Development Association, Transco, Trav